Chris Webb

The Auschwitz Concentration Camp

History, Biographies, Remembrance

Chris Webb

THE AUSCHWITZ CONCENTRATION CAMP

History, Biographies, Remembrance

ibidem-Verlag
Stuttgart

Bibliografische Information der Deutschen Nationalbibliothek
Die Deutsche Nationalbibliothek verzeichnet diese Publikation in der Deutschen Nationalbibliografie; detaillierte bibliografische Daten sind im Internet über http://dnb.d-nb.de abrufbar.

Bibliographic information published by the Deutsche Nationalbibliothek
Die Deutsche Nationalbibliothek lists this publication in the Deutsche Nationalbibliografie; detailed bibliographic data are available in the Internet at http://dnb.d-nb.de.

Cover design: Tom Nixon

∞
Gedruckt auf alterungsbeständigem, säurefreien Papier
Printed on acid-free paper

ISBN-13: 978-3-8382-1106-0

© *ibidem*-Verlag
Stuttgart 2018

Alle Rechte vorbehalten

Das Werk einschließlich aller seiner Teile ist urheberrechtlich geschützt. Jede Verwertung außerhalb der engen Grenzen des Urheberrechtsgesetzes ist ohne Zustimmung des Verlages unzulässig und strafbar. Dies gilt insbesondere für Vervielfältigungen, Übersetzungen, Mikroverfilmungen und elektronische Speicherformen sowie die Einspeicherung und Verarbeitung in elektronischen Systemen.

All rights reserved. No part of this publication may be reproduced, stored in or introduced into a retrieval system, or transmitted, in any form, or by any means (electronic, mechanical, photocopying, recording or otherwise) without the prior written permission of the publisher. Any person who does any unauthorized act in relation to this publication may be liable to criminal prosecution and civil claims for damages.

Printed in Germany

Dedicated To :

Mr Marian Koszewski from Kościan—Survivor of Auschwitz and Gusen camps.
I met him in Kościan in September 2005, thanks to Artur Hojan and Cameron Munro.

Frank Bright who survived Auschwitz, although his Father and Mother did not.
He kindly shared the story of the Brichta family with me, part of which is included in this book.

For **Freya Isabel**

I therefore became Commandant of the Quarantine Camp which
was to be built at Auschwitz.
It was far away, in the back of beyond, in Poland.

Rudolf Höss
Commandant of Auschwitz

We had read the name of Auschwitz on the labels on the trucks—
trucks or wagons—trucks. But nobody of us knew
what Auschwitz meant.

Primo Levi
Italian Jew who was deported to Auschwitz in 1944,
but survived.

Foreword

I have known Chris Webb since 2003. I myself had been involved in Holocaust research for many years prior to this, though on a purely private basis. It was in 2003 that I came across the Aktion Reinhardt Camps (ARC) website. I sent an inquisitive email to the website enquiring about becoming a member. A very enthusiastic response came back from Chris, welcoming me to the fold.

The website was run on a very devolved basis—if you wanted to contribute something you went ahead and did it. There was some proof checking and review of facts, but those who wanted to contribute could. And so the website and interest grew. It generated the most extensive research undertaken to date on the three Aktion Reinhardt Camps. As I was to discover, it was Chris who was the real driving force behind the website.

We met for the first time on the ARC field trip to Poland in 2004 and we have met several times each year since then, as well as undertaking research trips to Poland and the United States of America, and swapping research material and ideas by email. Chris has always provided excellent feedback on my research efforts. He has been researching the Aktion Reinhardt Camps and the Holocaust in general for over 40 years.

I have met many researchers and talked to many institutes of Holocaust research around the world. Almost all agree that the ARC website is still the most comprehensive and user-friendly website on the Holocaust. Since the ARC website was frozen some years ago, existing on the web but not being added to, Chris has moved on to other projects, including setting up H.E.A.R.T. and the Holocaust Historical Society. He has also written a trilogy of books on Bełżec, Sobibór and Treblinka, that have been published by Ibidem-Verlag and he has self-published other Holocaust related works.

Chris joined the Tiergarten 4 Association in 2015, of which I am the Chairman and founder. The Tiergarten 4 Association is a Berlin registered association which researches and publishes works on

Nazi war crimes, with a focus on the Warthegau, Chełmno, Aktion Reinhardt Camps, gas vans, Sonderkommando 1005, other Concentration Camps, euthanasia institutes and War crimes trials. The Tiergarten 4 Association has an extensive library of some 20,000 books and more than a million pages of original documents relating to the Nazi period and War crimes trials. Some of these documents have been consulted in producing this book on Auschwitz.

Chris has also very generously given his time and expertise to Holocaust education in the UK. He has given many lectures at Universities and has more recently acted as a consultant and guide to Auschwitz and Kraków, where he has imparted his knowledge about the Camp in particular and the Holocaust in general. It is thus an opportune moment for Chris to publish his book on 'The Auschwitz Concentration Camp, History, Biographies, Remembrance.'

As with all of his works, in his book on the Auschwitz Concentration Camp, Chris produces a fine balance between detailing the sufferings of the victims and the actions and characters of the perpetrators. He manages in a concise form to give an excellent overview of all aspects of Auschwitz and its many complex of camps.

The book will be useful both for those coming to the Holocaust for the first time, and those seasoned researchers like myself, who have read many books on Auschwitz. Although the number of existing published works on Auschwitz is vast, this book on the Auschwitz Concentration Camp is a very worthy addition to the bibliography of one of the most important Camps established by the Nazis.

Cameron Munro
Tiergarten 4 Association
Berlin
March 2017

Author's Introduction

The Author—Auschwitz-Birkenau January 2017
Photograph: Taken By Mark Handscomb

This book was inspired by my recent visits to Auschwitz-Birkenau whilst acting as a guide for the University of Teesside in 2016 and 2017. I have now visited the site four times and every visit brings new things to learn and understand. It remains a sobering and humbling experience, from my first visit in 2004, up to the current day, and these experiences will stay with me for life.

This book has been constructed using the excellent book by Danuta Czech, *'Auschwitz Chronicle'* to tell the chronological history of the Concentration Camp, from its conception in 1940 to its demise in 1945. This is the best way to chart the development of the police Camp which became the greatest cemetery without a grave in the history of mankind. Whilst the *'Chronicle'* has been used as the foundation, accounts from both survivors and members of the Camp garrison, some of which have never been published in book form to date, tell the heartbreaking story of life and death, in the most infamous of places, created by man.

This work covers the establishment of the Camp, its development from a Security Police prison holding Polish political prisoners to the industrial mass killing of a large portion of the Jewish race in Europe. The story is told from all sides; the Polish prisoners, the Jews, the Germans, the Resistance workers, the survivors and the victims, the heroes and the villains. Biographies of the perpetrators and remembrance for both the survivors and the victims. Chronological tables of the deportations and details of some of the survivors, and the post-war statements and Trials, all tell the story of the hell called Auschwitz.

My first visit to Auschwitz was made in 2004, as part of a group visiting many of the major Holocaust related sites, including former Camps such as Płaszów, Treblinka, Sobibór, Bełżec, Trawniki, Poniatowa, and Majdanek. I was lucky enough to be guided around Auschwitz by the Swedish expert Börje Hallström, who joined us on the trip. He had visited the Camp and the surrounding area many times before, and he passed on his knowledge freely, for which I am most grateful.

In terms of thanking people, I would first like to thank Tom Nixon from Teesside University who designed the book cover, with such consummate skill. I was delighted to renew my working relationship with Tania Mühlberger, who once again proof read and copy edited this book in her exemplary style, I am blessed to know her. For introducing me to Tania and for being instrumental in the great privilege of inviting me to work with Teesside University, I must thank Professor Matthew Feldman. Our long standing friendship is a source of much joy. I must also thank Mark Handscomb and Lucy Jolly, for our three trips to Auschwitz, along with the students from Teesside University who made the journey to Poland. Mark very kindly took some photographs of me on the ramp in Birkenau, in freezing weather in January 2017, specifically for this book.

I am also indebted to Cameron Munro, the founder of the Tiergarten 4 Association in Berlin, who very kindly wrote the foreword to this book, and provided information used in this work. He was part of the ARC group which toured the Auschwitz-Birkenau murder factory in 2004, and along with the late Artur Hojan, produced a study of the Auschwitz sub-camps, which was completed in 2009, but to date is unpublished. Artur also obtained some original items of correspondence from Auschwitz for me, which have been included in this work.

Cameron Munro is a dedicated researcher on the Holocaust and we have worked together on many projects and research trips, in the United Kingdom, Europe and the United States of America. From the same organization I must also pay thanks to Robert Parzer, who supported my many requests for information and documents. I thank Robert wholeheartedly for all of his efforts.

I am grateful for the support of a number of people helping me with my research. I must place on record my thanks to Frank Bright, who survived Theresienstadt and Auschwitz, before settling in the UK after the War. He very kindly sent me his fantastic account of his families' experiences growing up in Nazi Germany. Both of Frank's parents were murdered in Auschwitz. I am sincerely grateful to him for sharing this tragic story with me. His full account was first published online on the Holocaust Education and Research Team (H.E.A.R.T.) website during 2008. In a similar vein, I must also thank Dr. Thomas Nowotny, for providing me with the account of Max Block, who perished in Auschwitz during 1944, also for the H.E.A.R.T. website in 2012.

I must also place on record my thanks to the late Sir Martin Gilbert, who inspired me greatly with his research on the Holocaust, and who kindly donated maps to aid me in my research. His sad passing in 2014 was a great loss.

During the writing of this book, I must express my thanks to Piotr Setkiewicz from the Auschwitz-Birkenau State Museum, who helped me with a number of questions. I am also grateful for the assistance given to me by Miriam Haardt, Deputy Senior Librarian at the Wiener Library, in London, who helped me with my research into transports to Auschwitz, from a number of European countries occupied by the Nazis.

A big thank-you to my publisher, ibidem-Verlag, who are a real pleasure to work with. I am extremely appreciative of their continual support, and the kindness and patience of Valerie Lange and Florian Bölter. This is my fourth published work with them, and I am proud that we have such a productive working relationship.

My wife Shirley, my daughter Heather and son-in-law Mark all deserve a mention in supporting my research and published works, over the many years. They mean the world to me.

To everyone who has supported me with my life-long interest in the Holocaust—I thank you all.

Abbreviations

AK – Armia Krajowa – Polish Home Army

ARC – Aktion Reinhard Camps website

BBC – British Broadcasting Corporation

GFH – Ghetto Fighters House, Israel

H.E.A.R.T. Holocaust Education Archive Research Team

HHS – Holocaust Historical Society, UK

KL – KonzentrationsLager – Concentration Camp

NA – National Archives, Kew, London

PPS – Polish Socialist Party

RSHA – Reich Security Main Office

SD – Sicherheitsdienst – Security Service

SIPO – Sicherheitspolizei – Security Police

SS – Schutzstaffel – Protection Squad

TAP – Secret Polish Army

TOW – Military Organization Union (Polish)

USHMM – United States Holocaust Memorial Museum

WL – Wiener Library, London

WVHA – Administration and Economic Main Office of the SS

YVA – Yad Vashem Archives

Contents

Foreword 7

Author's Introduction 9

Abbreviations 13

Part I The Hell Called Auschwitz 17

    Chapter I Auschwitz Main Camp 1940 18

    Chapter II Auschwitz Main Camp 1941 29

    Chapter III Selected SS Personnel 39

    Chapter IV Auschwitz I Mass Murder By Gassing 1941–1942 44

    Chapter V Auschwitz-Birkenau 1941–1942 55

    Chapter VI Auschwitz-Birkenau 1943 84

    Chapter VII Auschwitz-Birkenau 1944 104

    Chapter VIII The Sonderkommando Revolt Auschwitz-Birkenau October 1944 179

    Chapter IX Auschwitz-Birkenau October–December 1944 186

    Chapter X Evacuation and Liberation January 1945 200

Part II Perpetrators, Survivors, Victims and Aftermath 223

    Chapter XI Biographies—Perpetrators 224

    Chapter XII Transports to Auschwitz Remembrance, Survivors and Victims 276

    Chapter XIII War Time Reports About Auschwitz-Birkenau ... 333

    Chapter XIV Post War Testimonies 359

    Chapter XV Post War Trials 387

    Chapter XVI Epilogue 398

Illustrations	413
Documents, Drawings, Maps and Sources	443
Appendix I Equivalent Ranks	461
Appendix II Glossary of Nazi Terms	463
Selected Bibliography	469
Sources and Acknowledgements	473
Index of Names	477

Part I
The Hell Called Auschwitz

Chapter I
Auschwitz Main Camp
1940

The *Baedekers* Guide to the *Generalgouvernement* published in 1943, provides a description of Auschwitz, the German spelling for the Polish town of Oświęcim, (ironically containing—although slightly mis-spelled—the word "schwitzen...aus" which is literally to sweat profusely—something also associated with decay. Tragically symbolic, it is here associated with the emaciated, tired, and extremely malnourished physique of the prisoners, and for those selected—the after effect of the gassing of the many thousands of Jews in this Concentration Camp) which is located in southern Poland, some 31 miles west of Kraków:

The railway to Kraków continues north-east past Auschwitz (348 kilometers from Vienna), an industrial town of 12,000 inhabitants, the former capital of the Piast Duchies of Auschwitz and Zator, whence a secondary railway runs via Skawina to Kraków.[1]

It was here near the Polish town of Oświęcim that the Nazis in 1940, created the infamous Auschwitz Concentration Camp, utilizing former Polish army barracks in the Zasole district. The *SS-Oberführer* Arpad Wigand, who was based in the *Höhere SS- und Polizeiführer Südost* offices in Breslau, today Wrocław, had identified the site of Zasole, with its military bases and excellent rail connections just outside of the town of Auschwitz in the fork of the Soła and Vistula rivers, as a suitable place to build a Concentration Camp for Poles arrested by the German Security forces.[2]

In early January 1940, *SS-Oberführer* Richard Glücks, the Inspector of Concentration Camps ordered *SS-Sturmbannführer* Walter

---

[1] Baedekers, *Das Generalgouvernement*, Leipzig 1943, p. 10.
[2] *Auschwitz—Nazi Extermination Camp,* Interpress, Warsaw 1985, p. 15.

Eisfeld from Sachsenhausen Concentration Camp to inspect the military barracks, and the commission concluded that the barracks were unsuitable for conversion into a Concentration Camp. This view, however, was not shared by the *HSSPF* office in Wrocław, and another inspection commission was ordered.

On February 21, 1940, *SS-Oberführer* Richard Glücks informed *Reichsführer-SS*, Heinrich Himmler, that the inspection of the barracks had recommended, that with certain modifications, the barracks could be used and that a quarantine camp could begin functioning immediately. Negotiations commenced with *Luftwaffe* General Halm, regarding the transfer of these barracks to the *SS*.

Another inspection, this time, under the command of *SS-Hauptsturmführer* Rudolf Höss, also from Sachsenhausen Concentration Camp took place in Zasole, on April 18 and April 19, 1940. Rudolf Höss advised *SS-Oberführer* Richard Glücks, that the accommodation of the eight two-storey and fourteen single-storey brick barracks framing the north and south side of the large exercise yard, could be utilized as a Concentration Camp.[3]

On April 27, 1940, following the inspection report prepared by Rudolf Höss, Himmler ordered Richard Glücks to establish a Concentration Camp at Auschwitz and on May 4, 1940, Höss was officially appointed the first Commandant. One of his first acts was to acquire from the Mayor of Auschwitz, 300 local Jews who worked at the site, making it ready to accept the first intake of prisoners.

Rudolf Höss described his task on taking up his appointment:

> My task was not an easy one. In the shortest possible time, I had to construct a transit camp for ten thousand prisoners, using the existing complex of buildings which, though well constructed, had been completely neglected, and were swarming with vermin. From the point of view of hygiene, practically everything was lacking. I had been told in Oranienburg, before setting off, that I could not expect much help, and I would

---

[3] Robert Jan van Pelt and Deborah Dwork, *Auschwitz 1270 To the Present,* Yale University Press, New Haven and London 1996, p. 168.

have to rely largely on my own resources. In Poland I would find everything that had been unobtainable in Germany for years![4]

However, the reality was that in constructing Auschwitz Concentration Camp, Rudolf Höss was facing considerable problems even in obtaining the basics:

> Whether it was a question of bread or meat or potatoes, it was I who had to find them. Yes, I even had to visit the farms, in order to collect straw. Since I could expect no help of any kind from the Inspectorate, I had to make do as best I could on my own. I had to organize the trucks and lorries I needed and the fuel for them. I had to drive as far as Zakopane and Rabka to acquire cooking-pots for the prisoners' kitchen, and to the Sudetenland for bed-frames and mattresses.[5]

SS-Unterscharführer Pery Broad, who was a member of the Political Section in Auschwitz, wrote an account of his experiences in the Camp and he handed it over to the British authorities after the War. It became known as the 'Broad Report.'

His description of the main camp at Auschwitz states:

> The Auschwitz Concentration Camp, known in Poland as the 'Camp of Death' was located near the city of the same name in the marshy tract between the Vistula and a tributary, the Soła. It was opened in 1940. Old military barracks and factory buildings formed the core of what later became a very large complex of buildings.

At first there was only the so-called Auschwitz base camp, situated on a road along the Soła connecting the village of Rajsko with Auschwitz. From the street, next to the main gate, could be seen the luxurious quarters of the Commandant *SS-Obersturmbannführer* Höss. The entrance was barred, and *SS* guards checked every soldier and civilian entering or leaving. To the right of the gate were the guard barracks and diagonally across from that the headquarters building. The view of the prisoner compound was obstructed by a long concrete wall, above which could be seen the guard towers and

---

[4] Rudolf Höss, *Commandant of Auschwitz*, Pan Books London and Sydney 1980, p. 116.

[5] *KL Auschwitz Seen by the SS*, Panstwowe Muzeum W Oswiecimiu 1978, p. 40.

gables of the dreary red-brick buildings. Most of the twenty-eight blocks of the compound housed prisoners. Some were used as hospitals, offices, storerooms and for other purposes. The prisoner kitchen was also in the compound. The compound was surrounded by two high, electrified barbed-wire fences, which at night were brightly lit. In addition there were large searchlights on the towers. A 10-foot-wide gravel strip, the so-called neutral zone, ran along the inner fence, and anyone found there was fired at. About 20,000–25,000 persons were confined in the base camp.[6]

The infamous *Rapportführer* (Roll-Call Leader) Gerhard Arno Palitzsch, arrived on May 20, 1940, from Sachsenhausen Concentration Camp, with 30 convicted criminals, mostly German, who were given serial numbers 1–30, and placed in Block 1. These 30 men were the *Kapo's* who were to supervise the prisoners and maintain control, in a brutal fashion, as an extension to the *SS* forces. Among the thirty men were Bruno Brodniewitsch, who was given Serial Number 1, and he was appointed Camp Senior.[7]

Forty prisoners from the Dachau Concentration Camp, near Munich arrived in Auschwitz on May 29, 1940, the so-called *Aussen-Kommando*, under the command of *SS-Unterscharführer* Beck. This *Kommando* consisted of one German *Kapo,* and thirty-nine Polish prisoners, most of them gymnasium students from Łódź. They were housed in the kitchen barracks and were put to work erecting the first temporary barbed wire fence around the camp.[8]

On June 14, 1940 the first transport of prisoners arrived in Auschwitz, these were 728 Polish men from the prison in Tarnów, on the orders of the *SIPO* and *SD*[9] Commander in Kraków. One of the prisoners was Wiesław Kielar, who described the journey in his book '*Anus Mundi*' and extracts from his book are quoted here:

---

[6] B. Naumann, *Auschwitz*, Pall Mall Press, London 1966, pp. 162–163.
[7] Danuta Czech, *Auschwitz Chronicle*, Henry Holt and Company, New York 1990, p. 10.
[8] Ibid., p. 10.
[9] SIPO (Sicherheitspolizei) and SD (Sicherheitsdienst)—German Security Forces .

> We tried to stay together and until now, we had been lucky. This time too. Here we were, just as we had been in our prison cell: Tadek Szwed, Djunio Beker, Romek Trojanowski and I, sitting on a bench, each clutching the small bundle they had allowed us to bring from Tarnów prison...... the policemen escorting us were decent, they allowed us to talk to each other and to smoke, if we wanted to. But we were not permitted to go near the windows.

This was an historic day for the Third Reich:

> We arrived in Kraków about midday. The whole station was festooned with swastikas. There was excitement and undisguised rejoicing among the Germans. From the loudspeakers came the blare of military music and strident speeches: Victory! Paris had fallen—it was June of 1940.

The journey continued:

> We traveled on.... We stop for a long time at some station. It turns out that this is the frontier between the *Generalgouvernement* and the Reich. We continue our journey. Next we stop at what, judging from the number of trucks on either side of the train, must be a major station. The name of the place, written in large letters on the station building, is, Auschwitz.... Some dump or other. We don't think about it anymore because now our train has started to move again. Presumably we're being shunted into a siding since the train curves sharply, so that the wheels squeal remorselessly.

The transport had arrived at Auschwitz Concentration Camp:

> From the other side of the window comes the sound of voices shouting in German, of feet running and stamping. Suddenly the doors of our carriage are flung open. Someone on the platform shouts at the top of his voice: "Everybody out!" Our escorts assist us to climb out of the train in their own way. They bring the butts of their carbines down on our backs with resounding blows. We all dash like mad towards the one and only exit. One by one we jump down from the high carriage and land directly at the feet of scores of *SS* men; they are lined up in rows leading towards a high fence which encircles a large building. Beaten, pushed and terrified by the *SS* men yelling at us, we rush like a flock of panicking sheep through the open gate.

Wiesłav Kielar continued his account of arrival:

> Suddenly the striped man commanding us stepped smartly up to a group of *SS* men standing a little to one side. At a short distance from

them he came to attention, clicking his heels and taking off his cap in one swift movement; then he proceeded to talk rapidly in German, none of which we understood. One of the SS men, pointing at a nearby building, muttered something in reply without removing his pipe from his mouth. As soon as he had finished, Stripey once more clicked heels, put on his blue sailors cap, did a regulation about turn and returned to his previous position. Another command rang out. All the stripeys fell out and lined us up near the building.

After we had been divided up into small groups we were led into the basement where all our personal belongings were taken away; this included the removal of hair from every part of our body, followed by a bath in ice-cold water. We were handed a cardboard tab with a number which was to replace our names from now on. My number was 290. Romek Trojanowski 44, and Edek Galinski's 537. Thus in a perfectly simple manner, we became numbers.[10]

These first prisoners were quarantined in the building of the former Polish Tobacco Monopoly, near the railroad siding, which was separated from the rest of the buildings by barbed wire fences. This was only a temporary measure, and this building was designated for the SS guards at a later date. On the day that this first transport arrived at Auschwitz, the outside commando from Dachau were leaving and those departing saw the arrival of the first transport from Tarnów.

On July 6, 1940, the first escape from Auschwitz concentration camp took place. Polish prisoner Tadeusz Wiejowski, who was born on May 4, 1914, in Kołaczyce, near Kraków, escaped from the camp. The escape was discovered during the evening roll call. Wiesłav Kielar recalled the brutal roll-call that took place that day:

> We stand in rows in a large square behind the hospital block. The *Kapo's* are having a hard time counting us. The SS men too. The roll call won't tally. Maybe someone has escaped. They keep counting, but don't get the correct figure. They are furious. They vent their fury on us. We stand to attention, side by side, at arm's length, hands folded behind our heads, elbows turned back as far as possible. Thus we stand for an hour, maybe more, maybe less, because time has lost all meaning.... A group of SS men approach, among them is *Rapportführer* Palitzsch, young and

---

[10] Wiesław Kielar, *Anus Mundi,* Penguin Books, Harmondsworth, England 1980, pp. 3–5.

slim in a beautifully cut uniform, his unpleasant face covered with pimples.... Pale with fear, Baworowski interprets, "A prisoner has escaped Wiejowski—the person who helped him get away is to come forward."
No-one came forward, the *SS* ordered the prisoners to stand there, until someone does. Kielar's account continues:
The *SS* men have left, Leo Wietschorek[11] is practicing sport with us. It is getting dark, consequently we manage to cheat. The *Kapo's* who seem to have grown tired, slope off, one after the other, back to the block. After a while Leo returns ... he's shouting "Knees bend!" ..... Night has fallen, from the river dampness, sticky and cold, comes creeping towards us... we shiver as if we have an attack of malaria, and this burning in our stomach, if one could only get some coffee. Someone asks for permission to go to the toilet. Permission refused, we piss in our trousers.
Dawn, now the cold is so cruel that our teeth chatter loudly... suddenly the sun appears behind the block. It turns warm. For a change they make us fold our hands behind our heads. The longed-for sun, now grows into a hated tormentor. Somebody collapses, Leo rushes over to him, he beats him with his stick, but it no longer has much effect. After a while another man passes out, and still another. From the sky a veritable fire pours down.... Many pretend to faint.... I decide to try the same trick I fall down on my face. What a relief!
I can hear the gravel crunching under the approaching feet, a hand pushes something under my nose... it's the sick-bay *Kapo*, his small penetrating eyes blink at me with understanding. Before Leo arrives they carry me to the sick bay. In the room some dozen bodies are lying on the floor. There is coffee too. Bock, the sick-bay *Kapo* gives me some tablets. I swallow them and fall asleep immediately.
Stehappell (standing-up roll call) continued until 2 p.m.—thus I managed to get out of four hours of it. Next day we are transferred from Quarantine to Block 2.[12]

During this first 'punishment roll-call', the first public flogging occurred. The flogging was carried out on a stand made in the camp carpentry workshop. Those flogged were prisoners interrogated by SS members of the Political Department—the Camp *Gestapo*, on

---

[11]   Leo Wietschorek, is one of the German criminals brought from Sachsenhausen Concentration Camp. Serial Number 30.
[12]   Wiesław Kielar, *Anus Mundi*, Penguin Books, Harmondsworth, England 1980, pp. 15–17.

suspicion of assisting Tadeusz Wiejowski[13] in his successful escape attempt. The beatings were carried out by *Rapportführer* (Roll-Call Leader) Gerhard Palitzsch, with a stick four centimeters in diameter.[14]

The following day on July 7, 1940, the Jew, David Wingoczewski became the first prisoner to die in Auschwitz, as a result of standing in the punishment roll-call. He arrived in Auschwitz on June 20, 1940 from the prison in Nowy Wiśnicz, suffering various serious ailments and signs of ill-treatment.[15]

Wilhelm Brasse, who was born on December 3, 1917, in Żywiec, was of Austrian and Polish descent. He learnt to be a photographer in Katowice. After the German occupation, he refused to sign the *Volksliste* (ethnic German register) and he tried to cross into Hungary. He was arrested on the Polish-Hungarian border and was sent to Auschwitz Concentration Camp on August 31, 1940. He was tattooed with the Prisoner Number 3444. Later on, because of his photographic skills he was selected to work in the Photographic Identification Unit, where he took photographs of the new arrivals, for individual camp records. He recalled the early days of construction work in the Auschwitz Camp:

> The prisoners had to carry stones. It was very difficult, hard labor. And we were beaten. But not enough construction materials had been provided to complete the task, so a typical Nazi solution was found—theft. I worked at demolishing houses that used to belong to Polish families. There was an order to take building materials such as bricks, planks and all kinds of other wood. We were surprised the Germans wanted to build so rapidly and they did not have the materials.
> The Camp quickly developed a culture of theft, not just from the local population, but from within the institution itself. The German *Kapos* would send us inmates off and say, 'Go and steal cement from another work *Kommando*. We don't care about the other guys.' And that is what we did. Planks or cement would be stolen from another *Kommando*. In

---

[13] Tadeusz Wiejowski hid for a year in Kołaczyce, re-arrested, sent to prison in Jaslo. He was shot in an abandoned oil well near Gorlice.

[14] Danuta Czech, *Auschwitz Chronicle*, Henry Holt and Company, New York 1990, p. 17.

[15] Ibid., p. 17.

the Camp lingo that would be called 'organizing', but we had to be careful not to get caught.[16]

Jerzy Bielski, Prisoner Number 243, who was also a member of the first transport of Polish political prisoners that arrived in Auschwitz from Tarnów, recalled the *Kapo* Ernst Krankemann, who arrived at the Camp in the second batch of German criminals transferred from Sachsenhausen Concentration Camp on August 29, 1940:

> First time I saw him, they were rolling the square between the two blocks, and because it was a very heavy roller, the twenty or twenty-five people in the unit were unable to pull it. Krankemann had a whip and would hit them. 'Faster you dogs!' he said.

Jerzy Bielski continued:

> As evening fell, one of them collapsed on his knees and could not get up. Then Krankemann ordered the rest of the penal *Kommando* to pull the giant roller over their prostrate comrade. I had got used to seeing death and beatings, but what I saw then just made me cold. I just froze.[17]

On September 22, 1940, the *SIPO* and *SD* Commander of Warsaw sent 1,705 men, 1139 who were caught in round-ups on the streets of Warsaw and 566 men from Pawiak Prison, to Auschwitz. Stanislaw Debski, whose real name was Stanislaw Dubois, a young active member of the Polish Socialist Party, was given serial number 3904. Konstanty Jagiello, also a member of PPS, and active in the Red Scouts was given number 4007. Tomasz Serafinski, whose real name was Witold Pilecki, was given number 4859. Pilecki was chief of staff of the underground organization of the Secret Polish Army (*TAP*). Pilecki, with the approval of his immediate superior, joined a group of people who were to be arrested during a street round-up in Warsaw, to get into Auschwitz Concentration Camp with the aim of establishing a resistance group within the Camp, which will provide

---

[16] Laurence Rees, *Auschwitz—The Nazis and the Final Solution*, BBC Books, London 2005, p. 38.
[17] Ibid., p.40.

mutual aid to prisoners and establish contacts with the outside world.[18]

Witold Pilecki, a month after his arrival in the Camp, organized a group which took the name of Military Organization Union (*TOW*) and was based on the system of five member cells. Its members included Edward Ciesielski, Lieutenant Kacperski, Captain Henryk Bartosiewicz and Cavalry Captain Wlodzimierz Makalinski. The main focus of this group was organizing food, warm clothing, keeping up prisoners morale and spreading news from the outside world, as well as sending to Warsaw reports about the conditions in the Camp itself.[19]

Witold Pilecki escaped from the bakery squad on April 27, 1943. The purpose of his escape was to take out documents regarding the crimes committed there and to provide an eyewitness account of what was happening in Auschwitz, and to help the underground organization plan for liberating the Camp. One of his last acts in captivity was to entrust the leadership of his group to Major Zygmunt Boncza-Bohdanowski[20] and Captain Henryk Bartosiewicz.[21]

At the end of November 1940, Rudolf Höss, and the Head of Office D-III of the *Wirtschafts- und Verwaltungshauptamt (WHVA)*— the Administration and Economic Main Office of the *SS*, Major Heinrich Vogel, submitted a report to *SS-Reichsführer* Heinrich Himmler, investigating the possibilities of establishing agricultural enterprises in the area around the Auschwitz Camp.

On the basis of this report, Himmler decided to create an *SS* farm district, in the third zone, which included the villages of Babice, Broszkowice, Brzezinka, Budy, Harmeze, Plawy and Rajsko. In this farm district, an experimental agricultural station for the East was

---

[18] Danuta Czech, *Auschwitz Chronicle*, Henry Holt and Company, New York 1990, p. 29.
[19] Barbara Jarosz, *Auschwitz*, Interpress, Warsaw 1985, pp. 137–138.
[20] Executed at the Black Wall on October 11, 1943.
[21] Barbara Jarosz, *Auschwitz*, Interpress, Warsaw 1985, p. 138.

to be built with laboratories, a plant breeding station in Rajsko, as well as cattle, poultry and fish-breeding facilities.[22]

On December 19, 1940, the Archbishop of Kraków, Prince Adam Sapheia, sent a letter to the parish office in Auschwitz, addressed to the Commandant of Auschwitz Concentration Camp, seeking permission to read a Holy Mass at Christmas for the Catholic prisoners. On receipt of the letter from the Archbishop, the local priests, Wladyslaw Gross and Rudolf Schmidt presented the letter to Rudolf Höss, in person. The Commandant however, refused permission as the rules for Concentration Camps did not allow for religious observance.

Rudolf Höss did however approve that approximately 6,000 food packages weighing about two pounds each could be sent to all prisoners on Christmas Eve. Packages were indeed put together from local donations and from the funds set aside by Archbishop Sapheia, but many of the packages did not reach the prisoners until after the new year.[23]

---

[22] Danuta Czech, *Auschwitz Chronicle*, Henry Holt and Company, New York 1990, pp. 37–38.
[23] Ibid., p. 40.

Chapter II
Auschwitz Main Camp
1941

During early January 1941, Dr. Otto Ambros, a member of the board of the I.G. Farben company and responsible for the Buna Division (Synthetic Rubber) and Head Engineer, Wilhelm Biedenkopf, visited the State Planning Office in Kattowitz to look at maps and charts of various sites in Upper Silesia, in order to select an appropriate site for the construction of four Buna factories to produce 30,000 tons of synthetic rubber per year.

The area around Auschwitz seemed desirable since the confluence of three rivers meant the water and raw materials, such as lime, coal and salt were available in the region. In addition, the high population density and the existence of a Concentration Camp were also crucial, since this provided the necessary labor force for the construction of the plants. After a tour of the area, Dr. Ambros selected the town of Dwory, some 4 miles from Auschwitz as the chosen site for the Buna complex.[24]

In an edict dated January 2, 1941, Reinhard Heydrich, the chief of the *Reichssicherheitshauptamt* (*RSHA*)—The Reich Security Main Office, announced that Heinrich Himmler had agreed to the classification of the Concentration Camps into three categories; Auschwitz I was designated a Class I Camp for less serious prisoners, whilst Auschwitz II, which had not yet been constructed was deemed a Class II Camp, for prisoners charged with serious crimes.

Hermann Göring, the *Reichsmarschall* and Commissioner for the Nazis 'Four Year Plan' issued guidelines for the construction of the Buna factory complex in Auschwitz. Hermann Göring requested that Himmler arranged for the speedy evacuation of the Jews from the area, in order to free up living space for the workers, who were to be employed in building the Buna works. Göring estimated that

---

[24]   Ibid., p. 43.

between 8,000 to 12,000 workers would be needed to undertake this work.

Witold Pilecki, who is mentioned in the previous chapter, became very ill during February 1941, he had a very high temperature of almost 40 degrees Celsius. He was taken to Block 15 and laid on the floor in Room 7. Attacked by lice, which he fought off, after three days and three sleepless nights he sought help. Through a male nurse, Tadeusz Burski, he sent a note to the Polish Doctor Wladyslaw Dering. Dr. Dering came with another doctor and examined Pilecki and diagnosed an inflammation of the left lung, and had Pilecki transferred to Block 20. After a bath and injection Pilecki found himself in a clean bed, and could sleep at last. Due to strict cleanliness and isolation, there were no lice and no danger of typhus. After ten days, the illness passed its critical stage and he was able to get out of bed, though still of course very weak. He was kept on as a male nurse in the Hospital block.[25]

It was during the month he worked in the Hospital, that Pilecki was able to see for himself the effectiveness of the Hospital as one of the two main branches of the resistance organization he had created. The Hospital was run by a German criminal prisoner Hans Bock, although he had never studied medicine, he was kind-hearted and courageous in the face of *SS* brutality.

The Prisoners' Hospital at first occupied Block16, in the Auschwitz Main Camp, a little later it took over Block 15 and by the end of 1940, Block 20 as well. Bock was supported by the Polish doctors and in agreement with *SS* doctors Max Popiersch fought for and obtained important privileges for the Hospital. Conflicts arose between the *SS* doctors and the Political Department, who considered that the whole Camp came under their jurisdiction. There were a number of striking examples of these conflicts. For example, the Political Department sent a Russian prisoner named Zolotov, who was an informer to the Hospital as a nurse and to spy on the doctors. *SS*-Doctor Friedrich Entress was informed by a Polish doctor that although there was not a vacancy, he was demanding to be taken in,

---

[25] Jozef Garlinski, *Fighting Auschwitz*, Fontana Collins 1975, p. 51.

because the Political Department wanted it. Dr. Entress reacted by kicking the spy out and going immediately to see Camp Commandant Rudolf Höss. Entress returned from this meeting and confirmed that only the Senior Medical Officer and himself had any authority over the affairs of the Hospital.[26]

The role of the Hospital in the history of Auschwitz was very important, and it deserves recording. Dr. Wladyslaw Dering, was a Polish doctor, who was noisy, brusque, and difficult but a good doctor and he became an important figure in the Hospital. But he was not the first, the earliest doctor was Dr. Stefan Pizlo, who entered the Camp on the very first transport from Tarnów Prison on June 14, 1940.

The first Hospital clerk was Kazimierz Szczerbowski; the first pharmacist was Wlodzimierz Lachowicz, who was assisted by Marian Tolinski. When Lachowicz died of typhus in 1942, Tolinski took over his role. A laboratory was established beside the Hospital and was directed until the final days of the Camp by Witold Kosztowny. Dr. Glogowski worked there for a few weeks before he was accepted into the Hospital. For a short time too, Professor Antoni Jakubski was employed there. Professor Jakubski was 62 years old when he entered Auschwitz, and he was probably the oldest prisoner to survive and see the liberation in January 1945.[27]

On February 28, 1941, in Berlin, the program for the visit to Auschwitz was planned. Present at the meeting were Himmler, Karl Wolff, who was Himmler's chief of staff, *SS-Sturmbannführer* Heinrich Vogel, and *SS-Untersturmführer* von Thermann. The inspection members will fly from Berlin's Tempelhof Airport to Gleiwitz. They will tour the Camp and then leave for Breslau, to attend the 42nd birthday celebrations of *SS-Gruppenführer* Erich von dem Bach-Zelewski. Himmler and his entourage will stay overnight in the Hotel Monopol, in Kattowitz.

Heinrich Himmler, the *SS-Reichsführer*, carried out his first inspection tour of Auschwitz, on March 1, 1941. Himmler and his group

---

[26] Jozef Garlinski, *Fighting Auschwitz*, Fontana Collins 1975, pp. 53–54.
[27] Ibid., p. 54.

were accompanied by the *Gauleiter* and Governor of Upper Silesia, Fritz Bracht, the Higher SS and Police Leader in Breslau, *SS-Obergruppenführer* Ernst Schmauser, as well as *SS-Oberführer* Richard Glücks, who according to Rudolf Höss had arrived in Auschwitz, prior to Himmler's visit. Also present were leading representatives of the firm of I.G. Farben.

Following the comprehensive tour of the Camp Heinrich Himmler ordered Rudolf Höss to expand Auschwitz Concentration Camp in order to hold 30,000 prisoners. He also ordered the construction on the site of the village of Birkenau, a Camp to hold 100,000 Soviet Prisoners of War. He further instructed Höss to make available 10,000 prisoners for I.G. Farben for the construction of the industrial plant in Dwory near Auschwitz. Himmler was also keen to cultivate the development of agricultural projects and to expand the Camp workshops.[28]

One rather unusual occurrence took place around Easter 1941 for one prisoner. Wladyslaw Bartoszewski, a Polish political prisoner was in the hospital Block 20, when two SS men approached him and told him to get out. Then having passed a cursory medical he was about to be released from captivity, he was taken to the Camp chancellery where the clothes he was wearing when he entered the Camp, were returned to him. Wladyslaw takes up the story:

> They didn't give me back my golden cross, they kept that as a souvenir. I had to sign a form that he had no complaints about his stay in the Camp. Together with three other Poles who were released that day, Wladyslaw Bartoszewski was escorted by a German guard to Auschwitz railway station and put on a train. As the train pulled away he felt keenly 'those first minutes of freedom.' Ahead of him lay a lengthy journey home, back to his mother in Warsaw.[29]

On Holy Saturday, April 12, 1941, the evacuation of the villages of Babitz, Birkenau, Broschowitz, Budy, Harmense, and Rajsko was

---

[28] Danuta Czech, *Auschwitz Chronicle*, Henry Holt and Company, New York 1990, pp. 50–51.
[29] Laurence Rees, *Auschwitz—The Nazis and the Final Solution*, BBC Books, London 2005, pp.46–47.

completed. This operation took five days to complete, and no warning was given to the residents, and they were robbed of their possessions and property. Thus the Auschwitz Concentration Camp had taken over the area between the Sola and Vistula rivers.[30]

Rudolf Höss and Karl Fritzsch selected 10 prisoners from Block 2 as hostages and condemned them to death by starvation, in retaliation for the escape of a prisoner from the Camp. Among those selected were the Polish political prisoners:

Marian Batko (11795)
Wincenty Rejowski (3301)
Antoni Suliga (7883)
Stefan Otulak (7904)
Tadeusz Kustra (12906)
Jan Scheffler (11860)
Franciszek Bobla (1075)
Stanislaw Opasiak (9638)
Adam Giermakowski (12889)
Jozef Nocko (12929)

All of the above were locked up together in a cell in the cellar of Block 11, where they were given nothing to eat or drink. The cell was opened a few days later and Marian Batko, originally from Kraków, was the first to die on April 27, 1941; the rest of those incarcerated died by May 26, 1941.[31]

Father Maksymilian Rajmund Kolbe arrived in Auschwitz on May 29, 1941. He was arrested in the Franciscan monastery in Niepokalanów and was incarcerated in the Pawiak prison in Warsaw on February 17, 1941, along with other monks from that order. Transported to Auschwitz, he was given prisoner number 16670.[32]

On June 17, 1941, Rudolf Höss selected another ten prisoners from Block 2 and condemns them to starve to death in retaliation for the escape of Antoni Jedlinski. Those condemned are as follows:

Boleslaw Pinski (16761)

---

[30] Danuta Czech, *Auschwitz Chronicle*, Henry Holt and Company, New York 1990, p.58.
[31] Ibid., p. 59.
[32] Ibid., p. 65.

Aleksander Paszkowski (13953)
Roman Orzel (12922)
Wasyl Fediuszko (7354)
Witales Loposki (9608)
Wojciech Szczepanek (13939)
Franciszek Juszczyk (12322)
Antoni Grzesiak (11858)
Stanislaw Wysocki (13220)
Jan Pajor (11852)

The above mentioned prisoners starved to death between June 19, 1941 and June 27, 1941, in the bunker of Block 11.[33]

Commandant Rudolf Höss, once again on June 24, 1941, selected another ten hostages from among the prisoners in Block 2, in retaliation for another prisoner's escape. He condemned them to starve to death in the bunker of Block 11. The names of the Polish prisoners were :

Albert Bies (14033)
Piotr Prozorowski (12195)
Marcin Domino (14440)
Wlodzimierz Krat (8749)
Wladyslaw Glab (14243)
Stanislaw Markiewicz (12116)
Marian Sosniczka (16626)
Stanislaw Ungier (12959)
Roman Hejduk (17207)
Feliks Krolik (16741)

Six days later on June 30, 1941, the bunker cell was opened and their deaths were confirmed.[34]

On July 3, 1941, 80 Polish political prisoners were sent to Auschwitz by the *SIPO* and *SD* in Kraków and they were executed in the gravel pits near the theatre building. Among those executed were

---

[33] Ibid., p. 67.
[34] Ibid., p. 69.

some unwell prisoners from Block 15. Also included in those murdered were the former Mayor of Kraków, Dr. Boleslaw Czuchajowski (17365) and Karol Karwat (17349).[35]

A few hundred Russian Prisoners of War were incarcerated in Block 11, on July 18, 1941. They were put to work excavating sand in the gravel pit, behind the Camp kitchen, next to the SS Block Leaders room. Within the space of a few days this entire group was murdered, either from gun shots from small-calibre weapons or the *Kapo's* killed them with blows from shovels or picks.[36]

One of those who witnessed the murder of these Russian Prisoners of War was Jerzy Bielski. In Auschwitz he was given the Prisoner Number 243. He was a member of the first transport of Polish political prisoners that arrived in Auschwitz from Tarnów. He recalled what happened:

> Prisoner *Kapo's* beat them mercilessly, kicked them, clubbed them, they would fall to the ground. It was a macabre scene. I have never in my life seen anything like it. Neither did I later on, even though I remained in the camp for a long time after. I saw an SS man, a junior officer walking around the gravel pit with a pistol in his hand, it was sadism. "You dogs, you damn Communists, you pieces of shit," horrible words like these. And from time to time he would direct the pistol downwards and shoot.[37]

Karl Fritzsch selected 15 hostages on July 29, 1941, from among the prisoners in Block 14, in retaliation for an escape by a prisoner from the Camp. They were condemned to death by starvation in the bunker of Block 11. During this selection Father Maksymilian Rajmund Kolbe stepped out of the line of prisoners and asked Karl Fritzsch to take him instead of the prisoner Franciszek Gajowniczek (5659). The prisoners were incarcerated in Block 11.[38] Father Maksymilian

---

[35] Ibid., p. 70.
[36] Ibid., p. 74.
[37] *Auschwitz—The Nazis and the Final Solution* – BBC 2005.
[38] Danuta Czech, *Auschwitz Chronicle*, Henry Holt and Company, New York 1990, p. 76.

Rajmund Kolbe, on August 14, 1941, was killed with a phenol injection by Hans Bock, the Block Senior in the prisoners infirmary.[39]

On October 8/9, 1941, the construction of the Prisoner of War Camp in Birkenau was commenced. In retaliation for an escape on October 27, 1941, from Block 18a, ten hostages were selected from that block and they were condemned to death by starvation in the bunker of Block 11. The following were selected:

Henryk Kozlecki (11278)
Jan Skierniewski (21157)
Wladyslaw Maciag (20908)
Jozef Tomczak (21373)
Stanislaw Kocek (21173)
Stefan Kisniewicz (16189)
Zdislaw Witamborski (13882)
Franciszek Roller (21086)
Pawel Olszowka (21062)
Waclaw Kieszkowski (14634)

Six of the above men died from starvation between October 31, 1941 and November 10, 1941. Jan Skierniewski, Jozef Tomczak, and Franciszek Roller were shot on November 11, 1941. However, Henryk Kozlecki was released from the bunker into the Camp on October 29, 1941. This was the only instance of a prisoner condemned to death by starvation, being released from the bunker back into the Camp.[40]

During October 1941, Polish prisoner Kazimierz Smolen witnessed the arrival of Soviet Prisoners of War in Auschwitz, and he later recalled:

> It was already snowing—extraordinary to have snow in October—and the Soviet Prisoners of War were unloaded from trains about three kilometers from the Camp. They had to give all their clothes away and jump into barrels with disinfectant, and naked they went to Auschwitz Main Camp. Usually they were completely emaciated. Once at the main

---

[39] Ibid., p. 80.
[40] Ibid., p. 100.

Camp, the Soviet prisoners became the first inmates to have their prison numbers tattooed on their bodies.[41]

One of those Soviet Prisoners of War who arrived in Auschwitz during October 1941, was Pavel Stenkin, who had been captured by the Germans a mere two hours after the invasion of the Soviet Union on June 22, 1941. He remembered his initial impressions of life in the Camp:

> The average living time for a Soviet prisoner at Birkenau was two weeks. If you got something eatable, you must swallow it. Raw potato or not—it doesn't matter...... when it was time to get up in the morning, those who were alive moved, and around them would be two or three dead people ..... it was death, death, death. Death at night, death in the morning, death in the afternoon. There was death all the time.[42]

The Polish national holiday of November 11, 1941, saw mass executions in the courtyard of Block 11, against the 'Black Wall' or 'Wall of Death' take place. 151 inmates were shot by Roll Call Leader, Gerhard Palitzsch. The prisoners were killed by a shot to the base of the neck.[43]

On November 20, 1941, Commandant Rudolf Höss ordered the cessation of cremating corpses in the crematorium in Auschwitz *Stammlager*. He ordered that the corpses of inmates and Russian Prisoners of War should henceforth be buried in the mass graves in Birkenau.[44]

The poultry and fish farm begun in the spring on the site of the evacuated village of Harmense, where an outside *Kommando* had been working. It was one of the first sub-camps to be established on December 8, 1941. Fifty inmates were housed there. The Director of the farm was *SS-Unterscharführer*, Bernard Glaue. An angora rabbit

---

[41] Laurence Rees, Auschwitz—*The Nazis and the Final Solution*, BBC Books, London 2005, p. 80.
[42] Ibid., pp. 80–81.
[43] Danuta Czech, *Auschwitz Chronicle*, Henry Holt and Company, New York 1990, p. 105.
[44] Ibid., p. 108.

facility was also moved there. This was previously located in the vicinity of the Camp, in a storage area, between farm buildings.[45]

On December 18, 1941, in Block 11, where the Penal Company was located, 11 Jewish prisoners died. They were:

Chaim Ackermann (22355)
Rubin Opel (22935)
Herbert Guttman (23618)
Isaak Oppel (24271)
Juda Gutwein (23618)
Anschel Rausen (24326)
Gerson Ring (24333)
Richard Spira (24441)
Stanislaw Borski (24508)
Moses Eichenstein (24531)
Olmer Rubin (24574)[46]

---

[45] Ibid., p. 114.
[46] Danuta Czech, *Auschwitz Chronicle*, Henry Holt and Company, New York 1990, p. 118.

Chapter III
Selected SS Personnel

At the head of Auschwitz Concentration Camp stood the Camp Commandant, who was responsible for everything connected to the Camp, including the maintenance of security. The Camp Commandant was at the same time the Commander of the *SS* garrison and the head of the numerous *SS* economic enterprises.

The first Commandant of Auschwitz Concentration Camp was *SS-Obersturmbannführer* Rudolf Höss from May 4, 1940 until November 11, 1943, when he was transferred to the post of Head of the Office D-I in the *WVHA* in Oranienburg. He was succeeded by Arthur Liebehenschel on November 11, 1943. Liebehenschel only served as the Commandant for 6 months and he was replaced by *SS-Sturmbannführer* Richard Baer on May 11, 1944, who served as the Commandant until the Camp was liquidated in January 1945.

After the division of the Auschwitz Camp into three different camps, the Commandants of Birkenau (also known as Auschwitz II) were *SS-Sturmbannführer* Fritz Hartjenstein from November 22, 1943 until May 8, 1944, when *SS-Hauptsturmführer* Josef Kramer succeeded him. The Commandant of the sub-camp at Monowitz, also known as Auschwitz III was *SS-Hauptsturmführer* Heinrich Schwarz, who held this post until the Camp's liquidation in January 1945.

Rudolf Höss was supported by his Adjutant Josef Kramer, who transferred to Auschwitz from Mauthausen Concentration Camp in Austria. Kramer was captured by the British Army when they liberated Bergen-Belsen in April 1945. Kramer was known in the British press as 'The Beast of Belsen'.

The role of the First Camp Commander was held by Karl Fritzsch, who was transferred from Dachau Concentration Camp near Munich and the Second Camp Commander was Franz Xaver Maier, who was transferred to Auschwitz from the *SS* Death's Head Division.

The Director of Administration was Max Meyer who had previously served in the Concentration Camp Inspectorate, and the role of Bursar was performed by Herbert Minkos, who had previously served in Buchenwald Concentration Camp in Weimar. Other posts such as Senior Food Clerk was undertaken by Willi Rieck who arrived in Auschwitz from Dachau Concentration Camp and Otto Reinicke was in charge of Housing Administration who previously had served in Flossenburg Concentration Camp.

Maximillian Grabner was the Director of the Auschwitz camp's Political Department, who had previously served in the *Kattowitz Gestapo*. One of the most notorious individuals in the Political Department was *SS-Scharführer* Friedrich Wilhelm Boger. Known and referred to as the 'Tiger of Auschwitz', he was in charge of escapes, and was feared for his brutal interrogations. He even invented a contraption for beating prisoners, called the 'Boger Swing'. Maximilian Grabner, the feared head of the Political Department was relieved of his post on December 1, 1943 and repaced by Hans Schurz. Another member of the Political Department was the young Hans Stark, who was in charge of registrations, and who was given leave from Auschwitz to sit school exams.

The direct management of the Auschwitz Concentration Camp, responsible for such matters as accommodation, food and clothing for the prisoners, the prisoners work and security and camp discipline, came under the responsibility of the *SS-Schutzhaftlagerführer*.

The first *SS-Schutzhaftlagerführer*, Karl Fritzsch, held the rank of *SS-Hauptsturmführer* and had several roll-call leaders to assist him, as well as Block Leaders. The most infamous roll-call leader was Gerhard Palitzsch, who arrived from Sachsenhausen Concentration Camp. Karl Fritzsch served in this post until the end of 1941, and it was Fritzsch who was responsible for carrying out the experimental gassings of Soviet Prisoners of War in a bunker in Block 11 during late August 1941. Fritzsch was succeeded in this post by *SS-Hauptsturmführer* Hans Aumeier, who held this post until August 18, 1943. Hans Aumeier was replaced by *SS-Hauptsturmführer* Heinrich Schwarz, up to November 1943 when he was replaced by *SS-Obersturmführer* Franz Johann Hofmann. Hofmann held this post until June 1944, when *SS-Hauptsturmführer* Franz Hössler carried out the same role up to the liquidation of the Camp.

The chief *Lagerführer* of the men's Camp in Birkenau was *SS-Obersturmführer* Johann Schwarzhuber and the Women's Camp was under the supervision of Franz Hössler. In the women's Camp in Birkenau, the function of chief Supervisor was held by Johanna Langefeld during the period March 26, 1942 until October 8, 1942. She was then succeeded by Marie Mandel, who retained this post until November 1944, when she was replaced by Elisabeth Volkenrath, who performed this role until the Camp was liquidated in January 1945. One of the most infamous female guards was Irma Grese, who was well-known for her cruelty to the women inmates. Grese was captured by the British Forces at Belsen Concentration Camp and was tried and executed in Hamelin prison on December 13, 1945.

One of the most notorious members of the guard personnel, mentioned above, was Gerhard Palitzsch who held the rank of *SS-Hauptscharführer* and he performed the role of *Rapportführer* (Roll Call Leader). He was generally regarded as the most brutal and cruel member of the *SS* Garrison. He carried out thousands of executions at the 'Black Wall' in the courtyard of Block II. Palitzsch boasted that he was responsible for the deaths of 25,000 people, which has never been substantiated. His name is forever part of the bloody history of Auschwitz. He was eventually transferred to a sub-camp at Brno, but then arrested by the *SS*, and subjected to disciplinary proceedings. He was sent to the front and was apparently killed in action near Budapest during December 1944.

Another member of the *SS* Garrison who deserves special mention is *SS-Hauptscharführer* Otto Moll, who was in charge of the penal company and later in charge of the Jewish *Sonderkommando* that cremated corpses near the Bunkers I and II in Birkenau. After managing the Gleiwitz sub-camp, he was recalled by Rudolf Höss to manage the crematoria in May 1944, when the mass deportation of Hungarian Jews took place. A number of prisoners accounts all present a picture of him as one of the Third Reich's most brutal and cruel murderers. He submitted a plan, as the Red Army drew near to liquidate the Camp by bombing, in what became known as the 'Moll Plan'. He was tried by the Allies after the War, at the trial of the *SS* Garrison at Dachau, where he was found guilty of War Crimes and executed on May 28, 1946.

Among the most well known members of the *SS* personnel in Auschwitz within the medical profession, was Dr. Josef Mengele, who arrived at the Camp on May 30, 1943. Dr. Mengele was not only responsible for sending thousands of individuals to their deaths after being selected at the unloading ramps, he also carried out pseudo-scientific research on twins and dwarfs, killing many of them in the name of medical research.

The *SS-Standortarzt* was responsible for the health and well-being of the *SS* garrison and providing health care for the prisoners, throughout the Auschwitz Camp complex. The *SS* garrison doctor was in charge of the medical officers of the *SS* detachments, the Camp doctors, the *SS* dentists and the Camp pharmacist. The garrison doctors were *SS-Hauptsturmführer* Dr. Max Popiersch from the start of the Camp, until September 1941. He was replaced by *SS-Hauptsturmführer* Siegfried Schwela, who died on May 10, 1942 from typhus. He was in turn replaced by Dr. Franz Bodmann, who was the Women's Camp doctor in Auschwitz.

On August 17, 1942, Dr. Kurt Uhlenbrock took over the position of *SS* Garrison Doctor, but like Schwela he contracted typhus and was replaced on September 6, 1942 by *SS Obersturmbannführer* Dr. Eduard Wirths, who retained this post until January 18, 1945.

A number of other medical professionals featured heavily in the history of Auschwitz Concentration Camp, such as Professor Carl Clauberg, who was a Professor in gynecology at the University of Königsberg. He arrived in Auschwitz in April 1943 and carried out mass sterilization experiments in Block 10. Another, was Dr. Johann Kremer, who went to Auschwitz during August 1942, to carry out research on hunger. Kremer kept a journal of his time in Auschwitz, where he conducted selections for the gas chambers.

Dr. Horst Schumann, who was involved in the T4 euthanasia programme, went to Auschwitz on July 28, 1941 and selected 575 prisoners to be taken to the T4 Institute at Sonnenstein-Pirna to be gassed. In November 1942, he returned to Auschwitz to carry out mass sterilization experiments on men and women using x-rays.

One of the most feared *SS* members of the medical staff was Josef Klehr, who was the Head Medical Officer in the prisoner's infirmary in the main Camp. He participated in the killing of prisoners with phenol injections into the heart, in Block 20.

Whilst there will be a detailed section on the biographies of the most important figures in the Camp's personnel, it must be recognised that circa 8,000 *SS* male and *SS* female personnel served at Auschwitz throughout its five year existence. The vast majority of these held German citizenship, the so-called *Reichsdeutsche*, whilst others were ethnic Germans, the so-called *Volksdeutsche*.

Chapter IV
Auschwitz I
Mass Murder By Gassing 1941–1942

On July 28, 1941, a special medical commission arrived at Auschwitz in order to carry out a selection of prisoners within the framework of the 'Euthanasia Programme,' run by Viktor Brack. This secret organization was based at the address of *Tiergartenstraße 4*, in Berlin, and was responsible for the programme that carried out euthanasia of the mentally ill, chronically sick, and the so-called asocials within the Third Reich. This was until Adolf Hitler brought the programme to a close in 1941. This programme was extended to include Concentration Camps, and this committee inspected all invalids, and the chronically ill, who were selected by the Camp administration under the pretext of transferring them to another Camp, supposedly with better working conditions.

One of the doctors of this special medical commission was Dr. Horst Schumann, who was the Director of the Grafeneck Euthanasia Institute in Württemberg and then he performed a similar role in the T4 Institute at Pirna / Sonnenstein, near Dresden. Dr. Schumann was later to return to Auschwitz to carry out sterilization experiments on both male and female prisoners.

Most of the prisoners selected by this commission came from Block 15, the convalescent block, where sick and exhausted prisoners and those incapable of working were sent when an *SS* doctor no longer wanted them to remain in the prisoners' infirmary. Some of the prisoners registered voluntarily, because there was a rumor circulating in the Camp that the inmates selected for this transport were to be relocated to a sanatorium.

A total of 573 inmates, most of them Poles were selected, and at the last moment two German *Kapos* were added to the transport: Johann Siegruth, Prisoner Number 26, the one-armed Head *Kapo* of the lumber yard, and Ernst Krankemann, Prisoner Number 3210, the Block Senior of Block 11 and *Kapo* in the road construction labor camp. Following Dr. Schumann's orders, the transport was sent to *Schloss Sonnenstein*, a castle near Pirna, under the watchful eye of Roll Call Leader Franz Hössler. On his return, Franz Hössler reported to Rudolf Höss, that the prisoners were gassed in a bathroom, where carbon monoxide gas was introduced through the showerheads. Also Franz Hössler claimed that during the transport to Sonnenstein that Krankemann was murdered and that Siegruth committed suicide.[47]

Whilst Rudolf Höss attended a conference in Berlin to discuss the Jewish Question at the end of August 1941, *SS Hauptsturmführer* Karl Fritzsch used the gassing agent *Zyklon B*, to murder Russian Prisoners of War in the basement of Block 11. Wiesław Kielar, in his book *Anus Mundi* described the scene:

> Outside Block II Palitzsch was waiting for us. It was getting dark. The heavy wooden door of the penal company opened. We pushed the trucks into the yard and turned them around, facing the gate. Waiting in the yard was the entire *SS* retinue with *Lagerführer* Fritzsch and Camp Doctor Entress at the head. We stood expectantly while the *SS* men conferred for a time, after which they summoned Gienek.

They were handed gas masks. Palitzsch and several *Blockführers* also put on their gas masks. Together they approached the entrance to the block cellars. They stayed down there for rather a long time.......Palitzsch was the first to reappear, behind him the rest of the *SS* men. They had taken off their gas masks, which meant the gas was already diffusing. After a while Obojski and Teofil returned as well.

Wiesław Kielar described what happened next:

> Now we were divided into groups, each with its own special task. Some went down into the bunkers in order to fetch the corpses out of the cells, others carried them up the stairs where yet another group of nursing orderlies undressed them. The rest were ordered to haul the naked corpses a little farther into the yard, ready for loading onto the waiting trucks......

---

[47] Danuta Czech, *Auschwitz Chronicle*, Henry Holt and Company, New York 1990, p. 75.

> Downstairs it was stifling and reeked of dead bodies. All the cells were open, and in them we saw corpses of the gassed, crowded together and standing up. It was a little less crowded where the sick had been. A few corpses lay in a heap directly behind the door. We began with them. It was difficult to pry apart the bodies that were clinging together. One by one we dragged them into the corridor, from where the others carried them up the stairs.
> The deeper we penetrated into the cells, the harder it became to fetch out the corpses. Pressed together in the small cells, they stood, although they were dead, with the same countenance they had had, presumably, two days earlier. Their faces were blue, almost purplish. Wide open eyes threatened to pop out of their sockets; their tongues protruded between their open lips; their bared teeth gave an eerie appearance to their faces.

The nightmare went on:

> To begin with, two of us carried one corpse. As a result there was confusion on the narrow stairs, people getting in each other's way. We made only slow progress, we began to work singly. Instead of carrying the corpses, we dragged them behind us by a hand or foot. Now our work progressed much faster and more smoothly. The whole bunker was disinfected with chlorine, which made our labors easier still. True, the strong smell of chlorine made one's eyes smart, but at least it reduced the stench of the putrefying corpses. The greatest problem was getting the bodies up the stairs. Their heavy heads bumped against each step with a dull thud; their limp extremities caught on protruding steps and thresholds. Upstairs, in the corridor next to the washroom, we flung the bodies on the floor, here other prisoners undressed them while we turned back to fetch another load. Before very long I discovered that the air up there was considerably better, moreover the work of undressing seemed to be less arduous.
> Therefore, having dragged out another corpse, I began to undress it. However, it turned out that taking garments off limp and distended bodies was not at all easier than transporting them; but at least there was a little more fresh air here, and it was somewhat cooler. Out of pockets fell money, notes, letters, photographs, several bits and pieces, keepsakes and cigarettes; in other words, the sort of things one was allowed to keep in a prison camp. All these belongings now lay on the floor, mingled with excrement and wet chlorine, forming a veritable rubbish heap. From time to time, one of the *SS* men would rummage with his boot in this junk, which had been the prisoners' most cherished keepsakes. Whenever an *SS* man discovered something valuable he

would pick it up in mock-disgust, play about with it for a bit, and when he fancied himself unobserved, quickly slip it into his pocket. All we helped ourselves to were belts, which we needed for work and which anyway, we had official permission to take.

The plunder of the dead continued:

> The naked corpses, once they had been dragged across the steps out into the yard, had to undergo a special treatment. Closely supervised by SS men, dentists peered into the mouth of every corpse. When they found gold crowns, gold teeth or other gold work, they pulled them out with forceps. It didn't take long for a small wooden box to be filled, to the undisguised satisfaction of the SS.
> One of the *Blockführers* was struggling with the hand of a huge prisoner in an attempt to remove a wide wedding ring from his finger. The German was so drunk that he could not manage it. He stood there, cursing obscenely and looking around helplessly. Suddenly he noticed a shovel by the wall, which someone had forgotten to take away. Here was the solution to his problem. With one blow he chopped all five fingers off the blue hand. The wedding ring rolled along the floor. With a coarse laugh he picked it up and dropped it virtuously into the box, not without first having kicked the hacked-off stumps in the direction of the corpses. These mutilated fingers made a far more harrowing impression on me than dozens of dead bodies being loaded on platforms.[48]

Once the method of gassing had been determined, the Camp administration needed to find a suitable building to carry out the exterminations. The Camp authorities had installed a crematorium in an old ammunition depot, and in June 1940, August Schlachter, the head of the construction office in the Camp, an architect from Biberbach, obtained an advanced double-muffle, coke-heated furnace from J. A. Töpf and Sons, for *RM* 9,000.[49]

On September 16, 1941, another trial gassing took place and 900 Soviet Prisoners of War were gassed in the morgue of the old crematorium, as recalled by Rudolf Höss in his memoirs:

---

[48] Wiesław Kielar, *Anus Mundi*, Penguin Books, Harmondsworth, England 1980, pp. 62–65.
[49] Robert Jan van Pelt and Deborah Dwork, *Auschwitz 1270 To the Present*, Yale University Press, New Haven and London 1996, pp. 176–177.

> I have a clearer recollection of the gassing of nine hundred Russians which took place shortly afterwards in the old crematorium, since the use of Block II for this purpose caused too much trouble. While the transport was detraining, holes were pierced in the earth and concrete ceiling of the mortuary. The Russians were ordered to undress in an anteroom; they then quietly entered the mortuary, for they had been told they were to be deloused. The whole transport exactly filled the mortuary to capacity. The doors were then sealed and the gas shaken down through the holes in the roof. I do not know how long this killing took. For a little while a humming sound could be heard. When the powder was thrown in there were cries of "Gas," then a great bellowing, and the trapped prisoners hurled themselves against both the doors. But the doors held. They were opened several hours later, so that the place might be aired. It was then that I saw, for the first time, gassed bodies in the mass. The killing of these Russian prisoners of war did not cause me much concern at the time. The order had been given, and I had to carry it out. I must even admit that this gassing set my mind at rest, for the mass extermination of the Jews was to start soon and at that time neither Eichmann nor I were certain how these mass killings were to be carried out.[50]

SS-Unterscharführer Pery Broad provided a description of the crematorium:

> The old Auschwitz crematorium stood at a distance of approximately 100 meters from the Camp. It was said to have originally been a storehouse for turnips. The stone building was surrounded on three sides by earthern embankments on which grass, young trees and beautiful flowers were planted. A level concrete block served as its roof. The area in front of the crematorium was closed in by a high wall with two large gates, the entrance and the exit. Thus when wagons loaded with corpses, brought from the mortuary of Block 28, arrived of an evening to be unloaded, the whole place was hidden from the eyes of unwanted onlookers. A stranger would not so easily have guessed that the rectangular mound planted with many coloured flowers, was in reality the crematorium—unless he noticed the thick metal pipe bent at right angles, which projected from the roof and emitted a monotonous humming. But even then he would hardly know that this was the ventilation pipe, which made the air in the mortuary at least a little more bearable.

---

[50] *KL Auschwitz Seen by the SS*, Panstwowe Muzeum W Oswiecimiu 1978, pp. 93–94.

> The square chimney, which stood some meters away and was connected by underground flues with the four ovens, also had quite an ordinary appearance. But the smoke did not always rise above the chimney in transparent, bluish clouds. It was sometimes pressed down to the ground by the wind. And then one could notice the unmistakeable, penetrating stench of burnt hair and burnt flesh, a stench that spread over many kilometers. When the ovens, in which four to six bodies could be burnt at the same time, were stoked up and dense, pitch-black smoke coiled upwards from the chimney, or when at night the tall flame issuing from the chimney was visible from afar, then there was no doubt as to the purpose of the mound.[51]

The first transport of Jews from Beuthen, on February 15, 1942, destined to die in the gas chambers of Auschwitz arrived at the unloading platform of the Camp's siding. *SS-Unterscharführer* Pery Broad again gave a comprehensive account of this event in the Broad Report:

> Then a sad procession walked along the streets of the camp. It had started at the railway siding, located between the garrison storehouse and the German Armaments Factory. There, at the ramp, cattle vans were being unloaded, and people who had arrived in them were slowly marching towards their unknown destination. All of them had large, yellow Jewish stars on their miserable clothes. A few guards without guns, but with pistols well hidden in their pockets escorted the procession to the crematorium.
> Both sides of the big entrance gate to the crematorium were wide open. Suspecting nothing the column marched in, in lines of five persons, and stood in the yard. Somewhat nervously the SS guard at the entrance waited for the last man to enter the yard. Quickly he shut the gate and bolted it. Grabner and Hössler were standing on the roof of the crematorium. Grabner spoke to the Jews, who unsuspectingly awaited their fate.
> "You will now bathe and be disinfected, we don't want any epidemics in the camp. Then you will be brought to your barracks, where you'll get some hot soup. You will be employed in accordance with your professional qualifications. Now undress and put your clothes in front of you on the ground".
> They willingly followed these instructions, given to them in a friendly warm-hearted voice. Some looked forward to the soup, others were glad

---

[51] Ibid., pp. 156–157.

that the nerve-racking uncertainty as to their immediate future was over and their worst expectations were not realized. All felt relieved after their days full of anxiety. Grabner and Hössler continued from the roof to give friendly advice, which had a calming effect upon the people. The first lines entered the mortuary through the hall. Everything was extremely tidy. But the special smell made some of them uneasy. They looked in vain for showers or water pipes fixed to the ceiling. The hall meanwhile was getting packed. Several *SS* men had entered with them, full of jokes and small talk. They inobtrusively kept their eyes on the entrance. As soon as the last person had entered, they disappeared without much ado. Suddenly the door was closed. It had been made tight with rubber and secured with iron fittings. Those inside heard the heavy bolts being secured. They were fastened together with screws, making the door air-tight. A deadly paralysing terror spread among the victims. They started to beat upon the door, in helpless rage and despair, they hammered on it with their fists. Derisive laughter was the only reply. Somebody shouted through the door, "Don't get burnt while you make your bath"! Several victims noticed that covers had been removed from the six holes in the ceiling.

They uttered a loud cry of terror when they saw a head in a gas-mask at one opening. The 'disinfectors' were at work—one of them was *SS-Unterscharführer*, Adolf Theuer, decorated with the Cross of War Merit. With a chisel and a hammer they opened a few innocuous looking tins which bore the inscription '*Zyklon*' to be used against vermin. Attention poison. To be opened by trained personnel only. The tins were filled to the brim with blue granules the size of peas. Immediately after opening the tins, their contents was thrown into the holes, which were quickly covered.

Meanwhile Grabner gave a sign to the driver of a lorry, which had stopped close to the crematorium. The driver started the motor and its deafening noise was louder than the death cries of the hundreds of people inside, being gassed to death. Grabner looked with the interest of a scientist at the second hand of his wrist watch. *Zyklon* acted swiftly. It consists of hydrogen cyanide in solid form. As soon as the tin was emptied, the pussic acid escaped from the granules. One of the men, who participated in the bestial gassing could not refrain from lifting for a fraction of a second, the cover of one of the vents and from spitting into the hall. Some two minutes later the screams became less loud and only an indistinct groaning was heard. The majority of the victims had already lost consciousness. Two minutes more and Grabner stopped looking at his watch. There was complete silence. The lorry had driven away.

The guards were called off, and the cleaning squad started to sort out the clothes, so tidily put down in the yard of the crematorium. Busy SS men and civilians working in the Camp were again passing the mound, on whose artificial slopes young trees swayed peacefully in the wind. Very few knew what terrible event had taken place there only a few minutes before and what sight the mortuary below the greenery would present. Some time later, when the ventilators had extracted the gas, the prisoners working in the crematorium opened the door to the mortuary. The corpses, their mouths wide open, were leaning on one another. They were especially closely packed near to the door, where in their deadly fright they had crowded to force it. The prisoners of the crematorium squad worked like robots, apathetically and without a trace of emotion. It was difficult to tug the corpses from the mortuary, as their twisted limbs had grown stiff with the gas. Thick smoke clouds poured from the chimney—this was the beginning in 1942.[52]

Filip Müller, was born during 1922, in Sered', Czechoslovakia and was deported to Auschwitz in April 1942. His prisoner number in the Camp was 29236 and he worked in the crematorium as a member of the *Sonderkommando*. He provided a detailed description of what he lived through and witnessed in the crematorium of Auschwitz I. He was ordered to the crematorium with his fellow prisoner Maurice, who had been deported to Auschwitz from the internment Camp at Drancy, near Paris, France:

> We had been running for about 100 meters, when a strange flat-roofed building loomed up before us. Behind it a round red-brick chimney rose up into the sky. Through a wooden gate the two guards led us into a yard which was separated from the outside world by a wall. To our right was the building we had seen, with an entrance in the middle. Above the door hung a wrought iron lamp. Under it stood an *SS* man who, according to his insignia was an *Unterscharführer*. He was still young, with sandy hair and a commanding presence, and I learned later that his name was Stark. In his hand he held a horsewhip. He greeted us with the words , "Get inside you scum!" Then belabouring us with his whip, he drove us through the entrance into a passage with several doors, which were painted pale blue.....

---

[52]   *KL Auschwitz Seen by the SS,* Panstwowe Muzeum W Oswiecimiu 1978, pp. 173–175.

The damp stench of dead bodies and a cloud of stifling, biting smoke surged out towards us. Through the fumes I saw the vague outlines of huge ovens. We were in the cremation room of the Auschwitz crematorium. A few prisoners, the Star of David on their prison uniforms, were running about. As the glow of the flames broke through the smoke and fumes, I noticed two large openings; they were cast iron incinerators. Prisoners were busy pushing a truck heaped with corpses up to them. Stark pulled open another door. Flogging Maurice and me, he hustled us into a larger room, next door to the cremation plant.

Filip Müller continued his grisly account:

We were met by an appalling sight of the dead bodies of men and women lying higgledy-piggledy among suitcases and rucksacks. I was petrified with horror..... a violent blow accompanied by Stark yelling, "Strip the stiffs!" galvanized me into action...... when Stark returned he ordered Maurice and myself to the cremation room. Handing each of us a long crow-bar and a heavy hammer, he ordered us to remove the clinker from the grates of those ovens which were not then in use. Neither Maurice nor I had ever done any work like this before, so we did not know what we were supposed to do. Instead of hammering the crow-bars into the clinker on the grates we thrust them into the ash pit and damaged the fire brick lining. When Stark discovered the damage we had done, he hustled us back into the room where the corpses were and fetched a prisoner called Fischl—later to become our foreman—who went on with cleaning the grates.

Filip Müller described the cremation process:

Coming from the room where I had been undressing corpses into the cremation room, there were two ovens on the left and four on the right. A depression roughly 20 to 25 centimeters deep and 1 meter wide ran across the room and in this rails had been laid. This track was about 15 meters. Leading off from the main track were six branch rails, each 4 meters long, going straight to the ovens. On the main track was a turn-table which enabled a truck to be moved onto the branch tracks. The cast-iron truck had a box—shaped superstructure made of sheet metal, with an overall height and width of just under 1 meter. It was about 80 centimeters long. An iron hand-rail went right across its entire width at the back. A loading platform made of strong sheet metal and not quite

2 meters long jutted out in the front; its side walls were 12 to 15 centimeters high. Open at the front, the platform was not quite as wide as the mouth of the oven, so that it fitted easily into the muffle. On the platform there was also a box-shaped pusher made of sheet metal, higher than the side walls of the platform and rounded off at the top. It was about 50 centimeters deep, 30 to 40 centimeters high and could be moved back and forth quite easily. Before the truck was loaded, the pusher was moved to the back of the platform. To move the truck from one track to another, one had to hold onto the turn-table to prevent the truck from jumping off the rails as it left the turn-table.

To begin with, the corpses were dragged close to the ovens. Then with the help of the turn-table, the truck was brought up to a branch rail, and the front edge of the platform supported by a wooden prop to prevent the truck from tipping during loading. A prisoner then poured a bucket of water on the platform to stop it becoming too hot, inside the red-hot oven. Meanwhile two prisoners were busy lifting a corpse onto a board lying on the floor beside the platform. Then they lifted the board, tipping it sideways so that the corpse dropped on the platform . A prisoner standing on the other side checked that the body was in correct position. When the truck was fully loaded two corpses were lying on either side facing the oven, while a third was wedged between them feet first. Now the time had come to open the oven door. Immediately one was overcome by the fierce heat which rushed out. When the wooden prop had been removed, two men took hold of the front end of the platform on either side pulling it right up to the oven. Simultaneously two men pushed the truck from behind, thus forcing the platform into the oven. The two who had been doing the carrying in front, having meanwhile nipped back a few steps, now braced themselves against the hand-rail while giving the pusher a vigorous shove with one leg. In this way they helped complete the job of getting the corpses right inside the oven. As soon as the front part of the pusher was inside the oven the truck with its platform was pulled back. In order to prevent the load of corpses from sliding out of the oven during this operation, a prisoner standing to one side thrust an iron fork into the oven pressing it against the corpses. While the platform—which had been more than three-quarters inside the oven—was being manoeuvred on its truck back onto the turn-table, the oven door was closed again.

The powers that be had allocated twenty minutes for the cremation of three corpses. It was Stark's duty to see to it that this time was strictly adhered to. All at once, while I busied myself with my ghoulish task, three prisoners started to scurry around crazily in front of the ovens......

by late afternoon the fire had reduced many of the dead bodies into ashes. Yet the bulk of them were still lying about because with three corpses going into each oven at intervals of twenty minutes, it was impossible to cremate more than fifty-four in one hour. I calculated that it would take quite a time before all the dead were cremated.[53]

Another prisoner who witnessed the gassing of prisoners in the crematorium was Josef Paczynski who recalled this for the BBC in their programme *'The Nazis and the Final Solution'* broadcast in 2005:

> I went into the attic of that building. I stood on a crate or something. I lifted a roof tile and I could see everything that was going on right there in front of me. And they were very polite with those people—very polite—undress—pack your things here—this there—that here.
> And then an *SS* man climbed onto the flat roof of the building, he put on a gas mask, opened the hatch and dropped the powder in. When he did this, in spite of the fact that these walls were very thick, you could hear a great scream from within—despite the thick walls.
> This took place at lunchtime, in the daytime. In order to stifle the screaming they had two motorcycles standing on the pavement near the crematorium. Engines revved up as far as they could go, to stifle the screams. To cover up the yelling they had these engines going, but they failed—they gave it a try but it didn't work. The screaming lasted for fifteen or twenty minutes it became weaker and weaker then went quiet.[54]

---

[53] Filip Müller, *Eyewitness Auschwitz*, Ivan R. Dee, Chicago 1979, pp. 11–17.
[54] Auschwitz—*The Nazis and the Final Solution* – BBC 2005.

Chapter V
Auschwitz-Birkenau
1941–1942

Following Heinrich Himmler's visit to Auschwitz in March 1941, he instructed Rudolf Höss to establish a Camp to hold 100,000 Soviet Prisoners of War in the nearby village of Brzezinka, in Polish or *Birkenau* in German. The construction began in October 1941. The *SS* commenced demolishing the farm buildings in Birkenau and assembling the materials needed to build the Camp.

The plan for the Prisoner-of-War Camp in Birkenau was approved by *SS-Sturmbannführer* Karl Bischoff, who had arrived in Auschwitz from *Amstgruppe C* of the *WVHA* in Berlin, and who subsequently became the head of the Central Construction Board of the *Waffen-SS* in Auschwitz. According to the plan, the site was to be divided by the main street of the Camp. A railroad platform was planned to run alongside the street. To the left of the street and platform would be a quarantine Camp, to the right, Administration Sections I and II. The whole site formed a rectangle surrounded by a barbed-wire fence and watchtowers. The dimensions of this rectangle were 787 by 1236 yards. The plan showed a total of 174 brick residence barracks in the three sections.

SS-Unterscharführer Pery Broad provided a description of the Camp in Birkenau in the already mentioned 'Broad Report':

> At a distance of five or six kilometers from the base camp, the notorious Camp of Birkenau was formed in 1941/42. It later contained 30,000 women prisoners and 50,000 to 60,000 men prisoners. If one went by train from Bielitz to Auschwitz in the evening, then one could see to the left an endless string of glaring lamps, like a string of beads, and a row of white-washed concrete posts, which formed the fence of the Birkenau Camp. The prisoners living quarters consisted of hundreds of windowless horse stables used as barracks, and of primitive stone houses.

The Camp was divided into three sectors. The first sector to be built housed women prisoners. Sector II was divided into six squares, which were used for different purposes. For example one square of this sector was used as a hospital, another served as the Gypsy Camp, while yet another contained the quarantine blocks for new arrivals. Sector III was still under construction when Auschwitz-Birkenau were hurriedly evacuated on January 17, 1945.

The wooden barracks, by now already finished, served as a weaving work-shop, and were occasionally used for housing prisoners. Conditions in Birkenau were considerably worse than in Auschwitz, where they were bad enough. Feet sank into a sticky bog at every step. There was hardly any water for washing. The prisoners slept, six in a bed, on wooden planks placed in three tiers. Most of the beds were without straw pallets. The roll call held twice daily, meant standing for hours in wet and cold weather with mire underfoot. If it rained in the daytime, the prisoners would be obliged to lie on the beds in their wet clothes. No wonder that several hundred of them died everyday.[55]

Rudolf Höss wrote in his memoirs about the Russian Prisoners of War engaged in constructing Birkenau:

> It was with these prisoners, many of whom could hardly stand, that I was now supposed to build the Birkenau Prisoner-of-War Camp. *SS-Reichsführer* ordered that only the strongest of the Russian prisoners, those who were particularly capable of hard work, were to be sent to me. The officers who accompanied them said these were the best available at Lamsdorf. They were willing to work, but were incapable of doing so, because of their weakened condition. I remember very clearly how we continually gave them food when first they arrived at the base camp, but in vain.... The Russians could endure the cold more or less, but not the damp and being constantly wet through. In the unfinished, simple stone barracks, hastily constructed in the early days of Birkenau, the death rate constantly rose.[56]

Auschwitz-Birkenau was destined to play a major part in the destruction of European Jewry and Rudolf Höss recalled in his memoirs how he was summoned to meet *RFSS* Heinrich Himmler in the

---

[55] *KL Auschwitz Seen by the SS,* Panstwowe, Muzeum W Oswiecimiu 1978, pp. 138–139.

[56] *KL Auschwitz Seen by the SS,* Panstwowe Muzeum W Oswiecimiu 1978, pp. 59–60.

summer of 1941, although he cannot remember the precise date. Himmler told Höss the following:

> The *Führer* has ordered that the Jewish question be solved once and for all and that we, the *SS*, are to implement that order. The existing extermination centres in the East[57] are not in a position to carry out the large actions which are anticipated. I have therefore earmarked Auschwitz for this purpose, both because of its good position as regards communications and because the area can be easily isolated and camouflaged. At first I thought of calling in a senior *SS* officer for this job, but I changed my mind in order to avoid difficulties concerning the terms of reference. I have now decided to entrust this task to you. It is difficult and onerous and calls for complete devotion, notwithstanding the difficulties that may arise. You will learn further details from *SS-Sturmbannführer* Eichmann of the Reich Security Head Office, who will call on you in the immediate future.
>
> The departments concerned will be notified by me in due course. You will treat this order as absolutely secret, even from your superiors. After your talk with Eichmann you will immediately forward to me the plans of the projected installations. The Jews are the sworn enemies of the German people and must be eradicated. Every Jew that we can lay our hands on is to be destroyed now during the War, without exception. If we cannot obliterate the biological basis of Jewry, the Jews will one day destroy the German people.[58]

The gas chamber in Auschwitz I had only a modest capacity and was totally inadequate to deal with the Nazis murderous intentions towards European Jewry and Birkenau presented the most ideal location. Adolf Eichmann, as Himmler had stated to Rudolf Höss, in the meeting described above, soon visited Auschwitz. Adolf Eichmann was the head of Jewish and Evacuation Affairs, Section IV-B-4, of the *Reichssicherheitshauptamt (RSHA)* in Berlin.

In Birkenau, a dwelling house belonging to Poles forcibly evacuated by the Germans, was identified by Adolf Eichmann during his

---

[57] At that time—August 1941, there were no extermination centres in the East, Chełmno the first was not operational until December 1941, thus Himmler might be referring to Einsatzgruppen shooting actions.

[58] *KL Auschwitz Seen by the SS*, Panstwowe Muzeum W Oswiecimiu 1978, p. 108.

first visit to Auschwitz, as being suitable. The farmhouse had its windows walled up, its doors strengthened and sealed by screwing them in place, and shafts drilled in the walls. On March 20, 1942, the converted farmhouse in Birkenau with its two gas chambers was put into operation. This gas chamber was known in the Camp as 'Bunker I.' The corpses of those gassed were then buried in mass graves, in the nearby meadow.[59]

Rudolf Höss described the selection of the former peasant farmstead, by him and Adolf Eichmann in more detail during the month of August 1941:

> We left the matter unresolved. Eichmann decided to try and find a gas that was in ready supply and would not entail special installations for its use, and to inform me when he had done so. We decided that a peasant farmstead situated in the northwest corner of what later became Section III in Birkenau would be the most suitable. It was isolated and screened by woods and hedges, and it was also not far from the railroad. The bodies could be placed in long, deep pits dug in the nearby meadows. We had not at that time thought of burning the corpses. We calculated that after gas-proofing the premises then available, it would be possible to kill about 800 people simultaneously with a suitable gas. Eichmann returned to Berlin to report our conversation to the *SS-Reichsführer*. A few days later I sent to the *SS-Reichsführer* by courier a detailed site plan and description of the installation.[60]

SS-Unterscharführer Pery Broad wrote:

> At some distance from the Birkenau Camp, which was growing at an incredible rate, there stood amongst pleasant scenery, two pretty and tidy looking farmhouses, separated from one another by a grove. They were dazzlingly whitewashed, cosily thatched and surrounded by fruit trees of the kind that usually grows there.... The attentative spectator might have noticed signs in many languages on the houses. The signs read: 'To Disinfection'. Then he might observe that the houses were windowless, but had a disproportionate number of remarkably strong doors, made air-tight with rubber and secured with screwed down bolts, while small wooden flaps were fixed near the bolts. Near the small

---

[59] Danuta Czech, *Auschwitz Chronicle*, Henry Holt and Company, New York 1990, p. 144.
[60] Ibid., p. 78.

houses there were several incongruously large stables, such as were used in Birkenau to accommodate prisoners. The roads leading to them bore the tracks of many heavily loaded vans. If the visitor discovered in addition, that from the doors there led a van track to some pits, hidden by brushwood fences, then he would certainly guess that the houses served some special purpose.[61]

Moshe Maurice Garbarz decribed the gas chamber known as Bunker I, also known in the Camp as the 'Red House':

> We saw a sort of barn closed on three sides, identical to those where our farmers keep the hay, and not far from it, three or four pretty little buildings like country houses, only the first of which was close enough to be clearly visible. The convoys arrived, adult men and little boys together, women, girls and babies together. They went completely naked in groups of twenty towards the little house. Despite the distance we could see that they were not afraid. A strange *Kommando* dressed in white, led them, four men only, plus two *SS*.
> When the people had entered the house, they were shut in by a fairly strong door. When the door was well and truly bolted an *SS* man passed with a can and disappeared from our eyes, hidden by the house. Then we heard a bang, that of someone opening a trap door, rather than a window. Twice after this bang, we heard the prayer 'Shema Israel,' then we heard cries, but very faintly.
> From time to time, at the last minute, just before disappearing behind the door, the people understood. I saw one group of men revolt. The case had been foreseen; a *Kommando* of four or five people was waiting beside the entrance and pushed them inside, while an *SS* man used his revolver to shoot some in the head. The external aspect of the little house was so ordinary that such incidents were very rare. In seven days I saw only one revolt with my own eyes. But others took place, for several times, from afar, we heard the same characteristic sound of a shot at point blank range.

The rectangle where we had the previous day installed the posts had been dug out and transformed into a kind of empty swimming pool with cleanly cut edges, about one meter fifty deep. The ground had been left around our posts to stop them falling. Some rails were installed, starting one meter from the little house. As soon as the Jews

---

[61] *KL Auschwitz Seen by the SS*, Panstwowe Muzeum W Oswiecimiu 1978, pp. 175–176.

were gassed, a new team came along and added rails as far as the edge of the swimming pool. The group also belonged to the *Sonderkommando*. The men of this *Kommando* ate well, they were properly dressed. They lived entirely separately and no longer returned to our camp to sleep. The SS said that in a week we would be enrolled with them. So I now had less than a week in which I had to try something, however desperate. We saw the special *Kommando* put platform trolleys on the rails. Then they brought out the men, women and children, who had been gassed to load them on these flat wagons. In order not to lose any on the way, they stacked them like sacks of flour, five width-ways and five length-ways. Their work was tough and their *Kapo*, a German, would not allow a moments rest. He was constantly crying, "*Schneller! Schneller!* (Faster, Faster) otherwise I'll wipe you out! I'll gas you on the spot!" and he kicked them. All the men, women and children were quickly thrown in the hole and covered with earth.[62]

During June 1942, another farmhouse in Birkenau became operational as a gassing facility, similar to Bunker I, but this time there were four gas chambers, two more than Bunker I. It was located to the west of the yet to be built Crematorium IV and V, and is known within the camp as Bunker II, or the 'White House'. The farmhouses originally belonged to the families Harmata and Wichaj, who were forced to vacate. One of the prisoner members of the *Sonderkommando*, Szlama Dragon described the conditions in Bunker II during December 1942:

> The next day on the morning of 10th December 1942, once all the *Kommando's* had gone to work, Moll arrived at Block 14 and gave the order "*Sonderkommando raus!*" It was thus that we learnt we were detailed, not to go to the rubber factory (*Buna*), but to a *Sonderkommando* and we did not realize what this was for, nobody had ever given us the slightest explanation of it. On Moll's order, we went out of the block and were divided into two groups of 100 men each to be marched out of the Camp by the SS.
> We were taken into a forest where there was a cottage covered with thatch, its windows bricked in . On the door leading to the interior of

---

[62] www. holocaustresearchproject.org. (H.E.A.R.T.)

the cottage was a metal plate with the inscription *'Hochspannung / Lebensgefahr'* (High Tension / Danger). Thirty or forty meters from this cottage there were two wooden huts. On the other side of the cottage there were four pits 30 meters long, 7 meters wide and 3 meters deep, their edges black with smoke.

We were then lined up in front of the house. Moll arrived and told us we would work here at burning old lousy people, that we would be given something to eat and in the evening we would be taken back to the Camp. He added that those who did not accept this work would be beaten and have the dogs set on them. The SS who escorted us were accompanied by dogs. Then he split us into a number of groups. I myself and eleven others were detailed, as we learnt later, to remove the bodies from this cottage. We were all given masks and led to the door of the cottage, when Moll opened the door, we saw that the cottage was full of naked corpses of both sexes and all ages.

Moll ordered us to move these corpses from the cottage to the yard in front of the door. We started work with four men carrying one body. This annoyed Moll, he rolled up his sleeves and threw a body into the yard. When, despite this example, we said we were incapable of doing that, he allowed us to carry them, two men to a body. Once the corpses were laid out in the yard, the dentist assisted by an SS man, pulled out the teeth and the barber, also watched by an SS man, cut off the hair.

Another group loaded the bodies onto wagons, running on rails, that led to the edge of the pits. These rails ran between two pits. Still another group prepared the pit for burning the corpses. First of all, big logs were put in the bottom. The logs are on the right along the wall of the undressing hut, then smaller and smaller wood in criss-cross fashion and finally dry twigs. The following group threw the bodies into the pit. Once all the bodies had been brought from the cottage to the pit, Moll poured kerosene over them in the four corners of the pit and set fire to it by throwing in a burning rubber comb (roughly fringed piece of rubber). That is how the corpses were burnt. While Moll was starting the fire, we were in the front of the cottage, on the north-west side and could see what he was doing.

After having removed all the bodies from the cottage, we were obliged to clean it thoroughly, washing the floor with water and spreading sawdust and whitewashing the walls. The interior of the cottage was divided into four parts by partition walls running across it, one of which could contain 1,200 naked people, the second 700, the third 400 and the fourth 200 to 250.⁶³

Richard Bock an *SS-Rottenführer* who worked in the Camp garage recalled witnessing a mass gassing at Bunker I in Birkenau:

> Holblinger said to me, "Richard, are you interested in seeing one of the actions?" I said, "Yes, very interested indeed," and he said "I'll take you with me this evening." We drove out to Birkenau, not to where the ramp was later, but where the train stopped on the big slope. It was a transport from Holland, and the Dutch Jews who came to Auschwitz were very elegant and rich. He parked his ambulance there and I sat in it pretending to be the co-driver.
>
> Then they drove them all off in a lorry to Bunker I, where there were four big halls. The halls did not have a proper roof, just a sloping top. At first, Holblinger did not have anything to do. Then they went into the hall and the new arrivals had to get undressed, and then the order came, 'Prepare for disinfection.' There were enormous piles of clothing in there, and there was a board running around so that the piles did not all collapse. And the new arrivals, the Dutch people, had to stand on top of this great heap of clothes to get undressed. Lots of them hid their children under the clothes and covered them up, then they shouted 'Get ready' and they all went out, they had to run naked approximately twenty yards from the hall across to Bunker I.
>
> There were two doors standing open and they went in there and when a certain number had gone inside, they shut the doors. That happened about three times, and every time Holblinger had to go out to his ambulance and they took out a sort of tin—he and one of his block chiefs—and then he climbed up the ladder and at the top there was a round hole and he opened a little round door and held the tin there and shook it and then he shut the little door again. Then a fearful screaming started up and approximately after about ten minutes it slowly went quiet.⁶⁴

Richard Bock continued his account:

> They opened the door—it was a prisoners' *Sonderkommando* who did that—then a blue haze came out. I looked in and I saw a pyramid. They had all climbed up on top of each other until the last one stood at the very top, all one on top of the other and then the prisoners had to go in

---

⁶³   www.holocaustresearchproject.org. (H.E.A.R.T.)
⁶⁴   Richard Holmes, *The World At War*, Ebury Press 2007, pp. 334–335.

and tear it apart. They were all tangled, one had his arm down by another's foot and then round it and back up again and his fingers were sticking in someone else's eye, so deep.

They were all tangled, they had to tug and pull very hard to disentangle all these people. Then we went back to the hall and now it was the turn of the last lot to get undressed, the ones who had managed to hang back a bit all the time. One girl with beautiful black hair, a beautiful girl, was crouching there and didn't want to get undressed and an SS man came up and said, "I suppose you don't want to get undressed," and she tossed her hair back and laughed a little. Then he went away and came back with two prisoners and they literally tore the clothes off her, then they each grabbed an arm and they dragged her across to Bunker I and pushed her in there. Then the prisoners had to check where the small children had been hidden and covered up. They pulled them out and opened the doors quickly again and threw all the children in and slammed the doors.[65]

Eva Votavova, from Slovakia was deported to Auschwitz in July 1942. She described her arrival at the *Judenrampe*. This unloading platform was located 1 kilometer south east from the entrance of the Camp at Birkenau:

When they opened the train carriages and forced us out, they shouted at us immediately. They were screaming in German. They were SS men who were dealing with us. We had to stand in line. Men had to step out first, then women and children, and then old people. I looked at my father, here, and I saw a sad look on his face. This is my last memory of him.[66]

Rudolf Höss in his memoirs summed up these early mass gassings in the converted farmhouses:

During the spring of 1942, hundreds of vigorous men and women walked all unsuspecting to their death in the gas chambers, under the blossom-laden fruit trees of the 'Cottage' orchard. This picture of death in the midst of life remains with me to this day.[67]

---

[65] Richard Holmes, *The World At War*, Ebury Press, 2007, pp. 335–336.
[66] Auschwitz—The Nazis and The Final Solution, BBC 2005.
[67] *KL Auschwitz Seen by the SS,* Panstwowe Muzeum W Oswiecimiu 1978, p. 100.

Some 400 prisoners brought from Warsaw and Kraków during 1940–41, on May 27, 1942, and were sent to the Penal Company, which from May 9, 1942, was located in Block 1, in Sector B-Ib. Prisoners who belonged to the Penal Company were distinguished by having a black patch in the shape of a circle sewn on their shirts and trousers, whilst those sent there in May 1942, had to have an additional red circle, which helped the Political Department keep a special eye, on these 'dangerous' prisoners. Zenon Rozanski, a prisoner, described what happened with this group of prisoners:

> A week later, eight men with red circles were called out after the morning roll call, sent to the central camp and shot there in Block No.11. Two days later another 10 'red circles' were called out after the morning roll call, and again came the news that they had all been shot. When for the third time prisoners from this group were summoned to the central camp, it became clear, that the wearers of the 'red circles' had been sentenced to death. The atmosphere in the company became heavy. The 'red circles' began to keep apart from the others. Every free moment one saw them gathered together and breaking off the conversation if anyone else approached them. During work periods they worked twice as hard.[68]

The news of the shootings at the central Camp reached the Penal Company through the underground, for Witold Pilecki, the network had several men there: Cadet Officer Stanislaw Maringe, Henryk Lachowicz, Jerzy Porazinski, Zenon Rozanski, Captain Chruscicki and his son Tadeusz Chruscicki. Pilecki was informed of the fact that the 'red circles' were doomed, and that an escape attempt had to be made.

The whole complement of the Penal Company worked near the River Vistula where they were building a canal known in the Camp as the *Königsgraben*. They toiled under the harsh leadership of *SS-Hauptscharführer* Otto Moll, assisted by a number of *Kapo's*. The Camp underground recognized that working near the River Vistula offered a good chance of escape for the doomed men and the underground were contacted on the other side of the river, to aid the escaping prisoners. Henryk Lachowicz took on the role of organizer

---

[68] Jozef Garlinski, *Fighting Auschwitz*, Fontana Collins 1975, p. 101.

and leader of the 'red circles' group of men. The plan was when Moll blew his whistle to cease work for the day, the men in the penal company were to jump the SS men, disarm them and run for the embankment by the Vistula. This action would be the signal for the other group of 'red circles' and for the rest of the prisoners to escape.

The whole complement of the penal company would have to force the embankment and swim across the river. The underground contacts on the other side of the River Vistula would from then on aid their wider bids for freedom. It was decided that the escape attempt would take place on June 10, 1942. It was a beautiful sunny day, but suddenly at circa 4:00 p.m. clouds appeared in the sky, and rain began to fall. The rain increased into a downpour and in the torrents of rain, it became almost impossible to see. Those in the know were not upset by this, as this bad weather could only increase their chances of escape. Bad weather such as this, would not curtail the working day.

But this time they were badly mistaken, unexpectedly Otto Moll came out of his hut, looked around and with one long shrill whistle gave the signal to knock-off work, although it was only half past four. Zenon Rozanski, who was on the verge of escaping himself, described what happened next:

> I turned my head to where Lachowicz was working with his group. They were by themselves, about 300 meters from the next group. What now? What would Lachowicz decide? Could the whole, carefully prepared operation be carried out now? I could feel cold shivers running down my spine. I stood motionless, as if hypnotized. Suddenly I heard a shout from the embankment. Several prisoners are rushing it. The figure of the guard disappears and soon after I see him on the ground. The escapees are running past him. The distance between me and where they are is a good 200 meters.
> A few meters from me Moll is standing, completely taken by surprise. If I move, I thought quickly, he will put a bullet into my head. The prisoners are running wildly from every side. The guards are throwing down their rifles and chasing them along the embankment. I can see plainly figures running across the wall and disappearing on the other side. Suddenly on the embankment appears *Kapo* Karl Dachdecker with other *Kapos*. He is holding an axe in his hand and shrieking savagely. A few meters from him the prisoner Henryk Pajaczkowski runs onto the wall.

65

Karl threw himself on him. For a moment they struggled. In the end, Pajaczkowski fell to the ground beneath Karl's blows. This was the turning point. The other prisoners running towards the embankment suddenly stopped and *Kommandoführer* Moll remembered that he had a pistol. Bullets began to whistle around the ears of the escapees. The order came: lie down.

The early signal to finish work early, had seriously affected the escape attempt. Only fifty prisoners with the 'red circles' under Henryk Lachowicz, had disarmed the *SS* guards and made a break for freedom. Thirteen fell in the attempt, and only nine crossed the River Vistula and found freedom. The Camp authorities exacted a bloody retaliation for the escape attempt:[69]

After the morning roll call, on June 11, 1942, more than 100 prisoners marked with a 'black circle' and several marked with 'red circles' were taken to work at the *Königsgraben* canal. Meanwhile circa 320 prisoners marked with 'red circles' stood with their knees bent and outstretched arms in the courtyard of the Penal Company. At 10:00 a.m. *Lagerführer* Hans Aumeier entered with a few *SS* men; he ordered all the prisoners assembled to point out the instigators of the escape attempt. He did not receive an answer, so he personally shot seventeen prisoners, and *SS Hauptscharführer* Hössler shot another three. In the afternoon, a few more prisoners with 'red circles' were brought from the prisoners' infirmary in Birkenau and put with the others. They undressed and took off their shoes, and their hands were tied behind their backs with barbed wire. After, *SS* guards led by Gerhard Palitzsch arrived, the group of circa 320 prisoners was taken to Bunker I and were gassed.[70]

A few days later on June 20, 1942, another audacious escape attempt from Auschwitz took place. In the afternoon, a Steyr 220, drove up to the barrier which separated the Camp's zone of interest from the outside world. In the car were two officers and two NCO's of the *SS*, armed with pistols and rifles, and wearing helmets. The *SS* man on guard at the barrier, seeing the officer's uniforms omitted the checking of passes, and let the car pass, shouting *Heil Hitler*.

The Steyr car sped quickly through the streets of Auschwitz town, crossed the bridge over the River Sola and turned north. Twice the car

---

[69] Jozef Garlinski, *Fighting Auschwitz*, Fontana Collins 1975, pp. 102–104.

[70] Danuta Czech, *Auschwitz Chronicle*, Henry Holt and Company, New York 1990, pp. 177–178.

met groups of working prisoners with SS guards. Several times the car took wrong roads and the driver had to turn back.

At the evening roll-call in the main Camp, it was discovered that four prisoners were missing, as was the Steyr motor car of SS-Captain Kreuzmann, in charge of the Motor Workshops and Garages. SS-*Hauptsturmführer* Hans Aumeier, who had just returned from Buna in time for the roll-call, screamed in rage that he had passed the Steyr on the road and that he had returned the salute of the officers riding in the car.

The SS-man who had let the car pass through the barrier was brought from the guard house and the numbers of the prisoners working at the Troops Supply Depot (*TWL – Truppenwirtschaftslager*) were checked. Four prisoners—Kazimierz Piechowski (918), Jozef Lempart (3419), Stanislaw Jaster (6438) and Eugeniusz Bendera (8502) were missing as was the Steyr 220 automobile bearing the license number SS-20868. Some 50 miles from Auschwitz the car was abandoned and concealed in a pit in the Sucha Forest near Saybusch.[71]

Returning to the subject of mass extermination, the SS knew that the gas chambers functioning in the two converted farmhouses in Birkenau, could only be considered as a temporary facility to achieve the 'The Final Solution' to the Jewish Question in Europe. Thus they started to plan the construction of four large gas chamber and crematoria facilities in Birkenau. On July 1, 1942, the Central Construction Administration of the *Waffen-SS* and Police in Auschwitz invited firms that had already carried out building work in Auschwitz to build new crematoria in Birkenau. The firms contacted were *Huta Hoch-und Tiefbau AG* and Lenz Industrial Construction Company of Silesia, in Kattowice. The incineration facilities were to be delivered and installed by the firm of J.A. Töpf and Sons, Erfurt. On July 15, 1942, the Lenz company declined to build the crematoria in Birkenau so the Central Construction Administration invited Huta Engineering to begin construction immediately.[72]

Heinrich Himmler, the *Reichsführer-SS,* began his second tour of inspection on July 17, 1942; this time a two-day visit of Auschwitz,

---

[71] Jozef Garlinski, *Fighting Auschwitz*, Fontana Collins 1975, pp. 99–100.
[72] Danuta Czech, *Auschwitz Chronicle*, Henry Holt and Company, New York 1990, pp. 190 and 197.

including the various camps, farms and projects in the vicinity of the Concentration Camp was undertaken. From his *Tagebuch* entry, he was accompanied on the trip by members of his own staff, Professor Wüst, Felix Kersten, Werner Grothmann and Josef Kiermaier. The entourage flew from Lötzen to Kattowice, where they were met by *Gauleiter* Fritz Bracht, *SS-Obergruppenführer* Ernst Schmauser and Commandant Rudolf Höss.[73]

Also present was *SS-Brigadeführer* Hans Kammler, the Head of *Amt C*, the construction department of the *SS*, in Berlin. On the first day of the inspection, Rudolf Höss outlined the arrangements of the Camps and their locations using maps. In the Construction Administration, Hans Kammler explained the projects under construction or those being planned, with the aid of maps, blueprints and models. Following this, Himmler and his entourage toured the whole Interest Zone, the farms and soil improvement projects, the dam construction, the laboratories and the plant breeding in Rajsko, the cattle breeding and nursery.

The inspection covered Birkenau, where they witnessed the prisoners at work, the accommodations, kitchens, and infirmaries where they saw the emaciated victims of epidemics. Himmler and his group went to the railway spur, adjacent to the main line, where they watched the selection of a transport from the Netherlands. Rudolf Höss recalled:

> Himmler very carefully observed the entire process of annihilation. He began with the unloading at the ramps and completed the inspection as Bunker II was being cleared of bodies. At that time there were no open pit burnings. He did not complain about anything.[74]

After witnessing the gassing, Himmler inspected the Buna plant and the installation of a sewage gas plant. In the evening of the first day, a dinner was held in the *Führerheim* in the town of Auschwitz, for all the guests and all the *SS* officers of the Auschwitz garrison. After

---

[73] *Der Dienstkalender Heinrich Himmler 1941/42*, Christians, Hamburg 1999, p. 491.
[74] Robert Jan van Pelt and Deborah Dwork, Auschwitz 1270 To the Present, Yale University Press, New Haven and London 1996, p. 319.

the dinner, Himmler, along with Rudolf Höss, Ernst Schmauser, Hans Kammler, and the Auschwitz Director Dr. Joachim Caesar went to a reception at the house of *Gauleiter* Bracht in Kattowice. At Himmlers' invitation, the wife of Rudolf Höss, also attended.

After breakfast with *Gauleiter* Brack and his wife, Himmler retuned to Auschwitz on July 18, 1942. He visited the kitchens, the women's camp, the workshops, the stables, 'Canada'—the so-called camp where the personal effects were sorted and stored, the *DAW* plant as well as the butcher shop and bakery. In the women's camp he witnessed the flogging of a female prisoner and a roll-call. There, *SS*-Chief Supervisor Johanna Langefeldt applied for the release of a few German women prisoners, which Himmler approved.

After the tour, a discussion was held in Höss's office, with Ernst Schmauser also present. Himmler informed Höss that the *SIPO* operations he had ordered must not be stopped. He ordered Höss to proceed faster with the construction of Birkenau and to kill the Jewish prisoners who were unfit for work. Himmler told Höss to prepare for the work of building armaments plants and to continue with the various agricultural projects. In recognition of his work and the progress made so far, Himmler promoted Höss to the rank of *SS-Obersturmbannführer*.[75]

On August 15, 1942, *SS-Sturmbannführer* Karl Bischoff, the Head of the Central Construction Administration approved an additional construction project for the Camp at Birkenau, that proposed to hold 200, 000 Prisoners of War. As a consequence of the decision to carry out the mass extermination of the Jews, and simultaneously to use Auschwitz as a reservoir of labor of Jewish prisoners selected from the transports to be employed for the benefit of German industry, this required changes to the previous plan to create space for housing the prisoners, as well as to erect appropriate extermination facilities.

Of the previous plan, only Section I remained, encompassing the Women's Camp in Section B-Ib and a Men's Camp in Section B-Ia.

---

[75] Danuta Czech, *Auschwitz Chronicle*, Henry Holt and Company, New York 1990, p. 199.

The second section B-II was to be to the right of these Camps, and next to these the third section, B-III—later called 'Mexico' by the Camp inmates. The fourth section, B-IV, which was never constructed, was planned to be to the left of Section B-I. Between Sections B-I and B-II was the main street of the Camp, where a railroad siding was planned for Section B-II. Except for the already built camp areas housing male and some female prisoners, the new sections were to consist of six camps each, separated from one another by fences with their own entrance gates and guard rooms for the SS men. Each of these sections was to hold 60,000 people; only the first section was planned to accommodate 20,000 people.

The entire Camp was to occupy a rectangular site of 790 by 2660 yards. Two crematoriums with gas chambers were planned for two rectangular sites at the western side of the Camp, to be built on the extension of the main street of the Camp and the railroad siding. In fact, four crematoriums with gas chambers were built and the construction of an additional crematorium was planned. Altogether, the plan encompassed 600 new buildings: residential, warehouses and office barracks, bathing facilities, laundry buildings, latrines, guard rooms and so on.

In an area of 432 acres, the following buildings were constructed: four large crematoriums with gas chambers; a delousing and bathing facility, the so-called 'Sauna'; about three hundred barracks for housing, administration, offices, latrines, laundry; a personal effects camp consisting of about thirty barracks for stolen property, which was known as 'Canada II' by the prisoners and the SS; a railroad siding with an unloading platform and a barbed-wire fence; 8 miles of drainage ditches and several miles of streets and roads.[76]

On August 19, 1942, Head Engineer, Kurt Prüfer, the representative of J.A. Töpf and Sons from Erfurt arrived at Auschwitz to conduct discussions with the Central Construction Administration regarding the construction of the crematorium ovens for incinerating corpses. During the discussions, it was agreed that a mechanic

---

[76] Ibid., p. 218.

Holik, would arrive from Buchenwald Concentration Camp on August 26 or 27 at the latest and another mechanic, Koch would arrive within fourteen days. The assembly of five triple-muffle crematorium ovens was to begin immediately. Walling in the ovens and constructing the chimney was to be done by the Köhler Company of Myslowitz, according to the plans and specifications drawn up by J.A. Töpf and Sons.[77]

A day later on August 20, 1942, the owner of the Köhler Company of Myslowitz and *SS-Obersturmführer* Josef Janisch of the Central Construction Administration went to one of the crematoriums in Birkenau to discuss details concerning the masonry for the five-triple-snout crematorium ovens and the chimney.[78]

One of the key members of the underground, Jozef Cyrankiewicz, was brought to Auschwitz on September 4, 1942, from Kraków. He was arrested during April 1942, in the secret office of the Kraków District *ZWZ*, and he spent the next 18-months in the Montelupich Prison in Kraków. Although only 31, he was one of the most prominent representatives of the *PPS* in occupied Poland. Before the war he had been the secretary to the Workers' District Committee of the Kraków Area—not a very important post, but he came to the fore through ambition and opportunity. Immediately on his arrival in Auschwitz, Adam Kurylowicz (18487) aided him, with the help of Dr. Rudolf Diem, to obtain a place in the Hospital, in Block 21, as a night clerk. In a very short space of time, Cryankiewicz became a member of the secret Fighting Organization of the *PPS* in the camp, and since he was a reserve officer, he also joined the Union of Military Organization.[79]

The Commandant's Office received written authorization on September 15, 1942, from Richard Glücks, the Head of Branch D of the *WVHA* for a trip by car to Łódź in the *Warthegau*, dated September 16, 1942. The purpose of the trip was to inspect an experimental facility of 'field ovens' to be used in connection with *Aktion*

---

[77] Ibid., p. 222.
[78] Ibid., p. 224.
[79] Jozef Garlinski *Fighting Auschwitz*, Fontana Collins 1975, p. 169.

Reinhardt. The following day Commandant Rudolf Höss, *SS-Untersturmführer* Franz Hössler and *SS-Hauptsturmführer* Walter Dejaco visited the extermination facility at Chełmno on the Ner, known to the Germans as *Kulmhof*. This is where *SS-Standartenführer* Paul Blobel, who had previously visited Rudolf Höss in Auschwitz, a little while after Himmler's visit, told Höss that the bodies buried in Birkenau had to be exhumed and cremated.

In June 1942, *SS-Gruppenführer* Heinrich Müller, the Head of the *Gestapo*, formally appointed Blobel to lead a *Kommando* with the task of erasing all traces of the mass executions carried out in the East. This grisly task was top secret, and was given the code name 'Sonderaktion 1005'. After his appointment, Blobel, along with a small squad of three or four men, began experimenting with different methods of burning bodies at Chełmno, in the *Waldlager* (Forest Camp).

Chełmno was the first Death Camp to use static gas chambers, although these were gas vans, rather than purpose-built gas chambers. This Camp became operational in December 1941, under the control of Herbert Lange, who served in the *Gestapo* office in *Posen*, today it is known as Poznan. After murdering Jews from the local communities, mass deportations took place from the Łódź (*Litzmannstadt*) ghetto. The Jews were taken to an abandoned palace on the edge of the village, next to the church. After undressing in the basement of the palace, the deportees were led through a brightly-lit corridor to a wooden ramp which led to the back of a vehicle—a gas van, with its back door open. The moment the last of the victims stepped into the vehicle the Germans locked the hemetic door. The driver connected the exhaust pipe with a vent in the floor of the gas van. After the engine had been started the exhaust gases spread quickly within the gas chamber, suffocating the people locked inside. The driver then took the suffocated victims to the Forest Camp (*Waldlager*) in the Rzuchów forest, where the corpses were buried in mass graves, that had been prepared in advance.[80]

---

[80] www. Holocaust Historical Society. org. uk. (HHS).

Blobel and his small team opened the mass graves and the first attempts to dispose of the corpses were carried out. Incendiary bombs were used, but these caused large fires in the surrounding woods. Then they experimented with cremating the bodies on wood in open fireplaces. The bones that remained were destroyed by a special bone-crushing machine. The ashes of the bodies and small fragments of bones were buried in the pits from which the bodies had been removed.[81]

In his memoirs, Rudolf Höss recalled his visit to Chełmno (*Kulmhof*):

> Hössler and I went to *Kulmhof* on a tour of inspection. Blobel had various makeshift ovens constructed, which were fired with wood and petrol refuse. He had also attempted to dispose of the bodies with explosives, but their destruction had been very incomplete. The ashes were distributed over the neighbouring countryside, after first being ground to a powder in a bone mill.... How many bodies lay in the mass graves at *Kulmhof* or how many had already been cremated, I was unable to ascertain.[82]

On September 21, 1942, the SS commenced the burning of the corpses in the open at Birkenau. At first the bodies were burned on wood piles on which 2,000 bodies were stacked at a time, and later they were burned in pits. In order to burn the bodies faster, they were first drenched with oil residue and then with wood alcohol. The pits burned day and night without a break.[83]

Otto Pressburger, one of the Jewish members of the *Sonderkommando* recalled his gruesome work near the gas chambers:

> We were digging holes. We really didn't know what they were for. It was only when the holes were deep enough that we started to throw the bodies into them. It was appalling. New bodies were lying here every

---

[81] Y. Arad, *Bełżec, Sobibór, Treblinka,* Indiana University Press, Bloomington and Indianapolis, 1987, p. 171.

[82] *KL Auschwitz Seen by the SS,* Panstwowe Muzeum W Oswiecimiu 1978, pp. 116–117.

[83] Danuta Czech, *Auschwitz Chronicle,* Henry Holt and Company, New York 1990, p. 242.

morning and we had to bury them. When summer came everything started to rot. It was terrible. The majority of the people working here were from my home city of Trnava. I knew all of them and every day there were less and less of them. They must still be buried around here somewhere. My brother and my father are buried here as well, you know.[84]

On the night of October 5, 1942, a massacre took place of French Jewesses in the Penal Company in Budy, and *SS-Unterscharführer* Pery Broad wrote about this in the 'Broad Report':

> Budy was a poor village, some four kilometers from Auschwitz Concentration Camp. A sub-camp belonging to Auschwitz was established there, to facilitate work in the fields, which then formed part of the Camp activity zone. The school, situated away from the road, and a large hut served as living quarters for the prisoners. The fact that at night the single barbed-wire fence was neither charged with electricity nor brightly illuminated, suggested that the prisoners there were less dangerous.
> It was a Camp for women. The ground floor of the school was occupied by the block and Camp seniors, both of whom were citizens of the Reich and former prostitutes. There was also a kitchen and an infirmary. Several German women prisoners with special duties in the Camp, and a considerable number of Jewish women, slept in the attic, which had two windows. But the majority of the women prisoners lived in the wooden building. Among them were Jewish, Ukrainian and Polish women, 300 to 400 altogether.
> Grabner's substitute, Criminal Office assistant Wosnitza (Georg), a criminal investigator and two clerks were told one morning, in the autumn of 1942, to pack quickly their typewriters and writing materials and get into the roomy car, waiting in front of the Commandant's office..... the car quickly drove in the direction of Budy. A few meters from the Camp it was stopped by a sentry. But on recognizing Grabner the guard apologized and explained that according to the Commandant's orders he was not to let any unauthorized persons pass through. The car proceeded to the Camp where Grabner made everybody get out. During the drive he had already hinted that a revolt had broken out at Budy.
> It was with a feeling of curiosity that the employees of Section II passed the gate of the Camp, the guard saluted them. They heard a particular

---

[84] Auschwitz—*The Nazis and the Final Solution*, BBC 2005.

buzzing and humming in the air. Then they saw a sight so horrible that some minutes passed before they could take it in properly. The square behind and beside the school was covered with dozens of female corpses, mutilated and bloody lying in complete chaos. All were covered only with threadbare prisoners undergarments. Half-dead women were writhing among the corpses. Their groaning mixed with the buzzing of immense swarms of flies, which circled round the sticky pools of blood and the smashed skulls. That was the origin of the strange humming sound which the newcomers had found so peculiar on their arrival. Some corpses hung in a twisted position on the barbed-wire fence. Others had evidently been thrown out from an attic window which was still open.

Grabner gave the order to find some women among those lying on the ground who could be interrogated to obtain their evidence as to what had happened. Wosnitza stopped around the corpses and tried in vain to find among the victims somebody who could talk. But he failed and so took as witnesses some of the less mutilated prisoners, who were just washing their wounds at the well. Their evidence was as follows:

The *SS* men, who acted as guards in the Camp, used to get the German women prisoners to maltreat the Jewish women. If the former did not comply, they were threatened with being driven through the chain of sentries and 'shot while escaping'. The bestial *SS* men regarded it as a pleasant pastime to look at the sufferings of the maltreated Jewesses. The result of this unbearable situation was that the German women always were in a state of fear, lest the tormented Jewish women take vengeance on them for their terrible lot. But the Jewish women, who mostly belonged to intellectual circles—some had formerly been students of the Sorbonne, or artists—never even thought of stooping to the level of the vulgar German prostitutes and of planning revenge, though it would have been understandable if they had done.

The evening before, one Jewess was returning from the lavatory and was on her way upstairs to the sleeping quarters. A German woman thought she had a stone in her hand, but that, of course, was only her hysterical imagination. At the gate below, a sentry was standing guard. As everybody knew, he was that woman's lover. Leaning out from the window, she cried for help, saying she had been hit by the Jewess. All the guards on duty immediately ran upstairs and together with the depraved German women prisoners they began to hit the Jewish women indiscriminately. They threw some women down the winding stairs, so that they fell in a heap, one upon the other. Some were thrown out of the window and fell to their deaths. The guards also drove the Jewish women from the barracks into the yard.

The German woman, who had instigated the butchering stayed behind in the bedroom with her lover. This may have been what she originally intended. The 'rebellion' was meanwhile mastered with bludgeons, gun butts and shots. Even an axe had been used as a weapon by one of the female *Kapo's*. In their mortal fear a few Jewish women tried to creep under the wire fence in order to escape the butchering. They got stuck and were soon killed. Even when all the women lay on the ground, the fiends drunk with blood, kept hitting the helpless victims again and again. They wanted, above all, to kill everybody, so as to destroy all witnesses of their atrocities.

At about 5 a.m. the Commandant was notified of the so-called 'rebellion', which had been successfully overcome. He drove to Budy and inspected the traces of the bloody orgy. A few wounded women who had hidden among the corpses, then rose and thought they were saved. But Höss soon left the Camp, after a short inspection. As soon as he left, the wounded women were shot.

The *SS* investigators and *SS* medical orderlies came later next morning 'to give medical help to the injured'. Some less seriously wounded women had managed to hide at the beginning of the tragic incident and not leave their hiding places so soon. They were interrogated and then 'looked after' by the orderlies. The criminal investigators did a lot of photographing of the scene. Only one copy of each photograph was later developed in the dark room under strict supervision. The plates had to be destroyed in the presence of the commandant and the photos were put at his disposal.

In an empty room the orderlies did their work. One after another, the victims with some traces of life still left in them were pulled into the room. A practised hold was applied and the syringe was inserted under the left breast. The patient collapsed and died some seconds after this 'treatment'. Two cubic centimeters of phenol, a cheap disinfectant was injected into the heart. Outside, on the stairs cowered an elderly woman. She had been in Concentration Camps for years owing to her religious convictions. She was to be re-educated according to the Nazi dogmas and made to reject 'the false teaching of the International Association of Bible Readers'. She was unable to forget what she had witnessed. The rest of the women looked on with terror as the half-dead as well as the living were pushed inside, while corpses were carried out by another door and were thrown on a wooden cart.

Six German women prisoners, who to a greater or lesser degree had participated in the atrocities, were taken to Block II together with the 'Axe Queen' Elfriede Schmidt, the favourite of the SS butchers. After the interrogation and confession of their guilt they lay, silenced for ever, in the mortuary of the crematorium. Only small, barely visible red dots under their left breasts betrayed the cause of their deaths. Their parents received properly worded letters of condolence from the Commandant. They were informed that their daughters had been on such and such day admitted to the prisoners hospital, suffering from such and such disease to which they succumbed 'in spite of the best medical care and treatment'.... The dossiers of the six murdered women were closed with the medical report on the course of their 'disease', and the circumstance which had led to their demise.[85]

SS-Doctor Johann Paul Kremer arrived at Auschwitz Concentration Camp on August 30, 1942 and he maintained a journal and his entry for October 24, 1942 recorded that 6 women from the Budy mutiny received injections (Klehr). During his interrogation in Kraków, where he stood trial, on July 30, 1947, Kremer elaborated on this entry in his journal:

> I was present once again at a killing with a phenol injection, this time of one of the six women from a group which was sentenced to death as a result of the so-called mutiny at Budy. The execution was performed by Klehr, in the dissecting room of the last block on the right—Block No 28. All these women were healthy, of German origin, I think. They were killed by Klehr in a sitting position. I was detached to be present at the executions in order to certify death. I looked on while the first of these women were killed and then left.[86]

Commandant Rudolf Höss had the final word on the revolt he recorded the murder of the French Jewesses as the 'bloodbath of Budy.'[87]

On October 27, 1942, in the Auschwitz *Stammlager*, 280 Polish prisoners were ordered to report to Block 3 the next day, after the

---

[85] *KL Auschwitz Seen by the SS*, Panstwowe Muzeum W Oswiecimiu 1978, pp. 161–166.
[86] Ibid., pp. 223–224.
[87] Danuta Czech, *Auschwitz Chronicle*, Henry Holt and Company, New York 1990, p. 249.

morning roll call. The following day on the 28th after the morning roll call and the departure of the labor squads, the 280 prisoners that were gathered in Block 3 were led to Block 11 under heavy *SS* guard and shot at the Black Wall. In addition in the morning, several prisoners employed as attendants in the prisoners' infirmary were also summoned by the Political Department, and taken to Block 11, and put with the other inmates who were to be shot.

These included Dr. Henryk Suchnicki and Leon Kukielka. When they found themselves in the group of condemned, they began to revolt and tried to escape from Block 11. Some of the prisoners were shot in the courtyard of Block 11, others died during the revolt from wounds incurred in the vestibule of Block 11. Before the execution, one prisoner gave prisoner Eugeniusz Obojski, who was summoned to the execution to perform the role of stretcher bearer, a secret message for his family, which he had found time to write. The secret message was discovered and Obojski was removed. The prisoners that had been executed, had arrived in Auschwitz from the Radom and Lublin districts by the Security Police (*Sipo*) and *SD*, after being arrested in retaliation for partisan operations in the Lublin district.

At around noon, *Rapportführer* (Roll Call Leader) Palitzsch visited Block 20 of the Prisoners Hospital and obtained the charts of the five prisoners held back by the prisoner attendants, who had not obeyed the summons to the Political Department. Following an order to close the block, the five prisoners were taken to the so-called treatment room on the ground floor and killed with phenol injections. On the orders of the Political Department, Polish political prisoner Eugeniusz Obojski, who had the prisoner tattoo number of 194 was locked in the bunker of Block 11.[88] Eugeniusz Obojski was later executed in Block 11 on January 25, 1943.[89]

Jews transferred to Auschwitz Concentration Camp from other Concentration Camps in the Reich, on October 30, 1942, were taken to the roll-call area of the *Stammlager* (Main Camp) where a selection took place, carried out by the labor manager. After the selection

---

[88] Ibid., pp. 259–260.
[89] Ibid., p. 313.

was completed, those deemed too weak to work were taken to the gas chamber in Birkenau, where they were murdered. Approximately 800 able-bodied prisoners were relocated to the new sub-camp built near the I. G. Farben works.

The new sub-camp near the construction site of the I. G. Farben works was in the village of Monowitz, whose residents had been forcibly evacuated. I. G. Farben had the sub-camp built, as no prisoners could be employed there from the end of August until the end of November because Auschwitz had been closed on account of the typhus epidemic. The sub-camp was called Buna and came under the jurisdiction of Auschwitz main Camp. During the initial stages, prisoners worked on erecting additional barracks, building latrines, and paving roads, while others were engaged in building the Buna plant.[90]

A few days later on November 2, 1942, approximately 150 prisoners, most of them Jews, were relocated to the newly constructed sub-camp at Chelmnek. The work consisted of clearing and enlarging a pond that was planned as a reservoir for the 'Bata' shoe factory, taken over by the Ota-Silesian Shoe Works. The prisoner workers were housed in Chelmnek-Paprotnik, a former wooden locomotive shed, to which a morgue had been added. The area around the locomotive shed was fenced with barbed-wire. The Commandant of this sub-camp was *SS-Oberscharführer* Josef Schillinger and he was succeeded by *SS-Oberscharführer* Wilhelm Emmerich. The prisoners were guarded by only six *SS*-men. Chelmnek sub-camp came under the jurisdiction of Auschwitz main Camp, until it was dissolved on December 9, 1942.[91]

On the same day, Dr. Horst Schumann returned to Auschwitz to develop a method whereby several men and women could be sterilized quickly and cheaply. This took place in Barracks No. 30 of the Women's Camp in Birkenau, Section B-1a, where an experimental station was set up where Dr. Schumann tested X-rays as a method

---

[90] Ibid., p. 261.
[91] Ibid., p. 262.

of sterilization. He also performed castrations at first in Block 21 and later in Block 10 in the main Auschwitz Camp.[92]

Luise Palitzsch, the wife of *Rapportführer* (Roll Call Leader) Gerhard Palitzsch died from typhus in a hospital in Katowice, on November 4, 1942, even though according to Helena Klys, a Polish girl aged 19-years of age, who worked as a nanny for the Palitzsch family, Frau Palitzsch was inoculated three times against the disease.[93]

On November 30, 1942, the *Sonderkommando* led by *SS-Untersturmführer* Franz Hössler, completed the gruesome task of removing all traces of the crimes committed in the gas chambers at Birkenau by emptying the mass graves and cremating the corpses. These mass graves contained the bodies of Jews who had arrived in transports from Upper Silesia and from Slovakia and other European countries prior to September 21, 1942, when the cremation of bodies commenced. The bodies of Russian Prisoners of War were also in these mass graves.[94]

With the completion of the cremation tasks in Birkenau, on December 3, 1942, approximately 300 Jews of the *Sonderkommando,* who had just cremated 107,000 bodies, were taken from Birkenau to Auschwitz I by *SS* guards. They were taken to the gas chamber in Crematorium I and murdered with gas, in order to eradicate any eye-witnesses as to what had taken place there.[95]

Three days later on December 6, 1942, a new *Sonderkommando* was formed with several dozen Jews from Section B-Ib in Birkenau assigned to it. Two of the prisoners selected were Meilech (Milton) Buki, Prisoner Number 80312, and Szlama Dragon, Prisoner Number 80359, who both survived the hell of Auschwitz-Birkenau and gave testimony after the War at various War Crimes trials. The following day on December 7, 1942, two Jewish prisoners escaped from the *Sonderkommando* in Birkenau. One was the Slovak Jew, Ladislaus

---

[92] Ibid., pp. 262–263.
[93] Piotr Setkiewicz, *The Private Lives of the Auschwitz SS*, Auschwitz-Birkenau State Museum 2015, p. 59.
[94] Danuta Czech, *Auschwitz Chronicle*, Henry Holt and Company, New York 1990, p. 275.
[95] Ibid., pp. 277–278.

Knopp, Prisoner Number 36816 and the Rumanian Jew Samuel Culea. They were both recaptured in Harmense, at 8.30 p.m. and were brought to the main guardhouse. They were executed in front of their *Sonderkommando* colleagues on December 11, 1942.[96]

Several trucks were sent on December 9, 1942, to the Chelmnek sub-camp to collect prisoners, as the sub-camp was closed and a day later two Jewish prisoners who had escaped from the *Sonderkommando* were captured and incarcerated in the bunker of Block 11. The two men, Bar Borenstein (74858) and Nojech Borenstein (74859) were both sent to Auschwitz from the Zichenau ghetto on November 14, 1942. They were both probably executed in public on December 17, 1942.[97]

Also on December 10, 1942, approximately 2,500 Jewish men, women and children arrived in Auschwitz from the transit camp at Malkinia, which is 97 kilometers from Warsaw. A total of 1976 people from this transport were murdered in the gas chambers.[98]

Among the prisoners on this transport from Malkinia on December 10, 1942, was Salmen Lewenthal who was drafted into the *Sonderkommando* in Birkenau. He was subsequently to become one of the organizers of the revolt by the *Sonderkommando* which took place on October 7, 1944. Salmen managed to bury a manuscript adjacent to Crematorium III, which was damaged in places, but was discovered during October 1962, and was published by the Auschwitz State Museum in 1971.[99]

On December 13, 1942, the first *RSHA* transport arrived in Auschwitz organized by the Central Resettlement Office, *Umwandererzentralstelle(UWZ)* headed by Hermann Krumey in Łódź, from the Zamość area. This was part of Odilo Globocnik, the *SS* and Police Leader for the Lublin District's plans to colonize the Zamość Lands with German and ethnic German settlers, having first moved out the

---

96	Ibid., pp. 280–283.
97	Ibid., p. 282.
98	Ibid., p. 283.
99	Danuta Czech, *Auschwitz Chronicle*, Henry Holt and Company, New York 1990, p. 283.

Polish residents. Hermann Krumey went on to serve with Adolf Eichmann, in the deportation of Hungarian Jews to Auschwitz during the summer of 1944. Another transport from Zamość, as part of this programme arrived in Auschwitz on December 16, 1942.[100]

The Political Department on December 16, 1942, uncovered the evidence of a resistance movement in the main Camp. They arrested the Clerk of Block 17, a Polish political prisoner Zdzislaw Wroblewski (1029) a former officer of the 1st Light Cavalry Regiment, because he was in possession of illegal records. He was locked up in the bunker of Block 11. At the same time, weapons were found hidden in a shed, near to the military supply camp. Wroblewski and Jozef Krall were tortured during harsh interrogations.[101]

Professor Dr. Carl Clauberg, on December 28, 1942, commenced his sterilization experiments on female prisoners in Barrack 28 of the Women's Camp in Birkenau, the women were housed in Barrack 27. Dr. Clauberg was the director of a gynaecological clinic in Silesia, and Himmler agreed to his request that he be allowed to carry out sterilizing women by injection, at Ravensbrück Concentration Camp, before transferring this work to Auschwitz.[102]

The next day on December 29, 1942 a most daring escape took place. Otto Küsel, who had been brought to the Camp from Sachsenhausen in May 1940, and was given Prisoner Number 2, escaped along with Jan Baras (564), Mieczyslaw Januszewski (711) and Dr. Boleslaw Kuczbara (4308). Otto Küsel, who was a Labor Manager in the Camp, drove a truck up to Block 24. He loaded four cabinets and he left the Camp without being stopped.

In an open field he opened up one of the cabinets and Mieczyslaw Januszewski got out, dressed in the uniform of an SS-man, armed with a rifle, and he took his place next to Küsel in the front of the truck. They left the Zone of Interest by showing a previously procured transit pass, and the other two escapees climbed out of the other cabinets. This daring escape was prepared with the support of

---

[100] Ibid., pp. 284–285.
[101] Ibid., pp. 286–287.
[102] G. Reitlinger, *The Final Solution*, Sphere Books, London 1971, p. 189.

the underground Polish Home Army and Janina Kaytoch, who lived in Auschwitz town. The four escapees were sheltered by the family of Andrezj Harat in Libiaz, prior to fleeing to the *Generalgouvernement*. Otto Küsel was however recaptured in Warsaw and was returned back to Auschwitz on September 25, 1943.[103]

---

[103] Danuta Czech, *Auschwitz Chronicle*, Henry Holt and Company, New York 1990, p. 292.

Chapter VI
Auschwitz-Birkenau
1943

On January 6, 1943, Protective Custody Commander, Hans Aumeier, Head of the Political Department, Maximilian Grabner, Roll Call Leader, Gerhard Palitzsch and Gerhard Lachmann, also from the Political Department, visited the roll-call area. Prisoners kept behind from the work-details were asked by *SS-Untersturmführer* Lachmann, "Who is the Colonel?" Colonel Karol Kumuniecki (8361) stepped forward and was taken off to Block 11.[104]

A transport from the Netherlands arrived at the Camp on January 24, 1943. 921 Jewish patients and medical personnel from the Jewish psychiatric hospital at Apeldoorne Bosch, arrived at the ramp. 869 people on this transport were killed in the gas chambers. Rudolf Vrba, whose real name was Walter Rosenberg, had arrived in Auschwitz on 30 June 1942, and he escaped with Alfred Wetzler on April 7, 1944. He wrote about the arrival of this transport:

> In some of the trucks nearly half the occupants were dead or dying, more than I had ever seen. Many obviously had been dead for several days, for their bodies were decomposing and the stench of disintegrating flesh gushed from the open doors. This, however, was no new novelty for me. What appalled me was the state of the living. Some were drooling, imbecile, live people with dead minds. Some were raving, tearing at their neighbours, even at their own flesh. Some were naked, though the cold was petrifying; and above everything, above the moans of the dying or the despairing, the cries of pain, of fear, the sound of wild, frightening, lunatic laughter rose and fell.
> Yet amid all this bedlam, there was one spark of splendid unselfish sanity. Moving among the insane were nurses, young girls, their uniforms torn and grimy, but their faces calm and their hands never idle. Their medicine bags were still over their shoulders and they had to fight

---

[104] Danuta Czech, *Auschwitz Chronicle*, Henry Holt and Company, New York 1990, p. 300.

sometimes to keep their feet: but all the time they were working, soothing, bandaging, giving an injection here, an aspirin there. Not one showed the slightest trace of panic. "Get them out!" roared the *SS* men. "Get them out you bastards!"

A naked girl of about twenty with red hair and a superb figure suddenly leaped from the wagon and lay, squirming, laughing at my feet. A nurse flung me a heavy Dutch blanket and I tried to put it around her, but she would not get up. With another prisoner, a Slovak called Fogel, I managed to roll her into the blanket. "Get them to the lorries!" roared the *SS*. "Straight to the lorries! Get on with it for Christ's sake!" Somehow Fogel and I broke into a lumbering run, for this beautiful girl was heavy. The motion pleased her and she began clapping her hands like a child. An *SS* club slashed across my shoulders and the blanket slipped from my numbed fingers. "Get on you swine! Drag her!"

I joined Fogel at the other end of the blanket and we dragged her, bumping her over the frozen earth for five hundred yards. Somehow she clung to the blanket, not laughing now, but crying, as the hard ground thumped her naked flesh through the thick wool. "Pitch her in! Get her on the lorries!" The *SS* men were frantic, for here, there was something they could not understand. Something that knew no order, no discipline, no obedience, no fear of violence or death.

We pitched her in somehow, then ran back for another crazy, pathetic bundle. Hundreds of them were out of the wagons now, herded by the prisoners who were herded by the *SS*; and everywhere, the nurses still working. One nurse walked slowly with an old, frail man, talking to him quietly, as if they were out in the hospital grounds. Another half-carried a screaming girl. They fought to bring order out of chaos, using medicines and blankets, gentleness and quiet heroism, instead of guns, sticks and snarling dogs. Then suddenly it was all over. The last abject victims had been slung into one of the overloaded lorries. We stood there, panting in the chill January air; and all our eyes were on those nurses. In unemotional groups they stood around the lorries, waiting for permission to join their patients.[105]

The next day on January 26, 1943, Hans Aumeier, Maximilian Grabner and Gerhard Palitzsch carried out another selection in the bunkers of Block 11. This ruthless selection was aimed at the underground members and intelligentsia. Those men executed were:

Colonel Edward Gott-Getynski

---

[105] M. Gilbert, *The Holocaust*, Collins London 1985, pp. 528–529.

Colonel Jan Karcz
Colonel Karol Kumuniecki
Cavalry Captain Wlodzimierz Kolinski
Wiktor Kolinski
Mieczyslaw Garbowiecki
Karol Karotynski
Henryk Suligorski
Marian Studencki
Tadeusz Radwanski
Heliodor Zalesny
Zbigniew Ruszczynski
Henryk Stirer
Kazimierz Superson
Boleslaw Borczyk
Eugeniusz Obojski[106]

Three days later on January 29, 1943, Head Engineer Prüfer from the firm J.A. Töpf arrived in Auschwitz to inspect the construction of Crematorium II, III, IV, and V in Birkenau. On the same day Karl Bischoff, Head of the Auschwitz construction department wrote to Hans Kammler, the Head of *Amt C*, the construction department of the *SS*, in Berlin:

> Crematorium Number 2: The completed furnaces have been started up in the presence of Engineer Prüfer from Messrs Töpf of Erfurt. The planks cannot yet be moved from the ceiling on account of the frost, but this is not important, as the gassing cellar (*Vergassungskeller*) can be used for that purpose. The ventilation plant has been held up by restrictions on rail transport, but the installation should be ready by February 20th.[107]

On February 1, 1943, the Camp authorities decided to train a group of Jewish prisoners for the operation of the crematoriums in Birkenau. They were housed in the main camp after undergoing a medical in Bunker 7 in Block 11. Among the 20 Jews selected was Henryk Tauber (90124). The next day this group of 20 prisoners were taken from Bunker 7, to the Crematorium 1 in the main Camp, where they

---

[106] See page 28.
[107] G. Reitlinger, *The Final Solution*, Sphere Books, London 1971, pp. 158–159.

were immediately put to work cremating the corpses that had accumulated there.[108]

Four days later on February 5, 1943, another transport of 1,000 Poles from the Zamość region arrived on Special Train Po 65, which departed from Zamość on February 3, 1943. From this transport, 417 people were murdered in the gas chambers, whilst the other 583 people were admitted into the Camp.[109]

Jozef Gawel (99088) along with 13 other prisoners were shot at the 'Black Wall' in the courtyard of Block 11, on February 19, 1943. Gawel, who was born on July 4, 1923, in Kurdwanowo, arrived in Auschwitz for the third time. It was determined during registration that he had first arrived on July 23, 1941 but he had escaped from the Camp in September 1941. On February 2, 1943, he had been brought to Auschwitz for the second time on a transport from Katowice and was given the Prisoner Number 99088. He escaped from the Camp for a second time but was re-arrested again and he arrived back in the Camp on February 15, 1943 and was given the number 102318, but this was cancelled and his old number 99088 was re-assigned to him.[110]

The first shipment of Gypsies from Germany arrived in Auschwitz on February 26, 1943. They were housed in the not yet completed Camp in Section B-IIe in Birkenau, which became known as the so-called Gypsy Family Camp B-IIe. A few days later, on March 1, 1943, the second Gypsy transport arrived and these people were also housed in the Gypsy Family Camp. From one end of the barracks to the other, connecting two chimneys, ran a flue, that divided the barracks. On both sides of the flue stood three storey wooden plank-beds. One family was accommodated on each plank-bed. The Gypsies draped the plank-beds with covers that they had brought with them.[111]

---

[108] Danuta Czech, *Auschwitz Chronicle*, Henry Holt and Company, New York 1990, p. 321.
[109] Ibid., p. 32.
[110] Ibid., p. 331 and p. 333.
[111] Ibid., p. 341.

On March 4, 1943, the *Sonderkommando* destined to work in Crematorium II, in Birkenau, was transferred from the main Camp to section B-Ib in Birkenau, after having been trained in Crematorium I in the main Camp. Among the people transferred were Henryk Tauber, Wladyslaw Biskup, Jan Agrestowski and Wladyslaw Tomiczek. The *Sonderkommando* was housed in Barrack 2, in Camp B-Ib. Also transferred on the same day was Mieczyslaw Morawa (5730) the *Kapo* of Crematorium I to Birkenau.[112]

August Brück arrived on March 5, 1943, from Buchenwald Concentration Camp, and he became a *Kapo* of the Crematorium in Birkenau and was given the Prisoner Number 106293. He started work without delay. During a test heating of the ovens in Crematorium II in Birkenau, August Brück explained the construction of the ovens to the prisoners in the *Sonderkommando* and described how they worked. The generators ran from the morning until 4 p.m. During this test a commission of high-level SS officers from Berlin arrived. Also present were members of the Camp's authorities, and functionaries from the Political Department. Also in attendance were engineers and employees of the firm J.A. Töpf in Erfurt, who had built the crematorium facilities.

Under their watchful eyes, members of the *Sonderkommando* stoked the fifteen retorts of the five crematorium ovens with 45 corpses. With a stop-watch in hand, the members of the commission timed the cremation of the corpses, which took 40 minutes, which was longer than expected. Thus the *Sonderkommando* were ordered to let the generators run constantly for several days, so the ovens could reach the desired temperature. These tests lasted from March 4, 1943, until 6 March 1943, under the stewardship of Head *Kapo* August Brück and Mieczyslaw Morawa, who returned to the main Camp, when the tests were completed.[113]

Approximately 2,000 Jewish men, women and children arrived in Auschwitz on March 13, 1943, from Ghetto 'B' in Kraków, and 1,492

---

[112] Danuta Czech, *Auschwitz Chronicle*, Henry Holt and Company, New York 1990, pp. 344–345.
[113] Ibid., pp. 345–346 .

of these were the first to be killed in the gas chambers of Crematorium II, while the remainder of the transport were admitted into the Camp. Three days later, another 1,000 Jewish men, women and children arrived in Auschwitz from the dissolved Ghetto B in Kraków. 959 Jews were murdered in the gas chambers. Three days later another 1,000 Jewish men, women and children arrived in Auschwitz from the dissolved Ghetto 'B' in Kraków. 959 Jews were murdered in the gas chambers.[114]

On March 22, 1943, the Central Construction Administration of the *Waffen-SS* and Police handed over to the Camp authorities the newly completed Crematorium IV. This crematorium was identical to that of Crematorium V. Both had an oven with eight combustion chambers and four fireboxes that could also be heated with gas, as well as three gas chambers—the third was divided into two smaller ones—with space for 1,500, 800 and 150 people respectively. The gas chambers were located in an above-ground part of the building. As with the so-called Bunkers I and II, the gas intake holes were in the outside walls. The holes were barred on the inside and could be closed from the outside with gas-tight drop doors.[115]

Mieczyslaw Morawa, on March 23, 1943, the *Kapo* of Crematorium I in the *Stammlager* was transferred to the position of *Kapo* of Crematorium IV, in Birkenau, where corpse cremation had now commenced. On the evening of the same day, approximately 1,700 Gypsy men, women and children housed in Barracks 20 and 22, were murdered in the gas chambers. These Gypsies came from the Białystok area and were kept isolated from the rest of the Camp in Barracks 20 and 22, because it was feared by the Camp authorities that they had contracted typhus.[116]

The Central Construction Administration of the *Waffen-SS* and Police in Auschwitz, on March 31, 1943, handed over to the Camp authorities Crematorium II, whose construction was identical to

---

[114] Ibid., pp. 352 and 354.
[115] Ibid., pp. 357–358.
[116] Danuta Czech, *Auschwitz Chronicle*, Henry Holt and Company, New York 1990, pp. 358–359.

Crematorium III. Both buildings had five ovens with three combustion chambers and two fireboxes per oven. As in Crematorium III, the gas chamber of Crematorium II was intended for 3,000 people and, like the undressing space, was situated below ground. In it were floor-to-ceiling columns consisting of several layers of thick, woven wire. The gas was poured into them from above, through openings in the ceiling. Next to the gas chambers was an elevator that transported the dead from the basement to the hall with the cremation ovens, which was situated on the ground floor. Crematorium III was handed over on June 25, 1943.[117]

On April 4, 1943, the Central Construction Administration of the *Waffen-SS* and Police in Auschwitz handed over to the Camp authorities the completed Crematorium V in Birkenau. Its construction was identical to Crematorium IV, which had already been handed over on March 22, 1943.[118]

Two days later, two Jews from Darmstadt, Pierre Braunschweig and Paul Guarien, who had been re-captured following their escape from the fifty-third *RSHA* transport of March 26, 1943 which left Le Bourget-Drancy, were destined for the Sobibór Death Camp, in south-eastern Poland.[119]

32 members of the *SS*-Garrison were awarded on April 20, the *Führer's* birthday, the Distinguished Service Cross, Second Class with Swords. Among the recipients were some of the most brutal *SS* men, such as Roll-Call Leader Oswald Kaduk, Herbert Kirschner and Gerhard Lachmann from the Political Department and medical orderlies Josef Klehr and Herbert Scherpe.[120]

The Camp authories arrested the underground fighter Helena Plotnicka, the wife of a miner who lived near the Camp, and the mother of five children, on May 19, 1943. She was devoted to helping the prisoners in the Camp, and she was arrested along with her 13-year old daughter Wanda. She was arrested for her resistance work

---

[117] Ibid., pp. 364–365.
[118] Ibid., p. 368.
[119] Ibid., p. 370.
[120] Ibid., p. 380.

with the surveyors Commando, whose *Kapo*, Stanislaw Dorosiewicz was an informer for the Political Department, and it was he who denounced her.

She was taken to Block 11, where she was brutally tortured. She was beaten unconscious, hung up with her hands tied behind her back, and red-hot oil was poured into her nose, her teeth were smashed out, her finger-nails were torn out, and she was starved and denied water in an attempt to force her to betray her contacts. Despite this brutality she was able to endure, she did not betray anyone. The Political Department lost interest in her and she was eventually released into the Women's Camp in Birkenau, where the other prisoners treated her with tender loving care and she regained her health. Unfortunately, she subsequently contracted typhus and she died on March 17, 1944. Her young daughter Wanda was released from the Camp.[121]

Dr. Josef Mengele arrived in Auschwitz-Birkenau on May 30, 1943, to take over the position of Camp Doctor in the Gypsy Family Camp. Mengele was a medical doctor with a doctorate in philosophy, and he was wounded on the Eastern Front. Dr. Mengele performed countless selections on the ramp. In the Gypsy Camp he conducted pseudoscientific research on twins and dwarfs, killing many of them for so-called research purposes.[122]

On June 25, 1943, the Central Construction Administration of the *Waffen-SS* and Police in Auschwitz handed over to the Camp authorities the completed Crematorium III in Birkenau. This facility was identical to Crematorium II, which became operational in March 1943.[123]

The Head of the Central Construction Administration of the *Waffen-SS* and Police, *SS*-Karl Bischoff reported to Heinz Kammler, the Head of *Amt C*, on June 28, 1943, the construction department of the *SS*, in Berlin, that Crematorium III was now operational and

---

[121] Jozef Garlinski, *Fighting Auschwitz*, Fontana Collins 1975, p. 150.
[122] Danuta Czech, *Auschwitz Chronicle*, Henry Holt and Company, New York 1990, p. 408.
[123] Ibid., p. 426.

that herewith all crematoria had been set up as commanded. He also provided information regarding the capacity on a 24-hour operation:[124]

	Crematoria	Cremation Capacity
1	Old Crematorium I (Auschwitz) 3 Double muffle cremation ovens	340 corpses
2	New Crematorium II (Birkenau) 5 Three muffle cremation ovens	1,440 corpses
3	New Crematorium III (Birkenau) 5 Three muffle cremation ovens	1,440 corpses
4	New Crematorium IV Eight muffle cremation ovens	768 corpses
5	New Crematorium V Eight muffle cremation ovens	768 corpses
	Total	**4,756**

Now that each of the four crematorium and gas chamber facilities were operational, Filip Müller a member of the *Sonderkommando* provided a detailed description of these facilities in his book 'Eyewitness Auschwitz' written after the War:

> My first working day in Birkenau was a hot summer's day. In the early hours of the morning the work teams stood in rows on the dusty Camp street, ready to march out. We were lined up near the gate, not far from the Camp orchestra. Chief *Kapo* August Brück, led the almost 200-strong crematorium team to work. This team, its *Kapos* walking in the first few ranks, was divided into four groups, one for each of the fourcrematoria . It was the job of a fifth group called the demolition team, to remove any remaining traces of the cremation pits near the bunkers—no longer needed since the installation of the new crematoria—by levelling them.
> Brück's tall and lean figure was striking. A *Reichsdeutscher*, he was roughly fifty-years old, taciturn, and walked with a slight stoop. His face

---

[124] Ibid., p. 429.

was square and wrinkled, with high cheekbones, and there was an alert look in his half-closed eyes. He had spent many years in Nazi prisons and Concentration Camps. In the spring of 1943, he had been transferred from Buchenwald to Birkenau, where it was his job to introduce *Sonderkommando* prisoners to the installations in the new crematoria. Furthermore he was responsible for the smooth and accident-free running of the establishment.

To the sound of the Camp orchestra playing a sentimental folk song, we marched off to work through the main gate. A few meters behind the gate our team reformed into three independent groups. The first, turning to the left, marched towards crematoria IV and V. A few meters behind walked the demolition team. The third group to which I belonged turned to the right. I noticed *Kapo* Mietek in the front rank, and my heart sank. I wondered if he would be as brutal and callous as he had been at Auschwitz.

On the way we went past the Women's Camp. On the left behind the barbed wire there were emaciated female figures busy loading soil into the wheelbarrows. But something else attracted my attention: at the end of the Camp of Birkenau behind barbed-wire fences, which had been put up on either side of the dusty road, two buildings stood out clearly, and towering above them a chimney. Presently we turned to the left and through an iron gate, we entered a yard. The long single-storey redbrick building of Crematorium II was only a few meters away in front of us. On one of its longer sides there was a projecting structure from which the square chimney rose up. The sight of it reminded me very forcibly of the transitoriness of life; but before long this lethal giant had become part of our daily life. Five underground channels connected it to the fifteen ovens, which were arranged in groups of three.

Filip Müller continued his account:

We were divided into separate teams. At first I worked in a group of twenty; we were engaged in levelling a large mound of earth. From the surface which was to be sown with grass seed, concrete shafts stuck out here and there. There could be no doubt that concealed under the mound of earth was a gas chamber. In the lunch break I ran across a mate of mine, whom I had first met at the beginning of 1943, during his 'training' as a stoker in the old crematorium at Auschwitz. Through a wooden door in the left wing of the building he took me into the coke store. From there we went along a narrow semi-dark corridor, past three doors—one of which led into the *Kommandoführer's* room—into the cremation plant. Five ovens, each with three combustion chambers, were installed here. Outwardly the fifteen arched openings did not significantly differ from those at the Auschwitz crematorium. The one important innovation consisted of two rollers, each with a diameter of 15 centimeters, fixed to the edge of each oven. This made it easier for the metal platform to be pushed inside the oven. The process of cremating corpses was similar to that in Auschwitz. The only way in which the death factory differed from the one in Auschwitz was its size. Its fifteen huge ovens, working non-stop, could cremate more than 3,000 corpses daily.[125]

Filip Müller went on with his tour:

> Using the lift which brought the corpses up we descended into the basement. The sight of the rooms down there made me shudder. Every detail had been devised with the sole aim of cramming up to 3,000 people into one room in order to kill them with poison gas. When we entered the morgue, we found lying in a heap some 200 emaciated corpses, all of whom had obviously died of hunger, disease or exhaustion. They had been thrown down the concrete chute from the yard into the mortuary basement.
> It was here that I met *Kapo* Jakob Kaminski. Stocky and red-faced, he was about thirty-two. He had come to Birkenau with a transport from Ciechanów towards the end of 1942. Self-confident, energetic and determined, he had the courage and the ability to lead others.......
> We left the mortuary and came to a huge iron-mounted wooden door; it was not locked. We entered a place which was in total darkness. As we switched on the light, the room was lit by bulbs enclosed in a protective wire cage. We were standing in a large oblong room measuring about 250 square meters. Its unusually low ceiling and walls were whitewashed. Down the length of the room, concrete pillars supported the ceiling. However, not all the pillars served this purpose: for there were others too. The *Zyklon B* gas crystals were inserted through openings into hollow pillars made of sheet metal. They were perforated at regular intervals and inside them a spiral ran from top to bottom, in order to ensure as even a distribution of the granular crystals as possible.
> Mounted on the ceiling was a large number of dummy showers made of metal. These were intended to delude the suspicious on entering the gas chamber into believing that they were in a shower room. A ventilating plant was installed in the wall; this was switched on immediately after

---

[125] Filip Müller, *Eyewitness Auschwitz*, Ivan R. Dee, Chicago 1979, pp. 57–59.

each gassing to disperse the gas and thus to expedite the removal of the corpses. At right angles to the gas chamber was the largest room in the extermination complex, the so-called changing room.

Measuring over 300 square meters, this underground room could accommodate more than 1,000 people. They entered from the yard, down wide concrete steps. At the entrance to the basement was a signboard, and written on it in several languages the direction: 'To the Baths and disinfecting rooms'. The ceiling of the changing room was supported by concrete pillars to which many more notices were fixed, once again with the aim of making the unsuspecting people believe that the imminent process of disinfection was of vital importance for their health. Slogans like 'Cleanliness brings freedom' or 'One louse may kill you' were intended to hoodwink, as were numbered clothes hooks fixed at a height of 1.50 meters. Along the walls stood wooden benches, creating the impression that they were placed there to make people more comfortable while undressing.

There were other multi-lingual notices inviting them to hang up their clothes as well as their shoes, tied together by their laces and admonishing them to remember the number of their hook, so that they might easily retrieve their clothes after their showers. There were further notices on the way from the changing room to the gas chamber, directing people to the baths and disinfecting room.[126]

Fifteen Ukrainian-SS from the 8th Company, which was assembled from Ukrainian volunteers on March 31, 1943, fled from the Camp during the night of July 3, 1943. They were fully armed. During the pursuit and battle that ensued in the area of Chełm Wielki, near Bierun, eight Ukrainian-SS were killed and one captured. Three of those in pursuit were killed, including two SS-men, Karl Rainicke and Stephan Rachberger.[127]

In Block 11, on July 28, 1943, a session of the Police Court-martial was held. Inmates from prisons in Silesia were incarcerated in Auschwitz. Four prisoners in advance of the Court—martial sessions were locked in the bunker. They were:

Jan Zakrzewski (107360)

---

[126] Filip Müller, *Eyewitness Auschwitz*, Ivan R. Dee, Chicago 1979, pp. 60–61.
[127] Danuta Czech, *Auschwitz Chronicle*, Henry Holt and Company, New York 1990, p. 434.

Jerzy Opilka (11482)
Franciszek Goszkowski (EH 4807)
Franciszek Rybinski (39865)
They were condemned to death and shot the same day.[128]

The police Court-martial sessions, which commenced in November 1941, deserves to be fully covered in depth, and *SS-Unterscharführer* Pery Broad recounted this in the Broad Report:

> The candidates for the Summary Court trial were led to a room in Block 11. A large room opposite was made ready for the court. A long table with water glasses on it and a row of chairs behind it, with the chairman's seat for Mildner in the middle, was the main feature of the room. Himmler and Hitler graciously looked down from the walls. Through both barred windows, which were not boarded up, one had a direct view of the tall barbed-wire fences. A concrete wall kept the rest of the Camp from view.
> The light-blue Opel Admiral car finally drove up to Block 11 and Mildner got out. With his upraised hand he pompously greeted the respectfully standing *SS* men, ascended the stone steps and entered the Block. He also greeted Grabner and Aumeier, who were allowed to participate in the session. Kauz carried in the heavy dossiers, '*Geheime Staatspolizei Kattowitz*,' was the formidable title on their covers. Mildner took his seat, *Sturmbannführer* Dr. Eisenschmidt sat next to him. The rest of those present merrily exchanged greetings, talked of old times and also took their seats at the table..... Mildner had opened the proceedings.
> With a self-satisfied smile he congratulated the Summary Court on its two hundredth session. Then he signalled the *SS* guard at the door to bring in the defendants. Kauz called the first name. The *SS* Guard repeated the name to the clerk, who was standing in the other room with the defendants. From among the softly murmuring crowd of people who, after long unspeakable torments, were waiting for their death sentence, a weak voice called '*Hier*' (Here) and one of the sunken-eyed creatures came reeling forward. The clerk helped him to the door of the court room. The clerk was a prisoner himself and a similar fate might soon be in store for him. The hapless person had to stand near the door. Mildner read out the reasons for the sentence: 'As a result of investigations carried out by the State Police, the Pole ... has been found guilty of acting against the laws of the German Reich by...'. This was the usual

---

[128] Danuta Czech, *Auschwitz Chronicle*, Henry Holt and Company, New York 1990, p. 448.

beginning, and it ended with the sentence pronounced in monotonous and unfeeling voice: 'The Police and Summary Court of the State Police Office in Katowice pronounces the death sentence.' With an expression on his face which brooked no criticism, the despot so brave in killing, looked right and left, accepting the consenting nods of his associates, as a matter of course. The sentenced man was not allowed to say a word.

Each case took up to one minute at the most. Kauz often had a hard task to find the dossier among the heap quickly enough. He perspired when Mildner showed his impatience by a discontented glance, or by drumming his fingers on the table. If the defendant, called to the court-room did not report immediately, the other prisoners would impatiently repeat the name. They were no longer eager to delay their end by unnecessary minutes.

The session was over in less than two hours: 206 out of the 210 had been sentenced to death, 4 were to be detained in the Camp. Mildner was in a hurry to get to the place of execution. He would never miss an execution, not for anything in the world. The condemned stood in the yard of Block 11, five persons in a line. That day the execution was to take place at the crematorium, instead of in front of the 'Black Wall,' on account of the great number of the condemned. A covered van backed out from the opened gate. Lockets and other cherished momentos, thrown away by the condemned, shortly before their death, lay scattered on the ground, a symbol of their final farewell to the world.... The van made its journey several times. As many people as possible were crowded into it every time.

Mildner's big blue car was already standing in front of the crematorium. The old Auschwitz crematorium stood at a distance of approximately 100 meters from the Camp. The condemned men and women stood in the yard before the crematorium. A wrought-iron lantern hanging above the entrance door gave a cosy impression, as if it hung over a door of a home.....

The prisoners of the Summary Court were conducted into the hall in groups of forty. They had to undress there. An *SS* guard stood at the door to the mortuary, where the execution was to take place. He led in ten people at a time. The shots and the thudding of heads when they hit the cement floor were audible in the hall. One could witness nerve-wracking scenes: mothers saying goodbye to their daughters; men, former officers, judging by their military carriage, shaking hands with their fellows for the last time, some people saying their last prayers.

The mass murder, more vile than could be imagined, was meanwhile going on in the mortuary. Ten prisoners went naked into the mortuary.

The walls were stained with blood, and in the background there lay the corpses of those already shot. A wide stream of blood was flowing towards the sink placed in the middle of the hall. The victims were obliged to step quite close to the corpses and formed a line. Their feet were stained with blood; they stood in puddles of it. Some cried out when recognizing a near relative, the father perhaps, among those lying on the floor and still groaning.

The right-hand man of the Camp Leader, *SS-Hauptscharführer* Palitzsch, did the shooting. He killed one person after another with a practised shot in the back of the head. The mortuary was getting more and more packed with corpses. Mildner, who was there together with his staff, watched with cold eyes, the executioner at his work. The corpses lay all around him too. The *SS* guard finally shouted from the hall that no-one was left outside. Then Palitzsch, stepping over the corpses, shot those who were still moving or groaning. He put down his gun at last, turned to his master and stood to attention, to signify that he had done his duty. Mildner looked at him with a significant, fiendish smile and then slowly raised his arm in the Nazi salute, remaining in that position for several seconds. Thus he acknowledged the services of his hangman.

Mildner turned to go. Raising his arm again and again to salute the *SS* men on his right and left, smiling jovially he reached the door, stepping over the corpses on his way out. The clerks of Section II were then kept busy writing the records of the executions. Cause of death—several shots through the chest, of these one through the heart and two through the lungs... thus ran the records.[129]

On September 25, 1943, the German prisoner Otto Küsel, who escaped from Auschwitz on December 29, 1942, and hid in Warsaw, before being re-captured and incarcerated in Pawiak Prison, was returned to Auschwitz. He was locked in Block 11, and was later released into the Camp on November 23, 1943.[130]

A transport arrived at Auschwitz-Birkenau on October 23, 1943, from the Bergen-Belsen Concentration Camp near Celle, in Ger-

---

[129] *KL Auschwitz Seen by the SS,* Panstwowe Muzeum W Oswiecimiu 1978, pp. 153–160.
[130] Danuta Czech, *Auschwitz Chronicle*, Henry Holt and Company, New York 1990, p. 493.

many. This transport consisted of 1,800 Polish Jews who had received passports for traveling to Latin American countries. Most of them paid considerable sums of money for these visas, and had been held in the Hotel Polski in Warsaw, with the blessing of the local *Gestapo*, before being shipped to Bergen-Belsen. They were known as the so-called 'Exchange Jews.' One of Adolf Eichmann's experts Dr. Seidl, from the *RSHA*, examined their documentation, and the Jews were informed that they were going to the Bergau Camp near Dresden and their luggage would follow them.

On arrival at the ramp in Birkenau, the men and women were separated. The women were taken to Crematorium II and the men were taken to Crematorium III. The *SS* carried out an examination of the travel documents, the Polish Jews were told that they must be disinfected.

The *SS* led the women and children to the undressing room in Crematorium II and they ordered the women to undress and the *SS* men started to remove their rings and watches. One woman in her desperation flung the clothes she has taken off at the head of *SS-Oberscharführer* Josef Schillinger and grabbed his revolver. She shot him and also shot and wounded *SS-Oberscharführer* Wilhelm Emmerich in the leg.[131]

Filip Müller was an eyewitness to this act of resistance:

> A panic broke out in the changing room. The young woman had disappeared in the crowd. Any moment she might appear somewhere else and aim her pistol at another of her executioners. The *SS* men realized this danger. One by one they crept outside—the wounded Schillinger was still lying unattended on the floor. After a while, a few *SS* men came in and dragged him hastily to the door. Then a third shot was fired: one of *SS* men pulling Schillinger let go of him and started to limp to the door as fast as he could. Then the light went out. Simultaneously the door was bolted from the outside. We, too, were now caught inside the pitch-dark room.......
>
> A man who was standing near us, had noticed we did not belong to their group. He spoke to us in the dark and wanted to know where we came

---

[131] Danuta Czech, *Auschwitz Chronicle*, Henry Holt and Company, New York 1990, p. 513.

from. 'From the death factory' one of my companions replied tersely. The man was very agitated and demanded loudly: 'I don't understand what this is all about. After all we have valid entry visas for Paraguay; and what's more we paid the *Gestapo* a great deal of money to get our exit permits. I handed over three diamonds worth at least 100,000 Złoty; it was all I had left of my inheritance. And that young dancer, the one who fired the shots a little while ago, she had to pay a lot more.
Suddenly the door was flung open. I was blinded by the glare of several searchlights. Then I heard Voss shouting: 'All members of the *Sonderkommando*, come out!' Greatly relieved we dashed outside and ran up the stairs and into the yard. Outside the door to the changing room two machine-guns had been set up, and behind them several searchlights. Steel-helmeted *SS* men were lying ready to operate the machine-guns. A horde of armed *SS* men were milling about the yard.
I was on my way to the cremation room when a car drew up and *Lagerkommandant* Höss climbed out. Then there was a rattle of machine-guns. A terrible blood-bath was wrought about the people caught in the changing room. A very few who had managed to hide behind pillars or in corners were later seized and shot. In the meantime, the 'disinfecting officers' had thrown their deadly *Zyklon B* gas down into the gas chamber where the credulous... had gone less than an hour earlier.
Next morning we learnt that Schillinger had died on the way to hospital while Emmerich had been wounded. The news was received with satisfaction by many Camp inmates; for in Section B2d of the Men's Camp, Schillinger had been regarded as an extremely brutal and capricious sadist. The body of the young dancer was laid out in the dissecting room of Crematorium II. *SS* men went there to look at her corpse before its incineration. Perhaps the sight of her was to be a warning, as well as an illustration of the dire consequences one moment's lack of vigilance might have for an *SS* man.[132]

Gerhard Wiebeck, an *SS* judge in Breslau, visited Auschwitz Concentration Camp as part of the investigations conducted by Georg Konrad Morgen into the conduct of Commandant Rudolf Höss. He was having an affair with a prisoner named Eleonore Hodys, whom he visited in the *SS* prison in the basement of the central administration block. In the post-War Auschwitz Trial in Frankfurt am Main, Wiebeck testified that Morgen succeeded in getting Hodys out of

---

[132] Filip Müller, *Eyewitness Auschwitz*, Ivan R. Dee, Chicago 1979, pp. 88–89.

Auschwitz, but a diary she kept contained incriminating statements about Grabner.[133] All of these things culminated in major developments in the Camps staffing, over the next few months.

Significant changes were made to the chain of command in Auschwitz on November 11, 1943 when Rudolf Höss was replaced by the former Chief of Office DI in the *SS-WHVA*, *SS-Obersturmbannführer* Arthur Liebehenschel, who on November 22, 1943, issued garrison order no. 53/43 which explained the new structure of the Auschwitz Concentration Camp complex:

Konzentrationslager Auschwitz I – *Stammlager*
Konzentrationslager Auschwitz II – Birkenau
Konzentrationslager Auschwitz III – *Aussenlager*

KL Auschwitz I embraced the main Camp, under the command of *SS-Obersturmbannführer* Arthur Liebehenschel. His adjutants were *SS-Hauptsturmführer* Viktor Zoller and *Schutzhaftlagerführer SS-Obersturmführer* Franz Johann Hoffmann.

KL Auschwitz II comprised of the Birkenau Camp and the branch camps attached to the farms. The Commandant of *KL* Auschwitz II was *SS-Sturmbannführer* Friedrich 'Fritz' Hartjenstein. The office of *Schutzhaftlagerführer* was performed by *SS-Untersturmführer* Johann Schwarzhuber in the Men's Camp and by *SS-Untersturmführer* Franz Hössler in the Women's Camp.

KL Auschwitz III comprised the ten branch Camps at Monowice, Jaworzno, Świętochłowice, Łagisza, Wesoła near Mysłowice, Goleszów, Libiak, Sosnowice and Brno. The Commandant of *KL* Auschwitz III, was *SS-Hauptsturmführer* Heinrich Schwarz, who had his headquarters in the sub-camp at Monowice.

The Commandants of *KL* Auschwitz II and III were subordinate to Liebehenschel, the most senior in rank, whilst the administration of all of the Camps was carried out centrally by the command of Auschwitz I.

---

[133] B. Naumann, *Auschwitz*, Pall Mall Press, London 1966, p. 258.

More changes took place on December 1, 1943, regarding an important figure forever bound up in the history of Auschwitz, Commandant Liebehenschel appointed *SS-Untersturmführer* Hans Schurz as the Director of the Political Department. Liebehenschel informed the *SS* garrison that Maximilian Grabner was returning to his former post as the *Gestapo* in Katowice. In truth, Grabner had been arrested for corruption and repeated abuse of office in Auschwitz.[134]

Six days later on December 7, 1943, during the night, a fire broke out in the barracks where the special commission sent to Auschwitz by *SS* Chief Heinrich Himmler, under the command of Dr. Konrad Morgen, deposited the evidence of valuables stolen by a number of *SS* men, during the extermination of the Jews. With the destruction of the barracks, the evidence was lost forever.[135]

On December 14, 1943, in Camp B-IIg in Birkenau, the construction of the barracks where the sorting of the personal effects took place, was completed. This warehouse complex was known in the Camp as 'Canada', by both the prisoners and *SS* men. The warehouse complex lies between Crematorium III and Crematorium IV and borders on the men's prisoners' infirmary, in Camp B-IIf , consisting of thirty barracks. In twenty-five barracks, the items taken from Jews were stored and sorted. The prisoners employed in 'Canada' lived in two barracks, the other three barracks were for administration.[136]

Two prisoners on December 21, 1943, who were both informers for the Camps' Political Department escape from Auschwitz I. One is the *Kapo* Stanislaw Dorosiewicz (18379) and the other is the Jew, Herz Kurcweig (65655) who worked in the Canada Commando. The two prisoners left the Camp on the pretext of wanting to show an *SS* man where the Communist resistance movement in the Camp met

---

[134] Danuta Czech, *Auschwitz Chronicle*, Henry Holt and Company, New York 1990, p. 537 .
[135] Danuta Czech, *Auschwitz Chronicle*, Henry Holt and Company, New York 1990, p. 541.
[136] Ibid., p. 546.

with resistance groups outside the Camp. The *SS* man was *SS-Rottenführer* Peter Jarosiewitsch from the Camp's Political Department. On the far bank of the River Soła, they killed him and disappeared.[137]

---

[137] Jozef Garlinski, *Fighting Auschwitz*, Fontana Collins 1975, p. 211.

Chapter VII
Auschwitz-Birkenau 1944

Salmen Lewenthal, a member of the *Sonderkommando* buried a manuscript, as mentioned in Chapter V, near Crematorium III, and it contained a report with the title '3000 naked people' which was discovered after the Second World War ended and is a fitting account to commence this chapter. The report buried in the ground was destroyed in places by dampness which seeped into the jar, containing the report. Thus there are words missing in the original document:

> This was at the beginning of 1944. A cold, dry lashing wind was blowing. The soil was quite frozen. The first lorry, loaded brimful with naked women and girls, drove in front of Crematorium III. They were not standing close to one another, as usual, no; they did not stand on their feet at all, they were exhausted, they lay inertly one upon another in a state of utter exhaustion. They were sighing and groaning.
> The lorry stopped, the tarpaulin was raised and they began to dump down the human mass in the way gravel is unloaded on the road. Those that had lain at the edge, fell upon the hard ground, breaking their heads upon ... so that they weakened completely and had no strength left to move. The remaining women fell upon them, pressing them down with their weight. One heard.... Groans.
> Those that were dumped down later, began to extricate themselves from the pile of bodies, stood ... on their feet and tried to walk... the ground, they trembled and jerked horribly with cold, they slowly dragged themselves to the bunker, which was called *Auskleidungsraum*, 'Undressing room' and to which steps led down, like to a cellar.
> The remainder of the women were taken down by men from the *Kommando* who swiftly ran upstairs, raised the fainted victims, left without help, extricated them carefully, crushed and barely breathing, from the heap of bodies and led them quickly downstairs. They were a long time in the Camp and knew that the bunker—the gas chamber was the last step leading to death.
> But still they were most grateful, with their eyes begging for mercy and with the movements of their trembling heads they expressed their thanks, at the same time giving signs with their hands that they were unable to speak. They found solace in seeing tears of compassion and

an expression of depression.... in the faces of those who were leading them downstairs. They were shaking with cold and ......

The women taken downstairs were permitted to sit down, the rest of them were led into this confined cold room, they jerked horribly and trembled with cold, so a coke stove was brought. Only some of them drew near enough to be able to feel the warmth emanating from the small stove. The rest sat plunged in pain and sadness. It was cold but they were so resigned and embittered with their lives that they thought with abhorrence of physical sensations of any kind. They were sitting far in the background and were silent.

Salmen Lewenthal continued his report regarding a girl from the ghetto of Bedzin, who had been deported to Auschwitz-Birkenau in the summer of 1943, and a few months later, spoke to him, as she lay helpless:

> She was left the only one of a numerous family. All the time she had been working hard, was undernourished, suffered the cold. Still, she was in good health and was well. She thought she would survive. Eight days ago, no Jewish child was allowed to go to work. The order came '*Juden, antreten!*' 'Jews, leave the ranks!' Then the blocks were filled with Jewish girls. During the selection nobody paid attention whether they looked well or not, whether they were sick or well.
>
> They were lined outside the block and later they were led to Block 25, there they were ordered to strip naked; allegedly they were to be examined as to their health. When they had stripped, all were driven to three blocks; one thousand persons in a block and there they were shut up for three days and three nights, without getting a drop of water or a crumb of bread, even.
>
> So they had lived for three awful days and it was only the third night that bread was brought; one loaf of bread weighing 1.40 kilogrammes for sixteen persons, afterwards ...... if they had shot us then, gassed us, it would have been better. Many women lost consciousness and others were only semi-conscious. They lay crowded on bunks, motionless, helpless. Death would not have impressed us at all then.
>
> The fourth day we were led from the block, the weakest were led to the *Krankenstube* (infirmary), and the rest were again given the normal camp ration of food and were left .... were taken... to life. On the eighth day, that is five days later, we were again ordered to strip naked, *Blocksperre* was ordained. Our clothes were at once loaded and we, after many hours of waiting in the frost, were loaded into lorries and here we were dumped down on the ground.

Such is the sad end of our last mistaken illusions. We have been, evidently, cursed in our mothers' wombs, since such a sad end fell to our lot.[138]

In January 1944, the Germans opened a brothel in Block 24, in the Auschwitz Main Camp. It occupied twenty rooms and was furnished with the cheap elegance of such places. Eleven German and nine Polish women were selected for this duty. They were promised that after six months they would be released. In fact after the six months they were taken to Birkenau and murdered.

Admission to the brothel was for Aryans only, but in practice its use was almost confined to Germans. It was conducted with characteristic German method. After their days work, the prisoners who wanted to visit the brothel stood in a queue, and bought tickets that cost a Mark each.

Each woman received six visitors a night, each visitor was allowed twenty minutes. At the end of fifteen minutes the woman who ran the house would go into the passage and call out, 'Get ready, 15 minutes gone.'[139]

Ryszard Dacko, who was 25 years old in 1943, and who worked in the Auschwitz *Stammlager,* as a fireman, recalled his visits to the Camp brothel. He spent time with a girl called Alinka:

> I wanted to be as close as possible to her, to embrace her. It was three and a half years since I was arrested; three and a half years without a woman. Alinka was a very nice girl—she was not ashamed of anything. She gave what one wanted.[140]

Otto Küsel who had escaped from the camp on December 29, 1942, and had hidden in Warsaw, before being re-captured and returned to Auschwitz in September 1943, was transferred along with another

---

[138] M. Gilbert, *The Holocaust,* Collins London 1985, pp. 649–651.
[139] Dr. Filip Friedman, *This Was Oswiecim*, United Jewish Relief Appeal, London 1946, pp. 39–40.
[140] L. Rees, *Auschwitz—The Nazis and The Final Solution*, BBC Books, Ebury Publishing 2005. p. 251.

111 prisoners to Flossenbürg Concentration Camp on February 9, 1944.[141]

The number of prisoners in the *Sonderkommando* in Birkenau was reduced by half on February 24, 1944, with the transfer of 200 of them to Lublin Concentration Camp, where they were shot and killed.[142]

SS-Obersturmbannführer Adolf Eichmann, from the *RSHA*, was in Birkenau on February 29, 1944, where he visited the Family Camp in Camp B-IIb. The Family Camp was established for Jews deported from the Theresienstadt ghetto during September 1943, when 5,000 Jews in two transports arrived in Birkenau, and were not subjected to the usual procedure on arrival, they were allowed to keep their own clothes, their heads were not shaven, there were no selections and families were kept together.

Dr. Leo Janowitz, the former Director of the Central Secretariat in the Theresienstadt ghetto, and Friedrich Hirsch, a teacher and children's attendant in the Family Camp reported to Eichmann. During the visit, Eichmann also conversed with Miriam Edelstein, the wife of Jakob Edelstein, the so-called Jewish Elder in the Theresienstadt ghetto, was probably in Germany. In fact this was a lie, Jakob Edelstein had been deported from Theresienstadt to Auschwitz in December 1943. He had been incarcerated in Block 11, along with other members of the *Judenrat*, and it was highly unlikely that Eichmann was not aware of this.

On March 5, 1944, the Jewish prisoners deported from Theresienstadt on September 8, 1943, and were now residing in the Family Camp were given postcards, and were ordered to write to their relatives, stating that they were healthy and that things were going well for them. They were not allowed to write that they soon would be transferred to the labor Camp in Heydebreck, and they were ordered

---

[141] Danuta Czech, *Auschwitz Chronicle*, Henry Holt and Company, New York 1990, p. 582.
[142] Ibid., p. 588.

also to date the postcards March 25–27. The completed postcards were despatched by the Political Department from March 25, 1944.[143]

Two days later, the Camp authorities decided to liquidate the first group of Jews living in the Family Camp. In order to carry on the pretense that the Jews from the Family Camp were to be transferred to labor Camps in the Reich, all those considered healthy were transferred to the Quarantine Camp B-IIa in Birkenau. The men and women were housed in separate blocks, and were allowed to take their personal belongings with them.[144]

Filip Müller described the destruction of the Family Camp members on March 8, 1944, in his memoirs '*Eyewitness Auschwitz*':

> Together with some hundred fellow prisoners I went on duty in the two death factories during the late afternoon of March 8, 1944. After dark, heavy trucks began to rumble into the yard of Crematorium II. SS men undid the tarpaulins and lowered the tailboards. Then they viciously clubbed the people with their truncheons as they were climbing and jumping down. A futher group of SS guards made them run the gauntlet into the underground changing room; the whole gruesome scene was illuminated by floodlights. Today the SS showed no consideration for the old, the sick or children, beating and clubbing everybody without mercy.....
>
> It was not long before the first 600 or so people were inside the crematorium changing room. There they had to wait for their fellow victims to arrive. The SS men had them where they wanted them and no longer paid any attention to them. Together with about thirty prisoners I was in the underground passage which linked the changing room to the gas chamber. After the gassing it would be our job to load the garments left behind on a truck in the yard.....
>
> The scene through the half-open door of the changing room was heartrending. Groups of desperate people were crowding around the fake signboards. When they were still living in the Family Camp they had heard many a tale about these strange rooms; but then, despite much obvious proof, they did not wish to know about them. Now they were here themselves and realized, too late, that all they heard was indeed true. They knew the signboards were fake, and in their frightened eyes

---

[143] Danuta Czech, *Auschwitz Chronicle*, Henry Holt and Company, New York 1990, p. 593.

[144] Ibid., p. 593.

I could read fear and despair. Young mothers were clasping their little ones to their breast, while older boys and girls clung weeping to their parents' legs.

Filip Müller continued his heartbreaking description:

> They began to bid each other farewell. Husbands embraced their wives and children. Everybody was in tears. Mothers turned to their children and caressed them tenderly. The little ones sensed that something frightening was about to happen. They wept with their mothers and held on to them. But gradually the people's sorrow changed to restlessness and agitation. When several SS leaders, among them *Lagerführer* Schwarzhuber and Dr. Mengele appeared in the doorway of the changing room, those standing near flew into a rage: suffering and sorrow gave way to unrestrained hatred for those men who had made false promises and given their word of honour that they would be taken to work at Heydebreck……
>
> Now a few people began to shout slogans, their cries growing louder as they were joined by their fellows: 'We want to live!' and they cried, 'We want to work!' Their angry voices echoed across the underground room. It was their stubborn will to live which made them regard this anteroom of death as a place from which they still might escape. When they saw that their appeals met with no response from the SS leaders, some of the men rushed towards the door. No doubt they wanted to confront Schwarzhuber and remind him of his word of honour.
>
> But their plan was foiled. Once they reached the door they were instantly shot by armed SS guards, some fifty of whom were in the crematorium that day. There was also a large number of *SS-Unterführer*, among them Boger, Buntrock, Baretzki, Hustek, Steinberg, Kurschuss, Schulz and Gorges. After the shootings, the SS men once more flung themselves upon the wretched crowd in the changing room; beating them about the head with their truncheons and using their Alsatians, they drove them into the back of the room. Then they erected machine-guns in front of them……

The SS must have realized that they could not afford to let the second lot of victims into the changing room where their fellow victims no longer bore any resemblance to God's image. Therefore *Oberscharführer* Voss stepped in front of the crowd in an endeavour to establish contact with them. Raising his hands pleadingly he turned to the people to get them to understand that they should be quiet.

Once there was silence he began to speak: 'Now, what is the meaning of all this, you Jews? Your hour has come. There is nothing in the world which can reverse your fate. It is entirely up to you. If you are sensible, you can spare yourselves and your children a great deal of distress..... everything will be much easier if you get undressed quickly and then move on into the next room. Or do you want to make your children's last moments needlessly distressing?

The atmosphere in the room was one of immense gravity. Most of the people now began to undress, but some were still hesitating. As soon as the executioners perceived this they pushed and shoved the crowd into the gas chamber, irrespective of whether or not they had taken off their clothes. Anybody offering resistance was mercilessly beaten to a pulp. Husbands, helpless themselves, crowded around their wives and children to protect them from the blows and also from the savage teeth of the dogs. There was chaos, as in the narrow space people pushed and shoved each other, *SS* men shouted and used their truncheons, and dogs barked and snapped ferociously.

What happened next must have surprised everyone witnessing these terrible scenes in Crematorium II:

> Suddenly a voice began to sing. Others joined in and the sound swelled into a mighty choir. They sang first the Czechoslovakian national anthem and then the Hebrew song 'Hatikvah'. And all the time the *SS* men never stopped their brutal beatings. It was as if they regarded the singing as a last kind of protest, which they were determined to stifle, if they could.

Filip Müller came to the conclusion that he wanted to die with his country-men in the gas chamber:

> In the great confusion near the door I managed to mingle with the pushing and shoving crowd of people who were being driven into the gas chamber. Quickly I ran to the back and stood behind one of the concrete pillars. I thought that here I would remain undiscovered until the gas chamber was full, when it would be locked.... My plan to die anonymously was frustrated. The people who had recognized me insisted on my explaining to them why I had decided to die with them. I implored them not to speak to anybody about my decision; for I knew it would

probably take some time before the gas chamber was sealed off..... during our conversation they told me that young Friedrich Hirsch, who had so devotedly cared for the young people in the Family Camp, had committed suicide.

Time seemed to stand still. The minutes dragged on, and there was no end, no release from torment in sight. Outside, at the doors to the gas chamber, stood Voss, Gorges and Kurschuss, and behind them SS guards with their dogs which barked incessantly, all of them obviously waiting for the next truck load of people to arrive. Through the open door I saw Schwarzhuber and Dr. Mengele stretching to look curiously over the guards' shoulders into the gas chambers. When they were recognized renewed shouts and curses sounded in the gas chamber.

Suddenly a few girls, naked and in the full bloom of youth, came up to me.... At last one of them plucked up courage and spoke to me: 'We understand that you have chosen to die with us of your own free will, and we have come to tell you that we think your decision is pointless; for it helps no one. We must die, but you still have a chance to save your life. You have to return to the camp and tell everybody about our last hours,' she commanded.

Before Filip Müller could answer, the girls took hold of him and dragged him still protesting to the door of the gas chamber. At the door they pushed him and he landed at the feet of the SS men standing there. Kurschuss recognized Filip Müller and he struck him with his truncheon. Filip Müller continued his account:

Kurschuss yelled at me: 'You bloody shit, get it into your stupid head, we decide how long you stay alive and when you die, and not you. Now, piss off to the ovens!' Then he socked me viciously in the face so that I reeled against the lift door. I took the lift upstairs and went into the cremation room. There my legs gave way under me, my head was spinning and I knew I was going to faint. When I came to, I was lying in the coke store. Some of my fellow prisoners helped me up and took me to the door for a breath of fresh air.

I could hear trucks driving into the yard: the second convoy had arrived. Again SS men were shouting, again dogs were barking .... The ambulance marked on the back and on both sides with the emblem of the Red Cross, entered the crematorium yard, but today it stopped behind the building, so as to remain unnoticed... the vehicle had stopped alongside the lawn behind the crematorium, where the concrete shafts projected, through which the pea-sized grains of *Zyklon B* gas was introduced. Near by the two 'disinfecting operators' were ready and waiting for their orders to pour in the gas crystals. But the time had clearly not yet come; for the two were chatting leisurely and lighting cigarettes. Although by now there were more than 1,000 people in the gas chamber, more were obviously expected. In fact before long a third convoy of trucks moved into the yard. Once more the people were driven into the changing room with the utmost brutality.

The end was near:

> After a while I heard the sound of piercing screams, banging against the door and also moaning and wailing. People began to cough. Their coughing grew worse from minute to minute, a sign that the gas had started to act. Then the clamour began to subside and to change to a many-voiced dull rattle, drowned now and then by coughing. The deadly gas had penetrated into the lungs of the people, where it quickly caused paralysis of the respiratory centre. Even before the door of the gas chamber was due to be opened, the *SS* guards with their dogs, the *Unterführer*, as well as several other *SS* men went across to Crematorium III. After they had left, the 'disinfecting operators' car with its Red Cross camouflage followed across to the crematorium yard. This meant the gassings were to be continued there.

Filip Müller described the unloading of the gas chambers after the mass gassing had taken place:

> On the order of an *SS* man I had taken the lift down again in the company of a few other prisoners. As we stepped out of the lift, *Lagerführer* Schwarzhuber and Dr. Mengele were standing outside the door to the gas chamber. The doctor was just switching on the light. Then he bent forward and peered through a peep-hole in the door, to ascertain whether there were still any signs of life inside. After a while he ordered the *Kommandoführer* to switch on the fans which were to disperse the gas. When they had run for a few minutes the door to the gas chamber which was secured with a few horizontal bolts was opened.
> Even before the bottom bar had been unbolted both wings of the double doors were bulging to the outside under the weight of the bodies. As the doors opened, the top layer of corpses tumbled out like the contents of an overloaded truck, when the tailboard is let down. They were the strongest who, in their mortal terror, had instinctively fought their way to the door, the one and only way out, had there been even the remotest possibility of getting out. It was the same every time the gas chamber was used.

Morever, the bodies were not evenly distributed throughout the chamber; most of them lay in heaps, the largest of which was always by the door. The spot where the gas came in was practically empty: no doubt the people had moved away from these places, because the gas smelled of burning metaldehyde and had a sickly-sweet taste. After a short time it produced an excruciating irritation of the throat and intense pressure in the head, before it took its lethal effect.

Filip Müller continued his detailed description:

> We had orders that immediately after the opening of the gas chamber we were to take away first the corpses that had tumbled out, followed by those lying behind the door, so as to clear a path. This was done by putting the loop of a leather strap around the wrist of a corpse and then dragging the body to the lift by the strap and thence conveying it upstairs to the crematorium. When some room had been made behind the door, the corpses were hosed down. This served to neutralize any gas crystals still lying about, but mainly it was intended to clean the dead bodies. For almost all of them were wet with sweat and urine, filthy with blood and excrement, while the legs of many of the women were streaked with menstrual blood.
> As soon as *Zyklon B* crystals came into contact with the air the deadly gas began to develop, spreading first at floor level and then rising to the ceiling. It was for this reason that the bottom layer of corpses always consisted of children, as well as the old and weak, while the tallest and strongest lay on top, with middle-aged men and women in between. No doubt the ones on top had climbed up there over the bodies already lying on the floor, because they still had the strength to do so and perhaps also because they had realized that the deadly gas was spreading from the bottom upwards. The people in their heaps were intertwined, some lying in each other's arms, others holding each other's hands; groups of them were leaning against the walls, pressed against each other like columns of basalt.

The *Sonderkommando's* grisly work went on:

> The carriers had great difficulty in prising the corpses apart, even though they were still warm and not yet rigid. Many had their mouths wide open, on their lips traces of whiteish dried-up spittle. Many had turned blue, and many faces were disfigured, almost beyond recognition, from blows. No doubt the subterranean labyrinth into which the gas chamber had turned when the lights went out, had led the people in their panic to rush all over the place, bump against each other, fall on

top of each other and trample one another, thus causing this confusion of tangled-up corpses. Among them lay the bodies of pregnant women, some of whom had expressed the head of their baby just before they died.
During the removal of corpses from the gas chamber, bearers had to wear gas-masks because the fans were unable to disperse the gas completely. In particular there were remnants of the lethal gas in between the dead bodies and this was released during cleaning out operations. It was terrible but also strenuous work to disentangle the corpses and then drag them away. It quickly made me sweat so that the glasses of my gas-mask steamed up..... when the bearers had begun to remove the corpses from the back of the gas chamber, I went to the pillar near which the girls had talked to me. There I found the girl Yana, who had asked me to take off her necklace and give it to her lover as a keepsake. She lay where she had said she would. I took off the necklace, pocketed it and left the room.[145]

On March 18, 1944, a marriage took place between an Austrian prisoner, Rudolf Freimel (25173) and a French woman, Margarita Ferrer Ray in the registry office in Birkenau. Rudolf Freimel, a Communist, a member of the Austrian underground group, had fought in the Civil War in Spain, and whilst there, he had met Margarita, and they had a son. The photographic laboratory even took a wedding portrait and the first floor of Block 24 was put at their disposal for twenty-four hours. The following day Margarita left the Camp, also taking their son. The wedding was the only case of its kind in the history of Auschwitz.[146]

Reports from London by the Associated Press on March 21, 1944, revealed that the Polish Information Ministry alleged that more than half-a-million people, mainly Jews, had been killed in the Auschwitz Concentration Camp, south-west of Kraków; in an extensive report, the Ministry had stated that the camp contained three crematoriums for the daily elimination of 10,000 corpses, and gas

---

[145] Filip Müller, *Eyewitness Auschwitz*, Ivan R. Dee, Chicago 1979, pp. 107–118.
[146] Jozef Garlinski, *Fighting Auschwitz*, Fontana Collins 1975, pp. 218–219.

chambers, where men, women and children had been killed within 10 to 15 minutes of their arrival in freight-cars.¹⁴⁷

The Allied airforce took photographs of Auschwitz for the first time on April 4, 1944. The photograph of Auschwitz I, the main Camp was taken by Lieutenant Charles Barry of the 60 Photo Reconnaissance Squadron, South African Airforce (SAAF) operating from a base in San Severo, Italy. Along with his navigator, Lieutenant Ian McIntyre, they flew in an unarmed de Havilland Mosquito IX aircraft. They flew at an altitude of 26,000 feet and photographed the main Camp, including the gas chamber building, the registration building and the family home of former Commandant Rudolf Höss. Other missions took place during 1944, photographing Birkenau and the I. G. Farben plant.¹⁴⁸

Two prisoners escaped from Birkenau on April 7, 1944, they were Walter Rosenberg (44070), who was born on September 11, 1944 and Alfred Wetzler (29162), who was born on May 10, 1918. Wetzler was born in Trnava, whilst Walter Rosenberg was born in Topoľčany.

Walter Rosenberg was a clerk in the Quarantine Camp in Section B-IIa and Alfred Wetzler carried out the same role in Section B-IId in Birkenau. Their duties enabled both men a certain degree of free movement within the Camp. This enabled them to collect detailed information on deportations, selections and the extermination process and some of the key figures involved.

With the aid of some prisoners from the construction *Kommando*, they constructed a so-called bunker in Section B-III (Mexico)—an excavated pit, well hidden by boards and pieces of wood from the barracks. They protected themselves against the guards' dogs by scattering gasoline-soaked tobacco around the pit. They waited for three days and nights in their hiding place until on the evening of April 10, 1944, they heard the long-awaited command, 'Vacate guard posts!' Only then did they leave their hiding place, which was barely 500 meters distance from the Block Commander's

---

¹⁴⁷ Danuta Czech, *Auschwitz Chronicle*, Henry Holt and Company, New York 1990, p. 599.
¹⁴⁸ www.World War II Today – 4 April 1944.

office, and crawled behind the circle of empty watchtowers of the 'outside chain.'[149]

They made their way south and with the help of local Poles reached Slovakia, and on April 24, 1944, in the town of Žilina, they met the local Jewish Council and handed them a report on the Auschwitz Concentration Camp. The Jewish Council promised the men that the report would be sent to Rudolf Kastner, the leader of the Hungarian Jews. Rosenberg subsequently saw the Papal Nuncio and also handed him a copy of his report on Auschwitz.[150]

On June 29, 1944, the 32-page Vrba-Wetzler Report (Rosenberg had changed his name to Rudolf Vrba) was sent to John McCloy, the American Assistant Secretary of War. Attached to the report was the request to bomb vital sections of the rail lines transporting the Jews to Auschwitz. This request fell on deaf ears. The transcription of the report below, excludes the paragraphs relating to the incarceration in the Concentration Camp in Lublin:

The Vrba-Wetzler Report

On the 13th April 1942, our group consisting of 1,000 men, was loaded into railroad cars at the assembly camp of Sered'. The doors were shut so that nothing could reveal the direction of the journey, and when they were opened after a long while, we realized that we had crossed the Slovak frontier and were in Zwardoń. The train had until then been guarded by Hlinka men, but was now taken over by SS guards. After a few of the cars had been uncoupled from our convoy, we continued on our way arriving at night at Auschwitz, where we stopped on a sidetrack. The reason the other cars were left behind was apparently the lack of room at Auschwitz. They joined us, however, a few days later.
Upon arrival we were placed in rows of five and counted. There were 643 of us. After a walk of 20 minutes with our heavy packs, we reached the Concentration Camp of Auschwitz. We were at once led into a huge barrack, where on the one side we had to deposit all our luggage and on

---

[149] Yuri Suhl, *They Fought Back*, Schocken Books, New York, 1975, pp. 205–206.
[150] Jozef Garlinski, *Fighting Auschwitz*, Fontana Collins 1975, p. 223.

the other side completely undress and leave our valuables behind. Naked, we then proceeded to an adjoining barrack where our heads and bodies were shaved and disinfected with Lysol. At the exit, every man was given a number which began with 28600 in consecutive order.

With this number in hand we were then herded to a third barrack where so-called registration took place. This consisted of tattooing the numbers we had received in the second barrack on the left side of our chests. The extreme brutality with which this was effected made many of us faint. The particulars of our identity were also recorded. Then we were put in groups of a hundred into a cellar and later to a barrack where we were issued striped prisoners' clothes and wooden clogs. This lasted until 10 a.m. In the afternoon our prisoners' outfits were taken away from us again and replaced by the ragged and dirty remains of Russian uniforms. Thus equipped we were marched off to Birkenau.

Auschwitz is a Concentration Camp for political prisoners under so-called 'Protective Custody.' At the time of my arrival, that is in April of 1942, there were about 15,000 prisoners in the Camp, the majority of whom were Poles, Germans and civilian Russians under protective custody. A small number of prisoners came under the categories of criminals and 'work-shirkers.'

Auschwitz Camp headquarters control at the same time the work Camp of Birkenau, as well as the farm labor Camp of Harmense. All the prisoners arrive first at Auschwitz, where they are provided with prisoners' matriculation numbers and then are either kept there, sent to Birkenau, or in very small numbers to Harmense. The prisoners receive consecutive numbers upon arrival. Every number is only used once, so that the last number always corresponds to the number of prisoners actually in the Camp. At the time of our escape, that is to say at the beginning of April 1944, the number had risen up to 180,000. At the outset the numbers were tattooed on the left breast, but later, due to their becoming blurred, on the left forearm.

All prisoners, irrespective of category or nationality, are treated the same. However, to facilitate identification, they are distinguished by various colored triangles, sewed on the clothing on the left breast, under the matriculation number. The first letter indicates the nationality of the prisoner. This letter (for instance 'P' for Poles) appears in the middle of the triangle. The colored triangles have the following meaning:

Red Triangle	Political prisoners under protective custody
Green Triangle	Professional criminals
Black Triangle	Dodgers—labor slackers—anti-socials

Pink Triangle	Homosexuals
Violet Triangle	Members of the religious sect of 'Bibelforscher'

The Jewish prisoners differ from the Aryan prisoners in that their triangle—which in the majority of cases is red—is turned into a David's star by adding yellow points.

Within the enclosure of the Camp of Auschwitz, there are several factories: a War production plant, *Deutscher Aufrustungswerk* (*DAW*), a factory belonging to the Krupp works, and one to the Siemens concern. Outside the boundary of the Camp is a tremendous plant covering several square kilometers named 'Buna.' The prisoners work in all the aforementioned factories.

The prisoners' actual living quarters, if such a term may at all be used, inside the Camp proper cover an area of approximately 500 by 300 meters surrounded by a double row of concrete posts about 3 meters high which are connected—both inside and out—with one another by a dense netting of high-tension wires fixed into the posts by insulators. Between these two rows of posts, at intervals of 150 meters there are 5 meter high watchtowers, equipped with machine-guns and searchlights.

In front of the inner high-tension circle, there is a further ordinary wire fence. Merely touching this fence is answered by a stream of bullets from the watchtowers. This system is called 'the small' or 'inner chain of sentry posts'. The Camp itself is composed of three rows of houses. Between the first and second row is the Camp street, and between the second and the third there used to be a low wall.

The Jewish girls deported from Slovakia in March and April 1942, over 7,000 of them, lived in the house separated by this wall up until the middle of August 1942. After these girls had been removed to Birkenau, the wall between the second and the third row of houses was removed. The Camp entry road cuts across the row of houses, while over the entrance gate, which is of course always heavily guarded, stands the ironic inscription 'Work Brings Freedom.' At a radius of some 2,000 meters the whole Camp is encircled by a second line called 'the big' or 'outer chain of sentry posts' also with watchtowers every 150 meters. Between the inner and outer chain of the sentry posts are the factories and other workshops. The towers of the inner chain are only manned at night, when the high-tension current is switched into the double row of wires. During the daytime the garrison of the inner chain of sentry posts is withdrawn, and the men take up duty in the outer chain. Escape through these sentry posts—and many attempts have been made—is practically impossible.

Getting through the inner circle of posts at night is completely impossible, and the towers of the outer chain are so close to one another—one every 150 meters, i.e. giving each tower a sector with a 75-meter radius to watch—that approaching unnoticed is out of the question. The guards shoot without warning. The garrison of the outer chain is withdrawn at twilight, but only after it has been ascertained that all the prisoners are within the inner circle. If the roll call reveals that a prisoner is missing, sirens immediately sound the alarm.

The men in the outer chain remain in their towers on the lookout, the inner chain is manned, and a systematic search is begun by hundreds of *SS* guards and bloodhounds. The siren brings the whole surrounding countryside to a state of alarm, so that by a miracle the escapee has been successful in getting through the outer chain, he is nearly certain to be caught by one of the numerous German-police and *SS* patrols.

The escapee is furthermore handicapped by his clean-shaven head, his striped prisoner's outfit or red patches sewn on his clothing, and the passiveness of the thoroughly intimidated inhabitants. The mere fact of neglecting to give information on the whereabouts of a prisoner, not to speak of extending help, is punished by death. Provided that the prisoner has not been caught sooner, the garrison of the outer chain of sentry posts remains on the watch for three days and nights, after which delay, it is presumed that the escapee has succeeded in breaking through the double circle. The following night the outer guard is withdrawn.

If the escapee is caught alive, he is hanged in the presence of the whole Camp; but if he is found dead, his body wherever it may have been located—is brought back to the Camp and seated at the entrance gate, a small notice clasped in his hands reading, 'Here I am.' During our two years' imprisonment many attempts to escape were made by prisoners but, with the exception of two or three, all were brought back dead or alive. It is not known whether the two or three escapees who were not caught actually managed to get away. It can, however, be asserted that among the Jews who were deported from Slovakia to Auschwitz or Birkenau, we are the only two who were lucky enough to save ourselves. As stated previously, we were transferred from Auschwitz to Birkenau on the day of our arrival. Actually there is no such district as Birkenau. Even the word Birkenau is new in that it has been adopted from the nearby birch forest (Brzezinski). The district now called Birkenau was, and is still called Rajska by the local population. The existing Camp center of Birkenau lies 4 kilometers distance from Auschwitz. The outer control zones of both Birkenau and Auschwitz meet and are merely separated by a railway track. We never found anything out about *Neu Berun*, probably about 30 to 40 kilometers away, which oddly enough, we had to indicate as the postal district for Birkenau.

At the time of our arrival in Birkenau, we found there one huge kitchen for 15,000 people and three stone buildings—two of which were completed and one under construction. The buildings were surrounded by an ordinary barbed-wire fence. The prisoners were housed in these buildings and in others later constructed. All were built according to a standard model: A house is about 30 meters long and 8 to 10 meters wide. Whereas the height of the walls hardly exceeds 2 meters, the roof is disproportionately high—about 5 meters, so that the house gives the impression of a stable surmounted by a large hayloft. There is no inner ceiling, so that the room reaches a height of 7 meters in the center, in other words the pointed roofing rests directly on the four walls. The room is divided in two by a partition running its whole length down the middle and fitted with an opening to enable communication between the two parts thus separated.

Along both sidewalls, as well as along the middle partition, two parallel floors, some 80 centimeters apart, have been built, which are in turn divided into small cells by vertical partitions. Thus there are three floors: the ground floor and the two built in the sidewalls. Normally three people live in each cubicle. As can be judged from the dimensions indicated, these cubicles are too narrow for a man to lie stretched out and not high enough for him to sit upright. There is no question of having enough space to stand upright. In this way 400 to 500 people are accommodated in one house or 'block' as they are also called.

The present Camp of Birkenau covers an area of some 1,600 meters by 500 meters which is surrounded—similar to Auschwitz—by a so-called small or inner chain of sentry posts. Work is now proceeding on a still larger compound which is to be added later, the purpose of this extensive planning is not known to us. Within a radius of 2 kilometers, as with Auschwitz, Birkenau is also surrounded by another chain of sentry posts, with the same type of watch system as at Auschwitz.

The buildings we found on our arrival had been erected by 12,000 Russian Prisoners of War, brought there in December 1941. In severe winter weather they had to work under inhuman conditions, as a result of which, most of them, with the exception of a small number employed in the kitchen, died of exposure. They were numbered from 1 to 12,000 in a series which had no connection with the ordinary Camp numbering system previously described. Whenever fresh convoys of Russian prisoners arrived, they were not issued the current Auschwitz prisoner numbers, but received those of deceased Russians in the 1 to 12,000 series. It is therefore difficult to estimate how many prisoners of this category passed through the Camp. Apparently Russians were transferred to Auschwitz or Birkenau on disciplinary grounds from regular Prisoner of War Camps. We found what remained of the Russians in a terrible state of destitution and neglect living in the unfinished building, without the slightest protection against the cold or rain. They died 'en-masse.' Hundreds and thousands of their bodies were buried superficially, spreading a stench of pestillance. Later we had to exhume the corpses and burn them.

A week before our arrival in Auschwitz, the first group of Jews reached the Camp—the women were dealt with separately and received numbers parallel to those of the men; the Slovak women received serial numbers from 1 to 8,000. 1,320 naturalized French Jews from Paris—they were numbered from 27,500 onwards. It is clear, therefore, that between this French group and our convoy no other men arrived in Auschwitz, since we have already pointed out that our numbers started with 28600. We found the 700 French Jews, who were still alive, in terrible condition, the missing 600 having died within a week after their arrival.

The following categories were housed in the three completed buildings:

1. The so-called '*prominencia*,' professional criminals and older Polish political prisoners who were in charge of the administration of the Camp.
2. The remainder of the French Jews, namely some 700.
3. The 643 original Slovak Jews, to whom were added a few days later, those who had been left at Zwardoń.
4. Those Russians who were still alive and housed in the unfinished building, as well as in the open air, and whose numbers diminished so rapidly, that as a group they are scarcely worth mentioning.

Together with the remaining Russian prisoners, the Slovak Jews worked at the construction of buildings, whereas the French Jews had to do spade work. After three days I was ordered together with 200 other Slovak Jews, to work in the German armament factories at Auschwitz, but we continued to be housed in Birkenau. We left early in the morning, returning at night and worked in the carpentry shop as well as on road construction. Our food consisted of one liter of turnip soup at midday, and 300 grams of bad bread in the evening.

Working conditions were inconceivably hard, so that the majority of the ill, weakened by starvation and the inedible food, could not stand it. The mortality rate was so high, that every day, our group of 200 had 30 to 50 dead. Many were simply beaten to death by the overseers—the *Kapos*—during work, without the slightest provocation.

The gaps in our ranks caused by these deaths were replaced daily by prisoners from Birkenau. Our return at night was extremely painful and dangerous, as we had to drag along, over a distance of 5 kilometers, our tools, firewood, heavy cauldrons, and the bodies of those who had died, or had been killed during the working day. With these heavy loads, we were forced to maintain a brisk pace, and anyone incurring the displeasure of one of the *Kapos* was cruelly knocked down, if not beaten to death.

Until the arrival of the second group of Slovak men, some 14 days later, our original number had dwindled to 150. At night we were counted, the bodies of the dead were piled up on flat, narrow—gauge cars or in a truck and brought to the Birch Forest where they were burned in a trench several meters deep and about 15 meters long.

Every day on our way to work we met a working party of 300 Jewish girls from Slovakia, who were employed on ground work in the vicinity. They were dressed in old Russian uniform rags and wore wooden clogs. Their heads were shaven and unfortunately we could not speak to them. Until the middle of May 1942, a total of four convoys of male Jews from Slovakia arrived at Birkenau and all received similar treatment to ours.

From the first and second transports 120 men were chosen—including myself—and placed at the disposal of the administration of the Camp of Auschwitz, which was in need of doctors, dentists, intellectuals and clerks. This group consisted of 90 Slovak and 30 French Jews. As I had in the meantime managed to work my way up to a good position in Birkenau—being in command of a group of 50 men, which had brought me a considerable advantage—I at first felt reluctant to leave for Auschwitz. However, I was finally persuaded to go and left. After eight days, 18 doctors and attendants, as well as three further persons were selected from this group of 120 intellectuals. The doctors were used in the 'sick building' or hospital at Auschwitz, while we three were sent back to Birkenau. My two comrades, Ladislav Braun from Trnava and Emanuel Gross from Vrbové, both of whom have since died, were sent to the Slovak block, while I was ordered to the French section, where we were employed collecting 'personal data' and at 'nursing' the sick. The remaining 99 prisoners were sent to work in the gravel pit, where they all died within a short time.

Shortly thereafter, a so-called 'sick building'—*Krankenbau* was set up. It was destined to become the much dreaded 'Block 7' where at first I was chief attendant and later administrator. The chief of this 'infirmary' was a Pole. Actually this building was nothing else than an assembly center for death candidates. All prisoners incapable of working were sent there. There was no question of any medical attention or care. We had some 150 dead daily and their bodies were sent for cremation to Auschwitz. At the same time the so-called selections were introduced. Twice weekly, Mondays and Thursdays, the camp doctor indicated the number of prisoners who were to be gassed then burned. These 'selections' were loaded into trucks and brought to the Birch Forest. Those still alive on arrival were gassed in a big barrack erected near the trench used for burning the bodies. The weekly 'draft' in dead from Block 7, was about 2,000 of whom 1,200 died of a 'natural death' and about 800 through 'selection.' For those who had not been selected, a death certificate was issued and sent to the central administration at Oranienburg, whereas for those selected, a special register was kept with the indication '*SB*' (*Sonderbehandelt* – Special treatment).

Until January 15, 1943, up to which time I was the administrator of Block 7 and therefore in a position to directly observe happenings, some 50,000 prisoners died of 'natural death' or by selection.

As previously described, the prisoners were numbered consecutively, so that we are able to reconstruct fairly clearly their order of succession and the fate which befell each separate convoy on arrival. The first male Jewish transport reaching Auschwitz for Birkenau was composed, as mentioned, of 1,320 naturalized French Jews bearing approximately the following numbers:

27400–28600	French Jews
28600–29600	In April 1942, the first convoy of Slovak Jews—our convoy
29600–29700	100 men—Aryans from various Concentration Camps
29700–32700	3 complete convoys of Slovak Jews
32700–33100	400 professional criminals from Warsaw prisons
33100–35000	1,900 Jews from Kraków
35000–36000	1,000 Poles—political prisoners

36000–37300	In May 1942,—1,300 Jews from Lublin Concentration Camp	
37300–37900	600 Poles from Radom, amongst them a few Jews	
37900–38000	100 Poles from Dachau Concentration Camp	
38000–38400	400 French naturalized Jews who arrived with their families *	
38400–39200	800 naturalized French Jews, the remainder of the convoy was gassed	
39200–40000	800 Poles—political prisoners	
40000–40150	150 Slovak Jews with their families. Outside of a group of 50 girls sent to the Women's Camp, all other members were gassed in the Birch Forest. Among the 150 men who came to the Camp, there was a certain Zucker and Viliam Sonneschein, both from eastern Slovakia	
40150–43800	Approximately 4,000 French naturalized Jews, almost all were intellectuals; 1,000 women were directed to the Women's Camp, while the balance of about 3,000 persons were gassed in the usual manner	

*The whole convoy consisted of about 1,600 individuals, of whom approximately 200 girls and 400 men were admitted to the Camp, while the remaining 1,000 persons (women, old people, children as well as men) were sent without further procedure from the railroad siding directly to the Birch Forest, and there gassed and burned. From this moment on, all Jewish convoys were dealt with in the same manner. Approximately 10 percent of the men and 5 percent of the women were allotted to the Camps and the remaining members were immediately gassed. The process of extermination had already been applied earlier to the Polish Jews. During long months, without interruption, trucks brought thousands of Jews from the various ghettos direct to the pit in the 'Birkenwald.'

400 Slovak Jews from Lublin, including Matej Klein and Number 43820, Meiloch Laufer from eastern Slovakia. This convoy arrived on June 30, 1942.

200 Slovak Jews—the convoy consisted of 1,000 persons. A number of women were sent to the Women's Camp, the rest were gassed in the Birch Forest. Among the prisoners sent to the Camp were: Jozef Zelmanovic – Snina, Adolf Kahan – Bratislava, Walter Reichmann – Sučany, and Esther Kahan – Bratislava.

2,000 Frenchmen, communists and other political prisoners, among whom was the brother of Thorez and the young brother of Leon Blum. The latter was atrociously tortured, then gassed and burned.

500 Jews from Holland, in the majority German emigrants. The rest of the convoy, about 2,500 persons gassed. About 300 so-called Russians under protective custody.

320 Jews from Slovakia. About 70 girls were transferred to the women's camp, the remainder—some 650 people gassed in the Birch Forest. The convoy included about 80 people who had been handed over by the Hungarian police to the camp of Sereď. Others from this convoy were: Dr. Zoltan Mandel—since deceased, Holz—christian name unknown, a butcher from Piešťany, Miklos Engel, from Zilnia and Chaim Katz from Snina, his wife and 6 children were gassed.

15,000 naturalized French, Belgian and Dutch Jews. This figure certainly represents less than 10 percent of the total convoy. This was between July 1, and September 15, 1942. Large family convoys arrived from various European countries and were at once directed to the Birch Forest. The special squad (*Sonderkommando*) employed for gassing and burning worked in day and night shifts. Hundreds of thousands of Jews were gassed during this period.

64800–65000	200 Slovak Jews. Out of this transport about 100 women were admitted to the Camp, the rest of them were gassed and burned**
65000–68000	Naturalized French, Belgian and Dutch Jews. Not more than 1,000 women were selected and sent to the Camp. The others, at the lowest estimate 30,000 were gassed
71000–80000	Naturalized French, Belgian and Dutch Jews. The prisoners brought to the Camp represent 10 percent of the total transport. A conservative estimate would be approximately 65,000 to 70,000 persons gassed
80000–85000	Approximately 5,000 Jews from various ghettos in Mława – Maków – Ciechanów – Łomża – Grodno – Białystok. For 30 full days truck-convoys arrived without interruption. Only 5,000 persons were sent to the Concentration Camp, all the others were gassed at once. The 'special squad' worked in two shifts, 24 hours daily and was scarcely able to cope with the gassing and burning. Without exaggerating it may be said that out of these convoys

	80,000 to 90,000 received 'special treatment.' These transports also brought in a considerable amount of money, valuables and precious stones
85000–92600	6,000 Jews from Grodno, Białystok, and Kraków, as well as 1,000 Poles. The majority of the Jewish convoys were directly gassed and daily about 4,000 Jews were driven into the gas chambers. During mid-January 1943, three convoys of 2,000 persons each, arrived from Theresienstadt. They bore the designation 'CU,' 'CR,' and 'R,'—the meaning of these signs is unknown to us. These markings were also stamped on their luggage. Out of these 6,000 persons, only 600 men and 300 women were admitted to the Camp. The remainder were gassed
99000–100000	End of January 1943, large convoys of French and Dutch Jews arrived; only a small portion of them reached the Camp
100000–102000	In February 1943, 2,000 Poles, mostly intellectuals
102000–103000	700 Czech. Later those still alive were sent to Buchenwald
103000–108000	3,000 French and Dutch Jews and 2,000 Poles. During the month of February 1943, two contingents arrived daily. They included Polish, French and Dutch Jews, who in the main, were sent to the gas chambers. The number gassed during this month can well be estimated at 90,000

**Among the newly arrived were: Ludwig Katz – Zilnia, Avri Burger – Bratislava, Poprad, Mikulas Steiner – Považská Bystrica, Fried – Trencin-Buchwald, Josef Rosenwasser – Eastern Slovakia, Julius Neuman – Bardejov, Sandor Wertheimer – Vrbove, Misi Wertheimer – Vrbové, Bela Blau – Zilnia.

On December 17, 1942, the 200 young Slovak Jews, the so-called 'special squad' employed in gassing and burning the condemned, were in turn executed at Birkenau. They were executed for having planned to mutiny and escape. A Jew betrayed their preparations. This frightful job had to be taken over by a group of 200 Polish Jews who had just arrived at the Camp from Maków. The men belonging to the 'special squad' lived separately. On account of the dreadful smell spread by them, people had but little contact with them. Besides they were always filthy, destitute, half wild and extraordinarily brutal and ruthless. It was not uncommon to see one of them kill another. This was considered by the others a sensation, a change. One simply recorded that number so and so had died. Once I was an eyewitness, when a young Polish Jew named Jossel demonstrated a 'scientific' murder on a Jew, in the presence of an SS guard. He used no weapon, merely his bare hands, to kill his victim.

At the end of February 1943, a new modern crematorium and gassing plant was inaugurated at Birkenau. The gassing and burning of the bodies in the Birch Forest was discontinued, the whole job being taken over by the four specially built crematoria. The large ditch was filled in, the ground levelled and the ashes used as before, for fertilizer at the farm labor Camp of Harmense, so that today, it is almost impossible to find trace of the dreadful mass murder which took place here.

At present there are four crematoria in operation at Birkenau, two large ones II and III, and two smaller ones IV and V.[151] Those of type II and III consist of three parts: i.e. (A) the furnace room; (B) the large halls; (C) the gas chamber. A huge chimney rises from the furnace room, around which are grouped nine furnaces, each having four openings. Each opening can take three normal corpses at once and after an hour and a half, the bodies are completely burned. This corresponds to a daily capacity of about 2,000 bodies. Next to this is a large 'reception hall' which is arranged so as to give the impression of the antechamber of a bathing establishment. It holds 2,000 people and apparently there is a similar waiting room on the floor below. From there a door and a few steps lead down into the very long and narrow gas chamber. The walls of this chamber are also camouflaged with simulated entries to shower rooms to mislead the victims.

The roof is fitted with three traps which can be hermetically closed from the outside. A track leads from the gas chamber to the furnace room. The gassing takes place as follows: The unfortunate victims are brought into the hall, where they are told to undress. To complete the fiction that they are going to bathe, each person receives a towel and a small piece of soap, issued by two men clad in white coats. They are then crowded into the gas chamber in such numbers, there is, of course, only standing room. To compress this crowd into the very narrow space, shots are often fired to induce those already at the far end, to huddle still closer together. When everybody is inside, the heavy doors are closed. Then there is a short pause, presumably to allow the room temperature to rise to a certain level, after which SS men with gas masks

---

[151] Incorrectly listed in the report as Crematorium I and II

climb on the roof, open the traps, and shake down a preparation in powder form out of tin cans labelled 'Zyklon B—For use against vermin,' which is manufactured by a Hamburg concern.

It is presumed that this is a 'cyanide' mixture of some sort, which turns into gas at a certain temperature. After three minutes everyone in the chamber is dead. No one is known to have survived this ordeal, although it was not uncommon to discover signs of life, after the primitive measures employed in the Birch Forest.

The chamber is then opened, aired, and the 'special squad' carts the bodies on flat trucks to the furnace room, where the burning takes place. Crematorium IV and V work on nearly the same principle, but their capacity is only half as large. Thus the total capacity of the four cremating and gassing plants at Birkenau amounts to about 6,000 daily. On principle only Jews are gassed. Aryans very seldom, as they were usually given 'special treatment' by shooting. Before the crematoria were put into service, the shooting took place in the Birch Forest and the bodies were burned in the long trench; later, however, executions took place in the large hall of one of the crematoria, which had been provided with a special installation for this purpose.

Prominent guests from Berlin were present at the inauguration of the first crematorium in March 1943. The 'program' consisted of the gassing and burning of 8,000 Kraków Jews. The 'guests'—both officers and civilians were extremely satisfied with the results and the special peephole fitted into the door of the gas chamber was in constant use. They were lavish in their praise of this newly erected installation.

At the beginning of March 1943, 45,000 Jews arrived from Salonika, 10,000 came into the camp (109000–119000), including a small percentage of women; some 30,000 however, went straight to the cremating facility. Of the 10,000, nearly all died a short time later, from a contagious illness, resembling malaria. They also died of typhus due to the prevailing conditions in the camp. Malaria among the Jews and typhus took such a toll among the prisoners in general that the 'selections' were temporarily suspended. The contaminated Greek Jews were ordered to present themselves and in spite of our repeated warnings many of them did. They were all killed by intra-cardial phenol injections administered by a lance-corporal of the medical corps.

Out of the 10,000 Greek Jews, some 1,000 men remained alive, and were later sent, together with 500 other Jews, to do fortification work in Warsaw. A few weeks later, several hundred came back in a pitiful state and were immediately gassed. The remainder presumably died in Warsaw. Four hundred Greek Jews suffering from malaria were sent for 'further treatment' to Lublin, after the phenol injections had been stopped, and it appears they actually arrived. Their fate is not known to us, but it can be taken for granted that out of the original number of 10,000 Jews not one eventually remained in the Camp.

Simultaneously, with the stopping of the 'selections', the murdering of prisoners was forbidden. Prominent murderers such as the Reich German professional criminals Alexander Neumann, Alexander Zimmer, Albert Haemmerle, Rudi Osteringer, Rudi Bechert and the political prisoners Alfred Klein and Alois Stahler, were punished for repeated murder and had to make written declarations that they had killed so and so many prisoners.

At the beginning of 1943, the political section of Auschwitz received 500,000 discharge certificates and we thought with ill concealed joy, that at least a few of us, would be liberated. But the forms were simply filled out with the names of those gassed and filed away in the archives.

119000–120000	1,000 Poles from the Pawiak Prison in Warsaw
120000–123000	3,000 Greek Jews, part of whom were sent to replace their comrades in Warsaw. The remainder quickly died off
123000–124000	1,000 Poles from Radom and Tarnów
124000–126000	2,000 from mixed Aryan convoys

In the meantime, ceaseless convoys of Polish and a few French and Belgian Jews arrived, and without exception, were dispatched to the gas chambers. Among them was a transport of 1,000 Polish Jews from Lublin, which included three Slovaks, one of whom was a certain Spira from Stropkow or Vranov.

The flow of convoys abrubtly ceased at the end of July 1943, and there was a short breathing space. The crematoria were thoroughly cleaned, the installations were repaired and prepared for further use. On August 3, the killing machine again went into operation. The first convoys consisted of Jews from Bendin and Sosnowitz and others followed during the whole month of August.

Only 4,000 men (132000–136000) and a very small number of women were brought to the camp. Over 35,000 were gassed. Of the aforementioned 4,000 men, many died as a result of bad treatment, hunger or illness; some were even murdered. The responsibility for these tragedies lies with the criminal Tyn, a Reich German, from the Concentration Camp of Sachsenhausen and the Polish political prisoner Mieczislaw Katerzinski (8516) from Warsaw.

The selections were introduced again and this time to a murderous extent, especially in the Women's Camp. The Camp Doctor, an *SS-Hauptsturmführer* and the son or nephew of the Police President of Berlin (we forget his name) outdid all the others in brutality. The selection system has been continued ever since until our escape.

137000–138000	At the end of August 1,000 Poles came from the Pawiak Prison and 80 Jews from Greece
138000–141000	3,000 men from various Aryan Transports
142000–145000	At the beginning of September 1943, 3,000 Jews arrived from Polish Labor Camps and Russian Prisoners of War
148000–152000	During the week following September 1943, family transports of Jews arrived from Theresienstadt

They enjoyed quite an exceptional status, which was incomprehensible to us. The families were not separated and not a single one of them received the customary and normal gas treatment. Their heads were not even shaven, they were able to keep their luggage, and were lodged in a separate section of the Camp,—men, women and children together.
The men were not forced to work and a school was even set up under the direction of Fredy Hirsch (Makabi, Prague). They were allowed to correspond freely. The worst they had to undergo was mistreatment at the hands of their 'Camp Eldest,' a certain professional criminal by the name of Arno Bohm (8). Our astonishment increased when we learned of the official indication given to this 'special treatment – SB' transport of Czech Jews with six months quarantine.
We knew very well what 'SB' meant (*Sonderbehandlung*), but could not understand the long period of six months' quarantine and the generally clement treatment this group received. The longest quarantine period we had witnessed so far was only three weeks. Towards the end of the six month period, however, we became convinced that the fate of these Jews would be the same as that of most of the others—the gas chamber. We tried to get in touch with the leader of the group and explain their lot and what they had to expect. Some of them declared—especially Fredy Hirsch, who seemed to enjoy the full confidence of his companions—that if our fears took shape, they would organize resistance. Thus some of them hoped to instigate a general revolt in the camp. On March 6, 1944 we heard that the crematoria were being prepared to receive the Czech Jews. I hastened to inform Fredy Hirsch and begged him to take immediate action, as they had nothing left to lose. He replied that he recognized his duty. Before nightfall I again crept over to the Czech

Camp, where I learned that Fredy Hirsch was dying. He had poisoned himself with luminol.

The next day, March 7, 1944, he was taken unconscious, along with his 3,791 comrades who had arrived at Birkenau on September 7, 1943, on trucks to the crematoria and gassed. The young people went to their deaths singing, but to our great disappointment nobody revolted. Some 500 elderly people died during the quarantine. Of all of these Jews only eleven twins were left alive. They were being subjected to various medical tests at Auschwitz, and when we left Birkenau they were still alive. Among the gassed was Rozsi Furst from Sered'. A week before the gassing, that is to say on March 1, 1944, everyone in the Czech group in the Camp had been asked to inform his relatives about his well-being. The letters had to be dated March 23 to 25, 1944 and they were requested to ask for food parcels.

153000–154000	1,000 Poles from Pawiak Prison
155000–159000	During October and November 1943, 4,000 persons from various prisons and smaller transports of Jews from Bendin and vicinity, who had been driven out of their hiding places; also a group of Russians under protective custody from the Minsk and Vitebesk regions. Some more Russian Prisoners of War arrived and, as stated, they as usual received numbers between 1 and 12,000
160000–165000	In December 1943, 5,000 men originating from Dutch, French and Belgian transports and for the first time Italian Jews from Fiume, Trieste and Rome. Of these at least 30,000 were immediately gassed. The mortality among these Jews was very high, and in addition the 'selection' system was still decimating all ranks***
165000–168000	On December 20, 1943, a further group of 3,000 Jews arrived from Theresienstadt****
169000–170000	1,000 people in small groups, Jews, Poles and some Russians and a small number of Yugoslavs
170000–171000	1,000 Poles, Russians and some more Yugoslavs
171000–174000	At the end of February and the beginning of March, 3,000 Jews from Holland, Belgium, and for the first time, long-established French Jews (not naturalized) from Vichy, in France. The majority of this transport was gassed immediately upon arrival

***The bestiality of the whole procedure reached its culminating point between January 10 and 24, 1944, when even young and healthy persons irrespective of profession or working classification—with the exception of doctors—were ruthlessly 'selected.' Every single prisoner was called up, a strict control was established to see that all were present, and the 'selection' proceeded under the supervision of the same Camp doctor (son or nephew of the Police President of Berlin) and the Commandant in Birkenau *SS-Untersturmführer* Johann Schwarzhuber. The infirmary had in the meantime been transferred from Block 7 to a separate section of the Camp, where conditions had become quite bearable. Its inmates nevertheless, were gassed to the last man. Apart from this group the general action cost some 2,500 men and over 6,000 women their lives.

****The convoy was listed under the same category as the one which had reached the Camp on September 7, i.e. '*SB*-transport'—Czech Jews with six months' quarantine. On their arrival, men, women and children all joined the September group. They enjoyed the same privileges as their predecessors. Twenty-four hours before the gassing of the first group took place, the latest arrivals were separated from the rest and placed in another part of the Camp, where they still are at present. Their quarantine ends on June 20, 1944.

Small groups of Bendin and Sosnowitz Jews, who had been dragged from hiding, arrived in the middle of March. One of them told me that many Polish Jews were crossing over to Slovakia and from there to Hungary, and that the Slovak Jews helped them on their way through.

After the gassing of the Theresienstadt transports, there were no further arrivals until March 15, 1944. The effective strength of the Camp rapidly diminished and men of later incoming transports, especially Dutch Jews, were directed to the Camp. When we left on April 7, 1944, we heard that large convoys of Greek Jews were expected.

The Camp of Birkenau consists of three building areas. At present only sections I and II are guarded by the inner chain of sentry posts, whereas section III is still under construction and uninhabited. At the time of our departure from the Camp (the beginning of April 1944), the following categories of prisoners were in Birkenau:

Section 1 – Women's Concentration Camp			
	Slav Jews	Other Jews	Aryans
1a and 1b	300 approx	7,000 approx	6,000 approx

Section II – Men's Concentration Camp			
2a Quarantine Camp	2	200 approx	800 approx
2b Jews from Theresienstadt	3,500 approx		
2c Presently uninhabited			
2d *Stammlager*	58	4,000 approx	6,000 approx
The Gypsy Camp			4,500 approx

Remarks

In addition to the 300 Slovak Jewish girls, approximately 100 are employed in the administration building of Auschwitz
One of the two Slovak Jews in the Quarantine Camp is Dr. Andreas Müller from Podolínec (Block Eldest)
The Gypsy Camp—the 4,500—this is the remainder of some 16,000 Gypsies. They are not used to work and die off rapidly.
No. 36832 Walther Spitzer, Block Eldest from Nemšová who came to Lublin from Birkenau.
No. 29867 Jozef Neumann, Overseer of the Corpse Crew from Snina.
No. 44989 Josef Zelmanovic, Staff from Snina.
No. 33049 Ludwig Sollmann, Clerk from Kežmarok.
No. 32407 Ludwig Eisenstädter, Tattooist from Krempachy.
Chaim Katz, staff from Snina
The internal administration of the Camp of Birkenau is run by specially selected prisoners. The 'Blocks' are not inhabited according to nationalities, but rather according to working categories. Each 'Block' is supervised by a staff of five, i.e. a Block Eldest, a Block Recorder, a male nurse and two attendants.

The Block Eldest

He wears an armband with the number of his block, and is responsible for order there. He has power over life and death. Until February 1944, nearly 50 percent of the Block Eldest were Jews, but this was stopped by an order of Berlin. They all had to resign with the exception of three Jews, who in spite of this order, were able to keep their posts.

The Block Recorder

He was the Block Eldest's right-hand, he does all the clerical work, keeping the index cards and records. His work is of great responsibility and he has to keep his ledgers with painful exactitude, as the index cards only indicate the number and not the name of the prisoners; errors are fatal. For instance, if the Recoder has noted down a death by mistake, and this often occurs with the unusually high mortality, the discrepancy is straightened out, by killing the bearer of the corresponding number. Corrections are not admitted. The Block Recorder occupies a key post, which is often misused.

Nursing and Room Duties

They consist in keeping the inside of the barracks clean and carrying out small manual jobs in and around the Block. Of course, there is no question of really taking care of the sick. The Camp Eldest supervised the whole Camp, he is also a prisoner. The post is at present held by Franz Danisch (No. 11182), a political prisoner from Königshütte, Upper Silesia. He is the undisputed master of the whole Camp and has the power to nominate or dismiss the Block Eldest's and Block Recorder's hand out jobs and so on.

Further we have a 'Chief Recorder' whose position is undoubtedly one of the most powerful in the Camp. He is in direct contact with Camp headquarters, receiving their orders and reporting on all matters. All Camp Recorders are directly subordinated to him and have to submit all their reports to him. The Chief Recorder of Birkenau is Kasimir Gork (No. 31029), a Pole from Warsaw, a former bank clerk. The supreme control over the Blocks lies in the hands of six to eight 'Block Leaders,' all SS men. Every night they hold roll calls, the result of which is communicated to the Camp Leader, *SS-Untersturmführer* Johann Schwarzhuber, from the Tyrol. This individual is an alcoholic and a sadist. Over him is the Camp Commander, who also controls Auschwitz, where there is a second subordinate Camp leader. The Camp Commander's name is Höss.

The Chief of the work squad or group is called the *Kapo*. During work the *Kapo* has full authority over his group of prisoners and not infrequently one of these *Kapos* kills a man working under him. In larger squads there may be several *Kapos*, who are then under the orders of a *Kapo* in-chief. At first there were many Jewish *Kapos*, but an order from

Berlin prohibited their being employed. Supreme control over work is carried out by German specialists.[152]

The first transport of Jews from Hungary from Budapest containing approximately 1,800 people and a second transport from Topoly containing 2,000 people arrived at Auschwitz on May 2, 1944. Out of the 3,800 people 2,698 were murdered in the gas chambers.[153]

On April 11, 1944, 2,500 Jewish men, women and children arrived in Auschwitz from Athens, Greece, in a *RSHA* transport. From this transport, 1,067 Jewish men, women and children were murdered in the gas chambers. Among this transport is Shlomo Venezia, who was selected to live and tattooed with the prisoner number 182727. He was drafted into the *Sonderkommando* and he provided some comprehensive descriptions of the Bunker Number 2 gas chambers, as well as Crematorium III, in his book 'Inside the Gas Chambers.' The description of his journey and arrival at Auschwitz are covered in the section 'Transports From Greece,' in Part II. He described how he was selected for the *Sonderkommando:*

> We spent three weeks in quarantine. Then one day, we saw some German officers arriving. We didn't often see Germans in the quarantine sector; in general it was the *Kapos* who maintained order. These officers stopped in front of our barracks and ordered the *Kapo* to get us to line up, as if for roll call. Each of us had to say what kind of job he was able to do. Even if we didn't have a trade or profession, everyone knew that he had to lie. When my turn came, I said I was a hairdresser. Leon Cohen, a Greek friend, who always stood close to us, said that he was a dentist, even though he had actually worked in a bank..... the Germans chose eighty people including myself, my brother and my cousins.[154]

Shlomo Venezia continued his account:

> The next day at around nine o'clock, we lined up and set off to sector BIId—this was the men's sector in Birkenau..... *Lager* d consisted of two rows of barracks. The first two buildings bigger than the others, were

---

[152] Carmelo Lisciotto – www. holocaustresearchproject.org. (H.E.A.R.T.)
[153] Danuta Czech, *Auschwitz Chronicle*, Henry Holt and Company, New York 1990, p. 618.
[154] Shlomo Venezia, *Inside the Gas Chambers*, Polity Press, Cambridge 2009, p. 52.

used as the kitchens. In the middle of all those huts was that of the *Sonderkommando*. When I went in, I saw a prisoner by himself, who seemed to be waiting for us....... Then he asked me if I knew the name of the *Kommando* to which we had been assigned. Since I didn't have the slightest idea, he told me we were in the *Sonderkommando*. 'What does *Sonderkommando* mean? Special detachment. Special why? Because you have to work in the Crematorium... where the people are burned.'[155]

Shlomo Venezia explained:

> This man was named Avraham Dragon. Actually, it was only when I saw him again sixty years later in Israel, that I found out what his name was. I told him this story, with the vague hope that he might be the person who had given me such a humane reception, and whom I had never seen since. He smiled at me; he was moved, and said that he had never forgotten the famished young Greek who had landed in the *Sonderkommando*.[156]

With the forthcoming major operation against the Jews of Hungary, significant changes were once again made to the chain of command at Auschwitz Concentration Camp on May 8, 1944: *SS-Obersturmbannführer* Arthur Liebehenschel, the Commandant of Auschwitz I and *SS* Camp Senior was transferred to the post of Commandant of Lublin Concentration Camp and *SS-Sturmbannführer* Fritz Hartjenstein, the Commandant of Auschwitz II, was transferred to the post of Commandant of Natzweiler Struthof Concentration Camp. Rudolf Höss, the former Commandant returned to Auschwitz, as *SS* Camp Senior, from his role as Head of Office D-1 in the *WVHA*. *SS-Hauptsturmführer* Josef Kramer, the Commandant of Natzweiler Struthof Concentration Camp, assumed the post of the Commandant of Auschwitz II.[157]

Rudolf Höss wasted no time in preparing the Camp to receive the transports of Jews from Hungary. He ordered the completion of a

---

[155] Shlomo Venezia, *Inside the Gas Chambers*, Polity Press, Cambridge 2009, pp. 52–54.
[156] Ibid., p. 54.
[157] Danuta Czech, *Auschwitz Chronicle*, Henry Holt and Company, New York 1990, pp. 621–622.

new unloading ramp, within Birkenau itself, to replace the *Alte Judenrampe*, and a three track rail siding to facilitate the mass extermination of the Jews, by bringing them closer to the massive crematoria and gas chambers. He also ordered that the inactive ovens in Crematorium V, be made ready for operation and that next to Crematorium V, three large and two small pits for the incineration of corpses be dug. Höss also instructed that Bunker II—the so-called 'White House' was to be put back into operation and that incineration trenches were dug next to it. He ordered that barracks that would serve as undressing rooms for men and women were to be constructed near the 'White House.' Rudolf Höss also brought back *SS-Hauptscharführer* Otto Moll from his post of running the sub-camp at Gleiwitz, to perform the role of Director of all Crematoriums in Birkenau.[158]

Filip Müller provided a detailed description of Otto Moll, in his book '*Eyewitness Auschwitz*':

> Moll was rather short and thickset. His chubby face was, as is often the case with gingery-blond people, covered with freckles. He wore a glass eye. In the *Sonderkommando* we used to call him 'Cyclops'. Moll was cruel, brutal and unscrupulous. For him, Jews were sub-human creatures and he treated them accordingly.[159]

Otto Moll, like Rudolf Höss, wasted no time in his preparations to receive the Jews from Hungary, and Filip Müller explained the changes he made to the *SS* personnel who worked in the crematoria:

> *SS-Unterscharführer* Karl-Fritz Steinberg was temporarily put in charge of crematoria II and III. Very soon he was relieved by *Oberscharführer* Erich Mühsfeldt, who came from Lublin. Soviet prisoners of war who had come to know him there, told us what a merciless, brutal, slave-driver this man with a harmless countenance and almost frail build, really was. Under him worked *Rottenführer* Holländer and Eidenmüller. Both were lean and lanky. Bunker V was under the management of *SS-Unterscharführer* Eckardt. He was about twenty-eight, tall, slim and blond. Born in Hungary, he spoke Hungarian like his mother tongue. His crony, Kell, who came from Łódź, spoke Polish as well as Yiddish.

---

[158] www.holocausthistoricalsociety.org.uk (HHS).
[159] Filip Müller, *Eyewitness Auschwitz*, Ivan R. Dee, Chicago 1979, p. 125.

Both had instructions to listen carefully to what the victims said on their last walk to the place of extermination, in particular, to watch out for the least sign of insubordination. Reinforcement for Crematorium IV and V—up to then mainly under the command of *Unterscharführer* Gorges and *Sturmmann* Kurschuss—came in the persons of *Unterscharführer* Robert Seitz, and a little later, *Scharführer* Hubert Busch.

The construction work at Birkenau around Crematorium V began with urgency:

> Soon after his arrival, Moll ordered the excavation of five pits behind Crematorium V, not far from the three gas chambers. An increasing number of prisoners were also employed on the site near Bunker V, to dig more pits there. Here, as well as at the crematorium yards wattle screens had been put up to prevent the curious from looking in at the death factories from the outside. The meadow behind the yard of Crematorium V, where thousands of spring flowers were in bloom, now turned into a strange building site, where some 150 prisoners were set to work.
> Vast supplies of shovels, spades, wheelbarrows, timber, pneumatic drills and other tools waited, ready to be used for excavating cremation pits, once the surveying work was completed. Accompanied by his henchmen, extermination expert Moll paced up and down the large site, giving instructions for the siting of the pits, a fuel depot, the spot where the ashes were to be crushed, and all the rest of the devices, which he had thought up for the extermination and obliteration of human beings. After only a few hours' sleep, a new day began and with it final preparations for the extermination campaign about to begin. The two new pits had considerably increased the capacity of the four crematoria at Birkenau. It was just a matter of adding the finishing touches. There was a constant stream of trucks delivering materials of all kinds, such as old railway sleepers, conifer branches, waste wood, beams, rags, large quantities of wood alcohol, barrels of waste lubricating oil, rammers, coarse and fine-meshed sieves, cement, wooden planks, boards and barrels of chlorinated lime. Wherever the fuel was stacked in the open, it was roofed over.

To increase the murder capacity even further, the 'White House' was put back in service:

> Three more cremation pits were dug in the back yard of Crematorium V, making up the five that Moll had ordered. In addition, the farmhouse which had served as a place of extermination in 1942, was put in running

order. Its four rooms served as gas chambers, while an additional four cremation pits were dug outside. The changing rooms were located in three wooden barracks, and the whole complex was known as Bunker V.

From the outset, the Camp authorities took rigourous care to obliterate all traces of their crimes. For this reason the ashes of the burnt corpses were thrown into fishponds or the River Vistula. In this connection Moll had thought up a new technique to expedite the removal of ashes. He ordered an area next to the pits adjoining Crematorium V and measuring 60 meters by 15 meters to be concreted; on this surface the ashes were crushed to a fine powder before their final disposal.[160]

Shlomo Venezia described the extermination process at the 'White House' in some detail:

> At around five the *Kapo* again ordered us to assemble. We obviously assumed that, at this time in the evening, 'assembly' meant we had finished that laborious day's work. But unfortunately this wasn't the case. We came back out of the Crematorium, but instead of turning right to go back to the barracks, they made us turn left, through the little forest of birches. I'd never seen this kind of tree in Greece, but in Birkenau, they were the only trees one saw surrounding the camp. As we walked along the path, all we could hear was the wind whistling through the silvery leaves. All of a sudden, murmurs started to reach us from behind. To begin with, the noise was very faint and faraway. We came to a little house called, as I later learned, Bunker 2, or the 'White House.' Just then the murmuring of voices became more intense.[161]
>
> It was a small farm with a thatched roof. We were ordered to stand opposite one side of the little house, near the road that ran in front of it. From where we were, we could see nothing, neither on the left or right. Dusk was falling; the murmurs had become the distinct sound of people coming towards us. I was curious, as usual, and went across to try and see what was happening. I saw entire families waiting in front of the cottage: young men, women and children. There must have been two or three hundred of them altogether. I don't know where they'd come from, but I suppose they'd been deported from a Polish ghetto.

---

[160] Filip Müller, *Eyewitness Auschwitz*, Ivan R. Dee, Chicago 1979, pp. 126–133.

[161] Shlomo Venezia, *Inside the Gas Chambers*, Polity Press, Cambridge 2009, pp. 56–57.

People were forced to get undressed where they were, in front of the door. The children were crying. You could feel the fear and dread; people were really helpless and terrified..... finally the people were forced to enter the little house. The door was closed. Once everyone was inside, a little truck, with the Red Cross sign on its sides, drove up. A rather tall German got out. He went over to the small opening high up on one of the walls of the little house. He had to climb onto a stool to reach it. He took a can, opened it, and threw the contents in through the little opening. Then he closed the opening and left. The shouts and crying had not stopped, and they redoubled in intensity after a few minutes. This lasted for ten or twelve minutes, then silence.

Shlomo Venezia continued:

Meanwhile we had been ordered to go around to the back of the house. When we arrived, I noticed a strange gleam coming from that direction. As I went over, I realized that the light was that of a fire burning in the ditches some twenty yards away. So the Germans sent us to the other side of the house, where the ditches were. They ordered us to bring the bodies out of the gas chamber and place them in front of the ditches. I didn't go into the gas chamber myself; I stayed outside, going back and forth between the bunker and the ditches. Other men from the *Sonderkommando*, more experienced than we were, had the job of laying the bodies out in the ditches in such a way that the fire wouldn't go out. If the bodies were packed in too densely, the air couldn't get through and there was a risk that the fire would go out or fade in intensity..... the ditches sloped down, so that, as they burned, the bodies discharged a flow of human fat down the ditch to a corner where a sort of basin had been formed to collect it. When it looked as if the fire might go out, the men had to take some of that liquid fat from the basin, and throw it onto the fire to revive the flames. I saw this only in the ditches of Bunker 2.[162]

Shlomo Venezia provided a detailed description of his experiences in the *Sonderkommando* in Crematorium III in Birkenau, in his book 'Inside the Gas Chambers,' which is a memorable and harrowing account:

The respite didn't last. The very next day, we had to set off to work again. I was sent to Crematorium III with a little group of about fifteen people. As I said I was a hairdresser, the *Oberkapo* who had met us when

---

[162] Ibid., pp. 57–60.

> we arrived at the Crematorium placed in my hands a pair of very long scissors, like the ones used by tailors to cut fabric. Then they directed us towards the room in which we were supposed to be working. The old hands very succinctly explained to us what we needed to do. The contact with the dead was immediate. The deportees of a previous convoy had just been gassed and the men in the *Sonderkommando* were already busy taking the corpses out of the gas chamber. They were laid out in a kind of atrium, before being taken up to the Crematorium ovens. This was where I had to cut off the hair of the dead bodies. There were three or four of us doing this job. Then two 'dentists' came along to extract the victims' gold teeth, which they kept in a little container that nobody could go near. One of them was my friend Leon Cohen, who had claimed he was a dentist. They gave him a dentist's forceps and a little mirror to see inside the mouth. I remember that, when he realized what it was he was supposed to do, he almost fainted. To begin with, when he worked on the first corpses, he went quite quickly, he opened their mouths and removed the gold teeth. But as he continued, it all became more difficult, since the corpses had had time to stiffen, and he had to force their jaws open.[163]

Shlomo Venezia then described the removal of the corpses from the gas chamber:

> Those given this task started by pulling the corpses out with their hands, but in a few minutes their hands were dirty and slippery. In order to avoid touching the bodies directly, they tried using a bit of cloth, but of course the cloth in turn became dirty and damp after a few moments. So people had to make do. Some tried to drag the bodies along with a belt, but this actually made the work even harder, since they had to keep tying and untying the belt. Finally, the simplest thing was to use a walking stick under the nape of the neck to pull the bodies along. There were no shortage of walking sticks, because of all the elderly people who were put to death.

He described the scene when the gas chamber was opened:

> I found it difficult to speak of those visions of the gas chamber. You could find people whose eyes hung out of their sockets because of the struggles the organism had undergone. Others were bleeding from everywhere or were soiled by their own excrement, or that of other people.

---

[163] Shlomo Venezia, *Inside the Gas Chambers*, Polity Press, Cambridge 2009, pp. 62–63.

> Because of the effect that their fear and the gas had on them, the victims often evacuated everything they had in their bodies. Some bodies were all red, others very pale, as everyone reacted differently.
>
> You found them gripping each other—everyone had desperately sought a little air. The gas was thrown onto the floor and gave off acid underneath, so every one tried to find some air, even if each one needed to climb on top of another until the last one died.... They were crammed in so tightly against one another that the smallest and weakest were inevitably suffocated.[164]

Sholomo Venezia described the whole extermination process in Crematorium III:

> Every time a new convoy arrived, people went in through the big door of the Crematorium and were directed towards the underground staircase that led to the undressing room. There were so many of them that we saw the queue stretching out like a long snake. As the first of them were entering, the last were still a hundred yards or so behind. After the selection on the ramp, the women, children and old men were sent in first, then the other men arrived.
>
> In the undressing room, there were coat hooks with numbers all along the wall, as well as little wooden planks on which people could sit to get undressed. To deceive them more effectively, the Germans told people to pay particular attention to the numbers, so that they would be able to find their things more easily, when they came out of the 'shower.' After a time, they also added an instruction to use the laces to tie shoes in pairs.... These instructions were generally given by the SS standing guard, but it sometimes happened that a man in the *Sonderkommando* could speak the language of the deportees and transmit these instructions to them directly. To calm people down and ensure they would go through more quickly, without making any fuss, the Germans also promised them they would have a meal just after disinfection. Many of the women hurried up, so as to be the first in line and get it all over with as quickly as possible—especially as the children were terrified and clung to their mothers. For them, even more than for the others, everything must have been strange, eerie, dark, cold.[165]

---

[164] Ibid., pp. 63–65.
[165] Shlomo Venezia, *Inside the Gas Chambers*, Polity Press, Cambridge 2009, pp. 66–67.

Shlomo Venezia described the actual gassing of the Jewish deportees:

> Once they had taken off their clothes, the women went into the gas chamber and waited, thinking they were in a shower, with the shower heads hanging over them... a woman would sometimes be seized by doubt when no water came out and went to see one of the two Germans outside the door. She was immediately beaten and forced to go back in; that took away any desire she might have to ask questions.
> Then the men too, were finally pushed into the gas chamber. The Germans thought that if they made thirty or so strong men go in last, they would be able, with their force, to push the others, right in. And indeed, herded by the rain of blows, as if they were so many animals, their only option was to push hard to get into that room to avoid the beating.
> The German whose job it was to control the whole process often enjoyed making these people, who were about to die, suffer a bit more. While waiting for the arrival of the *SS* man who was going to release the gas, he amused himself by switching the light on and off to frighten them a little more. When he switched off the light, you could hear a different sound emerging from the gas chamber; the people seemed to be suffocating with anguish, they had realized they were going to die. Then he would switch the light back on and you heard a sort of sigh of relief, as if the people thought the operation had been cancelled.
> Then finally the German bringing the gas would arrive. It took two prisoners from the *Sonderkommando* to help him lift the external trapdoor above the gas chamber, then he introduced *Zyklon B* through the opening. The lid was made of very heavy cement. The German would never have bothered to lift it up himself, as it needed two of us. Sometimes it was me, sometimes others.

Venezia Shlomo described the end of the gassing process:

> Once the gas had been thrown in, it lasted about ten to twelve minutes, then finally you couldn't hear anything anymore, not a living soul. A German came to check that everyone was really dead by looking through a peephole placed in the thick door—it had iron bars on the inside to prevent the victims from trying to smash the glass. When he was sure that everyone was well and truly dead, he opened the door and came out right away, after starting the ventilation system. For twenty minutes, you could hear a loud throbbing noise, like a machine breathing in air. Then finally, we could go in and start to bring the corpses out of the gas chamber. A terrible acrid smell filled the room. We couldn't

distinguish between what came from the specific smell of the gas and what came from the smell of the people and the human excrement.[166]

On May 15, 1944, the Camp authorities decided to liquidate the inhabitants of the Gypsy Family Camp, which was housed in B-IIe in Birkenau. There were approximately 6,000 men, women and children in this section. The Director of Camp B-IIe, Paul Bonigut, advised the Gypsies in secret, so that they could resist.

The next day, on May 16, 1944, vehicles drove up to Camp B-IIe and heavily armed SS-men surrounded the Camp. The SS-Officer in charge ordered the Gypsies to leave the barracks. Forewarned, the Gypsies armed with knives, spades, crowbars and stones refused to leave the barracks. After a conference in the SS-Block Leaders room, a whistle announced the end of the operation. The first attempt to liquidate the Gypsy Camp had failed.[167]

Also on the 16 May 1944, three freight trains of Hungarian Jews arrived at the Birkenau rail sidings. After unloading, they were taken to the Crematoriums to be gassed. These transports signal the commencement of the mass transports from Hungary, organized by Adolf Eichmann and his staff.

Two Jewish prisoners on May 27, 1944, escaped from Auschwitz II; Arnost Rosin (29858) and Czesław Mordowicz (84216) reached Slovakia, where they were arrested. The news of their arrest reached a secret organization that succeeded in collecting 10,000 crowns and buying their release from prison. The pair met with Alfred Wetzler and Rudolf Vrba (formerly Walter Rosenberg) where they discussed the destruction of Hungarian Jewry. They too compiled reports that were added to the Vrba-Wetzler Report and these reports found their way to England, Switzerland and the United States of America.[168]

The Camp Authorities took a decision to record the arrival of a transport of Jews at Birkenau during May 1944, with a series of some

---

[166] Ibid., pp. 67–69.
[167] Danuta Czech, *Auschwitz Chronicle*, Henry Holt and Company, New York 1990, p. 626.
[168] Ibid., p. 635.

200 photographs taken by Ernst Hoffmann, and Bernhard Walter, members of the Identification Service, which was located in Block 26 in Auschwitz I. Bernhard Walter was in charge of this section.

The photographs, taken on May 26–27, 1944, record the arrival and selection for labor or death in the gas chambers of Jews from the towns of Bilke, Tačovo, Uzhgorod, located in the area of Carpatho-Ruthenia. The photographs provided a unique record of how the Nazis transported to the newly constructed camp in Birkenau, hundreds of thousands of Hungarian Jews. How they were selected for forced labor, or selected to die in the gas chambers, by SS doctors. The photographs show the fit and healthy before and after the registration process, and the elderly, and the women and children going to, or awaiting their turn to enter the gas chambers. The photographs also showed the confiscation and sorting of the belongings that the deportees brought with them. The photographs stop short of the murder process itself.

The photographs were placed in an album, suitably captioned, and how it came to be discovered was one of the most remarkable stories of the Holocaust For this, we must thank former Auschwitz prisoner Lili Jacob, who found the album.

Lili Jacob was born on January 16, 1926, in Bilke, in the upper Ruthenian Carpathians, one of six children. On the last day of Passover in 1944, the Jews of Bilke were ordered to assemble in the yard of the large synagogue. All together there were about 10,000 Jews from Berehovo and the neighbouring communities. From the ghetto, four transports filled with men, women and children left for Birkenau.

When the selection began, at first Lili was able to stay with her mother in the line. However, after she was categorized as 'unfit for labor,' when Lili tried to follow her, an SS guard pushed her away. As she fought with him and screamed, the guard beat her with his rifle butt, bayoneted her savagely in the arm, and dragged her to the group selected for slave labor. When Lili looked back, her father and the older boys were gone. Her mother and the younger boys, who were clinging to her skirt, were being marched away....

Lili was the only survivor from her extended family that arrived on May 26, 1944. After the selection, Lili had to relinquish her clothes and possessions. After a shower, she received someone else's clothing, and the prisoner number A-10862 was tattooed on her left arm.

In December 1944, Lili was transferred from Birkenau to work in a clothing factory in Silesia; from there she was sent to an ammunition factory in Morchenstern (Smržovka) in the Sudetenland, which was a sub-camp of the Gross-Rosen Concentration Camp. During the final stages of the Second World War, she was transported from there to Mittlebau-Dora, near Nordhausen in Thuringia, Germany. Just before the Camp was liberated, she became infected with typhus and two Czech physicians fought to save her life.

Mittelbau-Dora was liberated by the American forces on April 9, 1945, and on this day Lili found the photograph album. The day the Americans arrived at Mittlebau-Dora, Lili was lying in the prisoners' hospital, recovering from typhus. From outside she heard the other prisoners shouting that the Americans had arrived to liberate the Camp. She went out to see what was happening and collapsed from weakness. Some of her fellow prisoners carried her to a deserted *SS* barracks and when she awoke she began searching for some warm clothes. In a cupboard near the bed, she found under a striped pyjama, the hard-covered album. As she opened it—she saw the photograph of the Rabbi of Bilke—Naftali Zvi Weiss. In shock she then recognized familiar faces from her hometown, as well as her beloved relatives, who had arrived in Birkenau one year before—relatives who had all perished.

The album that Lili Jacob found was 33 centimeters long and 25 centimeters wide. It had a beige-brown linen hard cover and consisted of fifty-six pages. The four edges of the album were fortified with black-colored metal. The measurements of the photographs were 8.2 x 11.1 centimeters. The photographs show the procedure of the arrivals of the transports from the beginning to near the bitter end. At the rear of the album there is a smaller section, which includes 63 photographs which record the visit of Heinrich Himmler to Auschwitz and various photographs of the sub-camps. Lili Jacob herself was photographed in the album, standing in front of the kitchen building in Birkenau, during a roll call.

In July 1945, Lili returned to her hometown of Bilke, with the album. When surviving relatives identified their loved ones who had perished in the photographs, Lili could not reject their pleas to have a momento of those departed, and gave away some of the photographs. In the same year Lili married Max Zelmanovic in Mukachevo, and three years later they emigrated to the United States of America.

Dr. Erich Kulka, the respected historian, found in the Jewish Museum in Prague during 1955, two boxes with the title 'Photographs from Auschwitz,' in which there were 203 glass plates. As a survivor of Auschwitz, Kulka immediately recognized the location of where the photographs were taken, and he commenced research into the origin of the photographs.

The photographs were published in several publications in the years that followed and following Dr. Erich Kulka's recommendation, Lili appeared with the album at the trial of former Auschwitz personnel in Frankfurt am Main during the mid-1960's. She appeared on December 3, 1964 with the album, but she refused the court president's request to leave the album as evidence.

With encouragement from Beate and Serge Klarsfeld, who published a limited edition of the 'Auschwitz Album' in 1980, Lili Jacob, on August 26, 1980, attended a festive presentation ceremony where the album was donated to the Yad Vashem. Lili presented the album with trembling hands to the Director, Yitzhak Arad. In her speech, Lili emphasized that she was giving the album to Yad Vashem, so that it might serve as an eternal guard, in the realization that the album belongs first and foremost to the Jewish people. She added that: 'I am gratefully relieved that this weight has been lifted from my heart and the album will be permanently exhibited at Yad Vashem.'

Lili Zelmanovic passed away on December 17, 1999, at the age of seventy-three.[169]

---

[169] *The Auschwitz Album*, Yad Vashem/ Auschwitz-Birkenau State Museum, 2002, pp. 72–86.

An eyewitness to the deportation of Jews from Hungary was Janusz (John) Wiernicki who wrote about his experiences in Auschwitz in the book, 'War in the Shadow of Auschwitz', published in 2001:

> The next day, I started my work early and, in the middle of a bright and sunny May morning, I arrived close to the fence line separating the hospital from the ramp. This was a good location for watching the unfolding human drama across the barbed wire fence. However, I had to be very careful to look out for any activity on the hospital grounds. I did not want to be caught unexpectedly by a wandering *SS* man who could cross the sport field.... After a careful check to make sure I was alone, I unwrapped my binoculars from the tissue paper used by the orderlies for hospital dressing and looked at the railroad platform.
> The '*Canada Kommando*' gathered in small groups, already stood in the middle of the platform waiting for the train. *SS* armed guards were stationed along the full length of the ramp. A military vehicle arrived and an officer stepped out. I immediately recognized *SS-Hauptsturmführer*[170] Dr. Heinz Thilo from my previous hospital selections where, as the *Lagerarzt* of the Birkenau hospital, he selected sick prisoners for gassing.[171]

His account continued:

> Two large army trucks entered the platform and were parked near the exit. Dr. Thilo, accompanied by another officer, paced the platform and occasionally looked at his watch. A large number of *SS* personnel stood in small groups, talking in loud voices and laughing at the same time. All sergeants and corporals carried large wooden sticks. Then I also recognized my old adversary Stefan Baretzki, who was now one of the *SS-Blockführer's* at the Men's Camp....
> Suddenly I noticed excitement among the people gathered on the platform. The incoming black locomotive pulling a long line of cattle cars whistled from the distance and then slowly puffed its way along the railroad ramp. Then it stopped and unexpectedly released clouds of white steam from one of its side cylinders. For a second, the whole ramp, train, *SS* guards and prisoners were lost in the clouds of white and foggy mist.

---

[170] Incorrectly stated that Dr. Heinz Thilo, was an *SS-Obersturmführer* in rank.
[171] J. Wiernicki, *War in the Shadow of Auschwitz*, Syracuse University Press 2001, p. 156.

All of the people standing on the platform looked from a distance like dark and menacing shadows waiting anxiously for their victims as in *Dante's Inferno*.

When trains were unloaded from the track adjoining the Men's Camp and the hospital area, the view was completely obstructed by the long line of boxcars.... But when the incoming Jewish transports were unloaded from the middle track, closer to the Women's Camp, the dramatic ramp selections were clearly visible from the hospital grounds. Only then did I have a chance to use my binoculars and watch the drama unfolding before my eyes. This time, the train arrived on the middle track.

The horror of the arrival at the Birkenau ramp was about to begin:

> The train stopped. In the small windows of the cattle cars appeared human faces. Women with begging, sad eyes, unshaven men with fear and frustration pained on their faces, gazed with suspicion at the reception group on the platform. They all looked exhausted after their long journey. Thirsty, they pleaded in strained voices: '*Wasser*... Water!' The SS man walked slowly along the train, banging at each door with a wooden stick: 'All quiet and all out. Leave your luggage behind ...Keep Moving!' He screamed in a loud voice.
>
> '*Canada*' men opened the door of each cattle car. The people inside each car, tired, thirsty, and squeezed very tight for many days and nights, pushed towards an opening... men pushed harder and they were first on the ground. Women and children made the second wave. The sick and old were left behind lying helplessly on the dirty floors of the cattle cars among piles of luggage, blankets and human excrement.
>
> I looked closer at the railroad cars. The signs were in Hungarian. This was a Budapest transport. The '*Canada*' men jumped into the cattle cars and tried to assist the invalids and the sick. With a mixture of compassion and indifference, they gently guided disabled persons to descend from the high steps of the cattle cars to the railroad ramp.
>
> Once unloaded, SS guards with huge dogs inspected the empty cattle cars. They went from car to car. Whenever the guard found a person left behind, he let the dog attack the victim who, frightened by the ferocious animal, gathered all of his or her strength and desperately jumped screaming from the cattle car.
>
> People were helplessly lying on the ground, crying for mercy or help from members of their families or close friends.... One of the *SS Oberscharführer's* called out in a reasonably friendly voice: 'Please be calm, ladies and gentlemen. Form a column of five—men on the right side,

women and children on the left.' The friendly tone of his voice had a calming effect on the crowd.

The selection for life or immediate death was about to commence:

> Dilligently, they formed two long columns along the full length of the railroad platform. I noted also a small group of men with Red Cross armbands standing on one side. They were the Jewish doctors who arrived with the transport and who waited their turn for selection. All groups were facing Dr. Thilo. As soon as the men were formed in an orderly column, five abreast, each person was told to move forward, one at a time and face the doctor. After a brief assessment of each individual, the *SS* doctor started to move his finger. As he turned his face toward me, I really appreciated my new binoculars. Although, the platform was quite a distance away from the hospital fence, with my new equipment I could see him very well. However, I was disappointed when I looked at his face and his eyes. I expected to see a spark of humanity, anguish, contempt, perhaps even anger or hate. What I actually saw was a calm bureaucratic indifference. His face was expressionless and impersonal. His eyes were cold. He just stood there, in the middle of the platform, with his left arm behind his back holding his leather gloves and with his right arm outstretched in front, flicking his finger from left to right.
> Young, robust and healthy men moved to the right while the older men were forming a new column behind the army truck on the left. '*Canada*' men helped sick and disabled men to climb on the truck. Within a half-hour, the job was finished. The *SS* man heading the column made a sign to the driver of the truck. The long line of old men moved and walked silently behind the truck carrying the sick and disabled people. They crossed the rail lines as they walked towards the entrance to the Women's Camp. In front of the *SS* guard post, they turned right and walked along the railroad tracks towards the entrances to Crematoria II and III. The short column of young men followed the first group and walked in the same direction. After a few hundred yards the truck and the column of old men turned right and entered the courtyard of Crematorium III. The column of healthy young men bypassed the entrance to the crematoria and marched farther down the winding road to the bath house.'[172]

Then the women faced the ordeal of selection:

---

[172]   The bath house was the Sauna where new arrivals were received.

The women left behind on the platform were confused and scared. Families had been torn apart. Children cried and, in voices full of emotion, called 'Daddy, Daddy!' The women and children waved to the departing men.... The men's eyes reflected both resignation and fear. Wailing and screaming was heard everywhere, the *SS* men on the platform tried to reassure the women.... I was so close that I could hear *SS* men barking orders and some of their loud remarks.

Dr. Thilo was already selecting women left behind on the platform. Young and healthy girls stayed on the right. Older women, grandmothers, and grand-daughters below the age of fourteen were left together on the left. Sometimes the doctor stopped the selection process and talked to the people.

A young, beautiful, tall woman, well-dressed, slender, with dark long hair, who had been sent to the right side, pleaded in a highly emotional and loud voice with the doctor for permission to join her mother and grandmother sent to the left side. Dr. Thilo seemed to be accommodating in this case. He smiled, moved his head in an affirmative way, and let her join her family. Unknowingly, she had selected death.

'Canada' men helped old women, invalids and small children to climb on the second truck .... The doctor reached the end of the women's column and sent mostly young and healthy girls to the right. Immediately upon completion of the selection, the column of young women from the right side was led by an *SS-Unterscharführer* across the railroad tracks directly to the Women's Camp. The long line of mothers, grandmothers, and children followed the second truck heading towards Crematorium III. A Red Cross ambulance passed the marchers. Inside, cannisters with *Zyklon B* were delivered by *SS* men to the crematoria.

The arrival process was nearly complete:

'Canada' men were left behind on the platform to collect and sort out all of the luggage. Thrown in large piles in front of each cattle car, the mountains of suitcases offered tempting opportunities for theft. Large and small, expensive and cheap, made of leather or plywood, the tossed luggage was sorted out by 'Canada' men under the watchful and suspicious eyes of the *SS* guards. Damaged and half-opened suitcases full of clothes, food, jars of fat, bread, sausages and bottles of wine lay on the platform, in the middle of cleaning activities, tempting both prisoners and the *SS* guards....

The train stood empty on the platform. Dr. Thilo left with his driver, the people had gone, and only small groups of 'Canada' men worked diligently to make room for the next transport. There was a whistle on the platform signalling the beginning of train-cleaning activities. A special squad of *'Canada'* men went to each car to clean the floor and wash the walls. The cleaning crew threw out the cars trash, human excrement, soiled underwear, and corpses left abandoned and covered by pillows and blankets. Stiff bodies of infants, hidden by terrified mothers before their departure, were collected in a separate pile for transport to the crematoria.

The 'special handling' of the Budapest transport was coming to an end. Then I heard the whistle. The train moved backward. Wheels turned slowly as the steaming locomotive pushed the long line of cattle cars towards the main watchtower. *SS* guards holding automatic weapons still guarded the remaining suitcases, coats, briefcases, parcels and the damaged half-open trunks. Occasionally, a *Kapo* with a yellow armband crossed the platform, screaming at the few remaining *'Canada'* men to work faster.

I watched the arrival of this transport for almost two hours. There were approximately twenty cattle cars with eighty persons in each car. One thousand six hundred people: men and women, old and young, adults and children, and infants were 'processed' by efficient and business-like camp administrators.[173]

The arrival of a transport on May 29, 1944, from Oradea-Nagyvárad, Northern Transylvania, which was then part of Hungary, following the Second Vienna Award in 1940, brought a very important witness to Auschwitz. On this transport was Dr. Miklós Nyiszli, and his wife Margareta and daughter Susanna. In his post-war account, he described the journey and arrival at the hell that was Birkenau:

May 1944. Inside each of the locked cattle cars, ninety people were jammed. The stench of the urinal buckets, which were so full they overflowed, made the air unbearable. The train of the deportees. For four days, forty identical cars had been rolling endlessly on, first across Slovakia, then across the territory of the *Generalgouvernement,* bearing us towards an unknown destination.....

Leaving Tatra behind us, we passed the stations of Lublin and Kraków. During the war these two cities were used as regroupment camps—or, more exactly, as extermination camps for here, all the anti-Nazis of Europe were herded and sorted out for extermination. Scarcely an hour

---

[173] J. Wiernicki, *War in the Shadow of Auschwitz*, Syracuse University Press 2001, pp. 156–161.

out of Kraków, the train ground to a halt, before a station of some importance. Signs in Gothic letters announced it as 'Auschwitz,' a place which meant nothing to us, for we had never heard of it.

Peering through a crack in the side of the car, I noticed an unusual bustle taking place about the train. The SS troops who had accompanied us until now were replaced by others. The trainmen left the train. From chance snatches of conversation overheard, I gathered we were nearing the end of our journey. The line of cars began to move again and some twenty minutes later stopped with a long strident whistle of the locomotive.

The convoy had arrived at Birkenau:

> Through the crack I saw a desert-like terrain: the earth was a yellowish clay, similar to that of Eastern Silesia, broken here and there by a green thicket of trees. Concrete pylons stretched in even rows to the horizon, with barbed wire strung between them from top to bottom. Signs warned us that the wires were electrically charged with high tension current. Inside the enormous squares bounded by the pylons stood hundreds of barracks, covered with green tar-paper and arranged to form a long, rectangular network of streets as far as the eye could see. Tattered figures, dressed in the striped burlap of prisoners, moved about inside the camp. Some were carrying planks, others were wielding picks and shovels, and farther on, still others were hoisting fat trunks onto the backs of waiting trucks.
>
> The barbed wire enclosure was interrupted every thirty or forty yards by elevated watch towers, in each of which an SS guard stood leaning against a machine-gun mounted on a tripod. This was then Auschwitz Concentration Camp....... I glanced around the car at my companions. Our group consisted of some twenty-six doctors, six pharmacists, six women, our children and some elderly people, both men and women, our parents and relatives. Seated on their baggage or on the floor of the car, they looked both tired and apathetic, their faces betraying a sort of foreboding that even the excitement of our arrival was unable to dispel. Several of the children were asleep. Others sat munching the few scraps of food we had left. And the rest, finding nothing to eat, were vainly trying to wet their desiccated lips with dry tongues.

The unloading of the cattle cars was about to begin:

> Heavy footsteps crunched on the sand. The shout of orders broke the monotony of the wait. The seals on the cars were broken. The door slid slowly open and we could already hear them giving us orders. "Everyone

get out and bring his hand baggage with him. Leave all heavy baggage in the cars." We jumped to the ground, then turned to take our wives and children in our arms and help them down, for the level of the cars was over four and a half feet from the ground.

The guards had us line up along the tracks. Before us stood a young SS officer, impeccable in his uniform, a gold rosette gracing his lapel, his boots smartly polished.... I surmised from his arm-band that he was a doctor. Later, I learned that he was the head of the SS group, and that his name was Dr. Mengele.

In the moments that followed we experienced certain phases of what, at Auschwitz, was called 'selection.' As for the subsequent phases, everyone lived through them according to his particular fate. To start, the SS quickly divided us according to sex, leaving all children under fourteen with their mothers. So our once united group was straightaway split in two. A feeling of dread overwhelmed us. But the guards replied to our anxious questions in a paternal, almost good-natured manner. It was nothing to be concerned about. They were being taken off for a bath and to be disinfected, as was the custom. Afterwards we would all be reunited with our families.

Doctor Miklós Nyiszli was able to look around and take stock of the situation:

While they sorted us out for transportation I had a chance to look around. In the light of the dying sun the image glimpsed earlier through the crack in the box car seemed to have changed, grown more eerie and menacing. One object immediately caught my eye: an immense square chimney, built of red bricks, tapering towards the summit. It towered above a two-storey building and looked like a strange factory chimney. I was especially struck by the enormous tongues of flame rising between the lightning rods, which were set at angles on the square tops of the chimney..... so the 'factory' was a crematorium. A little further on I saw a second building with its chimney; then almost hidden in a thicket, a third, whose chimneys were spewing the same flames. A faint wind brought the smoke towards me. My nose, then my throat, were filled with the nauseating odour of burning flesh and scorched hair..... meanwhile the second phase of selection had begun. In single file, men, women, children, the aged had to pass before the selection committee. Dr. Mengele, the medical 'selector' made a sign. They lined up again in two groups. The left-hand column included the aged, the crippled, the feeble, and women with children under fourteen. The right-hand column consisted entirely of able-bodied men and women, those able to work. In this latter group I noticed my wife and fourteen year-old daughter. Those too sick to walk, the aged, the insane, were loaded into Red Cross vans. Some of the elderly doctors in my group asked if they could also get into the vans. The trucks departed, then the left-hand group, five abreast, flanked by SS guards, moved off in its turn. In a few minutes they were out of sight, cut off from view by a thicket of trees. The right-hand column had not moved. Dr. Mengele ordered all of the doctors to step forward; he then approached the new group, composed of some fifty doctors, and asked those who had studied in a German university, who had a thorough knowledge of pathology and had practiced forensic medicine to step forward.

Doctor Miklós Nyiszli decided to act:

> I broke ranks and presented myself. Dr. Mengele questioned me at length, asking me where I had studied, the names of my pathology professors, how I had acquired a knowledge of forensic medicine, how long I had practiced. Apparently my answers were satisfactory, for he immediately separated me from the others and ordered my collegues to return to their places.[174]

The Doctor was taken in Dr. Mengele's car along the main road to the Camp Office, where Dr. Mengele spoke with Dr. Sentkeller, A prisoner, and Doctor Miklós Nyiszli continued his account:

> Inside, several people with deep, intelligent eyes and refined faces, wearing the uniform of prisoners, sat working at their desks. They immediately rose and came to attention. Dr. Mengele crossed to one of them, a man of about fifty, whose head was shaved clean. Since I was standing a few steps behind the *Hauptsturmführer*,[175] it was impossible for me to hear what they were saying. Dr. Sentkeller, a prisoner, and as I learned later the F Camp doctor, nodded his head in assent. At his request I approached another prisoner's desk. The clerk rummaged for some file cards, then asked me a number of questions about myself, recorded the answers both on the card and in a large book, and handed the card to an SS guard. Then we left the room...... a guard took me to another barrack, on the entrance to which was written: 'Baths and Disinfection,' where I and my card were turned over to still another guard. A prisoner approached me and took my medical bag, then searched me

---

[174] Dr. Miklós Nyiszli, *Auschwitz*, Granada Publishing Limited, St. Albans 1973, pp. 25–28.

[175] In his account, Dr. Mengele's rank was incorrectly stated as an *Obersturmführer*.

and told me to undress. A barber came over and shaved first my head, then the rest of my body, and sent me to the showers. They rubbed my head with a solution of calcium chloride, which burnt my eyes so badly that for several minutes I could not open them again.

The registration process was nearing its end:

> In another room my clothes were exchanged for a heavy, almost new jacket, and a pair of striped trousers. They gave me back my shoes, after having dipped them in a tank containing the same solution of calcium chloride. I tried on my new clothes and found they fitted me quite well—I wondered what poor wretch had worn them before me. Before I could reflect any further, however, another prisoner pulled up my left sleeve and, checking the number on my card, began skilfully to make a series of little tattoo marks on my arm, using an instrument filled with a blue ink. A number of small, bluish spots appeared almost immediately. "Your arm will swell a little," he reassured me, "but in a week that will disappear and the number will stand out quite clearly." So I Dr. Miklós Nyiszli, had ceased to exist; henceforth I would be, merely, Concentration Camp Prisoner Number A 8450.[176]

Upon completion of the registration process, Doctor Miklós Nyiszli was transferred to the sub-camp at Monowitz, and at the end of June 1944, he was assigned by Dr. Mengele to work in the laboratory and the autopsy room located in Crematorium III.[177] We will hear much more from Doctor Nyiszli, about his time in the heart of the death factory, later on.

Dr. Edmund Veesenmayer, the Reich Plenipotentiary to Hungary, on June 17, 1944, sent a telegram to the Reich Foreign Minister, Joachim von Ribbentrop, that as of June 17, approximately 340,000 Jews had been deported from Hungary to the Reich territory. This number could be doubled by the end of July, according to the current estimates, without producing great traffic congestion, and later a total of approximately 900,000 could be reached.[178]

---

[176] Dr. Miklós Nyiszli, *Auschwitz*, Granada Publishing Limited, St. Albans, 1973, pp. 29–30.
[177] Danuta Czech, *Auschwitz Chronicle,* Henry Holt and Company, New York 1990, p. 636.
[178] Danuta Czech, *Auschwitz Chronicle,* Henry Holt and Company, New York 1990, p. 648.

Edward 'Edek' Galinski, born on October 15, 1923, who was brought to Auschwitz with the first transport of Polish prisoners from the prison in Tarnów on June 14, 1940, and given prisoner number 531, escaped from the Camp, on June 24, 1944, along with female prisoner Mala Zimetbaum. She was born on January 26, 1918, in Brzesko, and was deported to Auschwitz from the Malines Camp in Belgium.[179]

Edek Galinski's escape plan required an *SS* uniform, and in mid-February 1944, he entered into an agreement with *SS-Rottenführer* Edward Lubusch,[180] who hailed from Bielsko-Biała, and was formerly Edek's *Kommandoführer*, to supply him with an *SS* uniform and weapon. Wiesław Kielar, who had arrived in the same transport as Edek from Tarnów prison, described how Edek and Mala left Birkenau on June 24, 1944, in a daring bid for freedom:

> I had worked out a plan whereby Edek and Mala were to go on Saturday, and on Monday, if their escape had been successful, Jozek and I would follow them. Edek and Mala were to make a stop in Kozy. There they would hand the uniform and the pass to Szymiak, who would have to bring them to where Jozek worked....
> We parted between Sectors A and B of the Women's Camp directly opposite the street leading to the guardhouse, where the little Slovak girls were already on duty at the barrier. As though nothing was the matter, we did not even shake hands, just a few words. "Goodbye. We'll wait for you in Kozy. If there are any changes, I'll let you know by the old man. So long!" He gave a tug at his overalls, tossed his toolbox from one hand to the other and walked straight up to the little guardhouse.
> I went to Sector A. When I had passed the kitchen and the sauna, I turned around to watch Edek . He walked past the guardpost without any difficulty, reported his departure and proceeded with firm steps down the road, along the ramp, parallel to my sector.... Just a few yards from the main guardhouse I turned right, jumped across the ditch and made my way towards a pile of drain pipes that were stocked in this corner. Taking out my rule, I pretended to be measuring the pipes. From this spot I had an excellent vantage point. On the left was the sick bay,

---

[179] Ibid., p. 650.
[180] Edward Lubusch was found with false papers, as he was preparing to join the Polish resistance, he was stripped of his rank and shot. Jozef Garlinski, *Fighting Auschwitz*, Fontana Collins 1975, p. 196.

behind it the wires and the road along the ramp on which I briefly glimpsed Edek's figure before he disappeared inside the tall gate of the building that straddled the road. After a while I saw him again, this time accompanied by another prisoner, Jurek no doubt. Both in overalls, both carrying toolboxes, they were now walking in my direction towards the Women's Camp guardhouse. Once they had entered there, I lost sight of them.

Wiesław Kielar continued watching:

> Apparently Jurek stayed at the guardpost, while from behind the building the solitary figure of Edek emerged, walking quickly towards the potato bunker. Glancing around carefully he caught sight of me, made a vague movement with his hand, then reached into the box, probably to take out the duplicate key. He turned the key in the lock and slipped inside......
> Mala walked swiftly along the main camp road. As she passed the sick bay, a woman who was running along the hospital fence called something to her. With an impatient gesture Mala indicated she was in a great hurry. Limping Perschel was just coming out the guardhouse door. He said something to Mala, she assiduously held his bicycle for him, one of the two propped up against the bicycle stand. Swinging his game leg over the bicycle frame, he pressed the pedal with his sound leg and rode off.
> At last, they were coming. Stocky Jurek side by side with a short figure in overalls, carrying a heavy lavatory pan. Mala was already bending down under this load. I gave a sign to Edek. He had been waiting for it because moments later he emerged from the bunker. Brushing some invisible dust from his *Rottenführer's* uniform, he approached the side of the road and waited for the others to reach him. Jurek stopped in front of the *SS* man at regulation distance, executed a regular about-face and marched back.
> Mala stayed behind with Edek. He let Mala walk ahead, while he moved a few steps behind her, casual, normal, as one would often see an *SS* man escorting a prisoner. Slowly they left the camp. I followed them with my eyes for a good three hundred yards until I lost sight of them because the road turned slightly to the right and disappeared behind the building of the potato bunker.
> The worst was behind them. Now all they had to do was to cross the outer cordon, where there was a barrier, and beyond it freedom awaited them. I was damp all over. My knees were weak, my throat was constricted. It took a great deal of courage. No doubt they were by now

passing their last obstacle, the barrier at which there was always an SS man on duty. Once they had passed that without being stopped, they were free.[181]

But the escape of Edek and Mala did not end well. The pair were recaptured on July 6, 1944 and were brought back to Auschwitz the next day by the Bielitz *Gestapo*, and incarcerated in Block 11. Wiesłar Kielar managed to receive a letter from Edek, which in camp slang was known as a 'stiff.'

> I received a stiff from Edek. Strictly speaking Jurek received it with the instruction to convey its contents to me. In it Edek described their failure.... They were arrested in the Zywiek Mountains where they had run into a border patrol. They were taken to Bielsko and put in jail without being recognized, because Edek continued to wear the SS uniform. At present they were being interrogated daily. The Politicals treated them with unexpected leniency. Mala had even been offered coffee and cake. They wanted to find out how they had escaped and particularly where they had obtained the uniform and weapon.

The Political Departments soon reverted to their normal behaviour:

> A few days later Jurek, who had contacts with Auschwitz, brought another note from Edek. It was very brief and had been written in a much more depressed mood. The Politicals had stopped playing with them. Zbyszek, who also had close contacts with Edek, knew accurate details. They beat Edek's bare feet with a metal rod. Mala too, was no longer handled with kid gloves. Boger was in charge of the interrogations.[182]

Edek and Mala showed great courage and Wiesłar Kielar was informed of their hopeless position:

> Two or three days later I received another note from Edek. It had been written in an even more sombre mood than the one before. He told me they were waiting for their sentence, that they had betrayed no one, that Mala was keeping up her courage. They expected the worst. But they were determined the executioner would not get them alive... he asked me to reassure Lubusch that he had nothing to fear.[183]

---

[181] Wiesław Kielar, *Anus Mundi*, Penguin Books, Harmondsworth, England 1980, pp. 235–239.
[182] Ibid., pp. 248–249.
[183] Wiesław Kielar, *Anus Mundi*, Penguin Books, Harmondsworth, England 1980, p. 251.

The Camp Authorities executed Edek in the Men's camp and Mala in the Women's Camp on September 15, 1944. Wiesłar Kielar witnessed the execution of Edek Galinski, his close friend:

> Roll call was coming to an end. Now as was customary on these occasions, all of us went to where the gallows stood and formed a huge square around the gallows. I stood as near as possible to the small room from which Edek would be led to his doom. After a while the door opened and Edek appeared. There was complete silence. All that could be heard was the crunching of gravel under the boots of Edek, the condemned man, walking towards the gallows, and Jupp, the executioner....... Bravely Edek mounted the scaffold and immediately climbed on the stool that had been placed under the gallows. The noose touched his head.
> The command 'Attention' was given. After a while an SS man silently stepped forward and read out the sentence in German. At this moment Edek standing on the stool, sought the opening of the noose with his head; then he vigorously kicked away the stool and hung. He kept his word. He would not deliver himself alive to the hangman.

The SS were taken by surprise by Edek's actions, but soon recovered:

> But the SS men would not permit such a demonstration. They began to shout, and the Camp *Kapo* understood them at once. Grasping Edek around the middle, he placed him back on the stool and loosened the noose. The German finished reading the sentence in German, and began muddling it in Polish..... he was in a hurry. Edek waited until he had finished. In a moment of utter silence he suddenly cried out in a choking voice: "Long live Poland-!" He broke off in the middle of a word. Quickly Jupp pulled away the stool, and this time the noose was pulled tight. Edek's body tightened, twitched and then remained hanging limply, his head dropped to one side. He was no longer alive. The body circled slowly and bobbed slightly on the thick rope. The rays of the setting sun cast a bloody hue over the huge black water tank. I could not keep my eyes off this sight.[184]

Mala Zimetbaum was to share the same fate as Edek Galinski. Wiesłar Kielar was told of what happened to Mala, by a little Slovak girl runner, the next day:

---

[184] Ibid., pp. 252–253.

Just like Edek, Mala was determined to prevent the SS men from executing the sentence. As she was standing on the scaffold under the gallows, while the sentence was read out, she slashed her wrists with a razor blade. But as with Edek, they would not allow her to die, in the way she had chosen. *Rapportführer* Taube rushed up to her, and she slapped his face with her blood-streaming hands. The enraged SS men almost trampled her to death in front of the whole Women's Camp.

The sentence was duly executed, but not in the way laid down in the regulations. She died on the way to the crematorium on the handcart pulled by women prisoners, who were unable to spare her this last suffering. One of these women was the little Slovak. She wept, wiping away her tears with her sleeve. I found no words to comfort her.[185]

At the end of June 1944, Doctor Miklós Nyiszli, was transferred back to Birkenau, to work in Crematorium III, performing autopsies for Doctor Mengele and he recalled the transfer to the heart of the death factory in his memoirs:

> He drove up and was received by the barracks guard, then sent for me and asked me to join him in his car..... for about twelve minutes we drove through the labyrinth of barbed wire and entered well-guarded gates, thus passing from one section to another. We left the camp and skirted the Jewish unloading ramp for about 300 yards. A large armoured gate in the barbed wire opened behind the guard. We went in: before us lay a spacious courtyard, covered with green grass. The gravel paths and the shade of the pine trees would have made the place quite pleasant had there not been, at the end of the courtyard, an enormous red brick building, and a chimney spitting flames.
>
> An SS man ran up and saluted Dr. Mengele. Then we got out, crossed the courtyard and went through a large door into the crematorium..... "Is the room ready?" Dr. Mengele asked the guard. "Yes sir," the man replied... the room in question was freshly whitewashed and well lighted by a large window, which, however, was barred. The furnishings, after those of the barracks, surprised me: a white bed, a closet, also white: a large table and some chairs. On the table, a red velvet tablecloth. The concrete floor was covered with handsome rugs.
>
> We then passed through a dark corridor until we reached another room, a very bright, completely modern dissecting room, with two windows. The floor was of red concrete: in the center of the room, mounted on a concrete base, stood a dissecting table of polished marble, equipped

---

[185] Ibid., p. 255.

with several drainage channels. At the edge of the table a basin with nickel taps had been installed; against the wall, three porcelain sinks. The walls were painted a light green, and large barred windows were covered with green metal screens to keep out flies and mosquitoes.
We left the dissecting room for the next room: the work room. Here there were fancy chairs and paintings; in the middle of the room, a large table covered with a green cloth; all about comfortable armchairs. I counted three microscopes on the table. In one corner there was a well-stocked library which contained the most recent editions. In another corner a closet, in which were stowed white smocks, aprons, towels and rubber gloves. In short, the exact replica of any large city's institute of pathology.[186]

Doctor Mengele then explained to Doctor Nyiszli that in addition to his laboratory and anatomical work he was responsible for the medical care of all the *SS* personnel who worked in the crematoriums—about 120 men—as well as the *Sonderkommando*—about 860 prisoners. He was allowed to circulate among the four crematoria without a pass from 7:00 a.m. to 7:00 p.m. and he would have to make out a daily report to the *SS* Camp Commandant and a report to *SS-Oberscharführer* Erich Mühsfeldt, the Chief of the *Sonderkommando*, listing the number of ill, bed-ridden and ambulatory patients.[187]

Doctor Nyiszli was later on invited to dinner by the *Kapo*-in-chief of the crematorium and he described the living conditions of the *Sonderkommando*:

> As a matter of fact, it was almost dinner time. I followed them up the stairs to the second storey of the crematorium where the prisoners lived: an enormous room, with comfortable bunks lining both walls. The bunks were made of unpainted wood, but on each one silk coverlets and embroidered pillows shone. This colourful, expensive bedding was completely out of keeping with the atmosphere of the place. It had not been made here, but left by members of earlier convoys, who had brought it with them into captivity. The *Sonderkommando* were allowed to draw it from the storerooms and use it.

---

[186] Dr. Miklós Nyiszli, *Auschwitz*, Granada Publishing Limited, St Albans 1973, pp. 39–40.
[187] Ibid., p. 41.

The whole room was bathed in a dazzling light, for here they did not economize on electricity, as they did in the barracks. Our way led between the long row of bunks. Only half the *Sonderkommando* was present; the other half, about a hundred men, was on the night shift. Some of those here were already in bed asleep, while others were reading.

The table awaiting us was covered with a heavy silk brocade tablecloth; fine initialled porcelain dishes; and place settings of silver: more objects that had once belonged to the deportees. The table was piled high with choice and varied dishes, everything a deported people could carry with them into the uncertain future; all sorts of preserves, bacon, jellies, several kinds of salami, cakes and chocolate. From the labels I noticed that some of the food belonged to Hungarian deportees. All perishable foods automatically became the property of the legal heirs, of those who were still alive, that is the *Sonderkommando*.[188]

Doctor Nyiszli described the extermination process in his memoirs:

> The strident whistle of a train was heard coming from the direction of the unloading platform.... I approached my window, from which I had a direct view onto the tracks, and saw a very long train. A few seconds later the doors slid open and the box cars spilled out thousands upon thousands of the chosen people of Israel. Line up and selection took scarcely half an hour. The left hand column moved slowly away.
>
> Orders rang out, and the sound of rapid footsteps reached my room. The sounds came from the furnace rooms of the crematorium: they were preparing to welcome the new convoy. The throb of motors began. They had just set the enormous ventilators going to fan the flames, in order to obtain the desired degree in the ovens. Fifteen ventilators were going simultaneously, one beside each oven. The incineration room was about 500 feet long: it was a bright whitewashed room, with a concrete floor and barred windows. Each of these fifteen ovens was housed in a red brick structure. Immense iron doors, well-polished and gleaming, ominously lined the length of the wall.

The Jewish people selected to be murdered in the gas chambers, were approaching the crematorium:

> In five or six minutes the convoy reached the gate, whose swing doors opened inwards. Five abreast, the group entered the courtyard. They advanced with slow, weary steps. The children's eyes were heavy with

---

[188] Dr. Miklós Nyiszli, *Auschwitz*, Granada Publishing Limited, St Albans 1973, pp. 43–44.

sleep and they clung to their mother's clothes. For the most part the babies were carried in their father's arms, or else wheeled in their carriages. The SS guards remained before the crematorium doors, where a poster announced: 'Entrance is Strictly Forbidden to All Who Have No Business Here, Including SS.'

The deportees were quick to notice the water faucets, used for sprinkling the gas, that were arranged about the courtyard. They began to take pots and pans from their luggage, and broke ranks, pushing and shoving, in an effort to get near the faucets and fill their containers.... The SS guards who received the convoys were used to the scene. They waited patiently till each had quenched his thirst and filled his container. Slowly they began to re-form their ranks. Then they advanced for about 100 yards along a cinder path, edged with green grass, to an iron ramp, from which 10 or 12 concrete steps led underground to an enormous room dominated by a large sign in German, French, Greek and Hungarian: 'Baths and Disinfection Room.'

The room into which the convoy proceeded was about 200 yards long: its walls were whitewashed and it was brightly lit. In the middle of the room, rows of columns. Around the columns, as well as along the walls, benches. Above the benches, numbered coat hangers. Numerous signs in several languages drew everyone's attention to the necessity of tying his clothes and shoes together. Especially that he not forget the number of his coat hanger, in order to avoid all useless confusion upon his return from the bath.

There were 3,000 people in the room: men, women and children. Some of the soldiers arrived and announced that everyone must be completely undressed within ten minutes. The aged, grandfathers and grandmothers; the children; wives and husbands were all struck dumb with surprise. In ten minutes all were completely naked, their clothes hung on the pegs, their shoes attached together by the laces. As for the number of each clothes hanger, it had been carefully noted.

Doctor Nyiszli witnessed the final journey into the gas chambers:

> Making his way through the crowd, an SS man opened the swing-doors of the large oaken gate at the end of the room. The crowd flowed through it into another, equally well-lighted room. This second room was the same size as the first, but neither benches or pegs were to be seen. In the center of the rooms, at thirty yard intervals, columns rose from the concrete floor to the ceiling. They were not supporting columns, but square sheet-iron pipes, the sides of which contained numer-

ous perforations, like a wire lattice. Everyone was inside. A hoarse command rang out: "*SS* and *Sonderkommando* leave the room." They obeyed and counted off. The doors swung shut and from without the lights were switched off.

The final chapter of the tragedy for the living was about to take place:

> At that very instant the sound of a car was heard: a deluxe model, furnished by the International Red Cross. An *SS* Officer and a *Sanitätsdienst Gefreiter (SDG)* stepped out of the car. The Deputy Health Officer (*SDG*) held four green sheet-iron cannisters. He advanced across the grass, where every thirty yards, short concrete pipes jutted up from the ground. Having donned his gas mask, he lifted the lid of the pipe, which was also made of concrete. He opened one of the cans and poured the contents—a mauve granulated material—into the opening. The granulated substance fell in a lump to the bottom. The gas it produced escaped through the perforations and within a few seconds filled the room in which the deportees were stacked. Within five minutes everybody was dead.

The *Sonderkommando's* hell on earth now commenced:

> The ventilators, patented 'Exhator' system, quickly evacuated the gas from the room, but in the crannies between the dead and the cracks of the doors, small pockets of it always remained. Even two hours later it caused a suffocating cough. For that reason the *Sonderkommando* group which first moved into the room was equipped with gas masks. Once again the room was powerfully lighted, revealing a horrible spectacle. The bodies were not lying here and there throughout the room, but piled to a mass to the ceiling. The reason for this was that the gas first inundated the lower layers of air and rose but slowly towards the ceiling. This forced the victims to trample one another in a frantic effort to escape the gas. Yet a few feet higher up the gas reached them..... I noticed that the bodies of the women, the children, and the aged were at the bottom of the pile; at the top the strongest. The bodies that were covered with scratches and bruises from the struggle which had set them against each other, were often interlaced. Blood oozed from their noses and mouths; their faces bloated and blue, were so deformed as to be almost unrecognizable. Nevertheless, some of the *Sonderkommando* often did recognize their kin....
> The *Sonderkommando* squad, outfitted with large rubber boots, lined up around the hill of bodies and flooded it with powerful jets of water.

This was necessary because the final act of those who die by drowning or by gas is an involuntary defecation. Each body was befouled, and had to be washed. Once the bathing of the dead was finished, the separation of the welter of bodies began.

They knotted thongs around the wrists, which were clenched in a vice-like grip, and with these thongs they dragged the slippery bodies to the elevators in the next room. Four good-sized elevators were functioning. They loaded twenty to twenty-five corpses to an elevator. The ring of the bell was the signal that the load was ready to ascend. The elevator stopped at the crematorium's incineration room, where large sliding doors opened automatically. The Commando who operated the trailers was ready and waiting. Again straps were fixed to the wrists of the dead, and they were dragged onto specially constructed chutes which unloaded them in front of the furnaces.

Members of the *Sonderkommando* then shaved the hair from the corpses and then the corpses were sent to the 'tooth-pulling' commando, who were stationed in front of the ovens. These former dental surgeons, equipped with a lever and pliers, extracted gold teeth, gold bridgework and fillings. Doctor Nyiszli recalled:

> The gold teeth were collected in buckets filled with an acid which burned off all pieces of bone and flesh. Other valuables worn by the dead such as necklaces, pearls, wedding bands, and rings, were taken and dropped through a slot in the lid of a strongbox. When the last gold tooth had been removed, the bodies went to the incineration commando. There they were laid in threes on a kind of pushcart made of sheet metal. The heavy doors of the ovens opened automatically; the pushcart moved into a furnace heated to incandescence.
>
> The bodies were cremated in twenty minutes. Each crematorium worked with fifteen ovens, and there were four crematoriums... nothing but a pile of ashes remained in the crematory ovens. Trucks took the ashes to the Vistula, a mile away, and dumped them into the raging waters of the river.[189]

Otto Winklemann, the Higher SS and Police Leader in Budapest[190] on June 30, 1944, reported to Dr. Edmund Veesenmayer, that the

---

[189] Dr. Miklós Nyiszli, *Auschwitz*, Granada Publishing Limited, St Albans 1973, pp. 45–51.

[190] Mark C Yerger, *Allgemeine-SS*, Schifer Military History, Atglen PA 1997, p. 48.

deportation of Hungarian Jews from Zone IV had been completed and that a total of 381,661 had been deported from Zone 1 – IV.[191]

On July 2, 1944, in order to disguise the impending destruction of the Theresienstadt Family Camp, located in sector B-IIb in Birkenau, the Camp Authorities ordered a selection. Dr. Josef Mengele selected 3,080 young, healthy, able-bodied men, women and young people. Among those selected, approximately 2,000 women were destined for camps in Natzweiler-Struthof and Hamburg, whilst 1,000 men were designated for Sachsenhausen Camp. The young people were earmarked for vocational training.[192]

Five days later, 1,000 of the female Jews, previously selected by Doctor Mengele, from the Theresienstadt Family Camp were led to the sauna. After a bath, their hair was shorn, and they were given striped prisoner's uniform. They were then loaded onto waiting trains at the ramp, and transported to the Sachsenhausen Concentration Camp, and then subsequently onto Schwarzheide, to work in an aircraft factory.[193]

On July 10, 1944, Doctor Nyiszli explained in his memoirs that early one morning, he received a telephone call, the day before the Theresienstadt Family Camp was liquidated on July 11, 1944, to report immediately to the 'pyre' to collect all the medicines and eyeglasses that were there. What he witnessed at the 'pyre' was beyond normal imagination:

> The pyre was located about five or six hundred yards from Number IV crematorium, directly behind the little birch forest of Birkenau, in a clearing surrounded by pines. It lay outside the Concentration Camps electric barbed wire fence, between the first and second line of guards. Since I was not authorized to venture so far from the actual confines of the Camp, I requested some sort of written permission from the office. They issued me with a safe conduct good for three persons, for I planned on taking two men with me, to help carry the material back to the crematorium.

---

[191] Danuta Czech, *Auschwitz Chronicle*, Henry Holt and Company, New York 1990, p. 654.
[192] Ibid., p. 656.
[193] Ibid., p. 659.

We set off in the direction of the thick twisting spiral of smoke..... our path took us past the crematorium. After showing the SS guards our safe conduct, we passed through an opening cut in the barbed wire and reached an open road. The surrounding countryside—a patchwork of bright green, grassy clearing—seemed peaceful. But soon my watchful eyes discerned, about a hundred yards away, the guards of the second line, either lounging on the grass or sitting beside their machine guns and police dogs.

We crossed a clearing and came to a small pine forest. Once again we found our way blocked by a fence and a gate strung with barbed wire. A large sign, similar to those on the crematorium gates, was posted here: **Entrance Is Strictly Forbidden To All Those Who Have No Business Here, Including SS Personnel Not Assigned To This Command.**

In spite of this sign, we entered without the guards even asking for our pass. The reason was simple: the SS guards on duty here were from the crematoriums, and the 60 *Sonderkommando* men who worked at the pyre were also crematorium personnel from number II. At present the day shift were on.

Passing through the gate, we reached an open place which resembled a courtyard, in the middle of which stood a thatched-roof house, whose plaster was peeling off. Its style was that of a typical German country house, and its small windows were covered with planks. As a matter of fact, it no doubt had been a country house for at least 150 years, to judge by its thatched roof, which had long since turned black, and its often replastered walls..... in any case, it was now used as an undressing room for those on the way to the pyre. It was here that they deposited their shabby clothes, their glasses and their shoes.

It was here that the 'surplus' from the 'Jewish Ramp' was sent, that is, those for whom there was no room in the four crematoriums. The worst kind of death awaited them. Here there were no faucets to shake the thirst of several days' voyage, no fallacious signs to allay their misgivings, no gas chamber, which they could pretend was a disinfecting room. Merely a peasant house, once painted yellow and covered with thatch, whose windows had been replaced by planks.

Behind the house, enormous columns of smoke rose skyward, diffusing the odour of boiled flesh and burning hair. In the courtyard a terrified crowd of about 5,000 souls; on all sides thick cordons of SS, holding leashed police dogs. The prisoners were led, three or four hundred at a time, into the undressing room. There, hustled by a rain of truncheon blows, they spread out their clothes and left by the door at the opposite side of the house, yielding their places to those who were to follow.

What greeted the doomed Jews was a scene from Dante's Inferno:

> Once out of the door, they had no time even to glance around them or to realize the horror of their situation. A *Sonderkommando* immediately seized their arms and steered them between the double row of *SS* who lined the twisting path, which, flanked on either side by woods, ran for 50 yards to the pyre, which until now had been hidden by trees.
> The pyre was a ditch 50 yards long, six yards wide and three yards deep, a welter of burning bodies. *SS* soldiers stationed at five-yard intervals along the pathway side of the ditch, awaited their victims. They were holding small calibre arms—six millimeters—used in the Concentration Camp for administering a bullet in the back of the neck. At the end of the pathway, two *Sonderkommando* men seized the victims by the arms and dragged them for 15 or 20 yards into position before the *SS*. Their cries of terror covered the sounds of the shots. A shot, then, immediately afterwards, even before he was dead, the victim was hurled into the flames.
> Fifty yards farther on a scene similar in all respects was being enacted. *Oberscharführer* Moll was in charge of these butchers. As a doctor, and as an eyewitness, I swear that he was the Third Reich's most abject, diabolic and hardened assassin. Even Dr. Mengele showed from time to time that he was human. During the selections at the unloading ramp, when he noticed a healthy young woman who above all wanted to join her mother in the left-hand column, he snarled at her coarsely, but ordered her to regain the right-hand group. Even the ace shot of the crematorium *Oberscharführer* Mühsfeldt fired a second shot into anyone who the first shot had not killed outright. *Oberscharführer* Moll wasted no time over such trifles. Here the majority of the men were thrown alive into the flames.
> Woe to any *Sonderkommando* by whose actions the living chain, which extended from the cloakroom to the pyre, was broken, with the result that one of the members of the firing squad was forced to wait for a few seconds before receiving his new victim. Moll was everywhere at once. He made his way tirelessly from one pyre to the next, to the cloakroom and back again.
> Most of the deportees allowed themselves to be led without resistance. So paralysed were they with fright and terror that they no longer realized what was about to happen to them. The majority of the elderly and the children reacted in this way. There were however, a goodly number

of adolescents among those brought here, who instinctively tried to resist, with a strength born of despair. If Moll happened to witness such a scene, he took his gun from his holster. A shot, a bullet often fired from a distance of 40 to 50 yards, and the struggling person fell dead, in the arms of the *Sonderkommando*, who was dragging him towards the pyre. Moll was an ace shot. His bullets often pierced the arms of the *Sonderkommando* men, from one side to the other, when he was dissatisfied with their work. In such cases he inevitably aimed for the arms, without otherwise manifesting his dissatisfaction, but also without giving any previous warning.

When the two pyres were operating simultaneously, the output varied from five to six thousand dead a day. Slightly better than the crematoriums, but here death was a thousand times more terrible, for here one died twice, first by a bullet in the back of the neck, then by fire.

I gathered up the medicines and glasses left behind by the victims. Dazed, my knees still trembling with emotion, I started for home, that is, for number I crematorium, which to quote Dr. Mengele himself, "was no sanatorium, but a place where one could live in a pretty decent way." After having seen the pyre, I was inclined to agree with him.[194]

Over the next two days, July 10 and July 11, 1944, the Camp Authorities carried out the final liquidation of the Theresienstadt Family Camp in Birkenau. On the first day, 3,000 women and children were taken to the gas chambers in Birkenau and were murdered there. On the second day, 4,00 Jewish men and women from the Family Camp shared their fate.[195]

Following in the footsteps of Edek and Mala, another couple escaped from the camp. Polish prisoner Jerzy Bielecki, who was born on March 28, 1921, was amongst the first transport of prisoners from the prison in Tarnów, on June 14, 1940, to arrive in Auschwitz. He was given prisoner number 243, and Polish Jewess Cyla Stawiska, who was prisoner number 29558, escaped on July 21, 1944. Cyla, who born on December 29, 1920, arrived in Auschwitz from the ghetto in Zambrów on January 19, 1943. After their successful escape, the pair

---

[194] Dr. Miklos Nyiszli, *Auschwitz*, Granada Publishing Limited, St Albans 1973, pp. 69–73.

[195] Danuta Czech, *Auschwitz Chronicle*, Henry Holt and Company, New York 1990, pp. 662–663.

hide themselves near Miechów, where they survive until the liberation by the Red Army.[196]

On July 28, 1944, a transport of more than 1,000 prisoners from the Lublin Concentration Camp arrived in Birkenau, some six days after leaving Lublin. The transport was guarded by SS and soldiers of the *Wehrmacht*. The prisoners were led on foot from Lublin in the direction of Kraśnik. In Ćmielów they were loaded into freight cars and transported to Auschwitz-Birkenau.[197]

Rudolf Höss, who returned to Auschwitz to oversee the liquidation of the Hungarian Jews, left Auschwitz on July 29, 1944. Richard Baer, the *Kommandant* of Auschwitz *Stammlager* now holds the rank of Senior Officer in the Camp hierarchy.[198]

During the evening roll call on August 2, 1944, in the Gypsy Family Camp B-IIe in Birkenau, SS doctor Josef Mengele ordered all Polish doctors and nurses to step forward and he transferred them immediately into the Penal Company, which was located in Camp B-IId in Birkenau. When the roll call had been completed, the Gypsy Family Camp was surrounded by armed SS men.

Trucks then drove into the Gypsy Camp and transported 2,897 defenceless men, women and children to the gas chambers. Filip Müller was an eyewitness as to how the Gypsies were liquidated:

One late evening several trucks rolled into the yard of Crematorium V. Gypsies who had remained in section B-IIe and were to be gassed that night had been crammed into the cargo space. On the running boards stood SS men who were accompanying the death convoy. When the vehicles stopped, they jumped down and opened the tail-boards. The people—there were a lot, easily 300 in all—climbed out and were sent into the changing room along a corridor lined with armed SS guards.

Meanwhile the trucks went back to transport more of the human cargo. After about twenty minutes a new convoy rolled up with more

---

[196] Ibid., p. 668.
[197] Jozef Marszalek, *Majdanek*, Interpress Warsaw 1986, p. 184.
[198] Danuta Czech, *Auschwitz Chronicle*, Henry Holt and Company, New York 1990, p. 672.

candidates for death. These people were also directed into the changing room, while the trucks went away again. The process was repeated two or three times more, until towards midnight, over 1,000 people were in the changing room of Crematorium V. The rest had been put in Crematorium III.

> When the first batch was in the changing room, several *SS-Unterführer* arrived and asked the people to go right to the back and undress. Simultaneously, *SS* men moved away from the door to the back part of the room and formed a sort of cordon in front of the crowd. After a time, members of the *SS* brass also made their appearance, among them the *Kommandant* of Auschwitz II, Kramer; *Lagerführer* Schwarzhuber; some *SS* doctors and other *SS* leaders. Even Moll, who led the extermination routine, ran busily around with his underlings, giving directions and orders......
> Towards midnight the changing room was full of people. With every minute that passed the alarm increased.... On all sides sounded cries of despair, lamentations, and reproachful accusations. Choruses of voices cried: "We're German citizens! We've done nothing wrong!' Others shouted: "We want to live! Why do you want to kill us?"
> There was another unusual thing, which I had never before witnessed in this ante-room of death. Numerous men were holding their wives in a tight embrace, pressed convulsively against them as if merged into one, passionately but despairingly making love for the last time. It was as if in this way, they wanted to say farewell to the most precious thing they had in the world, but also to their own life.
> One could see that most of the *SS* men had a bad conscience. They hadn't shown any scruples about annihilating Jews, the killing of whom was now a daily routine for all of them, yet they clearly found it unpleasant and distressing to help exterminate people with whom they had been on quite good terms up to now. But in this dismal place there was no room for sentiment. The extermination routine took its usual course. Moll and his helpers cocked their pistols and rifles and, in a way that allowed no misunderstanding, asked the people, who meanwhile had undressed, to leave the changing room at once and go into those three rooms in which they were to be gassed. As they took their last walk, many wept in despair, others crossed themselves and prayed to God, and yet others, who even now were unwilling to come to terms with their inevitable fate, turned to the *SS* men and gesticulating wildly, shouted without stopping: "We are German citizens! You can't do this to us!" For a while desperate shouts and cries could be heard coming

from the gas chambers, until the gas had done its deadly work and choked the last voice.[199]

Filip Müller and the other members of the *Sonderkommando* in Crematorium V were then ordered to proceed into another room by Moll:

> Even before the opening of the chamber after the gassing, Moll ordered all prisoners to go immediately to the two rooms between the changing room and the gas chambers. There, we were locked in, ostensibly because there had been an air-raid warning. This was nonsense of course, since through the barred windows we could see that the camp lights had not been switched off. Quite obviously we were locked up under a pretext, a fact which made us feel distinctly uncomfortable. Perhaps our last hour had come.
> The muffled sounds of two shots were ominous. Much to our surprise we were released a few minutes later, and herded into the changing room where we had to line up. Then Moll announced that *Kapo* Kaminski had been shot. The SS thought that he was planning to assassinate *Oberscharführer* Mühsfeldt and they had succeeded in forestalling him at the last minute.... The news of the shooting of Kaminski came as a severe blow to us all. Dazed and panic-stricken we ran back and forth between the changing room and truck, loading gypsy clothing, scarcely able to grasp that we had lost yet another of our best men.
> Among the bodies of dead gypsies in the pit waiting to be burned, we came across Kaminski's corpse. The SS had taken him to the pit and covered his body with fir branches. He had two bullet holes, one at the back of his neck and another in his left eye, which was completely shattered. We never learnt who denounced Kaminski.[200]

On August 6, 1944, a transport containing 71 prisoners who had been evacuated from the Lublin Concentration Camp arrived in Auschwitz. This particular transport left the Lublin Concentration Camp two weeks earlier, just before the camp was liberated by the advancing Red Army.[201]

---

[199] Filip Müller, *Eyewitness Auschwitz*, Ivan R. Dee, Chicago 1979, pp. 149–151.
[200] Ibid., pp. 151–152.
[201] Danuta Czech, *Auschwitz Chronicle*, Henry Holt and Company, New York 1990, p. 680.

The following day, August 7, 1944, heavy American airforce bombers carried out air-raids on the area surrounding Auschwitz. The chemical plants of the *Oberschlesische Hydrierwerke AG* in Blechhammer and the oil refinery some 12 miles northeast of Auschwitz were destroyed.[202]

We return to the work of Doctor Josef Mengele, and Doctor Nyiszli explained in his memoirs how Doctor Mengele carried out medical research on twins and dwarfs:

> Immediately after the transport, one of the SS men walks down the row of new arrivals, and looks for twins and dwarfs. The twins and the dwarfs are selected and place themselves on the right side. The guards lead this group to a special barracks. In this barracks good food and comfortable sleeping areas are available, hygienic conditions are acceptable and the prisoners are treated well. This is Block 14 in Camp B-IIf. From here the prisoners are led under escort to the research block. Here all experiments that can be conducted on a living person are conducted on the prisoners: blood tests, thigh punctures, blood transfers among the twins and a multitude of various other experiments. All painful and exhausting......
>
> Dwarfs are also experimented upon. These experiments—camouflaged as medical experiments—conducted in vivo, that is, on living persons, are far removed from the scientific examination of the problems of twins as such. They are relative and do not say much. The next stage of the experiments follows: analysis on the basis of autopsy. The comparison of normal and pathological or sick organs. For this, corpses are necessary. Since the autopsy and analysis of the individual organs must proceed simultaneously, the twins must die simultaneously. Thus they die simultaneously in the experimental block of the Auschwitz Concentration Camp... Doctor Mengele kills them.... This is the most dangerous criminal type, who in addition has an unlimited power. He sends millions to their deaths, since according to the German race theory these are not human beings, but rather beings of a lower order, who have a ruinous effect on humanity.[203]

The Slovak prisoner Miszutko, who was an informer in the Camp, was killed in the gas chamber on August 14, 1944. In six months he

---

[202] Ibid., p. 681.
[203] Ibid., pp. 691–692.

had lodged over 250 reports to the Political Department in the Camp. He had a particular hatred of Poles.[204]

An American airforce squadron consisting of 127 bombers and 100 Mustang fighters bombarded the I. G. Farben chemical plants near Auschwitz for 28 minutes, on August 20, 1944. Only one American bomber was shot down. Photographs taken of the raid show Auschwitz I and Auschwitz II.[205]

Five days later on August 25, 1944, American airforce reconnaissance aircraft took photographs at an altitude of 30,000 feet. They photographed the grounds of the I. G. Farben chemical works near Auschwitz to determine the level of damage incurred during the bombing raid on August 20, 1944.

At the edge of the photographs were Auschwitz I and Auschwitz II. In the photographs of Auschwitz II-Birkenau, the Women's Camp can be seen: the fencing, the watchtowers, the main gate with the guardroom, the railroad ramp within the Camp, and a freight train with 33 cars: prisoners on their way to the gas chambers in Crematorium II, where an open gate in the fence can also be viewed. In the photographs of Auschwitz I, all Camp buildings can be recognized, and prisoners can be seen standing in a row before the registration building.[206]

During August 1944, the Germans liquidated the Łódź Ghetto. For twenty-three consecutive days the Jews from *Litzmannstadt* arrived in Birkenau. Included in one of the last transports was the Chairman of the Łódź ghetto, Mordechai Chaim Rumkowski, who was deported on August 28, 1944. Some accounts say he was murdered in the gas chambers, whilst others claim he was murdered by members of the *Sonderkommando*, who hailed from Łódź.

The Camp resistance organization, on September 4, 1944, sent photographs from Birkenau to the Aid to Concentration Camp Prisoners (*PWOK*) organization in Kraków: the photographs showed

---

[204] Ibid., pp. 686–687.
[205] Danuta Czech, *Auschwitz Chronicle*, Henry Holt and Company, New York 1990, p. 692.
[206] Ibid., pp. 697–698.

the incineration of corpses in the open air, as well as a section of a forest where deportees undressed, before entering the gas chambers. The Camp resistance movement requested two rolls of film, in order to take more photographs.[207]

A transport of 1,019 Jews arrived in Birkenau on September 5, 1944, from the Westerbork Camp in Holland. Among the prisoners on this transport were the Frank family, who had hidden in a secret annexe in Amsterdam. Anne Frank, the author of the world famous diary, her father Otto, her mother Edith and her elder sister Margot. Otto Frank was the only member of the family to survive. He was liberated on January 27, 1945 by the Russian Army. His wife Edith, died in Auschwitz on January 6, 1945. Anne and Margot were transferred from Auschwitz to Bergen Belsen Concentration Camp on October 28, 1944. They both died from typhus on March 31, 1945.[208]

Rudolf Höss returned to Auschwitz on September 6, 1944, on orders from Himmler to investigate what was required to completely liquidate the Camp at Birkenau. He inspected the site personally, and sought the views of experienced *SS* men. One of them, Otto Moll, the Director of the Crematoriums put forward a plan of what needed to be done. His plan, which was called the Moll Plan, called for the use of motorized *SS* units, artillery to bombard the barracks, six bombers, and a large number of people to cart away the ruins, level the ground and create an innocent appearance. Moll volunteered to command the operation.[209]

One *SS* man, *Rottenführer* Joachim Wolf, warned the prisoners of what was being planned. He contacted Jozef Mikusz, one of the leading members of the resistance group *Zwiazek Organizacji Wojskowej (ZOW)* which had originally been founded by Witold Pilecki. Wolf's warning was in general terms, it was sent first to Kraków, and was used in a radio broadcast by the BBC, in the guise of a Reuters communiqué.[210]

---

[207] Ibid., p. 701.
[208] Bundesarchiv—Memorial Book online resource.
[209] Jozef Garlinski, *Fighting Auschwitz*, Fontana Collins 1975, p. 233–234.
[210] Jozef Garlinski, *Fighting Auschwitz*, Fontana Collins 1975, p. 234.

The I. G. Farben works in Dwory near Auschwitz was bombed for thirteen minutes on September 13, 1944. The American airforce squadron which consisted of 96 Liberator bombers encountered no German aircraft, but was met by strong anti-aircraft fire, and three bombers were shot down.

The bombers dropped 1,000 bombs from an altitude of circa 23,000 feet. Several fell on the compound of Auschwitz I. In the camp expansion area, four residential blocks of the SS, the clothing workshops, and half of Block 6—where female prisoners who worked in the SS offices in the main camp lived—were destroyed. 15 SS men in the SS residential blocks and 28 were seriously wounded. In Block 6, a female prisoner was killed and many were injured. 40, prisoners, of which 23 were Jews, were killed in the workshops: 55 were seriously injured and 13 were buried in the rubble.

Two bombs fell on Auschwitz II. One damaged the railroad embankment and the connecting track to the crematorium; the second destoyed a dugout between the tracks, killing 30 civilian workers. The bombs caused property damage in the I. G. Farben works, destroying part of the factory installations. The number of those killed or injured was approximately 300, including Camp prisoners who worked there.[211]

Aerial photographs taken during the bombing raid on I. G. Farben, show both Auschwitz I and Auschwitz II. According to experts a train consisting of sixty-five freight cars was identified standing on the railroad tracks in Birkenau; also visible was a column of deportees on the Camp street that moved in a north-south direction. The gas chambers and Crematorium IV were in operation and the gate leading there was open.[212]

In the evening of September 21, 1944, Kazimierz Smolen (1327) handed over to his fellow prisoner Reinhold Puchala (1172) a small package containing secretly prepared registers of the male and female prisoners who arrived in Auschwitz between May 20, 1944 and

---

[211] Danuta Czech, *Auschwitz Chronicle*, Henry Holt and Company, New York 1990, p. 708.
[212] Ibid., p. 708.

September 21, 1944. The package was to be given to Puchala's sister, with whom Reinhold was able to meet in secret, to Kazimierz Smolen's mother, Helena Smolen in Königshütte. The prisoners Tadeusz Wasowicz, Lucjan Rajewski, Tadeusz Szymanski and Jan Trebaczowski knew the documents were being handed over and knew the recipient's address. The reason why so many prisoners were aware of this operation was to increase the chances of someone surviving and being able to retrieve the documents.[213]

On September 23, 1944, two hundred Jewish prisoners of the *Sonderkommando* who were deployed on incinerating the corpses in the open pits were removed, once the pits had been covered over. The SS explained that they were being sent to the Gleiwitz sub-camp. The members of the *Sonderkommando* that were selected were given food supplies and were loaded onto freight cars that stood on a siding in Birkenau. But the train did not go to Gleiwitz sub-camp, the train instead moved onto a siding in Auschwitz I. Here the prisoners were led to a building where clothes and other goods were disinfected. The *Sonderkommando* members had their particulars recorded as if they were new arrivals.

In the evening, the supervisor of the *Sonderkommando*, Moll and the SS men who were guarding them drank schnapps, which they also offered to the prisoners. As soon as the prisoners were drunk, the room they were in was locked from the outside. *Zyklon B* was thrown in through a window, which killed them.[214]

---

[213] Ibid., pp. 714–715.
[214] Danuta Czech, *Auschwitz Chronicle*, Henry Holt and Company, New York 1990, pp. 715–716.

Chapter VIII
The Sonderkommando Revolt Auschwitz-Birkenau October 1944

The strength of the Crematorium personnel in October 1944, was as follows:

Squad 57B – Crematorium II	Day Shift	84 prisoners
	Night Shift	85 prisoners
Squad 58B – Crematorium III	Day Shift	84 prisoners
	Night Shift	85 prisoners
Squad 59B – Crematorium IV	Day Shift	84 prisoners
	Night Shift	85 prisoners
Squad 60B – Crematorium V	Day Shift	72 prisoners
	Night Shift	84 prisoners
Total		**663 prisoners**

Filip Müller was an eyewitness to the causes of the revolt by the *Sonderkommando* and what took place on October 7, 1944:

> One afternoon towards the end of September 1944, all prisoners quartered in Crematorium IV had to line up in the yard where *Scharführer* Busch, *SS-Unterscharführer* Gorges and a few SS men of the political department, including *Oberscharführer* Hustek, were waiting. Busch spoke first. He informed us that he needed 200 men for a team in another camp; accommodation and food there were good. At any rate considerably better than Birkenau. Then he invited all who wished to join this team to step forward. In the yard there was deathly silence. Not one prisoner moved......
> A few minutes passed while the SS conferred about what to do next. Then Busch and Gorges stepped forward and began to pick out one prisoner after another, lining them up on the opposite side and noting down

their numbers. Almost all who had an 'old' number escaped selection. A little later, several armed *SS* guards led the selected prisoners away.

During the following night our forebodings became certainty. For the first time in the history of Auschwitz, *SS* men took over the duties of the *Sonderkommando* prisoners in Crematorium II, in order to cremate the corpses of prisoners selected that afternoon.

However, the *SS* were not as skilled as members of the *Sonderkommando* and the corpses were not completely cremated, and some of the *Sonderkommando* recognized the remains of their colleagues selected by Busch and Gorges:

> As we had feared there was another selection. It came on October 7. A few days earlier, *Scharführer* Busch had called together the Crematorium V and Bunker V *Kapos* and informed them he needed 300 men for a rubble clearance team. They were allegedly to be employed in an Upper Silesian town which had been badly damaged by enemy bombs. Busch requested the *Kapos* to let him have a list with the names and numbers of 300 prisoners within twenty-four hours.

Scharführer Busch had taken the easy option and shifted this terrible 'life or death' dilemma onto the *Kapos* who now had to make this terrible decision:

> The 300 prisoners selected by the *Kapos* were mainly Hungarian and Greek Jews. Even before the list was handed to Busch, some of these prisoners selected contacted our Resistance leaders and declared that not one of the 300 was prepared to let himself be slaughtered without resistance. They thought the time for the planned rebellion was now and requested the entire *Sonderkommando* to throw in their lot with them, and to do so whether or not the rest of the Camp were to join in. Their answer was waiting for them …. Any uprising, the message went, was to be avoided at all costs, because it might have disastrous consequences for the whole Camp.

The *Sonderkommando* men condemned to death, were preparing for rebellion:

> Two days came and went after the handing over of the list. Nothing happened. The 300 men were on tenter-hooks and tried to hide their growing nervousness behind an increasing bustle of activity. Surreptitiously they began to collect things like rags, wood-alcohol, oil, and other fuel, and to take them concealed under their clothing into Crematorium IV. After evening roll call they made last minute preparations for setting Crematorium IV on fire, by stuffing rags soaked in oil and

wood-alcohol in between the rafters and the felt roof, under the three-tier wooden bunks and in the coke store.

Filip Müller recalled that the following twenty-four hours were fraught with suspense:

> Next day, October 7, 1944, the sky was blue and cloudless. Towards midday *Scharführer* Busch, *SS-Unterscharführer* Gorges and several other SS men and guards arrived in the yard in front of Crematorium IV. All prisoners were ordered to line up, with the exception of fourteen who were away on their various jobs and who, in any case, were not affected by the selection. Then Busch began calling out the first few numbers on the list, starting with the highest and working his way down to the lowest. Those selected for 'transfer' were made to stand on the opposite side of the yard, those not concerned, once they had been called, were allowed to return to Crematorium V. Since I had the lowest number of all assembled in the yard I was still standing there waiting to be called.
>
> Now and then when Busch called a number, nobody stepped forward, although he would repeat the number loud and clear. When shortly before the end of the selection there was only a small group of about ten men left, it struck Busch that something was amiss, and that at least a dozen prisoners must be hiding somewhere. He therefore despatched a few of the guards to Crematorium IV to try and track them down. The guards were just leaving when quite suddenly from out of the ranks of selected prisoners they were pelted with a hail of stones. Some SS men were wounded, but others managed to dodge the stones and were drawing their guns and starting to shoot blindly into the crowd of prisoners. Two more SS men had managed to get away to the camp street where they grabbed two bicycles leaning against the camouflage fence, and sped off in the direction of the Camp.

The revolt had started, he recalled:

> Meanwhile Crematorium IV had been set on fire, the roof was blazing in several places, flames leaping out and clouds of smoke rising into the sky. Within five minutes of the start of the fighting, the Camp siren began to wail. Shortly afterwards several trucks arrived, and steel-helmeted SS guards, many of them still in their vests, spilled out: swiftly they surrounded the yard and set-up their machine-guns.
>
> All this time I was still in the yard where prisoners were now milling around aimlessly and panic-stricken, while from all sides they were met by a shower of bullets. One by one they fell to the ground fatally injured. Finally a large number raced towards the barbed wire to try and break

through. I ran to Crematorium IV and a few meters away from the door, threw myself to the ground. The shooting continued unabated. I had only one thought: to reach the crematorium without getting hurt. Taking my courage in both hands I stood up, bounded forward and flung myself through the door into the cremation room. I was by now completely out of breath. The crematorium was still burning fiercely. The wooden doors were ablaze, several of the wooden beams were charred and dangling from the ceiling, and there was a fire raging in the coke store. The windows on the opposite wall were riddled with bullet holes. Outside the firing continued, bullets hit the ovens and ricocheted in all directions.

Filip Müller needed to seek refuge from the bullets:

> In a flash I remembered a place where I would be safe from bullets: inside the flue leading from the ovens to the chimney. I lifted one of the cast-iron covers, climbed down and closed the cover behind me. Inside the flue there was no room to stand upright; I stretched out trying to catch my breath. From outside I could still hear the rattle of machine-guns.[215]

At the sounds of shots and explosions *Kommando* 57B in Crematorium II started to fight. The *Reichsdeutsche Oberkapo*, and one of the *SS*-men were thrown into the burning furnace alive; another *SS* man was beaten to death. The prisoners grabbed a few weapons and cut the wires of their own fence and those of the Women's Camp. Through the fence, they made a mistake and instead of turning north-east in the direction of the River Vistula, they turned south-west in the direction of the Rajsko sub-camp. Their chances of escape were greatly reduced, as they stayed within the Camp's jurisdiction. In the other two Crematoriums III and V, they did not take part in the revolt, as the *SS* guards acted swiftly to control the situation.

Shlomo Venezia described what happened in Crematorium III:

> From our crematorium, it was possible to see a strange cloud of smoke rising from Crematorium IV. But we were too far away and had no

---

[215] Filip Müller, *Eyewitness Auschwitz*, Ivan R. Dee, Chicago 1979, pp. 152–156.

means of communication to understand what was happening. A German set off the alarm bell and very soon we were all shut off inside the crematorium where we worked. The situation was pretty much the same in Crematorium II, except for the fact that, from there, many men tried to escape. Unfortunately they didn't get very far.

Lemke (Chaim) Pliszko, the *Oberkapo* of Crematorium III intervened as described by Shlomo:

> Lemke had told me to go down into the basement with one of the Russians and wait for the German guard.... We went down, the Russian lit up a cigarette and suddenly brought out from under his clothes a dagger and an axe and showed them to me, gesturing to me to choose between them... clutching this axe and trembling with fear, I had to wait until the German came down. But he never did come down, since he must have been warned of what was happening in Crematorium IV and must have suspected that we were laying a trap for him.[216]
> After a skirmish in the wood near Crematorium IV, nearly all the escaping prisoners lay dead. Those who had fled south-west were pursued and surrounded in a barn near Rajsko. The SS set fire to the barn and shot the prisoners as they ran out. The bodies of the members of the *Sonderkommando* who had been killed were brought back and laid out in the area of Crematorium IV. There were about 250 of them, including Jozef Deresinski from Luny, Zalman Gradowski from Suwałki, Ajzyk Kalniak from Łomża, Lajb Langfus from Warsaw, Lajb Panusz from Łomża, Josef Dorebus from Drancy, and Jozef Warszawski, the leader, who hailed from Warsaw.[217]

When the remainder were counted it was determined that twelve members of the *Sonderkommando* were missing. The SS men wanted to pursue them, but at that very moment the air-raid sirens began to wail. Frustrated by this, the SS shot on the spot some 200 prisoners of the two crematoriums that had revolted. In the evening, after the all-clear had been sounded, the SS patrols with dogs, set off in search of the missing twelve. The prisoners who had escaped managed to cross the River Vistula, but they were exhausted and sought refuge in an empty building. They were found by the SS, and

---

[216] Shlomo Venezia, *Inside the Gas Chambers*, Polity Press, Cambridge 2009, pp. 116–117.
[217] Jozef Garlinski, *Fighting Auschwitz*, Fontana Collins 1975, p. 239.

killed. Their bodies were also brought back to the Camp. Three *SS* men lost their lives, *Rottenführer* Rudolf Erler, who was born on August 31, 1904, *Rottenführer* Willi Freese, who was born on September 30, 1921, and *Rottenführer* Jozef Purke, who was born on February 28, 1903.[218]

On October 10, 1944, three female Jewish prisoners employed in the *Weichsel-Union Metallwerke*, Ella Gartner, Ester Wajsblum, and Regina Safin were arrested in the Women's Camp of Auschwitz I. They were charged with stealing explosives from the depot of the plant and giving them to the prisoners of the *Sonderkommando*. The members of the *Sonderkommando* fashioned primitive grenades from these explosives and used them during the revolt on October 7, 1944.

Also on October 10, 1944, fourteen prisoners of the *Sonderkommando* were arrested and locked in the bunker of Block 11, in Auschwitz I. Among them were Jankiel Handelsman from Radom, one of the organizers of the uprising, who was sent to the Camp on March 4, 1943, in an *RSHA* transport from Drancy; the prisoner Wrobel, a Polish Jew, who received the explosives from the female prisoners; and five Russian Prisoners of War, who had been transferred from the Lublin Concentration Camp and had been drafted into the *Sonderkommando* on April 5, 1944.

The interrogation by the *SS* functionaries of the Camp's Political Department, Hans Draser, Karl Broch and others was conducted with great harshness. With the arrest of these fourteen prisoners, 198 prisoners now worked in the *Sonderkommando*. This workforce was divided into three squads of 66 prisoners each and they worked in Crematoriums II, III, and V. They continued to work in day and night shifts with 33 prisoners in each.

Two more female prisoners were arrested in the Women's Camp in Birkenau on the charge of having contact with the *Sonderkommando* and transporting explosives there. One of those arrested, the female Polish Jew, Roza Robota, worked in 'Canada' the

---

[218] Ibid., p. 240.

personal effects camp, which bordered on the compound of Crematorium IV. Roza Robota passed the stolen explosives onto Wrobel.

Two days later on October 12, 1944 , two more female prisoners were arrested in Birkenau, suspected of supplying the *Sonderkommando* with explosives. In the evening of January 6, 1945, four female Jewish prisoners, Ella Gartner, Ester Wajsblum, Regina Safin and Roza Robota were hanged in the Women's Camp of Auschwitz. They were condemned to death because they assisted the uprising on October 7, 1944, by members of the *Sonderkommando,* by supplying explosives.

The execution took place in two stages. Two female prisoners were hanged during the evening roll call in the presence of both male and female prisoners who worked on the night shift at the *Weichsel-Union Metallwerke.* The other two female prisoners were executed after the return of the squad that worked the day shift. The sentence was delivered by the First Protective Custody Commander, Franz Hössler.[219]

---

[219] Danuta Czech, *Auschwitz Chronicle*, Henry Holt and Company, New York 1990, p. 775.

Chapter IX
Auschwitz-Birkenau
October–December 1944

Frantisek Brichta, who was born on October 7, 1928 in Berlin, was deported from the Theresienstadt ghetto on October 12, 1944, along with his mother Toni[220], who was born on June 22, 1892, also in Berlin. His father Hermann, who was also incarcerated in Theresienstadt was deported to Auschwitz as well, on September 29, 1944, where he was murdered in the gas chambers. The family had lived in Prague, but were deported to Theresienstadt on July 13, 1943. After the War, Frantisek settled in the United Kingdom and he changed his name to Frank Bright. Frank very kindly made his account of his life known to me, in both words and pictures. I am honoured to present part of his account in this chapter:

> On October 12, 1944, we boarded a third class railway carriage, similar to that which had brought us from Prague to Theresienstadt 15 months ago. Our luggage consisted of the same large duffle bags, but now there were only two of us. Luggage was put on the floor, some could put theirs on the luggage rack. We sat on long wooden, slatted, varnished, curved seats, not uncomfortable, used even in peacetime for long journeys by the below second class humanity. Decidedly more comfortable than the pitch dark cattle truck which normally entered and left the ghetto, with frightened human freight. Why we were so privileged, I don't know.....
> All I remember of the departure is the locking of the train doors. Now I had been on trains in pre-War days, but never one that had been locked and there had never been the unease, the apprehension, the foreboding that comes from sitting in a sealed compartment, not knowing one's destination, not knowing what to expect. Although there was a large window, there was nothing to see. We were into October and it gets dark early in those parts. There was the rhythmic clanging of steel wheels against the joints between the steel rails. We were on our way.[221]

---

[220] Listed as Tonca Brichtova, on the Czech website www.holocaust.cz
[221] Frank Bright unpublished memoirs—written communication with Chris Webb – February 2008.

Frank Bright continued describing their journey and subsequent arrival at Auschwitz-Birkenau Concentration Camp:

> We in our compartment may have been squashed but we did have a seat and large windows to look out of. Most of the time it was dark, we travelled through the night. I probably fell asleep. Mother probably looked forward to meeting father again, but how and what, any new and different circumstances, and they had been separated in the ghetto, must have caused her great anxiety.
>
> Day dawned. We were passing through a dull, flat landscape. And then the train slowed down and all of a sudden we were in a large area defined by concrete posts, wire and wooden towers in the distance. Some people say that they saw the sign *'Arbeit macht Frei'* over a gate, but we saw nothing like it. We couldn't, we went underneath it. The scene was most odd, weird, abnormal and therefore frightening, certainly not welcoming, just the opposite, something one would have avoided if at all possible. Only it wasn't possible. What we saw in the distance were watch towers and concrete posts with horizontal lines, the electrified high-tension barbed-wire which became familiar and our narrow horizon for the next seven months. Then somebody shouted: 'This is a Concentration Camp.' He was right. Before the war from early 1933, onwards, Jews had been taken to Dachau, Sachsenhausen, and so on and some had been released on the condition that they would emigrate and they would not breathe a word of their experience anywhere. Not all were given the opportunity to emigrate. Our fellow traveller had been one of those. He recognized the trappings of such a place alright. There were groups of men in the distance, as well as close by, and *SS* women. I had seen plenty of *SS* men, even in pre-war Berlin, in their black uniforms, riding boots and caps with an embossed skull in dull metal finish, but never women, and these women had walking sticks and looked aggressive.
>
> Now the large window of our compartment was fixed but it did have a sliding ventilation window. Suddenly some frighteningly emaciated faces appeared under the window and shouted for bread to be pushed through this ventilation window. Opposite me sat an old man and his daughter, they had brought with them plenty of bread. They considered what to do. There wasn't much time for that. These thin people in prison garb with a haggard look were obviously stepping out of line from where they had seen our train and it was clear from the urgency of their voices that they were taking risks and were driven by desperation caused by hunger. The old man decided against pushing a loaf, or part of it, through the ventilation window, because if the situation was that bad

then they, he and his daughter would need all the bread themselves. This picture has never left me. From it I have tried to learn and put into practice that if one sees a need and is in a position to help, then do so right away, one may not have the chance to do the good deed later. An hour later, at most, this man was dead, the bread and everything else he had possessed, he had to leave on the train, from where it was collected and taken to '*Kanada.*'

The train had reached its 'Journeys End:'

The train had come to a halt, the seal on the door was removed, we were ordered out. Others remember the shouting, screaming, threats, whips being brandished, snarling dogs. Nothing like that occurred at the arrival of our transport, there was no need to. Obviously there was utter confusion, but trusties, prisoners doing the dirty work for the SS, not that I blame them, everybody clings to life and if this particular lot hadn't done it, then others would have. Surely the blame for the system rested squarely on the SS and the German people who supported this way of life, or death. One can hardly blame it on the victims. These trusties, for want of a better word put us into two long columns, one made up of men, the other of women, some six abreast. As there were 1,500 of us, then there must have been two columns 125 persons long, quite a length, it didn't take long to form, the prisoners who got our long column into line, had done this before. There was a wide gap between these two columns, enough for a truck to pass through.
The trustee prisoners or the SS, I cannot remember which, asked whether there were any blind, lame, infirm or sick who needed a lift into the camp. Those who felt that they answered that description stepped out and were helped up into the rear of the lorry. At the time I thought it was a rather decent act to help the old, blind and infirm, but I soon learned to suspect any such outward sign of civilized behaviour....
In the melee of leaving the train and being put into one of the two columns, I became separated from my mother. Anyway my mother was in the column to the left of mine. Both of us were near the front of each column. As always I was a bit slow, was overwhelmed by it all and didn't see my mother, but my mother saw me. She left her place in the column, walked over to me, shook my hand, and returned to her place. Her column went forward first, one at a time, until one came across an SS-Officer, with several assistants either side of him. I couldn't see exactly what was happening but some of us went to the left and some to the right. I had seen my mother go to the left.

It didn't seem to take all that long for the left column of women to be processed and then it was our turn. I was, as I said, near the front and when it was my turn I walked forward until I got to the SS-Officer in charge. According to the accounts of others, he would look at one, just for a second, the process was quite quick, and indicate with his finger, where the person in front of him was to turn. I cannot remember any of that, I didn't take that in. I had seen my mother go to the left and so I simply turned left too.

I was called back. Obviously the officer's assistant had watched his finger and saw it point to the right, even if I had not. So I was called back and told to go to the right. I had been chosen to live, or rather, not so much to live, as to work and to work until I died of exhaustion by which time I would look like the prisoners who had asked for bread about an hour earlier. It was really a postponement.

On the right I waited for further directions with the others who had also been told to turn right. There weren't many of us.... Those 45 or so who had waited until the whole of our transport had been selected one way or another were now marched to the next stage of the process, taking our clothes off, thereby losing our last shirt, shower, shaving off of all hair on our bodies and the issue of prison garb which in our case was not the striped clothing. On the way to stage one, the SS soldiers asked us for watches. They were quite polite about it, they just said we weren't going to need them any more. They, of course, knew better. Once taken off and put on one big heap they were out of their reach. Some of us handed them over.

We had to wait outside one of the large halls, women were still inside, who had been shorn. A door was open and we looked in. I had never seen a naked young woman, but these beings looked utterly and completely like the shop window dummies, deprived of all sexual appeal, which I had seen. Except that is for the 'shearer,' one could hardly have called her a hairdresser, since her job was to get rid of all feminine tresses. She had a full head of wavy black hair. Odd, since one of the reasons for removing hair was to deprive lice of a foothold. Lice lay eggs on human hair and lice carry the typhus bacillus which is no respecter of person and the Germans were frightened of typhus outbreaks.

Once we were inside we were told to remove our clothes and put them in a pile, or piles, except for shoes or boots, which were retrieved. That made sense, we were earmarked for work, some like us, within the jurisdiction of other main Camps, Gross-Rosen in our case. It was winter, we would need shoes to move and work more efficiently and, since everybody had a different size shoe, it was best to keep them.....

> Different people describe the next steps in different sequences and I cannot remember. Did we have our hair removed before or after the shower? I don't know. Arnost Reiser says that it was done professionally and that his crowd was painted with carbolic to disinfect any cuts. That is not what I remember. By the time it was my turn, and I was very hairy, the barber's safety razor was very blunt, although there must have been plenty of replacement blades, as every arrival would have carried a supply, he did a 'dry' job and it was painful to have all hair removed from chest, legs, arms, armpits, testicles and anus. I cannot remember the carbolic at all. Then there was the short shower. I cannot remember whether we were given any soap, just a rinse would not have removed any dirt. There was nothing to dry oneself with, exposed to a Polish winter's blast at an open door, one would normally have caught pneumonia. There was nothing normal about our situation and we didn't.[222]

Then Frank and the other new arrivals were given 'new' clothes:

> Then came new clothes, a misnomer. Reiser says that there was a deliberate mismatch of sizes, but I cannot remember that. Underpants were short, wide, ill-fitting and tightened with string. They were made from prayer shawls. That may have had its root in wanting to insult the Jewish religious procedure, but as they were made of the finest wool, it did us a good turn. I received no shirt, instead I was handed a thin blanket to wrap around me and to tuck into the trousers. The trousers too were ill-fitting, made for a short but wide man and held up with string. The jacket was black, very old, had been worn by many others, who had probably died in it. Disinfection by stream had made the fabric brittle and a very large cross had been painted in red paint on its back. Exposure to the elements had made the paint brittle, bits had fallen off. Each of us was also issued with a cap, for the doffing of, the most important part of our used or second hand attire.

Frank Bright now experienced life in Auschwitz:

> We were then marched off to an empty wooden hut, or block, but before we could enter we had an extended period of instruction by the *Blockälteste* on the removal of our hat, or beret, with a flourish, to be carried out whenever an *SS*-man of any rank approached, as a sign of deference. There was also a knack in putting it back on again. This too

---

[222] Frank Bright unpublished memoirs—written communication with Chris Webb – February 2008.

had to be done quickly and pulled to one side, it was not to sit centrally on one's head like a yarmulke.

We were then let go, but warned not to go too far. If there was a roll-call one had to rush back to the block to which one had been allocated. If taken short and one found oneself in a strange block and there were more in that block than its allotted number then the surplus would be killed. A preferred method by some *Blockälteste* or *Kapo*s endowed with unlimited powers, was to put a spade across the unfortunate's throat and step sharply on the spade thus severing the head. Gruesome but quite possible.

I didn't stray far, it was dark outside by then apart from the gloomy light given off by the bulbs attached to the concrete posts with bent tops to which the barbed wire was attached. The wire was actually attached to porcelain insulators. It was the insulators which were attached to the posts. The insulators were necessary because of the high voltage in the exposed barbed wire. I saw just one man in the wire, his body twisted by the electric shock. Presumably he couldn't take it any more.

I didn't have far to go or to look to see the squat rectangular chimney belching black smoke. By that time I had heard what had happened to those who had been directed to the left by the moving finger. I stood there by the flickering flames licking above the top of the chimney and thought to myself: 'Which of these flames is my mother?'—but not feeling the immensity of her loss, the slaughter of innocent blood who had thought of herself as German until 1933, had played her part for Germany in the 1914–1918 War, had given gold for an iron ring in support of the Kaiser's War, had been proud of her brother in the German navy, the *Kriegsmarine*, being awarded the Iron Cross and who knew and had said so on many occasions that Hitler would not let her survive the War. It did also occur to me that my father, who must have arrived at the very same place a fortnight earlier, would have suffered the same fate and that I was from now on, on my own and quite unprepared for that, but I didn't cry or have strong feelings. The automatic mechanism of self-preservation, the shutter to feelings which could hinder that had already come down quite firmly and the numbness with which one confronted this valley of the shadow of death where there was no comforter, took years to lift.

When I returned to my hut we were all assembled in a corner next to the door, a wooden box was pointed at us, we were told it was an X-ray machine and would we voluntarily hand over any weapons found on our person. We may have been confused, downhearted, miserable, frightened and some were now deeply concerned about siblings, parents, wives, girlfriends, relatives, and so on but we were not stupid and to be treated as if we were, was just annoying. I did however, find a horseshoe sewn into my new old jacket which was removed. I suspect that it had not been sewn in for luck, but at heart level to protect the previous owner from blows—it would have spread the impact.

Frank Bright now described the living conditions in the block:

> The first night was horrific. There was a rendered brick heating duct running the length of the hut, something like 1 meter high and 1.5 meters wide, dividing the hut in two and, while these huts had been stables for horses, which is what we assumed they may have been, that would have been a heating duct, but of course now it was as cold as was the concrete floor on which we had to lie with a thin blanket over something like five people.
> What kept us awake and disturbed us, were people coming in inspecting our shoes. On the other hand we were not permitted to leave the block at night and had to relieve ourselves into a huge tub, or wide half barrel with two holes through which a wooden rod, like a broomstick was passed. Unfortunately I and another fellow were ordered to lift it and carry it to the cesspit and empty it. As it was full to the brim spilling was unavoidable and some of it went over us……..
> The next day we were told by our *Blockälteste,* or hut elder, that we were very lucky indeed, a good job in a factory was waiting for us, and that we would be leaving in a few days' time. While we didn't know what he was talking about, what he really knew, how reliable it was and seeing is believing—it sounded good, anything must be better than this hell hole.
> We also experienced our first '*Selektion,*' another inspection of the state of our bodies, a daily routine, carried out by Doctor Mengele, or his deputy. Having been passed fit at the so-called ramp on arrival did not guarantee future survival. If one's ribs started to show through the skin, one was taken to a hut and from there to the gas chamber. A '*Selektion'* was an unnerving experience.
> As we realized some time later we had not been tattooed, because only those who were to stay and work within the Auschwitz territory or boundary were thus marked. The property in our bodies had been pre-destined, probably before we had even left the ghetto, to pass to the jurisdiction of another Concentration Camp and it was that other Concentration Camp which was to number us. Because we were in transit we had nothing to do. On my walks, always within easy return to my hut, I was once spoken to by a more permanent inmate, which in a way

was a contradiction like so many things there, in striped garb, though I can't remember what small colored triangle provided a clue to his category, we had not been told anyway, it could have been a homosexual, it could have been a murderer, he was not a Jew. He was German and enquired where had I come from and when I told him he asked whether we were *'anständige Leute'*—decent people. I assured him that we were indeed *'anständig'* such a virtue seemed out of place there, where the exact opposite ruled, but then it was just small talk.

My perception of what went on had not been completely deadened. Once I saw an elderly man being beaten by a young *Kapo* and felt terrible. There were other, less traumatic yet odd sights, like Russian Prisoners of War. They must have come from a particular region because all of them had the same features, fat necks, just like the cartoons depicting German bureaucrats. What were they doing in an Auschwitz transit camp? As I learned much later, Russian POW's were treated abominably, millions of them were starved to death in open enclosures. Here they seemed to be doing well and not subject to *'Selektions'* for the gas chamber, which they would have passed anyway.

Permanent occupants, if that is the right word for a transient hell, also had a more comfortable stay, if so I was told at the time, they were artists. Painters were treated generously by the German guards and officers in return for having their portraits painted. There was one Czech female artist who painted gypsy girls for Mengele, before they were gassed.[223]

Frank Bright recalled the events of his fateful second night in Auschwitz:

> The second night proved crucial and also proved that the forecast about our future had been correct. It was dark, that could have been as early as afternoon, it gets dark early in October in those parts, when we were told to stand along one side of the raised central platform or heating duct which divided the hut for no apparent purpose. The door near us opened, and a civilian with a couple of *SS* entered. The civilian wore the outfit which marked him as a Nazi Party member, a light gabardine coat with the round Party emblem in his lapel. The light was dim in these huts and even when the eye got used to it, one couldn't see well and far, but it seemed that he was looking at us from a distance and then pointed his arm towards individuals, as if closer contact would be distasteful; if it had to be done, it had to be done from a distance.

---

[223] This was probably Dina from Prague as mentioned by Dr. Nyiszli in his memoirs on page 52.

That was it, we were being chosen. Those who had been pointed at then crossed the brick heating duct barrier and assembled at the Party member's side. I happened to be close to the door and when 'it was my turn to be pointed at, I seem to remember actually jumping across. There were two hitches. Firstly there was not enough of us, Dr. Mengele had not played the game.

The man in the raincoat was undoubtedly the manager of VDM of Friedland, Southern Silesia, formerly of Hamburg, who had been promised 165 Jewish '*Metallarbeiter*,' skilled workers in metal, and there was only a quarter of that number to chose from, but we didn't know that there should have been more of us. Secondly he had been promised a mathematician. The reputation of Theresienstadt as a never ending source of intellectuals must have permeated German society, so that by their reckoning there must have been at least one mathematician even among the few to come out alive after Dr. Mengele had done his worst— he had 95 out of every 100 gassed on arrival.....

What the manager of VDM really needed was a technician who would find and list the properties of each propeller blade using the apparatus provided, so that when three or four blades were to be fitted to a hub of any one engine their eccentricities would cancel out and there would be no resultant vibrations. To use a mathematician for such work was rather a waste of talent, but then if you could have the best of Jewish expertise then why not go for it, the cost was the same. However, when asked, no mathematician raised his hand.

That was a grave disappointment to all, may be the Auschwitz system of providing the German industry with Jewish labor of every skill imaginable wasn't perfect after all. Later in Friedland, when the German Air Force asked for an electrical engineer merely to operate a spot-welding machine, they got a professional engineer who, pre-War, had been in charge of an electricity generating station.

However, in our present, or the manager's predicament, the Auschwitz reputation was saved. One of our group remembered that one of us had failed the '*Selektion*' that morning and was in another hut to be taken to the gas chamber, when they had a few minutes to spare and that this unfortunate being was a mathematician. A messenger was quickly sent to that hut of the condemned and the man was reprieved.[224]

As already explained, an insufficient number of men had been allowed to survive on arrival. The next transport from the ghetto, 'Er,' which left

---

[224] This was probably Otto Fischer from Prague, born August 3, 1909, who Frank Bright found on the transport list after the War.

on October 16, 1944, fared marginally better. 117 out of 1,500 survived, or, say, 58 men. That, added to our 39, still didn't add up to the 165 needed or asked for by the factory's manager.

Frank Bright explained that according to the list of prisoners transferred from Auschwitz to Gross-Rosen Concentration Camp, of which Friedland was a branch, several former inmates of the ghetto of Łódź, and some Slovak and a few Hungarian Jews were added. That was something that he had to wait another 60 years to find out about these facts:

> On the appointed day, it was October 19, 1944, we were marched to the sidings, this time it was a cattle truck / boxcar for us, given a ration of bread, and stuffed, literally, into the cattle truck, standing room only. To start with at least, we didn't mind, a small price to pay, if it took us away from the smoking chimney stacks. The train rattled along all night.
> At some time in the morning, we had no idea what time it was, we stopped, the doors were slid open, the sun shone in, we were ordered out onto a platform of a small town railway station. I had stood in a dark corner and didn't know what had been going on. Others, like Arnost Reiser, who had been close to the one small ventilation window, said that we had stopped at another Friedland, now Frydlant in the Czech Republic, and close to what is now Poland, where they hadn't expected us and the train driver had to retrace his steps to deliver his cargo of slave laborers where we were expected. Arranged into a column, five or six abreast, we were marched to our new abode.[225]

On October 27, 1944, a truck driven by *SS-Rottenführer* Johann Roth and Private Willi Frank from Łódź sitting beside him, started out from the central Camp. On the platform, in the box containing wood used to make the gas, Ernst Burger (23850), and the Austrian Bernard Swierczyna (1393) were hidden. The truck went through the main gate without being halted and stopped by the *SS* Motor Workshops. There unseen, three other members climbed aboard and crawled into the box. They were Rudolf Freimel (25173), Czeslaw Duzel (3702), and Zbigniew Raynoch (60746). The whole operation of

---

[225] Frank Bright unpublished memoirs—written communication with Chris Webb – February 2008.

loading was made easier by the early morning mist, and was overseen by Ludwig Vesely (38169), a prisoner who worked at the SS Motor Workshops.

Johann Roth was to have smuggled the above-mentioned prisoners out of the camp, when he drove the dirty clothes to the laundry in Bielsko, and was to have dropped off the escapees in the village of Leki. However, he betrayed the escape attempt and informed the Political Department. The truck with the hidden prisoners was stopped by the barrier at the control hut. Several SS men from the Political Department climbed in and the truck was driven directly to Block 11. When the prisoners grasped the unfortunate turn of events, they all took poison. Raynoch and Duzel died, but the others survived and were locked in the bunkers of Block 11. The SS man Frank was also arrested.

In the truck that had gone to Bielsko, armed SS traveled to Leki Zasole, located four miles from Auschwitz, where Konstanty (Kostek) Jagiello, Tomasz Sobanski, Franciszek Dusik, Kazimierz Ptasinski were waiting in an inn belonging to Julian Dusik. Jagiello and Sobanski both escaped from Auschwitz on June 27, 1944, and they set up a resistance organization to aid other prisoners, who have escaped from Auschwitz.

They had with them five sets of civilian clothing for the escaping prisoners, and were looking out for the truck when it drove up, not with the prisoners escaping but with armed SS men. During the operation, Konstanty Jagiello was killed by machine-gun fire, as was Jan Galoch, the 70-year old gardener, whilst Tomasz Sobanski was able to escape. Franciszek Dusik, his uncle Julian Dusik, his daughter Wanda and Kazimierz Ptasinski were arrested and taken to the *Gestapo* quarters in the town of Auschwitz. Kazimierz Ptasinski managed to escape during the first night because the *Gestapo* quarters in an old rectory was poorly guarded. The interrogations that followed were carried out partly in the Political Department in the Camp, and some were in the town's *Gestapo* quarters.[226]

---

[226] Jozef Garlinski, *Fighting Auschwitz*, Fontana Collins 1975, pp. 248–249.

The following day, October 28, 1944, Transport EV left the Theresienstadt ghetto and it arrived in Auschwitz two days later on October 30, 1944, carrying 2038 Jews. Among those transported was the famous Kurt Gerson, also known as Kurt Gerron. He was born on May 11, 1897, in Berlin. He fought in World War I and was wounded several times. He studied medicine and obtained a degree, but left to pursue a career as an actor in 1920. He appeared in such films as *The Blue Angel* opposite Marlene Dietrich. He also appeared on stage, playing the role of London Police Chief Brown in the premiere production of *Dreigroschenoper* (Three Penny Opera), where he sang the song 'Mack the Knife,' in Berlin in 1928. Kurt Gerron was offered a trip to Hollywood, USA, but declined. He travelled to France, and later settled in the Netherlands; he directed films in both countries. After the German occupation of the Netherlands, he was interned in the Transit Camp at Westerbork in mid-1943.

He was deported from Westerbork on February 25, 1944, to the Theresienstadt ghetto near Prague. There he ran a cabaret called *'Karussell'* to entertain the ghetto inmates. He was subsequently forced by the Nazis to make a propaganda film showing how well the Jews were treated at Theresienstadt. The film was called 'The *Führer* Gives a City to the Jews.'

Kurt Gerron submitted a script to Karl Rahm the Commandant and the theme of the film was water. Berlin approved the theme and approval was given to start filming. Filming commenced on August 6, 1944, and was completed on September 11, 1944. The film was of course a grotesque lie, and once filming stopped the ghetto slipped back to its cruel regime of starvation and transports to Auschwitz. Upon arrival at Auschwitz on October 30, 1944, Kurt Gerson (Gerron) was murdered in the gas chambers of Birkenau.[227]

Following an earlier proposal from *SS-Standartenführer* Oskar Dirlewanger to Heinrich Himmler that former German criminals incarcerated in Concentration Camps should be enlisted in the *SS-*

---

[227] www.Holocaustresearchproject.org.

Sonderkommando, Dirlewanger was to leave Auschwitz Concentration Camp on November 7, 1944.[228]

On November 25, 1944, the dismantling of Crematorium II commenced. First to be removed was the motor which pumped the air out of the gas chambers. It was dismantled and sent to Mauthausen Concentration Camp in Austria. The pipes were transferred to the Gross-Rosen Concentration Camp. The following day, Heinrich Himmler ordered the destruction of all of the crematoriums in Auschwitz-Birkenau.[229]

The woodland demolition squad on December 5, 1944, was established in Birkenau, to which 50 female prisoners were sent. The squad worked on the grounds of the sauna and Crematorium IV. They filled in the pits and covered with grass the pits that were used to cremate the corpses of those killed in the gas chambers. They also sifted through the human ash remains before it was dumped in the River Vistula. Trees were then planted on the ground that has been levelled.[230]

The I. G. Farben plant in Dwory on December 18, 1944, was again attacked by the Allied airforce and three days after the attack, American air reconnaissance units took more aerial photographs to record the extent of the damage. Auschwitz I and Auschwitz II were to be seen at the edges of the photographs. In the enlarged photographs of Birkenau, the fences and watchtowers that surrounded the so-called 'Mexico' section have been removed. Also can be viewed the roofs of the gas chambers and the changing rooms, which were underground. The roof and chimney of Crematorium II was also demolished, as was the fence around Crematorium II, also the fence around Crematorium III has gone. The entire area was littered with rubble.[231]

---

[228] Danuta Czech, *Auschwitz Chronicle*, Henry Holt and Company, New York 1990, pp. 726 and 745.
[229] Danuta Czech, *Auschwitz Chronicle*, Henry Holt and Company, New York,1990, p. 754.
[230] Ibid., p. 759.
[231] Ibid., p. 766.

Another air raid by the American airforce took place on December 26, 1944, on the I. G. Farben works in Dwory. Several bombs fell on the *SS Lazarett*, which is near Birkenau, killing five *SS* men. Also the air-raid shelter set up for the nurses working in the *Lazarett* was destroyed. Two original registers of the prisoners in the infirmary of Auschwitz I from the year 1943, had been hidden in the shelter by Sister Maria Stromberger, an Austrian Red Cross nurse and Mother Superior to the nurses working in the *SS* sick bay. The registers were to be given to the *PWOK* in Kraków. Although Sister Maria was a patient herself in the *SS* sick bay because of an inflammation of her joints, she went to the air-raid shelter, and with the help of Mira, a 19-year old girl from Yugoslavia, they dug in the rubble until the registers were found.[232]

After the evening roll call on December 30, 1944, on the square in front of the kitchen in the central camp, Ernst Burger, Rudolf Freimel, Piotr Piaty, Bernard Swierczyna and Ludwig Vesely were hanged from a single beam, having been betrayed by *SS* man Johann Roth, in their escape on October 27, 1944. They died bravely, and despite their maltreated bodies, they managed to utter shouts that they had not betrayed anyone. These were the last executions in the Men's Camp at Auschwitz.[233]

The following day on December 31, 1944, Maria Stromberger managed to pass over to Natalia Szpak, the two original registers she recovered from the destroyed air-raid shelter.[234]

---

[232] Ibid., p. 768.
[233] Jozef Garlinski, *Fighting Auschwitz*, Fontana Collins 1975, pp. 249–250.
[234] Danuta Czech, *Auschwitz Chronicle*, Henry Holt and Company, New York 1990, p. 771.

Chapter X
Evacuation and Liberation
January 1945

On January 1, 1945, one hundred male and one hundred female Poles who were condemned to death by the Police Court Martial were shot to death in Crematorium V in Birkenau. The condemned were transported in two transports in a closed prisoner wagon from Block 11 in Auschwitz I. The men were executed first, then the women. *SS Camp Doctor Fritz Klein* handed over the condemned prisoners to *SS-Oberscharführer* Erich Mühsfeldt, who carried out the execution.[235]

Doctor Nyiszli was an eyewitness to this execution of the Polish men and women:

> Suddenly the purr of a powerful motor reached my ears, and a moment later a large brown van appeared. Used to transport prisoners, this van was called 'Brown Toni' by the Camp inmates, for it was painted a dark brownish color. A tall officer got out. I recognized him as Dr. Klein, an *SS* Major, one of the evil, bloody-handed Concentration Camp officials..... a hundred Polish prisoners, Christian men all, had been brought here to be murdered. *SS* guards took them to an empty room next to the furnace room and ordered them to undress immediately. Dr. Klein and *SS-Oberscharführer* Erich Mühsfeldt, meanwhile, took a stroll around the courtyard... now that there was no longer any *Sonderkommando*, the *SS* guards led the men to the *Ober's* revolver.
> Again the sound of 'Brown Toni's' powerful motor. A hundred new victim's arrived, all women, quite well dressed. They were sent to the same room where, only a few minutes before, the men had undressed. Then one by one the women were also taken to the *Ober's* waiting gun. They too were Polish Christians; they too had paid with their lives for minor infractions of the law. The cremation was carried out by the *SS*, who asked me to furnish them with rubber gloves for the job.[236]

---

[235] Danuta Czech, *Auschwitz Chronicle*, Henry Holt and Company, New York 1990, p. 773.
[236] Dr. Miklos Nyiszli, Auschwitz, Granada Publishing Ltd, St. Albans 1973, pp. 145–146.

Six prisoners, the so-called 'bearers of secrets' on January 5, 1944, were transferred from the Men's Camp in B-IId in Birkenau to Mauthausen Concentration Camp in Austria. Five of these men were Polish prisoners who worked in the *Sonderkommando*: Waclaw Lipka (2520), Mieczyslaw Morlawa (5730), Jozef Ilczuk (14916), Wladyslaw Biskup (74501), Jan Agrestowski (74545) and the Czech prisoner Stanislaw Slezak (39340). Slezak operated the X-ray machines in the experimental station of SS-Doctor Horst Schumann in camp B-Ia in Birkenau. They were all shot in the Mauthausen Concentration Camp's crematorium building on April 3, 1945.[237]

On the same day, the last session of the Police Court-martial of the Katowice *Gestapo* took place in Block 11. Seventy Poles, men and women were condemned to death. They were shot and killed the following day in Crematorium V in Birkenau. Among those killed were Wladyslaw Jasiowka from Sosnowitz, Stanislaw Kobylka from Rusce, Jozef Luczak from Wielun, Kazimierz Matjasinski from Sosnowitz, Jan Strychowski from Myslachowice and Adam Tods from Jezory. They left their names on the walls in the bunkers of Block 11.[238]

On January 14, 1945, the American airforce undertake its twelfth reconnaissance flight to determine the extent of the damage inflicted by the four previous bombings of the I. G. Farben works. Close examination of the enlargements reveal that Monowitz was still occupied, as the snow on the roofs of the barracks had melted and the paths between the barracks were free of snow.

Auschwitz I was still occupied, the snow had also melted on the individual barracks, with the exception of Block 10, the former experimental station of Professor Dr. Clauberg. In Auschwitz II, the section known as 'Mexico' was completely abandoned. The partly melted snow on the roofs on the barracks in Camp B-II, showed that these were still occupied. The condition of the gas chambers and Crematoriums II and III showed that these facilities were already

---

[237] Danuta Czech, *Auschwitz Chronicle*, Henry Holt and Company, New York 1990, p. 774.
[238] Danuta Czech, *Auschwitz Chronicle*, Henry Holt and Company, New York 1990, p. 774.

partially demolished, since the tracks in the snow, made by people and various vehicles in the area, pointed to major activity.[239]

The following day, January 15, 1945, seventy prisoners, former members of the *Sonderkommando*, now part of squad 104-B worked on removing the facilities from the crematoriums in Birkenau. The facilities removed were brought to a siding of the connecting railroad track and were transported to the Gross Rosen Concentration Camp. The prisoners also knocked holes in the walls of the crematorium buildings and the gas chambers, where explosives would be placed, in order to destroy the extermination centers.[240]

On January 17, 1945, following the decision to remove the healthy prisoners from the Auschwitz complex of camps, Commandant Richard Baer personally selected the leaders of the evacuation columns, from among members of the guard companies. He ordered them to ruthlessly liquidate all prisoners who attempt to escape during the evacuation, and to shoot any prisoner who fell behind.[241]

On the same day, the prisoners Jozef Cryankiewicz and Stanislaw Klodinski wrote in their last report to Teresa Lasocka and Edward Halon of the *PWOK* in Kraków:

> My Dear Ones!
> We are now experiencing the evacuation. Chaos. Panic among the drunken *SS*. We are trying with all political means to make the departure as tolerable as possible and to protect from extermination the invalids allegedly remaining behind. These objectives were—and possibly are—entirely clear.
> The march goes first in the direction of Bielsko. Later, a part is going towards the Sudenten (Leitmeritz), another part towards Gross-Rosen. The only train is taking the less seriously ill to Hanover. The intentions change from hour to hour, since they have no idea what orders they will receive. Radio propaganda is necessary. This type of evacuation means the extermination of at least half of the prisoners. A check by the Red Cross is necessary and, in the period of the 'interregnum' in the camp is

---

[239] Ibid., p. 778.
[240] Ibid., p. 779.
[241] Ibid., p. 783.

indispensible, so that some special commando of the SS doesn't simply wipe out the sick... we also enclose a number of documents.[242]

The evacuations start to take place in the Auschwitz sub-camps:

> The prisoners in Sosnowitz sub-camp were evacuated on January 17, 1945. Food left-overs were divided among the prisoners, and circa 4 p.m. they departed on foot in the direction of Gleiwitz and they continue onto Ratibor and Troppau. There, they were loaded onto freight cars and transported to Mauthausen Concentration Camp. This evacuation takes 16 days, 12 on foot. The prisoners were forced to pull handcarts loaded with the luggage of the SS guards. The SS murdered the weak who were unable to continue the march. During the evacuation the prisoners each received three potatoes and two pieces of cheese. Many prisoners died during this evacuation.[243]
>
> On the same day, approximately 3,200 prisoners who were healthy enough were marched out of the Neu-Dachs sub-camp. The route they took leads to Königshütte, Beuthen and Gleiwitz to the Blechhammer sub-camp. From there they were transported on January 21, 1945, to the Gross Rosen Concentration Camp. From there they were transported to Buchenwald Concentration Camp in Germany.[244]
>
> SS Camp Doctor Josef Mengele on January 17, 1945, closed his experimental medical research station in Camp B-IIf in Birkenau, ensuring that his files on research from his experiments on twins, dwarfs and cripples were 'secured.' At the same time SS-Doctor Fischer ordered the transport of the archive of the prisoners' infirmary from the main camp to outside Block 11, where the records were burnt, whilst in Birkenau the records from the Women's Infirmary met the same fate.[245]

On the same day, January 17, 1945, Shlomo Venezia a member of the *Sonderkommando* recalled how he managed to escape certain death:

> Quite unusually, on the evening of January 17, the SS guard accompanied us to the barrack and told us that we were strictly forbidden to leave. He even added, 'Really bad things will happen to anyone who even tries.' The fact that he felt it necessary to add something that was so obvious to all of us struck us as suspect—especially since on that day,

---

[242] Danuta Czech, *Auschwitz Chronicle*, Henry Holt and Company, New York 1990, p. 783.
[243] Ibid., p. 784.
[244] Ibid., p. 784.
[245] Ibid., pp. 784–785.

as we came back to the barrack, we crossed the path of several lines of prisoners leaving the camp as if they were going off to work, even though night was falling. On the road, I managed to ask someone discreetly, 'Was ist?' 'What's happening?' He whispered back to me '*Evakuieren.*' It wasn't hard for me to realize that, if everyone other than the *Sonderkommando* was being evacuated, and we were being strictly ordered not to move, they must be intending to trap us like mice and kill us. We went into the barrack, but no sooner had the German gone away than we came out again and mingled discreetly with the groups leaving the Camp.[246]

Shlomo continued his account:

> Several groups, each one of several thousand prisoners, had been formed, since it was impossible to send everyone to the same place. To begin with, we were sent to Auschwitz I, where we joined other prisoners, who were also ready to be evacuated. Night was already far gone. I found my brother-in-law in Auschwitz I, as well as other prisoners I knew, such as my brother-in-law's cousin, Joseph Mano, and others too. Everyone was given three portions of bread with a little bit of margarine for the road. To preclude anyone stealing mine, I elected to swallow the whole ration immediately and ensure that I'd have at least that in my belly.
>
> It was mid-winter; outside, everything was frozen or covered with snow. It was beastly cold. But I was happy knowing I was going to leave that place behind and especially that I'd managed to escape the liquidation planned for the *Sonderkommando*. From time to time, during the night, a German passed among the prisoners and yelled '*Wer hat im Sonderkommando gearbeitet?*' Who worked in the *Sonderkommando*? Of course, nobody replied.
>
> That night, the one preceeding what was called the 'death march,' I didn't sleep at all. There wasn't enough room for everybody and I spent the night huddled against the others, standing up. Even so I was lucky enough to manage to get inside a building, since some people spent the night outside.
>
> The next morning we left Auschwitz. In my column there must have been five or six thousand of us. We marched for days on end, always five by five, through the icy cold. At night we arrived in a village or a cowshed, and we had to do what little we could to find a decent place to rest

---

[246] Shlomo Venezia, *Inside the Gas Chambers*, Polity Press, Cambridge 2009, pp. 125–126.

for a while. The ones with the most practical sense managed to find a place indoors; the others had to stay outside. Many died of cold during the night, or their feet got frozen. If they could no longer walk, they were killed on the spot. We were dragging our feet, we were thirsty, cold, hungry, but we had to march, march and keep on marching. Those who dropped from exhaustion were left behind and were executed by the SS who brought up the rear. Other prisoners had to throw their bodies into the ditches.[247]

At one o'clock in the morning of January 18, 1945, forty prisoners, doctors and nurses were led from the Birkenau male prisoners' infirmary B-IIf and were forced to join the prisoners' column from Camp B-IId, who were preparing to march from the Camp. The remaining doctors were ordered to burn the files of the patients under the supervision of SS medical personnel.[248]

Among the prisoners ready to march out from Birkenau was Filip Müller, the former member of the *Sonderkommando*, and he recalled the evacuation:

> And then came that memorable January 18, 1945. There was great confusion throughout the Camp. Early in the morning columns of smoke could be seen rising in all parts of the Camp. Quite obviously the SS men were destroying card indexes and other documents. The prisoners who normally at this time of day were bustling about, seemed almost paralysed with inaction.
>
> The rumble of guns and the explosions of heavy shelling were very close. SS men on bikes and motor cycles were dashing back and forth on the snow-covered camp street where not long ago, long columns of men, women and children had dragged themselves along to their deaths.
>
> Certain that today we must die we watched the three SS men in the Crematorium—Gorges, Kurschuss and another *Unterführer*—with eagle eyes... in the course of the late afternoon a *Blockführer* came running to the Crematorium and shouted nervously 'Return to Camp everybody! At the double!'

---

[247] Shlomo Venezia, *Inside the Gas Chambers*, Polity Press, Cambridge 2009, pp. 126–127.
[248] Danuta Czech, *Auschwitz Chronicle,* Henry Holt and Company, New York 1990, p. 785.

We did not need to be told twice and ran right across the copse back to Camp B-IId where our mates from the demolition team had been quartered for some weeks. Chaos reigned here too.... But evening roll call did take place; it was to be the last one in Auschwitz. Thousands of us had lined up. For the first time I had the feeling of being a prisoner like any other.... Towards the end of roll call we were told to get ready for the transport. Then we were dismissed.....

Then before midnight the order to march was given. It was an exhilarating moment. Outside it was snowing and very cold. Some 20,000 prisoners formed up in a long marching column and flanked by armed *SS* guards set out into the night. The snow crunched under our feet, a cold wind blew into our faces. We talked about nothing but where they were taking us and what they intended to do with us.

Filip Müller was forced to march for a few days:

> We marched intermittently for a few days until we came to Loslau, where we were herded into open railway cattle trucks. Many people did not survive this long march in the bitter cold, without hot food or drink and without warm clothes. The physically weak and the sick lasted only a few hours. Anyone too exhausted to go on was shot by the guards and left by the wayside. Several prisoners managed to escape under the cover of darkness.
>
> In the open cattle trucks, exposed to the biting cold, we travelled for several days from Loslau to Mauthausen. We were strictly forbidden to leave our trucks. No rations were handed out. Under these harsh conditions it was not surprising that many died from cold or hunger during the transport. Some tried to escape by jumping from the moving train during the night, risking not only injury but also being picked off by the *SS* who had machine-guns and swivelling searchlights set up all along the train. When at long last our arduous transport arrived at the little station of Mauthausen in Lower Austria, we were taken to the Concentration Camp which was not far away. As we marched through the Camp gate, no one knew how many had escaped, died or had been killed since the evacuation of Auschwitz.[249]

Returning to January 18, 1945, the German prisoner Engelbert Marketsch, who was born on August 30, 1918, in Bleiberg, near Villach, who was a surveyor and architect by profession arrived in Auschwitz

---

[249] Filip Müller, *Eyewitness Auschwitz*, Ivan R. Dee, Chicago 1979, pp. 165–167.

from Mauthausen Concentration Camp. He received the prisoner number 202499. This was the last number to be assigned to a prisoner at Auschwitz.[250]

The departure of the female prisoners from the Women's Camp in Birkenau commenced towards morning. At short intervals columns of 500 women and children left the Camp, escorted by SS men. A total of 5,345 female prisoners exit the Camp on this day, among them 176 from Płaszów Concentration Camp, 1,169 from Camp B-IIc, and 4,000 from Camps B-IIb and B-IIe. They were taken to Auschwitz Main Camp and they waited there for the formation of evacuation columns to take place.[251]

On the same day, 800 prisoners were led out of Janinagrube sub-camp and force-marched to the Gross Rosen Concentration Camp. The prisoners, like the others, had no protection against the cold and they only received small portions of dry food for the 18-day march. Only 200 out of the 800 reached Gross Rosen, in a state of complete exhaustion.[252]

Columns of prisoners left the Birkenau Camp at specific intervals. The last column to leave the Camp of approximately 1,500 prisoners left Camp B-IId in the afternoon of January 18, 1945. The route of this column passed through Auschwitz, Rajsko, Rybnik and onto Wodzisław Śląski in Silesia. In the evening of the same day, the female prisoners in the Auschwitz Women's Camp, along with those prisoners who had joined them in Birkenau, set off in the direction of Rajsko. The female prisoners of the gardening and plant-breeding squads from the Rajsko sub-camp, joined the procession of the prisoners evacuated from Auschwitz-Birkenau, bringing up the rear. They marched to Wodzisław Śląski in Silesia. Only Eugenia Halbreich (29700) who sought refuge in the attic, next to the house of SS man Hermann Grell, remained in the Rajsko sub-camp.[253]

---

[250] Danuta Czech, *Auschwitz Chronicle*, Henry Holt and Company, New York 1990, p. 785.
[251] Ibid., p. 785.
[252] Danuta Czech, *Auschwitz Chronicle*, Henry Holt and Company, New York 1990, p. 785.
[253] Ibid., p. 786.

All of the prisoners of the Monowitz sub-camp were formed into columns of 1,000 prisoners in each and march off to Gleiwitz, whilst 850 prisoners remained in the prisoners' infirmary, including Dr. Czeslaw Jaworski, among other assistant doctors.[254]

The prisoners were evacuated from the Trzebinia sub-camp to Auschwitz, those who cannot proceed are left there. The remaining prisoners were marched to Rybnik, where they were loaded onto freight cars and after a four day journey arrived in Gross Rosen Concentration Camp. The transport was refused entry and was re-directed to Sachsenhausen Concentration Camp in Germany. After a short stay of only two weeks the prisoners were transferred to Bergen-Belsen Concentration Camp. During the enforced foot march, Arnost Tauber, Abraham Piasecki, and Karl Broszio escaped from the columns.[255]

The Camp Authorities in the sub-camp Gleiwitz I, conducted a selection, during which several dozen sick, lame and weakened prisoners were taken behind the barracks and shot. The prisoners were then led off on a forced march to Blechhammer sub-camp which took three days. On January 21, 1945, the remaining prisoners were again on the march, this time to Gross Rosen Concentration Camp. They arrived there at the beginning of February 1945. After several days they were transported to various Concentration Camps in Germany.[256]

The prisoners of Gleiwitz II sub-camp received the order to prepare for evacuation from the camp. The Director of the *Deutsche Gasrusswerke*, Schenk intervened so that the female prisoners received extra clothing. The columns of male and female prisoners marching out were escorted by *SS* troops under the direction of *SS-Hauptscharführer* Bernhard Rackers.

After a thirteen-mile march the prisoners were sheltered in a barn, however, the next morning with the advance of the Soviet Red Army, they returned to Gleiwitz. There they were loaded into open

---

[254]   Ibid., pp. 786–787.
[255]   Ibid., p. 787.
[256]   Ibid., p. 787.

freight cars and they travelled to Oranienburg, in Germany. The men were then sent to Sachsenhausen Concentration Camp and the women were sent to Ravensbrück Concentration Camp. Many female prisoners escaped, including one Anna Markowiecka, who jumped from the train and hid in the undergrowth. The SS guards fired shots at her, but they failed to hit her.[257]

The prisoners of the Bismarckhütte sub-camp were marched off under SS escort, which was under the direction of SS-Scharführer Hermann Christoph Klemann, who hailed from Hamburg. The prisoners reached Gleiwitz on January 20, 1945, where they waited for onward transportation.[258]

The Günthergrube sub-camp at about 10.00 p.m. was evacuated and the prisoners set off in the direction of the village of Kosztowo along side-roads. In the morning hours of January 19, 1945, near the village of Mikołów, they joined the columns of prisoners evacuated from Monowitz. The prisoners not killed en-route reached Gleiwitz sub-camp. On January 21, 1945, they were loaded onto open freight cars. The following day, January 22, 1945, the train stopped around noon at the station of Rzedowka. The SS guards under the direction of SS man Karl Kurpanik, ordered the prisoners to remove the dead from the freight cars. Once this had been completed the prisoners were led on foot to a nearby forest. 331 prisoners were shot in the forest.[259]

Approximately 450 prisoners left the Tschechowitz sub-camp at 7.00 o'clock in the evening, guarded by an armed SS escort. On January 20, 1945, they reached Wodzisław Śląski in Silesia. They were transported, along with other prisoners from Auschwitz, in open freight cars to Buchenwald Concentration Camp. Out of the 450 prisoners who evacuated, 300 survived the harsh journey.[260]

---

[257] Danuta Czech, *Auschwitz Chronicle*, Henry Holt and Company, New York 1990, pp. 787–788.
[258] Ibid., p. 788.
[259] Ibid., p. 788.
[260] Ibid., pp. 788–789.

In the evening of January 18, 1945, several hundred prisoners at the Golleschau sub-camp were evacuated from the camp, a second column of equal size left on January 19, 1945, and they aimed for Wodzisław in Silesia. From there they were transported to Sachsenhausen and Flossenburg in open freight cars. Almost half the prisoners died on this terrible journey.

At Auschwitz Main Camp during the day, columns of 100 prisoners in each, at timed intervals left the Camp. One of these columns consisted of male and female civilian prisoners who were detained in Block 11, by order of the Police Court-martial of the Katowice *Gestapo*. They were guarded by heavily armed *SS* escorts.[261]

The final biggest transport consisting of 2,500 prisoners departed from the Auschwitz Main Camp on January 19, 1945, at 1.00 o'clock in the morning. The prisoners were escorted by *SS* guards, under the direction of *SS-Obersturmführer* Wilhelm Reischenbeck. Near Rajsko, the last column joined up with 1,000 prisoners from Birkenau. Near the village of Brzeszcze, the procession joined with a column of 1,948 prisoners from the Jawischowitz sub-camp. The prisoners marched to Wodzisław in Silesia , where they were loaded into open freight wagons and sent to Mauthausen Concentration Camp in Austria, they completed their journey on January 26, 1945.[262]

The last group at 4 o'clock in the morning, consisting of 30 prisoner functionaries departed from Auschwitz Main Camp, in the direction of Wodzisław in Silesia, and they were loaded to the same transport to Mauthausen, as the earlier larger group.

On the same day, the Gleiwitz III sub-camp was evacuated, under *SS* escort. The march lasted several days and when they reached the left bank of the River Oder, the prisoners were marched via Cosel, to the Blechhammer sub-camp. Part of this group were sent to Gross Rosen Concentration Camp, a few escaped, and some returned to Gleiwitz.[263]

---

[261] Ibid., p. 789.
[262] Ibid., p. 789.
[263] Danuta Czech, *Auschwitz Chronicle*, Henry Holt and Company, New York 1990, p. 790.

380 prisoners were taken from the Gleiwitz IV sub camp on January 19, 1945, and led in the direction of the village of Sośnicowice. However, they were ordered back to Gleiwitz and then onto the Blechhammer sub-camp. From there some of the prisoners were transferred to Gross Rosen and Buchenwald Concentration Camps. 57 of the prisoners unable to continue were locked in the sick-bay. After several hours the Commander of the Gleiwitz IV sub-camp, *SS-Rottenführer* Otto Latsch returned to the camp along with Gustav Günther, a member of the *Organisation Todt*[264]. The two men set the sick-bay building on fire, in which the sick and exhausted 57 prisoners were locked in. The prisoners who jumped out of the windows were shot to death by the SS guards. Only two prisoners Dabrowski and Rosenfeld were able to survive, by hiding in the corpses.[265]

In the early morning hours of January 19, 1945, 202 prisoners left the Hubertushütte sub-camp, under SS escort. They arrived in Gleiwitz around 3.00 o'clock in the afternoon. They waited in Gleiwitz until other evacuated columns of prisoners arrived. Meanwhile in the Hindenburg sub-camp, SS Supervisor Juana Bormann ordered the women returning from work to be prepared for evacuation. The camp was evacuated and approximately 470 female prisoners reached Gleiwitz II sub-camp in the evening. Here they were loaded into open freight cars and transported to Gross Rosen Concentration Camp. Because Gross Rosen was overcrowded, the women were transported onto Bergen-Belsen Concentration Camp, on a journey that lasted two weeks.[266]

On the same day, 833 prisoners were evacuated from the Charlottengrube sub-camp, and they reached a farm near the River Oder,

---

[264] *Organisation Todt*, a para-military organization used for the construction of strategic highways and military installations, named after its head Fritz Todt, who after his death, was replaced by Albert Speer.
[265] Danuta Czech, *Auschwitz Chronicle*, Henry Holt and Company, New York 1990, p. 790.
[266] Ibid., pp. 790–791.

where they spent the night. The next day they marched back to Rydultowy, and from there they reached Wodzisław. They were loaded on open freight wagons and were transported to Mauthausen Concentration Camp in Austria.[267]

The liquidation of the Althammer sub-camp and the subsequent evacuation of the prisoners was personally supervised by Commandant Heinrich Schwarz of Monowitz. All the prisoners set off at 10.00 o'clock at night to Gleiwitz. Later an *SS* Division arrived in Gleiwitz, and held a roll call. A new Camp Senior was selected before the *SS* themselves abandoned the camp around January 25, 1945, forcing a good dozen prisoners to go with them. A local self-defence unit guarded the prisoners, until Russian forces liberated the camp. Among those who were liberated were Mieczyslaw Francuz, Aleksander Gelermann and the Lejbisz brothers.[268]

The Neustadt sub-camp was dissolved. The female prisoners were marched on foot to Gross Rosen Concentration Camp and from there they were transported to the Bergen-Belsen Concentration Camp in Germany. On the same day, approximately 1,000 prisoners were evacuated from the Fürstengrube sub-camp. The liquidation of the camp and the evacuation of the prisoners was supervised by Camp Commandant Max Schmidt. The march to Gleiwitz took 12 hours. In the evening the prisoners from Fürstengrube were sheltered in Gleiwitz II sub-camp.[269]

Forces of the Red Army marched into Jaworzno sub-camp and liberated approximately 400 prisoners who had been left behind in the Neu Dachs sub-camp, because they had been unable to march. In the morning hours, an *SS* Division arrived at the male prisoners' infirmary in Camp B-IIf in Birkenau. They selected prisoners to carry the corpses from the infirmary to the compound of Crematorium V. The *SS* set the corpses alight and departed from the Camp, having

---

[267] Ibid., p. 791.
[268] Ibid., p. 791.
[269] Danuta Czech, *Auschwitz Chronicle*, Henry Holt and Company, New York 1990, pp. 791–792.

first ordered the prisoners to remove valuable items from storerooms in the Personal Effects Camp.[270]

SS-Sturmbannführer Franz Xaver Kraus, received the order to liquidate immediately all prisoners who were unable to march from *SS-Obergruppenführer* Ernst Schmauser Higher SS and Police Leader in Breslau. Kraus from December 1944, was Head of the Auschwitz Liaison and Transition Office.[271]

Still on January 20, 1945, several SS Divisions remained in the vicinity of Birkenau. In the morning one of these Divisions entered the Women's Camp B-IIe and ordered the female prisoners to cook a midday meal for them. Under their uniforms most of the SS men were wearing civilian clothing, which they had obtained from the storerooms in 'Canada.' The midday meals were not eaten, as they received orders to march. Some of the healthier male and female prisoners decided to flee with them. They lifted the gate to Camp B-IIe and entered the SS Block Leader's room, which they started to demolish. Suddenly they noticed an SS Division approaching from a distance and they immediately returned to their section.

An SS Division under *SS-Rottenführer* Richard Perschel, the Labor Manager in the Women's Camp, entered the Women's Camp B-IIe. Perschel ordered all Jewish prisoners to leave their blocks, approximately 200 women came out. They were led in front of the camp gate and shot to death. Following this, the SS Division entered the prisoners' infirmary for men in Camp B-IIf, where they selected prisoners to carry cases of dynamite to Crematoriums II and III. The SS Division under *SS-Rottenführer* Perschel blew up the already partly demolished Crematoriums II and III, and they then departed from Birkenau.[272]

At 11:55 p.m. a number of prisoners escaped from the prisoners' infirmary in Camp B-IIf in Birkenau. Kazimierz Smolen (96238), Dr. Stanislaw Zasadzki (150155), Wladyslaw Rodowicz, Jerzy Bordzic, Alfons Budrowski and two female prisoners Wladyslawa Kaminski and

---

[270] Ibid., p. 792.
[271] Ibid., p. 793.
[272] Ibid., p. 794.

Janina Grzybowska made good their escape, and at 6:00 p.m. they arrived in Brzeszcze, where they found refuge with local Poles, until the Red Army arrived.[273]

The liquidation of the Blechhammer sub-camp took place on January 21, 1945. Approximately 4,000 prisoners were evacuated from the camp, as well as a number of prisoners from other sub-camps who were also assembled there. They were marched on foot to Gross Rosen Concentration Camp which they reached on February 2, 1945. During the march *SS* men murdered approximately 800 prisoners. *SS-Untersturmführer* Kurt Klipp directed the withdrawal. After a short five-day stay in Gross Rosen, the prisoners were transported to Buchenwald Concentration Camp in Germany. The *SS* escort returned to the Blechhammer sub-camp and proceeded to set it on fire. The *SS* men shot and threw grenades at the prisoners who fled the burning barracks.[274]

One of the prisoners incarcerated in the Blechhammer sub-camp was Dr. Alfred Oppenheimer, who had been forced to march from Gleiwitz sub-camp and he witnessed the return of the *SS* men to Blechhammer, and he recalled what happened next:

> There was a call, 'Hurry! The *SS* men are back!' The excitement and the fear—I felt no pain any longer. I dragged my two friends, and crossed to a place across the ground. These were the public lavatories. We stood there and peeped through the cracks to see what was going on in the camp. They started shooting from the towers, the watch-towers around the camp.
> The *SS* men set fire to the huts where the people took shelter and where they were in hiding. They stood facing the doors with machine-guns, and if anyone ran out of the burning huts, they were shot immediately by the *SS* men with those machine-guns. Those who did not run were burned alive.
> My friends and myself decided that they would be coming to the lavatories as well and set fire. Then we jumped through the seat into the pit, and this was the worst experience of my life. When we entered those pits of excrement, sinking, sinking slowly—and one did not know how

---

[273] Danuta Czech, *Auschwitz Chronicle*, Henry Holt and Company, New York 1990, pp. 794–795.
[274] Ibid., p. 795.

deep we were sinking. The excrement reached up to my chest, and all of a sudden, I felt solid ground under my feet.

The smell of the burning wood from the huts, the noise of the flames, and the half-burned people, those who were shot but not dead—they all formed this terrible experience, the worst I went through in those camps, far worse than the moment when a sentence of death was delivered against myself.[275]

Dr. Alfred Oppenheimer remained in the excrement pit for several hours:

> We heard voices, people speaking and saying the SS men had gone, that the gates were open. There were other prisoners of war, Jewish prisoners, also saved by some kind of miracle, because not all the huts were on fire. And then we cried out for help. A number of those Jewish prisoners came to help us, and pulled us out of this pit of excrement. We cleaned ourselves with snow. There was no water. We did what we could. Finally we were liberated by the Soviet Army.[276]

Also on January 21, 1945, an armed unit of the *Organisation Todt* entered the grounds of the Tschechowitz-Vacuum sub-camp. Approximately 100 prisoners who were unfit to join the evacuation had remained behind.

The members of the *Organisation Todt* ordered the prisoners to dig a pit, two yards deep and ten yards long, to bury the corpses of those that had died in the camp. Some hours later several SS men appeared and went to the sick-bay where they shot to death the bedridden prisoners. The SS men ordered the remaining prisoners to bring the murdered prisoners to the freshly dug pit, and to cover them with sacks of straw. Then the SS men shot at the prisoners carrying the sacks of straw. The SS men poured an extremely flammable liquid over the heap of corpses and straw sacks and then ignited it. Most of the prisoners involved in this were killed, but Erwin Habal (B-12457) and Dr. Josef Weil (B-12562) survived.[277]

---

[275] M. Gilbert, *The Holocaust*, Collins London 1985, pp. 772–773.
[276] Ibid., p. 773.
[277] Danuta Czech, *Auschwitz Chronicle*, Henry Holt and Company, New York 1990, p. 795.

On the same day five female prisoners attempted to escape from the Women's Camp B-IIe in Birkenau. They were detained by a drunken *SS* man in the so-called 'Death Gate.' He took the youngest woman into the guardroom. Two shots were heard and after a short time the woman ran out. She successfully defended herself and shot dead the drunken *SS* man. The women prisoners concealed themselves in a railroad car loaded with feathers and pillows that stood at the ramp. After spending the entire day in the railroad car they returned to the Women's Camp.[278]

Some Russian Prisoners of War who remained in the Birkenau Camp retrieved two weapons from a hiding place and shot several times into the air. The *Wehrmacht* was alerted by the shots and notified an *SD* Division, which arrived at the camp, and carried out a search for the guns. They failed to find any weapons. The German *Kapo*, Otto Schulz, informed the Germans that the man who fired the shots was the Russian Prisoner of War, Andreyev. The *SS* carried out a search but failed to locate him.[279]

The evacuation of the Golleschau sub-camp was completed on this day. The last group consisted of 96 sick and exhausted prisoners. They were transported in sealed freight cars to the Freudenthal sub-camp in Czechoslovakia. On January 29, 1945, the station supervisor in Zwittau informed Oskar Schindler, the Director of the munitions factory in Brüssen-Brünnlitz, that a wagon with Jewish prisoners had arrived at the station. Schindler ordered that this wagon must be sent to Brüssen-Brünnlitz, which was a sub-camp belonging to the Gross Rosen Concentration Camp. The wagon arrived, but the hinges and locks were frozen, and the doors had to be opened with great force. Half of the prisoners had frozen or starved to death.

The wife of Oskar Schindler recalled in her memoirs, the arrival of this transport:

> On the night of a terrible storm, when the temperature was 30 degrees below zero, a man came to speak with me in the middle of the night, while Oskar was still in Kraków. The man was in charge of transporting

---

[278] Ibid., p. 796.
[279] Ibid., p. 796.

250 Jews from Golleschau, a Polish mine of terrible repute. They were crammed into four wagons to be moved to another business, which had heard of the Russians' arrival, and had stranded them. If I refused them, they would have been shot.

I phoned Oskar, and asked for authorization to accept the Jews, which I received. I went out to find Schönborn, and we went straight to the station. It was snowing, and nearly dawn. We tried to open the locks of the wagons with large iron bars, but they were frozen shut. Schönborn went to find a welding machine, and with patience, we opened them up. The German Commander warned me of the sights, but I ignored him. What I saw remained in my nightmares: the men and women were indistinguishable, due to their thinness; they were almost skeletons and most weighed about 30 kilos. Their eyes shone like coals in the darkness. Twelve were dead and they had spent their last minutes, apparently in communion with God, searching for answers. The survivors were transferred to a sort of emergency hospital immediately, where they remained for two months. They needed special attention, and had not eaten for a long time, so they had to be fed slowly mouthful by mouthful, so they did not choke. As they improved, they were given a place at our factory, and were fed from the mill and our Black Market dealings. Our factory had become a refuge from the horrors of the Concentration Camps.[280]

Five Polish prisoners, on January 21, 1945, Tadeusz Balut (1259), Alfred Barabasch (62332), Wojeciech Kozlowski (26724), Mieczyslaw Zawadzki (8012) and Stanislaw Zaleski (1877) escaped from the Auschwitz Main Camp at 5:00 p.m.[281]

On January 22, 1945, in the morning an *SD* Division returned to Birkenau Camp B-IIf, and in Block 13 arrested the sleeping Russian Prisoner of War, Andreyev and five other Russian POW's who were accused of having fired shots the day before. They were led behind Block 14, made to stand next to a water channel, and then shot. As soon as the *SD* Division had departed, the other prisoners recovered one of the Russian POW's who had only been wounded in the head.

---

[280] Robin O'Neil, *Oskar Schindler—Stepping Stone to Life*, susaneking.com Texas, p. 166.
[281] Danuta Czech, *Auschwitz Chronicle*, Henry Holt and Company, New York 1990, p. 798.

The wound was treated by a prisoner doctor, Dr. Otto Wolken. The wounded prisoner was hidden in the block.[282]

At 9:00 a.m. on the same day, 80 male and female prisoners escaped from the Birkenau Camp and made their way towards the bridge in Babitz. The gun fire directed at them by the German *Wehrmacht* forces made them return to Birkenau. At around midday another group of male and female prisoners with children also attempted to leave the camp. They set off towards the *SS* barracks, where they meet an *SS* man who allowed them to proceed to the train station in Auschwitz town. Some railroad workers allowed some of the prisoners to board a train which was standing ready to depart for Kattowitz. The others dispersed, three female prisoners managed to reach the town without being arrested.[283]

The prisoners were evacuated from the Laurahütte sub-camp on January 23, 1945. On the railroad track near the foundry, a train was prepared into which the prisoners were loaded, also the civilian personnel were transported on the same train. The train stopped near the station of Rzędówka, where the *SS* escorts ordered the prisoners to retrieve the striped Concentration Camp clothing from the corpses who lay near the railroad tracks. The final destination for this transport was the Mauthausen Concentration Camp in Austria. The trip lasted five days and nights and 134 prisoners died en route.[284]

On the same day, over 1,200 prisoners were evacuated from the Eintrachthütte sub-camp. They waited the entire night on the railroad platform in Schwientochlowitz for a train to be prepared for them. Towards morning they were loaded onto several cattle cars, whose floors were thick with animal faeces. The journey to Mauthausen Concentration Camp took seven days.[285]

An *SS* Division arrived in the prisoners' infirmary Camp in B-IIf in Birkenau during the afternoon, and ordered the prisoners to carry

---

[282] Ibid., p. 798.
[283] Ibid., p. 798.
[284] Ibid., pp. 798–799.
[285] Ibid., p. 799.

the corpses of the shot Russian Prisoners of War to Crematorium V. The corpses were put in a large pile, and in the evening, the SS men set fire to it. Once this was completed they set 30 storeroom barracks in the Personnel Effects Camp (Canada) on fire. The prisoners in Camp B-IIf who were threatened by the fire, established a guard of healthy prisoners, and they ensured the fire did not spread to the infirmary Camp, which was only a few yards away.[286]

The next day, January 24, 1945, *SS-Sturmbannführer* Franz Xaver Kraus arrived in Birkenau with an SS unit and shot dead three prisoners, including the Dutch prisoner Dr. Ackermann.

On January 25, 1945, the Janinagrube sub-camp in Libiaz was liberated. There were 60 prisoners left behind, because they were ill. Polish people who lived near the camp provided first aid. The seriously ill were taken to the hospital. Meanwhile on the same day at 2:00 p.m. an *SD* Division arrived in the Women's Camp B-IIe and the Men's Camp B-IIf in Birkenau. They ordered all the Jews to leave their barracks. In Camp B-IIf *Kapo* Schulz identified Jews and drove them out of the barracks. Some of the Jewish prisoners were able to conceal themselves under the floors, in prepared hiding places.

Approximately 159 male and 200 female Jews were taken to the gate. Several Jewish prisoners were taken behind the Block Leader's Room, where they were shot to death, among them was the Jewish prisoner Harff from Cologne. They evacuated the Camp, but this transport was stopped by SS men who drove by in an automobile. The prisoners were ordered to go to the Auschwitz Main Camp, but the *SD* troops drove away with the *SS* men. Some of the prisoners obeyed this order, whilst some returned to Birkenau.[287]

Another *SD* Division arrived in the Auschwitz Main Camp. They ordered all sick prisoners to leave their blocks and made them line up near the main entrance gate, which bore the slogan '*Arbeit Macht Frei*' – Work Brings Freedom. The German Reich prisoners were made to line up in the front, behind them other nationalities and

---

[286] Ibid., p. 800.
[287] Danuta Czech, *Auschwitz Chronicle*, Henry Holt and Company, New York 1990, p. 800.

the Jewish prisoners bringing up the rear. Prisoners who could no longer walk were lined up separately. The *SD* unit combed the blocks and drove out all the prisoners and it was obvious that these prisoners were going to be shot. However, an automobile with *SS* men drove up, words were exchanged and the prisoners were ordered to return to the blocks. The *SD* Division departed with the *SS* men in great haste.[288]

At 1:00 a.m. on the morning of January 26, 1945, an *SS* squad ordered to eliminate all traces of the crimes committed, destroyed Crematorium V, the last of the crematoriums in Birkenau. Meanwhile the Red Army was advancing on Auschwitz and a number of air raids took place. Scattered *Wehrmacht* Divisions fled in panic towards Rajsko, in the direction of Bielsko.[289]

The retreating *Wehrmacht* troops on January 27, 1945 destroyed the railroad bridge over the Rivers Soła and Vistula, as well as the wooden bridge over the River Soła, which was opposite the main Camp, and was built by the prisoners.[290]

On the same day, an *SS* Division arrived in Fürstengrube subcamp, which contained 250 prisoners. They ordered 127 prisoners, who were able to walk, to leave the prisoners' infirmary and go into the wooden barracks. They were ordered to position themselves at the windows. The prisoners did not obey this order and positioned themselves on the other side of the barracks. The *SS* men began shooting and tossed in grenades. The *SS* set the barracks on fire and those prisoners who fled the burning barracks were shot to death. Then the *SS* entered the prisoners' infirmary and allowed 10 Aryan prisoners to leave for the camp kitchen. Then the *SS* set fire to the barracks and all the sick prisoners perished in the flames. After the liberation, those few that survived were taken to the Polish Miners Hospital in Mysłowice.[291]

---

[288] Ibid., p. 801.
[289] Ibid., p. 801.
[290] Ibid., p. 801.
[291] Danuta Czech, *Auschwitz Chronicle*, Henry Holt and Company, New York 1990, p. 803.

On Saturday January 27, 1945, at around 9:00 a.m. the first Russian soldier from a reconnaissance unit of the 100th Infantry Division of the 106th Corps arrived on the grounds of the prisoners' infirmary in Monowitz. The rest of the Division arrived half an hour later. The soldiers distributed bread among the sick. The same day a military physician, with the rank of captain, arrived and immediately organized medical treatment to be given. Of the 850 sick prisoners left behind during the evacuations, more than 200 of them had died by the day of liberation.[292]

In the afternoon of the same day, soldiers of the Red Army entered the vicinity of both Auschwitz Main Camp and Birkenau. Near the Main Camp they were met with resistance from the retreating German units. 231 Red Army were killed in close combat with the Germans for the liberation of Auschwitz, Birkenau and Monowitz. Two of them died in front of the gates of Auschwitz Main Camp. Among those killed was Lieutenant Gilmudin Baszrov.[293]

The first Red Army reconnaissance troops arrived in Auschwitz and Birkenau at around 3:00 p.m. and were greeted by joyous liberated prisoners. After the removal of mines from the surrounding area, soldiers of the 60th Army of the 1st Ukrainian Front, commanded by General Pawel Kuroczkin, marched into the Camp and brought freedom to the prisoners who survived. On the grounds of the Main Camp were 48 corpses and in Birkenau there were over 600 corpses of male and female prisoners who had died in the last few days of the Camps existence.[294]

At the time the Red Army arrived, there were 7,000 sick and exhausted prisoners in the Auschwitz, Birkenau, and Monowitz Camps. Dr. Otto Wolken remained in the Camp and was one of the organizers of the assistance measures for the prisoners. At the same time, he also secured various Camp documents that provided information on the crimes committed by the *SS* in the Auschwitz-Birkenau Concentration Camp. He reported the following numbers of

---

[292] Ibid., pp. 803–804.
[293] Ibid., p. 804.
[294] Ibid., p. 805.

surviving prisoners; Auschwitz—1,200 sick prisoners; Birkenau 5,800 prisoners, of whom 4,000 were women; Monowitz—600 sick prisoners.[295]

---

[295] Ibid., p. 805.

Part II
Perpetrators, Survivors, Victims and Aftermath

Chapter XI
Biographies—Perpetrators

Provided here are short biographical sketches of some of the *SS* men, women and Doctors who served at Auschwitz during the years 1940–1945. This is not a complete listing, but hopefully includes the major figures involved in the history of the Auschwitz Camp complex. The sources for these entries come from various works, which include books like the *'Auschwitz Chronicle'*, by Danuta Czech, *'KL Auschwitz Seen By The SS' 'The Private Lives of the Auschwitz SS'*, by Piotr Setkiewicz, *'Auschwitz'* by Bernd Naumann, and *'Who's Who in Nazi Germany'* by Robert S. Wistrich. Other works consulted were *'Fighting Auschwitz'* by Josef Garlinski, *'The Camp Men'* by French L. MacLean, and *'Commanders of Auschwitz'* by Jeremy Dixon.

Commandants

There were three Commandants and these have been listed in the order in which they performed this role:

HÖSS, Rudolf, Born on November 25, 1900, in Baden-Baden, Germany, to a strict Catholic family. His father's name was Franz, and his mother's name was Lina, formerly Speck. At the age of 15, he joined the German Army as a volunteer, serving in the 21st Regiment of Dragoons. He saw active service in the Turkish theatre of war, and the Palestine Front, where he rose through the ranks to become a non-commissioned officer and he received several medals.

After the German defeat in the Great War, he became a member of the *Freikorps*, in the Baltic Region, Upper Silesia and the Ruhr and he joined the Nazi Party in 1922. A year later in 1923, he was involved in the so-called *'Parchim Feme'* murder. A group of men, including Martin Bormann and Rudolf Höss, beat a local schoolteacher Walther Kadow to death, who was accused of betraying fellow Nazi, Albert Leo Schlageter, to the French authorities. Schlageter was arrested for carrying out acts of sabotage against the French, and he was executed on May 26, 1923. On May 31, Rudolf Höss, Martin Bormann and others murdered Walther Kadow and for this he was tried and found guilty. Höss was sentenced to 10 years in prison.

However, in 1928, he was released from Brandenburg prison in an amnesty and he joined the Artaman League in the same year. This was a nationalist 'back-to-the-land' movement that promoted clean living and an agricultural-based lifestyle. On August 17, 1929, he married another member of the Artaman League, Hedwig Hensel. The couple had five children, two boys, Klaus and Hans-Rudolf and three girls, Ingebrigitt, Heidetraut and Annegret, during the years 1930 to 1943.

Rudolf Höss was the longest serving Commandant in the history of Auschwitz. He was appointed by Heinrich Himmler, the head of the SS, to the post on May 4, 1940, and he performed this role until he was replaced by Arthur Liebehenschel on November 11, 1943. He took over from Liebehenschel as head of D-1 of the *WVHA*, but returned to Auschwitz in May 1944, to oversee the forthcoming liquidation of the Jews from Hungary, which bore the codename, '*Aktion Höss*'. He returned to his post with the *WVHA* on July 29, 1944. Rudolf Höss was characterized as an assiduous, petit-bourgeois executive, who organized mass murder with technical and administrative meticulousness.

On the eve of the defeat of Nazi Germany, Rudolf Höss disguised himself as a member of the German Navy under the name of Franz Lang. He worked on a farm near Flensburg. He was arrested by British troops on March 11, 1946. He was severely beaten to reveal his true identity. Höss testified at the Nuremberg War Crimes Trial, held during November 1945 and October 1946, as a witness for Ernst Kaltenbrunner, the Chief of the Reich Main Security Office and in the trials against Oswald Pohl, head of the *WVHA*, and the main figures of I. G. Farben.

On May 25, 1946, Rudolf Höss was handed over by the British Government to the Polish authorities and the Supreme National Tribunal tried him for War Crimes in Warsaw. The trial took place from March 11 to March 29, 1947, and Höss was sentenced to death on April 2, 1947. The sentence was carried out on April 16, 1947. He was hanged on a short drop gallows next to the crematorium in Auschwitz Main Camp, at the former site of the Camp's Political Department's barrack.

LIEBEHENSCHEL, Arthur, Born on November 25, 1901 in Posen, today Poznan, in Poland. He studied economics and public administration, and although too young to fight in the Great War, after it ended, he joined the *Freikorps* and served in the '*Grenzschutz Ost.*'

Arthur Liebehenschel also served in the Reichswehr and joined the Nazi Party in 1932, and two years later he joined the *SS*. After service in Lichtenburg, one of the so-called 'wild camps,' where he was an adjutant. He was then transferred to the Concentration Camps Inspectorate in Berlin. After the *WVHA* was created in 1942, he took over the newly formed Branch D, the Central Office for Concentration Camps, office D-I.

In November 1943, he succeeded Rudolf Höss as Commandant of the Auschwitz Main Camp and Garrison Senior. Liebehenschel was less harsh in his rule than Höss, and was considered by Heinrich Himmler as unsuited to carry out the extermination '*Aktion*' against the Jews of Hungary and was replaced by Rudolf Höss in May 1944.

He was transferred to the Lublin Concentration Camp where he took over as Commandant from Martin Weiss, although because of a heart disease he spent most of his time outside of the camp. After the evacuation of the camp on July 23, 1944, he went to Trieste where he served on the staff of Odilo Globocnik, the Higher *SS* Leader for the Adriatic Coast. Liebehenschel was arrested by American forces and was extradited to Poland where he stood on trial for War Crimes. The Supreme National Tribunal found him guilty and sentenced him to death. He was executed on January 24, 1948.

BAER, Richard, Born on September 9, 1911, in Floss, Bavaria. He studied to be a pastry cook but was unemployed until he joined the guard company at Dachau Concentration Camp in 1933. In 1939, he was transferred to the *SS* Death's Head Division where he sustained an injury. He was then assigned to the Neuengamme Concentration Camp to the post of Adjutant.

From 1943, he was the Adjutant to *SS* General Oswald Pohl, the Head of the *WVHA*, and from May 11, 1944, he was appointed the third and final Commandant of Auschwitz, a post he held until the camp was evacuated in January 1945. Richard Baer then replaced Otto Forschner as the Commandant of Dora-Mittelbau, until the end of the War. At the end of the Second World War, he went underground and lived near Hamburg under the name of Karl Neumann until 1960. He was arrested in December 1960, and he died of a heart attack on June 17, 1963, whilst in pre-trial detention.

Auschwitz Concentration Camp—Garrison Listed in Alphabetical Order

ALBERT, Roland, Born on April 21, 1916, in Schaessburg, Transylvania, Rumania. He joined the SS in 1941. At Auschwitz Concentration Camp he was the Commander of the 1st and 4th guard companies and the training company. He served in Auschwitz from January 1942.

AUMEIER, Hans, Born on August 20, 1906 in Arnberg, Upper Bavaria. He left school without any qualifications and found employment as an apprentice as a turner and fitter at a local rifle factory. He joined the Nazi Party in December 1929, and two years later joined the SA, before entering the SS, where he worked as a driver as part of Heinrich Himmler's staff.

After several assignments in various Concentration Camps including spells in Dachau, Buchenwald, Lichtenburg and Flossenbürg, he was transferred to Auschwitz, on February 1, 1942, where he performed the role of 'First Protective Custody Commander'. On August 18, 1943, he was found guilty of corruption, including the theft of gold from victims of gassings, and he was transferred to the Vaivara Concentration Camp in Estonia.

When that Camp was liberated he was transferred to the Grini Concentration Camp in Norway during January 1945. Aumeier was arrested by the Allied Forces on June 11, 1945. He was extradited to Poland where he stood on trial for War Crimes. The Supreme National Tribunal found him guilty and sentenced him to death. He was executed on January 28, 1948, in Montelupich Prison.

BARETZKI, Stefan, Born on March 24, 1919, in Czernowitz, Rumania, the son of a mechanic. His father died in the late 1930's. After completing elementary school he took up hosiery knitting, passed the trade examinations, and found employment as an operator in a hosiery mill in Czernowitz.

When the Second World War broke out he was 'resettled' and in the autumn of 1942, he was assigned to the *Waffen-SS* at Auschwitz, where he worked initially as a messenger, and then as a block leader. After the evacuation of the camp in January 1945, he was sent to the front, in the vicinity of Frankurt on the Oder. He was taken prisoner on May 6, 1945, but was released on August 17, 1945. After that he held a number of jobs in the coal and pumice industry. He was arrested and stood trial at the Frankfurt am Main trial in 1965. He was found guilty of War Crimes and was sentenced to life imprisonment.

BISCHOFF, Heinrich, Born on July 16, 1904, in Überruhr near Essen, the son of a miner. His early schooling was interrupted during 1917, when at the age of thirteen he too went to work in the coal mines. In 1921, his father had a fatal accident, and ten years later his mother died in 1931. Heinrich Bischoff joined the Nazi Party in October 1931, and he also became active in the *SA*, however, he was expelled from both of these organizations in 1934. After a period of unemployment he found work with a miners' association, and later he tended a furnace in a hospital.

In April 1940, he was drafted into the field artillery, from which he received a medical discharge. In July 1942, he was again called up, this time into the *SS* Death's Head unit at Oranienburg. After a few days he was transferred to Auschwitz Concentration Camp, where he was initially assigned to guard duty and later became a block leader.

He was taken prisoner by the American forces in May 1945, but was released on August 2, and he went back to working in the mines. He was working in the '*Heinrich*' mine in Essen, when it collapsed. He recovered from his injuries sustained in the collapse and until December 29, 1955, he worked as a mine guard and pump operator, until he suffered a heart attack, which forced him into retirement.

He died of a heart attack on October 26, 1964, and thus avoided the Frankfurt am Main War Crimes Trial.

BISCHOFF, Karl, Born on August 9, 1897, in Neuhemsbach, near Kaiserslautern. He joined the German airforce in 1917 and left two years later as a pilot. He studied building procedures and from 1935, obtained employment in the Luftwaffe Construction Bureau. During the initial phases of the Second World War he was involved in the building of airfields in France. During this time he met Hans Kammler, Head of *Amt C*, the construction department of the *SS*, who offered Bischoff a post in Auschwitz Concentration Camp.

On October 1, 1941, Karl Bischoff arrived in Auschwitz, where he became Chief of *Zentralbauleitung der Waffen-SS und Polizei Auschwitz*. He was responsible for the planning and construction of the Soviet Prisoner of War Camp at Birkenau. Bischoff was an extremely competent and dynamic bureaucrat, and he and his staff planned and constructed four huge crematoria, the technically complicated central sauna and the reception building in Auschwitz Main Camp. His work at Auschwitz was recognized and he was awarded the War Service Cross First Class. In April 1944, he left Auschwitz and became Chief of the construction bureau of the *Waffen-SS* in Silesia and Bohemia. He was never brought to trial and he died on October 2, 1950.

BOGER, Wilhelm, Born on December 19, 1906, in Stuttgart-Zuffenhausen, the son of a local merchant who did not enjoy the best of reputations. In the summer of 1925, after nine years of schooling and a three-year apprenticeship in a business firm, he was employed in a clerical position within the Stuttgart district office of the National German Commercial Employees Association.

After a spell in the *Hitler-Jugend* (Hitler Youth), he joined the Nazi Party and the *SA* in 1929. Until the end of 1929, he was also a member of the Artaman League, like Rudolf Höss, an organization that wished to substitute voluntary agricultural service for military service. In the years that followed, Wilhem Boger worked for a number of private business firms in Stuttgart, Dresden, and Friedrichshafen.

In 1930, while in Dresden, he joined the *SS* and two years later he lost his job and a year later, on March 5, 1933, as a member of the *SS*, he was called for duty in the auxiliary police of Friedrichshafen. On July 1, he was transferred to the Stuttgart political emergency police corps, and after another six weeks, to the Württemberg political police, also in Stuttgart. In October 1933, he moved to the offices of the Friedrichshafen political police. He attended the police training school in Stuttgart between the autumn of 1936, and the spring of 1937, where he sat the criminal police candidate examinations. He passed and was appointed Commissar in March 1937. At the outbreak of the Second World War he was transferred to the State Police Office in Zichenau; after three weeks he was put in charge of setting up and supervising the border police station in Ostrolenka, in Poland.

During 1939, Boger was arrested and charged with abortion, confined in a *Gestapo* prison, but released on December 19, 1940. A year later he was called-up to the 2nd *SS* and Police Engineer reserve unit in Dresden. After a brief training period, he was sent to the front, and in March 1942, he was wounded.

On December 1, 1942, Boger was transferred to the Auschwitz Concentration Camp, where he worked as a functionary for the Political Department. Here he became infamous for his brutal interrogation methods, such as the 'Boger Swing.' Wilhelm Boger stayed at Auschwitz until the evacuation in January 1945, when he accompanied prisoners to Germany.

He worked in the Political Department at Mittlebau Concentration Camp from February to March 1945. After Germany's collapse, Boger sought refuge in his parents' home in Ludwigsburg. However, on June 19, 1945, he was arrested by the American Military Police. Boger managed to escape from being extradited to Poland on November 22, 1946, which probably saved him from certain execution.

He lived in the vicinity of Crailsheim, as a farmhand using an assumed name, and in 1950, he was employed by the Heinkelwerke, an airplane company, as a supplies supervisor. The factory was located in his birthplace of Stuttgart-Zuffenhausen, and he used his own name.

Wilhelm Boger was arrested in 1958, and stood trial in the Frankfurt am Main Auschwitz proceedings. He was found guilty of War Crimes and sentenced to life imprisonment. He died on April 3, 1977, in Bietigheim-Bissingen Prison.

BREITWEISER, Arthur, Born on July 31, 1910, in Lvov, the son of a waiter. He attended a German elementary school and he graduated from secondary school in 1931. He studied law at the University of Lvov, receiving a Master's Degree in 1936. While a student, he joined the 'New German Party.' In June 1939, he became a legal adviser to the Municipal Employees' Association of Bromberg.

On September 1, 1939, he was arrested by the Polish police, but was freed by the German Army, when they invaded. He returned to Bromberg, where he found employment in the chamber of commerce, which dealt with inland waterways. During this period he joined the so-called 'Self-Protection League,' which as a body was incorporated into the *Waffen-SS* on November 1, 1939.

In May 1940, he was assigned to the Auschwitz Concentration Camp, where he worked in the disinfection section, which dealt with the disinfection of clothing, and was in charge of the stores where the cans of *Zyklon B* were stored. He also worked in the administrative office, and the billeting office.

Breitweiser was arrested by the American Forces at the end of the Second World War, and was interned in various camps, including Dachau. During December 1946, he was extradited to Poland to stand trial. The Supreme National Tribunal found him guilty and sentenced him to death on December 22, 1947. A month later, his sentence was commuted to life imprisonment, and on January 18, 1959, he was released and shipped back to Germany. He worked as a book-keeper in his brother-in-law's business. He was arrested and brought to trial in Frankfurt am Main, accused of participating in the first mass gassings in Auschwitz in October 1941. Due to insufficient evidence however, he was acquitted.

BROAD, Pery, Born on April 25, 1921, in Rio de Janeiro, Brazil, the son of a Brazilian businessman and a German woman. Soon after his birth, his mother took him to Germany, whilst his father remained in Brazil. Pery Broad attended primary and secondary schools in Berlin. As a reward for his early membership in the 'Hitler Youth,' he was awarded a gold membership pin. He graduated from high school in December 1940, and attended the Technical College of Berlin until December 1941, when he was forced to leave, because he could not renew his Brazilian passport, and residence permits were no longer being granted.

He volunteered to serve in the *Waffen-SS* and because of his myopia, he was sent to the Auschwitz Concentration Camp instead of serving on the front. He was initially assigned to guard duty in June 1942, and shortly after his arrival at the camp, he was transferred to the Political Department, where he stayed until the evacuation of the camp in January 1945. On May 6, 1945, he was arrested by the British Forces near Ravensbrück. After his release from British internment, in July 1953, he worked in the offices of a sawmill in Münsterlager and with a Brunswick manufacturer of electrical equipment, at whose Düsseldorf offices he was last employed. Broad stood trial in the Frankfurt am Main Auschwitz proceedings. He was found guilty of War Crimes and sentenced to 4 years hard labor. He died on November 28, 1993, in Düsseldorf.

BURGER, Willi, Born on May 19, 1904, in Munich. He was the Director of Department IV—Administration in Auschwitz Concentration Camp until his transfer in April 1943, where he was appointed the Director of *S-Amtsgruppe D IV* in the *WVHA*. He was sentenced to five years in prison at a post-war trial in Kraków. He was re-tried in Frankfurt am Main and sentenced to serve another eight years in prison.

CAESAR, Dr. Joachim, Born on May 30, 1901, in Boppard. He studied natural sciences and received a degree in agriculture. He joined the Nazi Party and the *SS*, and he became the Mayor of Holstein in 1933. Dr. Caesar from 1934, worked in the *SS* Training Office in the *Reich* Main Security Office (*RSHA*), which he later was in charge of.

In February 1942, he was posted to Auschwitz and in March 1942, he was appointed as the Head of all agricultural activies in Auschwitz Concentration Camp. He contracted typhus on October 13,

1942, a few days after his wife had died from the same disease. Heinrich Himmler followed the work that Dr. Caesar performed on experimental plant growing at Rajsko with great interest. After the Second World War ended he went into the laundry business and he died on January 25, 1974, in Kiel.

CAPESIUS, Dr. Victor, Born on July 2, 1907, in Reussmarkt, Rumania, the son of a Doctor. He graduated from secondary school in 1925, and studied pharmacy in Klausenberg. In 1931, he served the obligatory term in the Rumanian Army; however, he spent eleven months of this in Vienna completing his studies. He graduated from the University of Klausenberg in 1933.

Until August 1943, he worked as a representative for a subsidiary of I. G. Farben in Rumania; at the same time he also managed the hospital pharmacy of the Rumanian Army at Cernavode, which earned him a promotion to the rank of captain. On the basis of an agreement between Germany and Rumania, he was called up for service in the German Army in August 1943, but shortly afterwards, Dr. Capesius was assigned to the SS Central Medical Station at Warsaw as a pharmacist. He arrived in Auschwitz either at the end of 1943, or February 1944, via Medical posts in Berlin, Dachau and Oranienburg, he was put in charge of the SS pharmacy. When the camp was evacuated in January 1945, he was transferred to Berlin.

He was taken prisoner by the British Forces on Easter Sunday, 1945, at Schleswig-Holstein, but he was released in June 1946. He went to Stuttgart, but was unable to find employment because of his SS affiliations. He therefore enrolled in a course of electrical engineering at Stuttgart's Technical College. In the summer of 1946, he visited Munich and there he was recognized by a former inmate of Auschwitz and was reported to the authorities. He was arrested by the American Military Police, but their investigation into his past petered out, and by August 1947, he was once again at liberty. He found himself employed in a pharmacy in Stuttgart, but on October 5, 1950, he opened his own pharmacy in Göppingen and later also a cosmetic salon in Reutlingen. Capesius stood trial in the Frankfurt am Main Auschwitz proceedings. He was found guilty of War

Crimes and sentenced to 9 years hard labor. He died on March 20, 1985.

CLAUBERG, Dr. Carl, Born on September 28, 1898, in Wupperhof. He served as an infantryman in the Great War of 1914–1918, and he later studied medicine in Kiel, Hamburg, and Graz, receiving his Doctorate in 1925. He became Chief physician at the University Women's Hospital in Kiel. Clauberg joined the Nazi Party in 1933, and fully subscribed to the Nazi ideology. He was appointed to the post of Professor of Gynaecology and Obstetrics at the University of Königsberg, on August 30, 1937. Dr. Clauberg published a large number of scientific works in his field of expertise. By 1940, he had written over fifty research papers and several books.

He was appointed to the post of Director of a gynaecological clinic in Chorzów, Upper Silesia in 1940. Clauberg approached Heinrich Himmler, the Head of the SS, asking to be allowed to sterilize women using injections of chemicals into the uterus. Himmler accepted his proposal and he was put to work in Ravensbrück Concentration Camp, in July 1942.

In December 1942, Dr. Clauberg arrived in Auschwitz Concentration Camp, and in April 1943, he carried out his experiments in Block 10, in Auschwitz Main Camp. His experiments sought a cheap and efficient method of making women sterile, using injections of a corrosive liquid into the uterus, without using anesthesia. Dr. Clauberg fled from the advancing Red Army in January 1945, and made his way back to Ravensbrück Concentration Camp, where he resumed his sterilization experiments. It was estimated that he conducted sterilization experiments on about 700 women.

In 1948, he was tried in the Soviet Union and sentenced to 25 years in prison. He was freed in an amnesty in 1955, and he returned to Kiel, then in West Germany. He boasted of his 'scientific achievements' and the Central Council of Jews denounced him, and he was re-arrested, in November 1955. Dr. Clauberg died on August 9, 1957, in a Kiel hospital, shortly before his trial was due to commence.

DEJACO, Walter, Born on June 19, 1909, in Mühlau, Innsbruck, Austria. He was an Architect by profession and he arrived in Auschwitz in June 1940, and worked in the Central Construction Board in Auschwitz, under the control of Karl Bischoff. Dejaco was one of the officers who visited Chełmno in September 1942, with Rudolf Höss, to witness the disposal of bodies using 'roasts.'

Walter Dejaco was responsible for drawing up the blueprints for the Crematoriums in Auschwitz-Birkenau. At the end of the Second World War he was taken prisoner by the Russians but was released during 1949 or 1950. He was discovered in January 1962, running a construction business at Reute, in the Tyrol. Charges against him were preferred in 1963, but were later dropped. He was brought to trial in Vienna in 1972, but was acquitted. He died in 1978.

DYLEWSKI, Klaus, Born on May 1, 1916, in Finkenwald near Stettin, the son of a miner. He spent his youth in Kattowitz. His father had opted for Polish citizenship after World War One. Dylewski attended the German elementary school, a private secondary school in Pless, and the *Gymnasium* in Nicolai, from which he graduated in 1935. In the spring of 1936, he enrolled at the Danzig Technological Institute to study aviation engineering. In the autumn of 1938, he passed the qualifying examination for aircraft engineers. After completing his third year he changed over to mechanical engineering.

At the outbreak of the Second World War, he volunteered for the *SS* Home Guard Danzig and he stayed in Danzig during the Polish campaign. When the campaign was over he applied for release from the *SS*, in order to continue his studies. His application was not granted and he was transferred to the 1st Death's Head Infantry Regiment, which was being assembled at Dachau. Klaus Dylewski took part in the French Campaign in 1940, and on September 1, 1940, he was transferred to the *SS* detachment at Auschwitz, where initially he served in the guard unit. After a four month leave period to continue his studies he returned to Auschwitz, where he was assigned as an interpreter in the investigation office in the camp's Political Department, where he served until the summer of 1944.

In August 1944, he was put in charge of a machine-construction division of an underground factory in Nuremberg, and at the end of the Second World War he made his way to Munich, wearing civilian clothes. He worked on a farm, and later as a gardener's assistant in Hamburg, and until 1952, used the name Peter Schmidt. At the end of 1947, following his employment in Hamburg, he enrolled at the University of East Berlin, and received a degree. In 1950, he found employment as a trade-school teacher in Düsseldorf, and after that he worked in the same city as a technical consultant. Dylewski stood trial in the Frankfurt am Main Auschwitz proceedings. He was found guilty of War Crimes and sentenced to 5 years hard labor. He died on April 1, 2012, in Hilden.

EMMERICH, Wilhelm, Born on February 7, 1916, in Tiefenbach. He served in Auschwitz Concentration Camp from July 1940, until January 1945, mainly in the Employment Department IIIa as *Arbeitsdienstführer*. He participated in the selection of Jewish deportees in Birkenau. He was transferred to Dora-Mittlebau in January 1945. He died on May 22, 1945, in the *Reserve-Lazarett* in Schwarmstedt.

ENTRESS, Dr. Friedrich, Born on December 8, 1914 in Posen, today Poznań in Poland, where his father worked in the university library. Immediately after completing his university studies in Posen, he was assigned to Gross-Rosen Concentration Camp where he performed the role of camp physician, from January 3, 1941, until December 10, 1941.

On December 11, 1941, he took a similar post at Auschwitz Concentration Camp. Using the 'euthanasia order' as the reason, he organized the mass killings of prisoners with injections of phenol, directly into the heart. In this 'work,' as in all other operations, he was concerned with the perfection and efficiency of the killing machinery. He later entrusted the inhumane task of killing the prisoners, by this method, to *SS* Medical Officers like Josef Klehr, while he determined who was to be killed.

From October 21, 1943, to July 25, 1944, he was the garrison physician at Mauthausen Concentration Camp, and then from August

3, 1944, until the early days of January 1945, he returned to Gross-Rosen Concentration Camp, this time as the Senior Camp Physician. He was sentenced to death by an American Military Tribunal at Dachau in 1946, and he was executed on May 28, 1947 in Landsberg.

ERTL, Fritz Karl, Born on August 31, 1908, in Breitbrune, near Linz, Austria. He studied architecture at university. He was a member of the Reich Labor Service from August 1, 1934 until the October of the same year. He joined the Nazi Party on June 1, 1938 and a year later joined the *Waffen-SS*. In November 1939, he joined a cavalry regiment stationed near Kraków, the 8th *SS* Regiment 'Florian Geyer.'

On May 15, 1940, he was assigned to the *Waffen-SS* Construction Office at Auschwitz Concentration Camp. On November 1, 1941, he was appointed to the post of deputy of the Construction Office under Karl Bischoff. Ertl was instructed to draw up plans for the expansion of Auschwitz. In August 1942, Ertl chaired a meeting with Kurt Prüfer, an engineer from the firm J. A. Töpf, who manufactured crematoriums, also present was Robert Kohler, a smokestack expert. At the end of the meeting it was decided to construct five furnaces for Crematorium II. Ertl produced plans for Crematoriums II, III, IV and V.

On January 25, 1943, Ertl departed from Auschwitz, his work there was finished, and he trained as an engineer officer at the Radischko Training School and later on in the same year he saw action in anti-partisan warfare in Russia and during February 1944, in Croatia. On March 19, 1944, he was transferred to the *SS WVHA*, attached to *Amtsgruppe C* (Construction) stationed in Hungary, where he remained until May 1944. On August 15, 1944, Ertl achieved the rank of *SS-Untersturmführer* and was appointed head of the Construction Office in Breslau. In early 1945, he was transferred to Arnstadt to construct a headquarters.

In May 1945, he was captured by American forces but was soon released. He settled in Austria where he was untroubled until 1968, when preliminary investigations were started in Reutte, into his role in building the gas chambers at Auschwitz. In 1971, along with fellow Austrian Walter Dejaco, they were both indicted as war criminals.

The trial which began on January 18, 1972, saw both men acquitted, as they were both obeying orders. Ertl was released on March 10, 1972.

FISCHER, Dr. Horst, Born on December 31, 1912, in Dresden. He served in various *Waffen-SS* units including the 5th *SS* Panzer Division Wiking. He was posted to Auschwitz Concentration Camp from November 1942 to January 1945. He performed the role of head physician at the Auschwitz III-Monowitz Camp. He took part in numerous selections of Jews on the railroad platform ramp. Following the evacuation of Auschwitz in January 1945, he was transferred to Ravensbrück Concentration Camp. He remained in East Berlin after the war, practising medicine. He was eventually tried by the GDR Supreme Court, where he was found guilty and sentenced to death. Dr. Fischer was executed by guillotine on July 8, 1966.

FRANK, Dr. Willi, Born on February 9, 1903, in Regensburg, the son of a judge. His father was transferred to Munich and Willi Frank graduated from high school in Munich in 1923. After working for six months, he took up his studies at the Munich Technical College on November 2, 1923. A week later, Frank stated that he took part in the march to the *Feldhernhalle*, in Munich, which became known as the 'Beer Hall Putsch,' the failed Nazi Party attempt to seize power.

In 1927, having completed his course in mechanical engineering, he found employment with the company Maffei and Siemens-Schuckert. The depression forced the Siemens-Schuckert division in which he worked to close down, and he found himself unemployed. In 1931, he enrolled in the school of dentistry at the University of Munich, and took his qualifying examination in December 1934. The following November, he opened his own dental clinic at Bad Cannstatt, having received his degree two months earlier.

He applied for admission into the *SS* and worked as a dentist on the staff of the divisional headquarters South West. In 1940, he volunteered for the *Waffen-SS* and served on the Russian Front until January 1942, when he became ill. After his recovery he was assigned to the *SS* dental station of the Dachau Concentration Camp. From Dachau he was transferred back to the Eastern Front, to the *SS* field hospital in Minsk, and from there to the *SS* dental station at Wewelsburg.

From March 1943, until August 1944 he was the chief dental officer at the Auschwitz Concentration Camp. He subsequently held the same position at Dachau Concentration Camp, until Christmas 1944. Between Christmas 1944, until the end of the Second World War he served on the front-line in Hungary. He was taken prisoner by the American Forces, and was released in January 1947, and he resumed his dental practice at Bad Cannstatt. Dr. Frank stood trial in the Frankfurt am Main Auschwitz proceedings. He was found guilty of War Crimes and sentenced to 7 years hard labor.

FRESEMANN, Martin, Born on May 29, 1919, in the locality of Steenfelde, Leer district. By vocation he was a commercial assistant. He completed eight years of compulsory schooling. He joined the *Waffen-SS* from April 1936. He served at Sachsenburg Concentration Camp. He was posted to Auschwitz from September 1941 until February 1943. He performed the role of a health service orderly (*SDG*) in the 2nd and 8th sentry companies. He was transferred to a reserve battalion of *SS* combat engineers. His subsequent fate is unknown.

FRITZSCH, Karl, Born on July 10, 1903, in Nassengrub. He joined the Nazi Party and the *SS*. He saw service in Dachau Concentration Camp from 1935 to 1940. In May 1940, he was transferred to Auschwitz Concentration Camp, where he occupied the post as the first *Schutzhaftlagerführer*. In January 1942, he was transferred to Flossenbürg Concentration Camp and in 1944, to Mittelbau-Dora Concentration Camp. He was killed in action in May 1945.

GRABNER, Maximilian, Born on October 2, 1905, in Vienna, Austria. He joined the Austrian police in 1930 and on the outbreak of the Second World War, worked for the State Police Office in Kattowitz. He was transferred to Auschwitz in 1940, where he was appointed the head of the Political Department. He served in this post until October 1943, when he was removed following investigations by Dr. Konrad Morgen. A trial against Grabner began in October 1944, in Weimar, where he stood accused of killing 2,000 prisoners, 'beyond the general guidelines.' The *SS Sondergericht* (Special

Court) found him guilty and sentenced him to 12 years imprisonment. Grabner was extradited to Poland where he stood on trial for War Crimes. The Supreme National Tribunal found him guilty and sentenced him to death. He was executed on December 12, 1947.

GRESE, Irma, Ida, Ilse, Born on October 7, 1923, in Wrechen, Mecklenburg-Strelitz, the daughter of a dairy worker, she was the third born of five children. During 1936, her mother committed suicide after discovering that her husband Alfred had had an affair with a local pub owner's daughter. Irma Grese left school during 1938, and she found employment for two years as an assistant nurse in a sanatorium run by the *SS*. From mid-1942, she was a guard at the Concentration Camp for women at Ravensbrück. In March 1943, she was transferred to Auschwitz Concentration Camp, where she treated her charges in a most brutal fashion. In the second half of 1944, she was promoted to the role of *Rapportführerin*.

In January 1945, Grese accompanied a prisoner transport from Auschwitz to Ravensbrück Concentration Camp. In March 1945, she was posted to Bergen-Belsen Concentration Camp. She was arrested by the British Army on April 17, 1945. She was tried by a British Military Court, along with other members of the *SS*-Garrison of Bergen-Belsen. She was found guilty of War Crimes and was hanged on December 13, 1945, at Hamelin Prison.

GROENING, Oskar, Born on June 10, 1921, in Nienburg, Lower Saxony, the son of a skilled textile worker. After school, Groening trained as a bank clerk before joining the *Waffen-SS*, in 1940. He worked as a book-keeper until September 1942, when he was transferred to Auschwitz Concentration Camp. Groening's banking background was put to good use at the camp, where he was made responsible for the sorting, counting and transfer to Berlin, of the currencies brought by the arriving deportees to Auschwitz. In 1944, he was transferred to a front-line unit, where he saw active service in the Ardennes. He was wounded and later captured by the British Army on June 10, 1945, which was his birthday.

He was sent to the United Kingdom as a Prisoner of War, but was returned to Germany in 1947, where he found employment in a glass factory, where he worked his way up to become head of personnel. In September 2014, he was charged by State Prosecutors as having been an accessory to murder. The trial commenced on April 20, 2015 at the Lüneburg Regional Court. On July 15, 2015, he was found guilty and sentenced to serve 4 years in prison.

HANDLER, Werner, Born on July 27, 1913, in Leipzig. He was a bricklayer by vocation. He arrived in Auschwitz during October 1940, and he stayed there until January 1945. Initially he performed the role of *Blockführer*. From June 1943, he was the head of the prisoner kitchen in Birkenau. He was transferred to the Ravensbrück Concentration Camp. He was extradited to Poland after the war. He was found guilty of War Crimes and executed in March 1949.

HANTL, Emil, Born on December 14, 1902, in Mährisch-Lotschnau, the son of a factory worker. After completion of his schooling he was apprenticed in a bakery in Zwittau, where he later found employment in a textile factory. After a period of unemployment he performed agricultural labor and also joined a gymnastic association. After the incorporation of the '*Sudeten* District,' he, like all the members of the club, was automatically incorporated into the *SS*.

He was inducted into the *Waffen-SS* on January 26, 1940, and he was posted to the guard unit at Auschwitz Concentration Camp on August 1, 1940. At the camp he guarded the prisoner work details, worked in the hospital and he also served in Auschwitz III-Monowitz in the summer of 1944, and at the end of 1944 in the Jaworzno sub-camp.

In January 1945, Hantl deserted from his company at Beuthen, during the 'death marches' from Auschwitz, but afraid of being picked up as a deserter, he attached himself to an *SS* unit. He also deserted from this unit and he finally joined an *Organisation Todt* unit. He was taken prisoner, still serving as a member of the *Organisation Todt*, but was released after three weeks. The papers issued to him by the *Organisation Todt*, enabled him to keep his membership of the *Waffen-SS*, and his service at Auschwitz, a secret. After the war he worked as an agricultural laborer and then as a weaver at Marktredwitz. Emil Hantl stood trial in the Frankfurt am Main Auschwitz proceedings. He was found guilty of War Crimes and sentenced to 3 years, 6 months hard labor. He died on August 18, 1984, in Plochingen.

HARTJENSTEIN, Friedrich 'Fritz', Born on July 3, 1905, in Peine, near Brunswick. He commanded a platoon in 1938, at the Sachsenhausen Concentration Camp, and then during 1939, he was a manager at the Niederhagen-Wewelsburg labor camp. Between 1940 and 1942, he served in the *SS* Death's Head Division. During 1942, he was appointed Commandant of the *SS* garrison and from November 1943, he was the Commandant of Auschwitz II.

In 1944, he was transferred to the post of commandant at Natzweiler-Struthof Concentration Camp, he was arrested at the end of the war and was tried by the British at Wuppertal. He was found guilty of War Crimes and sentenced to death on June 5, 1946. He was again put on trial by the French authorities in Metz, and was again sentenced to death on July 2, 1954. He died in prison on October 20, 1954, before the execution could be carried out.

HÖCKER, Karl, Born on December 11, 1911, in Engershausen, near Lübbecke, the son of a building contractor, who was killed during World War I. After completing the *Volksschule*—elementary school—he served a four year apprenticeship in a business firm. After a period of unemployment lasting from the autumn of 1930, to the end of 1932, he was assigned to a work project, which lasted until April 1933.

In June 1933, he found work with a county savings bank in Preussich-Oldendorf; after that he worked at the county savings bank in Lübbecke. He joined the *SS* in October 1933, because as a member of the county bank he was forced to join a Party organization. The *SA* rejected him, so he joined the *SS*.

Karl Höcker joined the Nazi Party in 1937, and two years later in November 1939, he was assigned to the 9th *SS* Infantry Regiment in Danzig; six months later, he was transferred to an *SS* Death's Head unit in the Neuengamme Concentration Camp. At the end of 1943,

Höcker was appointed to the post of adjutant at Lublin Concentration Camp in Poland.

A year later, in 1944, he was transferred to Auschwitz Concentration Camp, where he performed the role of adjutant to Commandant, Richard Baer, who had just assumed control of the camp in May 1944. Karl Höcker stayed in Auschwitz until the evacuation took place in January 1945. He was then appointed to the post of adjutant at the Nordhausen Concentration Camp. The end of the war saw him as a member of a combat unit in the Hamburg area. He was arrested by the British Forces but was released at the end of January 1946.

Six years later, Karl Höcker brought charges against himself to the State Attorney of Bielefeld in order to obtain a de-Nazification hearing. On January 19, 1953, he received a nine-month sentence, but the amnesty law of 1954, saved him from serving his sentence. After being released, he became the chief cashier at the county savings bank in Lübbecke.

Karl Höcker stood trial in the Frankfurt am Main Auschwitz proceedings. He was found guilty of War Crimes and sentenced to 7 years hard labor. He died on January 30, 2000. In 2006, an album of photographs containing 116 photographs from his time at Auschwitz, was donated to the United States Holocaust Museum in Washington DC.

HOFMANN, Franz Johann, Born on April 5, 1906, in Hof, Saale, the son of a butcher. He left school in 1919, and went into the upholstery trade. From 1923 onwards, he held various jobs such as a waiter and a hotel porter. He joined the Nazi Party and the SS in mid-1932. His father ran an inn frequented by Party Members. After the Nazis came to power he took an auxiliary-police training course and on July 1, 1933, he joined the force. In September 1933, he was assigned to guard duty at Dachau Concentration Camp. On December 1, 1942, he was transferred to the Auschwitz Concentration Camp, where he became the third officer in charge, and in November 1943, he was made first officer in charge of Auschwitz I. In the interim he was acting officer in charge of the Gypsy compound in Birkenau.

In May 1944, he was transferred to the Natzweiler-Struthof Concentration Camp and at the end of the War he was in Guttenbach / Neckar and he attended a de-Nazification hearing in Rothenburg ob der Tauber. In December 1961, a court in Munich sentenced him to two life terms for two murders committed at Dachau Concentration Camp. Franz Johann Hofmann stood trial again in the Frankfurt am Main Auschwitz proceedings. He was found guilty of War Crimes and sentenced to life term with hard labor. He died on August 14, 1973, in Straubing prison.

HÖSSLER, Franz, Born on February 4, 1906 in Oberdorf. He left school to become a photographer and was later employed in a warehouse. After a period of unemployment he joined the Nazi Party and the *SS* in November 1932. He was assigned to Dachau Concentration Camp and in June 1940, Franz Hössler was transferred to Auschwitz Concentration Camp where he managed the kitchens.

In 1942, Hössler commanded the prisoners' squad at Międzybrodzie, near Żywiec, where prisoners built a rest-home for the *SS*, the so-called Sola-Hütte. The construction of the *SS* Resort commenced in 1940, and it was officially opened on April 21, 1941. Additional building work took place during 1942, under the command of Hössler. During September 1942, Hössler, Dejaco, and Höss went to Chełmno to witness the cremation methods being tested there by Paul Blobel. Hössler was immediately put in charge of the Jewish *Sonderkommando* that was used between September and November 1942, to exhume the mass graves adjacent to Bunker I and Bunker II, the converted farmhouses in Birkenau. The corpses once exhumed were then burnt on 'roasts' as witnessed in Chełmno.

From August 27, 1943, to January 1944, he was the camp leader of the Women's Camp in Birkenau, and after a short spell on one of Dachau's sub-camps, he returned once again to Auschwitz to manage the *Stammlager*, until the camp was evacuated in January 1945. He was transferred to Dora-Mittlebau Concentration Camp, and from there he went to Bergen-Belsen Concentration Camp.

The British Military Court at Lüneburg passed the death sentence on Franz Hössler for War Crimes, on November 17, 1945, at the trial of the *SS* garrison of Dachau Concentration Camp. He was executed on December 13, 1945, at Hameln Prison.

JAMBOR, Eduard, Born on July 13, 1900. He worked at Auschwitz Concentration Camp as a clerk to the *SS* Garrison surgeon. He was transferred to Berlin after the evacuation in January 1945. He died on July 24, 1945.

JOSTEN, Heinrich, Born on December 11, 1893, in Malmedy, which was German territory until 1918, and was part of Belgium until 1940, when the Germans invaded Belgium, and Malmedy was incorporated into the Reich. Heinrich Josten joined the *Allgemeine-SS* in 1933, and the Nazi Party shortly afterwards.

On August 20, 1939, he joined the *Waffen-SS,* and was assigned to Flossenburg Concentration Camp, where he served in the guard unit. After the outbreak of the Second World War, he spent a brief period on front-line duty in a *Waffen-SS* unit fighting in Poland. He was subsequently posted to Sachsenhausen Concentration Camp where he again served as a guard.

In November 1940, he was transferred to Auschwitz Concentration Camp, where he was appointed Commander of the 3rd *SS* Sentry Company. In December he was assigned as the Commander of the 2nd *SS* Sentry Company, a post he held until early 1941. In April 1941, he was appointed to the post of the Director of Arms and Military Equipment Section at Auschwitz. In this post he was responsible for the distribution of all firearms and technical military equipment for the entire *SS* garrison at Auschwitz.

Some time in late 1942, he was appointed to Department IIIa which was responsible for prisoner labor work gangs, and a year later in October 1943, he was made Deputy *Lagerführer* of the Auschwitz I Main Camp, succeeding Franz Johann Hofmann, and he was the last person to hold this position. On January 18, 1945, Josten was transferred to the Nordhausen Concentration Camp and in April 1945, he was subsequently posted to the Bergen-Belsen Concentration Camp, where he remained until the camp was liberated by the British Army.

He was extradited to Poland to stand trial in Kraków before the Supreme National Tribunal, where he was accused of taking part in the mass gassings of Hungarian Jews in Birkenau during 1944. He was also charged with shooting thirty-five inmates at the Auschwitz Main Camp and for taking part in the hangings. On December 22, 1947, he was sentenced to death and he was executed on January 24, 1948, in Montelupich Prison in Kraków.

JOTHANN, Werner, Born on May 18, 1907, in Eldenburg. He studied at university to become a construction engineer. He joined the *Allgemeine-SS* in May 1933, and joined the Nazi Party on May 1, 1937. He worked in a construction firm for several years while serving in the *SS* as a part-time member.

On March 31, 1941, he was called up for active service within the *Waffen-SS*. He was assigned to the Auschwitz Concentration Camp, where he served as a guard with the 5th *SS* Sentry Company. He served in various guard companies within Auschwitz-Birkenau. In April 1943, he was assigned to the Construction Department working under Karl Bischoff.

In November 1943, he took over the post of Director of the Special Construction Department at Auschwitz Concentration Camp and was thus responsible for general construction projects in the camp as well as the water supply there.

In the spring of 1944, he was informed of the planned liquidation of the Hungarian Jews, and was ordered to carry out a program of improvements in all four crematoria in Birkenau. He ensured that the firm J. A. Töpf installed additional elevators in Crematoria IV and V. Werner Jothann stayed at Auschwitz until the camp's evacuation on January 18, 1945, when he was posted to the *SS* Construction School for officers in Arolsen, where he remained until April 19, 1945. Jothann was never brought to trial for his activities in Auschwitz Concentration Camp.

KADUK, Oswald, Born on August 26, 1906, in Königshütte, Upper Silesia, the son of a blacksmith. He had five brothers, all of whom were killed during the Second World War. Oswald Kaduk attended public school in Königshütte and when his schooling was completed he became a butcher. For a year and a half he worked in the municipal slaughterhouse of his hometown. In 1927, after a brief period of unemployment he became a member of the municipal fire department of Königshütte, where he remained until being called up, after having volunteered to serve in the *Waffen-SS*, in the spring of 1940.

In 1942, after a fairly long illness, he was transferred to the guard detachment of the Auschwitz Concentration Camp. His first assignment there was that of block-leader. Later he became leader of a work detail. He remained at the camp until its evacuation in January 1945.

After the end of the War he assumed a false identity and found employment in a sugar refinery in Löbau. In December 1946, he was arrested by Soviet Millitary Police, after a former inmate of the camp had recognized him. On March 24, 1947, he was sentenced to death, but this was adjusted to a term of imprisonment of twenty-five years, by a Soviet Military Tribunal, for being a member of the *SS*. He was released from Bautzen prison on April 26, 1956 and he moved to West Berlin, where he worked as a male nurse. His patients called him *'Papa Kaduk.'*

Oswald Kaduk stood trial again in the Frankfurt am Main Auschwitz proceedings. He was found guilty of War Crimes and sentenced to a life term with hard labor. He died on May 31, 1997, in Langelsheim.

KIRSCHNECK, Hans, Born on June 14, 1909, in Eger, a small town in Czechoslovakia. When he completed his schooling he went to Prague University to study engineering. At the age of twenty-four he joined the *'Patriotsche Front der Sudetendeutschen'* which was headed by Konrad Henlein in 1933. Kirschneck's father was a German and young Hans was convinced that the Sudetenland should be part of Hitler's Reich. In 1933, he moved to Germany and joined the *SS* and in October 1938, he joined the Nazi Party.

In 1940, he joined the *Waffen-SS*, and was assigned to serve in the 4th *SS* Infantry Regiment. On May 15, 1942, he was posted to Auschwitz Concentration Camp, where he served as an engineer attached to the Construction Department. Hans Kirschneck worked on the construction of the Crematoriums in Birkenau, and along with Josef Janisch, they worked on the improvements program within Crematoria IV and Crematoria V. He worked on these up to May 15, 1944.

Kirschneck served for a brief time as a teacher at the Construction School in Arolsen and was then subsequently posted to the Construction Office of the *SS* and Police '*Silesia.*' In September 1944, he returned briefly to Auschwitz Concentration Camp, but was released from the *SS*, to serve as an engineer for the armed forces, the same month. His fate is unknown.

KITT, Bruno, Born August 9, 1906, in Heilsburg, Poland. He was Doctor of Medicine, head physician of the Women's Hospital in Auschwitz II-Birkenau, where he carried out selections of sick women for the gas chambers. He was also a physician at the Neuengamme Concentration Camp. At the trial of the Neuengamme camp garrison, the British Military Court found him guilty of War Crimes and sentenced him to death. He was hanged on October 8, 1946, in Hameln Prison.

KLEHR, Josef, Born on October 17, 1904, in Langenau, Upper Silesia, the son of a teacher at a reform school. After completion of his compulsory schooling he was apprenticed as a carpenter. In 1932, he joined the *Allgemeine-SS*, because of economic hardships. In 1934, he applied for a job at his father's institute, but there were no vacancies. Later however, he did obtain employment there as a porter. At the end of 1934, he found a job as a male nurse in a Silesian nursing home, and in mid-1938, he became an assistant prison guard at Wollau.

He was recruited into the *Waffen-SS*, after receiving his call-up notice in August 1939. He reached Auschwitz Concentration Camp, after stints in Buchenwald and then Dachau Concentration Camps, in January 1941. In Auschwitz he was assigned to the medical corps, and was later detailed to work in the Disinfection Squad. He also served in the Gleiwitz sub-camp.

After the evacuation in January 1945, he served briefly in Czechoslovakia, and on May 2, 1945, was taken prisoner by the American Forces in Austria. His *SS* membership earned Klehr a three-and-a-half-year term in a labor camp sentence by the Goeppingen de-Nazification court, but he won an appeal against this judgement. After this he worked as a carpenter in Brunswick.

Josef Klehr stood trial again in the Frankfurt am Main Auschwitz proceedings. He was found guilty of War Crimes and sentenced to a life term with an additional 15-years hard labor term. He died on August 23, 1988, in Leiferde.

KLEIN, Dr. Fritz, Born on November 1888, in Zeiden, Rumania, where he was a member of a German minority. He studied medicine and completed his military service in Rumania, finishing his studies in Budapest, after World War One ended. He lived and worked as a doctor in Siebenbürgen, where he also joined the Nazi Party.

In 1940, he once again served in the Rumanian Army, but in 1943, he became a German citizen and in May 1943, he joined the *Waffen-SS* and was posted to Yugoslavia. On December 15, 1943, he arrived in Auschwitz Concentration Camp, where at first he served as a camp doctor in the Women's Camp in Birkenau. Subsequently he worked as a camp doctor in the Gypsy Camp. He participated in numerous selections on the ramp, and for a short time he was also a doctor in the *Stammlager*.

In January 1945, Dr. Klein was transferred to the Neuengamme Concentration Camp, and then on to the Bergen-Belsen Concentration Camp. When the British Forces liberated the camp on April 15, 1945, he was taken into custody. At the trial of the Bergen-Belsen garrison at Lüneburg, he was found guilty of War Crimes, sentenced to death and hanged on December 13, 1945.

KNITTEL, Kurt, Born on September 23, 1910. He was the manager of Section VI—*Kulturabteilung*, in the commandant's office at Auschwitz Concentration Camp. He supervised the training and political education of the SS guard garrison. After the evacuation of the camp in January 1945, he was transferred to Mittelbau-Dora Concentration Camp.

KRAMER, Josef, Born on November 10, 1906, in Munich. He joined the Nazi Party in 1931, and a year later in 1932, he joined the SS. Kramer was employed in Concentration Camps from 1934, he was in

Dachau, Sachsenhausen and Mauthausen, before being sent to Auschwitz Concentration Camp in May 1940, as Adjutant to Rudolf Höss. In November 1940, he became the Camp Manager at the Natzweiler Concentration Camp and in October 1941, he was appointed as the Commandant of this camp. Josef Kramer returned to Auschwitz Concentration Camp, where he was Commandant of Auschwitz II-Birkenau from May 8, 1944 until November 1944. He was then transferred to the Bergen-Belsen Concentration Camp, to the post of Commandant. When the British Army liberated Bergen-Belsen Concentration Camp on April 15, 1945, they took Josef Kramer prisoner. The British Military Court in Lüneburg sentenced Josef Kramer to death on November 17, 1945, at the trial of members of the *SS* garrison at Bergen-Belsen Concentration Camp. He was executed at Hameln Prison, on December 13, 1945.

KRATZER, Theodor, Born on October 30, 1914, in Nuremberg. When he completed his education he became a bank clerk in a small local bank. In October 1933, at the age of eighteen he joined the Hitler Youth where he served as a youth leader until July 31, 1934. Whilst he was serving in the Hitler Youth he saw Hitler speak at a rally and in March 1934, he joined the *Allgemeine-SS*, and served as an unpaid part-time member.

On October 28, 1935, he joined the German Army and served with the 17th, 53rd, and 115th Artillery Regiments until March 1938. During this period, Kratzer decided to join the Nazi Party, and he joined with a group of friends on May 1, 1937. In April 1938, he became a full-time member of the *Allgemeine-SS*, and was assigned to the 2nd Company of *Standarte 'Deutschland.'* On April 21, 1939, now with his commission, he volunteered for service at Buchenwald Concentration Camp, where he served in the administration department until March 1941.

He was transferred to Auschwitz Concentration Camp on March 13, 1941, where he was appointed to the post of Director of the Section for the Administration of Prisoners Property. This section was established to store and account for the property belonging to the registered prisoners in the camp. This section was also responsible for the confiscation and disposal of the property of victims murdered in the gas chambers. This also included valuables, money, jewellery, and gold teeth from those victims. All this property was sorted and stored in the section at Birkenau, known as '*Kanada*,' and Kratzer was in charge of this section along with his deputy *SS-Hauptsturmführer* Georg Höcker.

Kratzer remained in this position until the camp was evacuated on January 18, 1945. From Auschwitz, Kratzer was transferred to the Dirlewanger Brigade, the notorious *SS* Penal Brigade, under Oskar Dirlewanger, made up of former convicts and even former concentratrion camp inmates. His eventual fate is unknown.

KREMER, Dr. Johann Paul, Born on December 26, 1883, in Stelberg / Cologne. He was an associate professor of anatomy at the University of Münster and had qualified for a professorship with a work called 'The Alteration of Muscle Tissue under Conditions of Hunger.' In August 1942, he went to Auschwitz Concentration Camp to carry out further research on hunger. For this purpose he selected so-called 'Moslems,' people who suffered from malnutrition and were extremely weakened, both spiritually and physically. During his stay in Auschwitz, Kremer kept a journal which was published after the War.

After the War, Dr. Kremer was extradited to Poland where he stood on trial for War Crimes. The Supreme National Tribunal found him guilty and sentenced him to 10 years in prison. He was returned to Germany and sentenced to another 10 years in prison. He died on January 8, 1965.

LANGEFELD, Joanna, Born on March 5, 1900, in Kupferdreh, the daughter of a blacksmith. In 1924, she moved to Mülheim and she married Wilhem Langefeld, but he died two years later from a lung disease. She moved to Düsseldorf where she gave birth to a son. Joanna Langefeld joined the Nazi Party in 1937, and then the *SS*. In March 1938, she applied for the post of a camp guard in the Lichtenburg Concentration Camp, which was the first *SS* run camp for women. She was transferred to the Ravensbrück Concentration Camp for women in May 1939.

In April 1942, Langefeld was transferred to Auschwitz Concentration Camp as the chief female supervisor, although Rudolf Höss was of the opinion she was unsuited for the role and placed a male *SS* officer in the role. From October 1942, she was transferred back to Ravensbrück Concentration Camp, but she was dismissed for being sympathetic to Polish inmates in April 1943.

On December 20, 1945, Langefeld was arrested by the American Army and in September 1946, she was extradited to Poland, where she stood on trial for War Crimes, before the Supreme National Tribunal. On December 23, 1946, she escaped from prison and found refuge in a convent. Around 1957, she returned to West Germany and lived with her sister in Munich. She died on January 26, 1974, in Augsburg.

LUCAS, Dr. Franz, Born on September 15, 1911, in Osnabrück, the son of a butcher. After his graduation from high school he decided to study Philology, but after four terms he switched to medicine, studying first in Münster, then in Rostock and Danzig. He joined the *SA* in 1933, and four years later on May 1, 1937, he joined the Nazi Party. He joined the *Allgemeine-SS* on November 15, 1937. He took his medical state examination in Danzig in 1942, the year in which he obtained his medical doctorate. At the end of a two month training course at the medical academy of the *Waffen-SS* at Graz, he was promoted to the rank of *Hauptscharführer* and became a doctor for the troops who served in a signals unit in Nuremburg. On December 15, 1943, he was transferred to the ecomomic and administrative headquarters of the *Gestapo (AMT DIII)*, and thereafter he became a Concentration Camp medical officer. At the end of 1943, or early 1944, Dr. Franz Lucas was transferred to Auschwitz Concentration Camp, where he says he spent only five months. From Auschwitz he was transferred to Mauthausen Concentration Camp in Austria.

In early 1945, he was threatened with a court-martial at the Sachsenhausen Concentration Camp. He escaped in March 1945, and with the help of a former prisoner from Norway, he was able to hide out until the end of the Second World War,when he went to Elmshorn. In Elmshorn he became chief of the local hospital's gynaecological clinic. He was discharged from this post in 1963, because he had failed to reveal his Concentration Camp past, when he was hired. After his dismissal he entered private practice. Dr. Franz Lucas stood trial in the Frankfurt am Main Auschwitz proceedings. He was found guilty of War Crimes and sentenced to 3 years and 3 months hard labor. He died on December 7, 1994, in Elmshorn.

MAIER, Franz-Xaver, Born on January 7, 1913, in Hausham. He served in the SS Death's Head Division at Buchenwald Concentration Camp. He transferred to Auschwitz in 1940, and was appointed to the post of second *Schützlagerführer*. He only held the post for a few months only, for he was charged with corrupt practices and court-martialed.

MANDEL, Maria, Born on January 10, 1912, in Münzkirchen, Upper Austria, the daughter of a shoemaker. After the *Anschluss* she moved to Munich, and joined the Nazi Party and the SS. She served in the Lichtenburg Concentration Camp, and on May 15, 1939, she was posted to the Ravensbrück Concentration Camp. On October 7, 1942, she was assigned to Auschwitz Concentration Camp, where she succeeded Joanna Langefeld, as *SS-Lagerführerin*. Maria Mandel was a music lover and established the Women's orchestra in the camp. In November 1944, she was transferred to the Dachau Concentration Camp, sub-camp Mühldorf. She returned to her home and was arrested by the US Army on August 10, 1945. Mandel was extradited to Poland where she stood on trial for War Crimes. The Supreme National Tribunal found her guilty and sentenced her to death. She was executed on January 24, 1948.

MENGELE, Dr. Josef, Born on March 16, 1911 in Günzburg, Bavaria. His father Carl Mengele ran an agricultural machinery factory, the largest employer in that area. At the age of 20, he joined the *Stahlhelm* (Steel Helmet), a militant nationalist organization formed by soldiers who had fought in World War One. In 1934, he joined the SA, and three years later joined the Nazi Party and the SS.

A convinced National Socialist while still a student in university, he studied in Munich, Bonn, Frankfurt, and Vienna. He completed his doctoral dissertation in 1935, at the Anthropology Institute of the philosophy department of the University of Munich; the title was 'The Racial Morphological Investigation of the Front Submaxilla Section in Four Racial Groups.' During 1938, he undertook work for his medical doctorate on genealogical research in lip, jaw, and gum fissures.

As a member of the newly founded *Institut für Erbbiologie und Rassenhygiene*—Institute of Hereditary Biology and Race Research, where he specialized in the study of twins and racial pedigrees, he volunteered for the *Waffen-SS* and served as a medical officer in France and Russia. He was awarded the Iron Cross 2nd Class and was wounded on the Eastern Front.

Declared unfit for frontline service he was transferred to Auschwitz Concentration Camp on May 30, 1943, where he performed the role of Camp Doctor of the Gypsy Family Camp in Birkenau. Mengele conducted innumerable selections of victims, proving himself to be a ruthless and pitiless enforcer of the 'Final Solution to the Jewish Question' at Auschwitz. In the camp Mengele continued to pursue his pseudo-scientific research into presumed racial differences, anomalies of giants and dwarfs, hunchbacks and other deformities. People afflicted with any sort of physical deformity would be killed for him,on their arrival in the Concentration Camp, in order to provide fresh material for his research. There was a special dissection ward where autopsies of murdered camp inmates were performed. Mengele was especially interested in medical experiments on twins, hoping to find a method of creating a race of blue-eyed Aryans that would realize the grotesque dreams of Nazi racial science. After the war, Mengele managed to escape from a British Forces internment hospital and with the aid of false papers fled via Rome to Buenos Aires. Mengele became one of the world's most wanted war criminals. Over the years Mengele was reported to have been seen by various eye-witnesses in Argentina, Brazil and Paraguay, and substantial rewards were offered for his capture. Mengele was naturalized as a Paraguayan citizen in November 1959.

Mengele was sought by the West German government for the next three decades but all efforts to locate and arrest him failed and in 1985, after a large reward had been offered in Israel for information leading to his arrest, it was announced that Mengele had most probably died in a swimming accident in Embu, Brazil, on February 7, 1979. In July 1985, a body presumed to be that of Mengele, was exhumed in Brazil and an autopsy by an international panel of forensic pathologists was carried out. They concluded that there was a high probability that it was indeed Mengele's last remains.

MEYER, Max, Member of the SS. He was transferred from the Inspectorate of Concentration Camps to Auschwitz Concentration Camp in 1940. He performed the role of the manager of the camp administration (*Verwaltungsführer*).

MÖCKEL, Karl, Born on January 9, 1901, in Klingental. Karl Möckel worked in various SS administrative positions and he was also head of Department W III in the *WVHA*. In April 1943, he took over from Willi Burger as administrative Director in Auschwitz. He held that post until the camp was evacuated in January 1945. He was tried by the Supreme National Tribunal in Kraków and he was found guilty of war crimes. He was executed on January 24, 1948.

MOLL, Otto, Born on March 4, 1915, in Hochen-Schönberg. Moll joined the SS on May 1, 1935 and served in Sachsenhausen Concentration Camp, before transferring to Auschwitz during May 1941. At first he supervised agricultural work, then he was leader of the prisoners' penal company (*Strafkompanie*). During 1942, he was in charge of the Jewish *Sonderkommando* which cremated corpses in pits near Bunkers I and II in Birkenau, when the purpose built facilities were not quite ready.

He was awarded the War Cross of Merit, First Class with Swords on April 30, 1943 for his criminal activities. He was manager of the Fürstengrube, sub-camp from September 1943 until March 1944. From March to May 1944, he was the manager of another Auschwitz sub-camp, Gleiwitz I. He was recalled from Gleiwitz sub-camp by Rudolf Höss, to assume the position of chief manager of the crematoria in Birkenau, which was being readied for '*Aktion Höss*,' the liquidation of the Jews from Hungary, in May 1944. Moll was also in charge of cremating corpses in the open.

Moll was the author of a plan to liquidate the gas chambers, crematoria and the Birkenau camp, using bombers and artillery, the so-called 'Moll Plan.' Moll returned to Gleiwitz sub-camp when the mass extermination of the Hungarian Jews ended. In January 1945, he was in charge of the evacuation of prisoners from Gleiwitz. He was posted to Dachau Concentration Camp and was put on trial, as part of the *SS* garrison at Dachau. He was found guilty of War Crimes and was sentenced to death on December 13, 1945. He was executed at Landsberg on May 28, 1946.

MULKA, Robert, Born on April 12, 1895, in Hamburg, the son of a post office assistant. After completion of the *Volksschule* and *Realschule*—a technical high school and a year of army service, he served an apprenticeship in a business firm. In August 1914, he volunteered to serve in the army; he served in France, Russia and Turkey, and he rose to the rank of lieutenant.

After the end of the Great War he joined the Baltic Guard, which was a right-wing paramilitary outfit. In 1920, he returned to Hamburg and business life. That same year the Hamburg District Court sentenced Mulka to eight months imprisonment and two years' loss of rights for failing to account for funds confiscated by him in the Baltic. During 1931, he founded his own import-export business. Mulka joined the Nazi Party in 1940 and later joined the *Waffen-SS*. He was assigned to Auschwitz at the beginning of 1942. In May 1942, he performed the role of adjutant to Commandant Rudolf Höss. He was arrested in March 1943, for making a critical remark about a speech by Propaganda Minister Josef Goebbels, but was released shortly afterwards.

He returned to Hamburg and volunteered for the *SS* North Sea command, until he was transferred to an *SS* Engineers school in the vicinity of Prague. He fell ill and was granted home leave and it was in Hamburg that he saw out the war. Between June 8, 1945, and March 28, 1948, he was interned in a number of camps. Mulka stood trial in the Frankfurt am Main Auschwitz proceedings. He was found guilty of War Crimes and sentenced to 14 years hard labor. He died on April 26, 1969, in Hamburg.

MÜNCH, Dr. Hans, Born on May 14, 1911, in Freiburg im Breisgau. His father Ernst was a forestry official. Münch studied medicine in Tübingen in 1933, and in 1936, he was awarded a scholarship and started working at the Institute of Hygiene in Munich and then in 1937 he worked in the main hospital in Munich.

Two years earlier in 1935, Münch had joined the *NSKK*, the National Socialist Motor Corps, and he joined the Nazi Party on May 1, 1937. He was awarded his doctorate in the summer of 1938 and the following year he performed emergency duties, where he took over small country practices, covering for doctors who had been drafted into the German Army. He worked in Steingarden until late 1940, then in Lechbruck until June 1943.

In June 1943, he applied to join the *SS*, and he was accepted and was employed as a physician in the medical department of the *SS* Main Office in Berlin. He trained briefly with a medical unit and then served in a military hospital. His experience as a bacteriologist with the Institute of Hygiene was noticed and he was seconded to serve in a Concentration Camp, though Münch maintained after the war, that he did not know where he was being sent to.

In September 1944, he arrived at Auschwitz Concentration Camp and he was assigned to the *SS* Hygiene department in the Rajsko sub-camp, where he was responsible for the prevention of epidemics. Münch claimed at his post-war trial that he became friends with Dr. Josef Mengele, who had arrived in May 1943, and it was Mengele who told him the true nature of Auschwitz Concentration Camp. This convinced Münch to request a transfer from Auschwitz, and he approached Dr. Eduard Wirths, with a request not to take part in selections. Wirths said he must take part, though Münch refused and said that he would only take orders from his superior Enno Lolling, the Head of the Medical Department *Amt D III*, in Berlin. Dr. Wirths backed down and Münch was allowed to continue working in the *SS* Hygiene department in Rajsko.

In June 1944, he was officially appointed as the deputy to *SS-Hauptsturmführer* Bruno Weber in the *SS* Hygiene department and used his position to help a number of prisoners escape from the gas chambers. When Auschwitz was evacuated in early January 1945,

Münch left with a group of prisoners and made their way to the Gross Rosen Concentration Camp, where they were joined by Dr. Mengele. During the 'death march' Münch supplied medicine and food to the prisoners and did what he could to help as many prisoners as he could.

Münch remained in Gross Rosen until March 1945, when he was transferred to Dachau Concentration Camp where he continued his work as a bacteriologist, but he left the camp just before the American Forces liberated the camp. In the summer of 1945, Münch gave himself up and reported to an American internment camp near Stuttgart. Within two months however, he was transferred to an internment camp for *SS* officers.

He was extradited to Poland from Germany in 1946, and on November 24, 1947, he stood trial before the Supreme National Tribunal in Kraków along with thirty-nine other members of the Auschwitz garrison. A number of witnesses came forward to testify in Münch's favour, they told the court that he helped many prisoners whenever he could, and risked his own life to help them. As a result of these testimonies Münch was the only defendant to be acquitted of all charges on December 16, 1947.

His acquittal was finally made official in March 1948, and he was released and returned to Germany, where he settled in Bavaria. He worked at a local hygiene company and he was called as a witness for the Auschwitz Trial held in Frankfurt am Main in 1964. He was interviewed many times by jounalists and by television documentary makers about his experiences at Auschwitz and his friendship with Dr. Josef Mengele. Münch even returned to Auschwitz for a documentary and signed a statement regarding the existence of gas chambers at Birkenau to combat Holocaust Denial. Hans Münch died in Allgau, Bavaria in 2001.

MÜHSFELDT, Erich. Born on February 18, 1913, in Neubrück, Brandenburg. He joined the *SS* in 1940, and was posted to Auschwitz Concentration Camp in August 1940. Initially he supervised a prisoners' squad and then was *a Blockführer*. He was transferred to the Lublin Concentration Camp on November 15, 1941. He was in charge of the crematorium at Lublin, and he took an active part in the mass murder of Jewish workers on November 3, 1943. This *Aktion* was known as *Aktion Erntefest* (Harvest Festival), and some 18, 000 Jews from the

Old Airfield Camp and the Lipowa Street camp were executed by shooting in specially dug pits near the crematorium. Mühsfeldt was transferred back to Auschwitz Concentration Camp in June 1944, he supervised the Jewish *Sonderkommando* in Crematoriums II and III, and later he became the overall manager of all of the crematoriums.

After the War, an American Military Court passed the life sentence upon him on January 23, 1947, for War Crimes committed at Flossenburg Concentration Camp. Mühsfeldt was extradited to Poland where he stood on trial for War Crimes. The Supreme National Tribunal found him guilty and sentenced him to death. He was executed on January 28, 1948.

ONTL, Friedrich, Born on August 25, 1909. He was the manager of the store in the *SS* hospital at Auschwitz Concentration Camp. In September 1942, he was chief clerk of the garrison surgeon's office. In July 1943, he held the post of *SS* sanitary orderly in the Auschwitz sub-camp 'Neu Dachs' at Jaworzno.

PALITZSCH, Gerhard Arno Max, Born on June 17, 1913, in Grossopitz-Tharandt, near Dresden. He was a member of the Nazi Party and the *SS* and of the Death's Head Formation. He served as a guard at Lichtenburg Concentration Camp. Then he served at Buchenwald and Sachsenhausen Concentration Camps rising from the role of *Blockführer,* to *Rapportführer.*

He was transferred to Auschwitz Concentration Camp in May 1940, and performed the role of *Rapportführer* there, and he became one of the most feared and brutal members of the *SS*-garrison. Part of his duties were to shoot prisoners at the 'Black Wall' in the yard of Block 11. He boasted that he killed 25,000 people, but that has never been corroborated. When the Gypsy camp was established at Birkenau, he managed this camp.

Palitzsch used to fill the prisoners with terror, as he proved to be extremely sadistic. He appropriated great quantities of money, valuables and clothes, taken from people sent to the camp. His wife Luise died from typhus on November 4, 1942, and despite the strict prohibition of relations with prisoners, he began an affair with a Jewess from Slovakia, in the Women's Camp. He was sent to the subcamp at Brünn, arrested by the SS, and after a disciplinary hearing he was sent to a front-line unit and was apparently killed in action in December 1944, near Budapest.

ROHDE, Dr. Werner, Born on June 11, 1904, in Marburg. He was a physician and dentist at Auschwitz Concentration Camp. He was responsible for numerous selections of prisoners who died in the gas chambers. He was transferred from Auschwitz to Natzweiler Struthof Concentration Camp. He was sentenced to death after the War in the trial of the SS garrison at Natzweiler before the British Military Tribunal in Wuppertal. He was executed on October 10, 1946.

SCHATZ, Dr. Willi, Born on February 1, 1905, in Hanover, the son of a dental technician. After graduating from secondary school in Hanover, he matriculated at Göttingen University, where he studied dentistry for ten terms. He graduated in 1932 and took his qualifying state examination. In the same year he also joined the Nazi Party, from which he was expelled in 1937, but not for political reasons. He practiced dentistry until 1940, when he was drafted.

In the summer of 1943, he was transferred to the *Waffen-SS,* and on January 30, 1944, he was promoted to *Untersturmführer* and transferred to Auschwitz Concentration Camp, where he became the second in charge dental officer. His immediate superior was Dr. Frank. Dr. Schatz remained in Auschwitz until the autumn of 1944, when he was transferred to the Neuengamme Concentration Camp. He was released by the British Forces from internment at the end of January 1946. He then returned to Hanover, and resumed his dental practice. Dr. Schatz stood trial in the Frankfurt am Main Auschwitz proceedings. He was acquitted. He died from cancer on February 17, 1985, in Hanover.

SCHERPE, Herbert, Born on May 20, 1907, in Gleiwitz, the son of an electrician. He completed his schooling and became a butcher's apprentice, and later worked in his father's business. After that he was unemployed for three years. From May 1933, until December 1935, he held various jobs: assistant policeman, market inspector, assistant customs clerk. Scherpe joined the Nazi Party and the SS in 1931, he became a member of an SS unit guarding gasoline stores at airfields. Later he was posted to an SS-Death's Head unit at Dachau. His unit fought in the French campaign, but because of his nearsightedness, he was sent to Oranienburg to the office of the inspector of Concentration Camps.

In the summer of 1940, after a ten-week training course as a medical orderly, he was transferred to the Auschwitz Concentration Camp. There he served in the prison hospital and in various subsidiary camps. He managed to desert after the evacuation of the camp in January 1945. At the end of the War he was interned briefly as an SS member but was released in July 1945. He worked as a porter in a Mannheim machinery plant when he was arrested. Scherpe stood trial in the Frankfurt am Main Auschwitz proceedings. He was found guilty of War Crimes and sentenced to 4 years and six months hard labor. He died on December 23, 1997, in Mannheim.

SCHILD, Helmut, Born on December 14, 1919. He arrived at Auschwitz from Mauthausen Concentration Camp in mid-1942. He served in the 3rd, 2nd, 8th and 6th guard companies.

SCHILLINGER, Josef, An SS Staff-Sergeant he performed the role of *Rapportführer,* commander of an outside working commando, at the Chełmek sub-camp, and head of the kitchen in the Men's Camp at Birkenau. He was also employed in guarding the transports of Jews from the unloading ramp to the crematoriums. On October 23, 1943, he was shot dead in the undressing room of one of the gas chambers, by a Jewess, brought on a transport from Bergen-Belsen Concentration Camp.

SCHLAGE, Bruno, Born on February 11, 1902, in Truttenau, near Königsberg, the son of a worker. Soon after his birth his parents moved to Itzehoe, where he grew up and attended elementary school. He completed his schooling in Rosengarten near Angerburg, where his parents had bought a farm. For a while, Schlage worked for the railways, later he became an apprentice to a mason. After attending a trade school he became a foreman working mostly on construction jobs outside of Germany. He was drafted into a police unit and assigned to the 22nd *SS* regiment.

At the end of 1941, he was posted to the Auschwitz Concentration Camp, where he stayed until the camp was evacuated in January 1945. During his time at the Camp he was a guard in Block 11, the notorious prison block, leader of a prisoner detail, and chief of the 3rd guard company. At the end of the War he spent more than four years in Polish prison camps; he was released in August 1949 and joined his family at Dehme. From October 1961, he worked as a caretaker. Schlage stood trial in the Frankfurt am Main Auschwitz proceedings. He was found guilty of War Crimes and sentenced to 6 years hard labor. He died on February 9, 1977, in Minden.

SCHMIDETZKI, Walter, Born on January 5, 1913, in Schran, near Rybnik, Upper Silesia. He joined the *Allgemeine-SS* in August 1934, and in September 1939, he was drafted into the *Waffen-SS*. He took part in active service at the front before joining the *SS-Totenkopfverbände* at the beginning of 1942.

On August 1, 1942, he was posted to Dachau Concentration Camp, where he served in the guard unit until December of that year. He then attended officer training school until February 1943, and was commissioned as an *SS-Untersturmführer* on February 18, 1943.

He was then posted to the Hinzert Concentration Camp, which was located some eighteen miles from Trier, where he served in the Administration Department. On February 14, 1944, he was transferred to the Flossenburg Concentration Camp, where once again he worked in administration.

On May 12, 1944, he was posted to Auschwitz Concentration Camp where he was appointed to the post of Head of the Disinfection Chambers at Birkenau. In June 1944, he was promoted to the rank of *SS-Obersturmführer,* and took over as head of the group of barracks, known to the prisoners and *SS*, as '*Kanada*.' From August 15, 1944, he was also appointed to the post of Director of the Camp's Administration at Auschwitz-III-Monowitz.

In January 1945, when Auschwitz was liquidated, Schmidetzki left the Camp with a small convoy of prisoners bound for Natzweiler Concentration Camp, where once again he performed an administrative role. He was there until Natzweiler was liberated by the American Army in April 1945.

Schmidetzki was handed over to the Polish authorities to stand trial. He was tried in Poland for War Crimes against humanity, whilst at Auschwitz. He was found guilty and sentenced to three years imprisonment on July 28, 1948.

SCHÖBERTH, Johann, Born on December 17, 1922, in Aufsess near Ebermannstadt, the illegitimate son of a farmer's daughter. His father, a miller's helper, did not take any interest in him, thus Schöberth was raised by his mother. He attended elementary school and three years of vocational school. At the age of fifteen he became a forest worker. He joined the *Hitler-Jugend*—the Hitler Youth. In February 1941, he was called up by the *Waffen-SS*, and was seriously wounded in Lapland in 1941.

In December 1942, having recovered, he was again wounded by a bullet in his pelvis, sustaining a spinal injury, and a bullet to the chest, which caused an injury to his lung. As a result, Schöberth was classified unfit for active duty. In the Spring of 1943, he was transferred to the Auschwitz Concentration Camp; there he was assigned to guard duty, the post office and the Political Department. He remained in Auschwitz until the summer of 1944, when he was assigned as a weapons technician to a unit of ethnic Germans, but once again he was wounded. Schöberth was arrested by the Russians but released from Soviet internment in August 1945. Schöberth stood trial in the Frankfurt am Main Auschwitz proceedings. He was acquitted.

SCHOLZ, Ernest, Born on April 30, 1911, in Cosel. By vocation he was a baker. He joined the *SS* in 1933. He served in Auschwitz Concentration Camp from 1940 until 1944, working as an electrician in

Department IV—*Technische Abteilung*, and later in the administration of the *SS* canteen, in the officers club (*SS-Führerheim*) and finally as a supply officer in the *SS* kitchens. His subsequent fate is unknown.

SCHULTE, Dr. Wilhelm, Born on March 27, 1907, in Elberfeld, near Wuppertal. He studied dentistry at university and in 1933, he passed his final exams and was awarded his doctorate.

In early 1934, he joined the *Allgemeine-SS* and three years later he joined the Nazi Party. He set up his own practice in Vienna, where he met his wife, and built up a successful business. He became a part-time member of the *SS* in Austria, and was appointed as a dentist with a local *SS* unit, shortly after the *Anschluss* with Germany in March 1938.

He joined the *Waffen-SS* on March 15, 1941, and trained as an officer, until he was commissioned in November 1941. In the same month on November 9, 1941, he was posted to Auschwitz Concentration Camp, where he served as one of the Camp's dentists at Auschwitz Main Camp until July 1942. On July 21, 1942, he was transferred to the 4th *SS* Panzer Grenadier Division '*Polizei*,' where he saw active service in Russia. In the spring of 1943, his regiment performed police duties in Czechoslovakia, Poland and Greece.

On May 20, 1944, Dr. Schulte was assigned to the 19th *SS* Grenadier Division, where he saw active service during the heavy fighting during the retreat from Leningrad and the Baltic States. Schulte surrendered to the Red Army in April 1945 and he was imprisoned by the Russians.

SCHULZ, Otto, Ludwig, Born on December 23, 1882, in the small town of Bellingen, in Stendal. At the age of twenty he joined the German Army and served in the infantry during the First World War. He saw front-line action in France and was wounded three times. He was awarded the 'Wound Badge in Silver.' He left the army in October 1919. In 1922, he studied agriculture and became a farmer in the Hamburg area.

Otto Schulz was called up on November 24, 1941, and he joined the *Waffen-SS*. Because of his military experience and training he was admitted to officer training, even though he was almost sixty-years old.

On April 20, 1942, he was assigned to the *SS-Totenkopfstandarte*. He was appointed as the Commander of the 7th *SS* Sentry Company at Auschwitz Concentration Camp and he served in this capacity until June 1942. He was then appointed as the Commander of the *SS* Sentry Company at Auschwitz-Monowitz. This sentry company not only guarded Monowitz itself, but the other nearby sub-camps. He remained in this position until May 1, 1943, when he was transferred to the Neuengamme Concentration Camp.

He served at Neuengamme until October 31, 1944, when he was retired and discharged from the *SS* at the age of sixty-two. He enjoyed a trouble-free retirement until his death. He was never brought to trial for his service in the Concentration Camps.

SCHUMANN, Dr. Horst, Born on May 11, 1906, in Halle on the Saale, the son of a general practioner. He joined the Nazi Party in 1930, and the *SA* in 1932. Schumann received his medical degree in Halle in 1933, and was employed in the health office in Halle during 1934. In 1939, when the Second World War began, he was conscripted as a subordinate physician in the *Luftwaffe*. He was summoned in 1939 by Viktor Brack, the head of the department T4 which was the code name for the program which carried out euthanasia of the mentally-ill, the disabled, Jews and the so-called a-socials.

In January 1940, Dr. Schumann took up the post at the Euthanasia Institute of Grafeneck, in Württemberg, where mentally ill and disabled people were killed by engine exhaust gas. In the summer of 1940, he became the Director of another T4 Euthanasia Institute at Pirna / Sonnenstein, near Dresden. Dr. Schumann belonged to a committee of doctors as part of the secret 14f-13 operation, who selected prisoners in various Concentration Camps, including Auschwitz, who were especially weak and incapable of working. They selected these individuals for death in the euthanasia institutes.

On July 28, 1941, Dr. Schumann went to Auschwitz for the first time, where he selected 575 prisoners to be taken to Sonnenstein and killed in the gas chamber. A year and a half later he returned to Auschwitz to test 'a cheap and rapid' mass sterilization method for men and women using X-rays. He carried out the experiments on 'young, healthy, and good looking' Jewish men, women, and girls, selected by himself. Hardly any of his 'patients' survived, the people died from burns, or from additional surgical procedures, exhaustion or shock.

He left Auschwitz in the middle of 1944, and went to the Ravensbrück Concentration Camp, where he continued his experiments. After the end of the War he surfaced in Gladbeck, where he registered with the police and was appointed municipal sport physician. With a refugee grant he opened his own practice in 1949.

In 1951, the authorities attempted to bring him to justice, but he was probably warned of his impending arrest and he escaped and worked as a doctor on a ship, as well as working in the Sudan, Nigeria and Libya to Ghana. Not until 1966, after the fall of Nkrumah, did Ghana extradite Dr. Schumann to West Germany. In September 1970, the trial against Schumann commenced, but in April 1971, the trial was interrupted because of his ill-health, and he was quietly released from custody. He died on May 5, 1983, in Frankfurt am Main.

SCHURZ, Hans, Born on December 28, 1913, in St. Salvator, Austria. He joined the police in 1936, and in June 1937, he was transferred to the Criminal Police (*KRIPO*), based in Berlin. In September 1939, Schurz joined the *Allgemeine-SS* and in December 1940, he was posted to the Reich Main Security Office (*RSHA*), where he was assigned to *AMT IV*, the *Gestapo*.

During November 1941, Schurz was assigned to the *Gestapo* Office in Cieszyn, Poland, a small town less than thirty miles from the Auschwitz Concentration Camp. During his time there he was responsible for sending suspected Polish resistance fighters to Auschwitz Concentration Camp.

On May 1, 1943, he was posted to Auschwitz Concentration Camp, where he was appointed to the post of Deputy Director of the Political Department, which was then under the stewardship of

Maximilian Grabner. However, in November 1943, Grabner was investigated by Dr. Konrad Morgen for corruption, and arrested and imprisoned. On December 1, 1943, Hans Schurz was officially appointed to replace Grabner, as the Head of the Political Department in Auschwitz, by the new Commandant, Arthur Liebehenschel. This was one of the most important and powerful posts in the camps hierarchy.

Schurz was posted to the Dora-Mittelbau Concentration Camp on January 18, 1945, when Auschwitz was liquidated. Hans Schurz was never brought to justice and a court in Vienna declared him dead on May 23, 1950.

SCHWARZ, Heinrich, Born on June 14, 1906, in Munich. At the beginning of the Second World War he was called up and served in the *Waffen-SS*. He was posted to Mauthausen Concentration Camp in Austria. During November 1941, he was transferred to the Auschwitz Concentration Camp where he performed the role of Manager of the Employment Section.

In November 1943, he was appointed as the Commandant of Auschwitz III-Monowitz. He stayed there until the evacuation in January 1945, when he was posted to Natzweiler-Struthof Concentration Camp, where he became the Commandant, succeeding Friedrich Hartjenstein. He was sentenced to death by the French Military Court and was executed on March 20, 1947.

SCHWARZHUBER, Johann, Born on August 28, 1904, in Tuetzing. He served at Dachau Concentration Camp after joining the SS. He served as a guard, then as a *Blockführer*. During 1938, he was transferred to Sachsenhausen Concentration Camp, where he performed the role of *Rapportführer*. In September 1941, he was assigned to Auschwitz Concentration Camp and in March 1941, he was appointed as the *Schutzlagerführer* of the Men's Camp in Birkenau.

In November 1944, he returned to Dachau, and then on January 12, 1945, he was transferred to Ravensbrück Concentration Camp. He was arrested by the British Forces on April 29, 1945, and was subsequently tried for War Crimes along with other members of the

Ravensbrück *SS*-garrison. He was found guilty and executed on May 3, 1947.

SCHWELA, Dr. Siegfried, Born on March 23, 1903, in Cottbus. He was commissioned into the *Waffen-SS* in September 1939, and was assigned to the *SS* Medical Department in Berlin. In 1940, he was posted to the Natzweiler-Struthof Concentration Camp, where he served as the Camp doctor.

In July 1941, he was transferred to the Auschwitz Concentration Camp where he was assigned to the Auschwitz Main Camp as a physician. He took part in selections for the gas chambers, and in September 1941, he ordered a mass selection from the hospital and 250 inmates were taken to Block 11. They were locked in a basement and murdered using the gassing agent *'Zyklon B.'*

On March 21, 1942, he took over the post as the Garrison Physician, succeeding Dr. Oskar Dienstbach. However, within eight weeks of this appointment, Dr. Siegfried Schwela contracted typhus and was admitted to the hospital in the camp, where he died on May 10, 1942.

SEIDLER, Fritz, Born on July 18, 1907, in Werdau. After serving in Sachsenhausen Concentration Camp between 1938 and 1940, he was posted to Auschwitz Concentration Camp in November 1940. He took over the post of second Camp manager. From October 1941 until March 1942, he held the post of deputy-manager of the Soviet Prisoner's of War Camp in Birkenau. He was transferred to Mauthausen Concentration Camp during 1944.

STARK, Hans, Born on June 14, 1921, in Darmstadt, the son of a police officer. At the age of sixteen years and five months, Hans Stark was accepted into the *Waffen-SS*, after his father had given his written permission. His first stint of service was with the 2nd *SS* Death's Head brigade 'Brandenburg' of Oranienburg; he was the youngest recruit there, where he received basic infantry training and schooling in National Socialist ideology and race history. After this he was assigned to guard duty in the Oranienburg Concentration Camp.

Hans Stark was later assigned to serve in the Buchenwald and Dachau Concentration Camps, and to the Honour Guard Battalion in Prague and to the *SS* regiment 'Westland', based in Munich. He suffered a compound thigh fracture in a riding accident and was again assigned to Dachau.

In December 1940, at the age of nineteen and a half, he was posted to Auschwitz Concentration Camp. During July 1941, he was assigned to the Political Department, where he was in charge of registrations. He was granted home leave from Christmas 1941, until March 1942, in order to sit his final examinations, which he passed.

He returned to Auschwitz but was once again granted school leave from November 1, 1942, until April 1, 1943, after which he was assigned to a front-line unit, although before joining his unit, he paid a 'farewell' visit to Auschwitz. While with the *SS* armoured unit '*Der Führer*', he was wounded. In the spring of 1944, Hans Stark attended the *SS* elite school at Klagenfurt. In January 1945, he was again wounded, and on May 2, 1945, he was taken prisoner by the Soviet Army in Berlin, but he managed to escape after two days.

In the autumn of 1946, Stark began to study agriculture; the Darmstadt de-Nazification chamber classified him as a minor offender. In February 1953, after passing a qualifying examination at Darmstadt, he became a teacher at two agricultural schools; he also worked as an agricultural consultant. Stark stood trial in the Frankfurt am Main Auschwitz proceedings. He was found guilty of War Crimes and sentenced to 10 years imprisonment. He died on March 29, 1991, in Darmstadt.

TAUBE, Adolf, Born on September 25, 1908, in Rudelsdorf in the Sudetenland. He was a clerk, before joining the *Waffen-SS* in 1940. He was posted to Auschwitz Concentration Camp as a guard during 1941. He was later posted to Birkenau where he performed the duties as a *Blockführer*, and *Rapportführer*. He was subsequently posted to Auschwitz III, and later to the Gleiwitz sub-Camp.

THILO, Dr. Heinz, Born on October 8, 1911, in Elberfeld. He joined the Nazi Party in December 1930 and the *SS* in 1934. He concluded his medical studies during 1935, in Jena. He then worked mostly as a gynaecologist within the *Lebensborn* organization from April 1938, until the end of 1941. He served at the front for six months and at the end of July 1942, he was posted to Auschwitz Concentration Camp.

From November 1942, until October 1944, Thilo was the physician for the prisoner's infirmary at Birkenau. According to Dr. Johann Paul Kremer, it was Dr. Thilo who coined the phrase that Auschwitz was the *'anus mundi'* (anus of the world) in his diary entry for September 5, 1942. Dr. Thilo participated in numerous selections on the ramp as well as in the infirmary camp. He also took part in the liquidation of the Family Camp for Czech Jews from Theresienstadt in March 1944.

During October 1944, he was transferred to the Gross-Rosen Concentration Camp, where he served as the camp physician until February 1945. He left the camp shortly before its liberation. He committed suicide on April 13, 1945, in Hohenelbe.

UHLENBROCK, Dr. Kurt, Born on March 2, 1908, in Rostock. He was sent to Auschwitz Concentration Camp in August 1942, as a result of a court-martial, in which he was accused of not caring properly for wounded soldiers in a field hospital. After a period of serving in the Economic Office D-III of the WVHA, which oversaw the deployment of doctors in the Concentration Camps. From August 17, 1942, until September 16, 1943, he functioned as *SS* Garrison Doctor. He carried out selections of unfit prisoners for the gas chambers.

Uhlenbrock was transferred out of Auschwitz in 1943. After the War he continued to work undisturbed in his practice in Hamburg. It was not until the Frankfurt am Main Auschwitz Trial that he was indicted and charged by witnesses of taking part in the selection of sick prisoners who were then put to death. During the trial proceedings the investigation of Dr. Uhlenbrock was dropped. He returned to his practice in Hamburg. He died on August 7, 1992, in Hamburg.

VETTER, Dr. Helmuth, Born on March 21, 1910, in Rastenburg. He worked as a Concentration Camp Doctor in Dachau, Auschwitz and Mauthausen. He was a former employee of the Bayer Company, which was a member of I. G. Farben. Dr. Vetter organized in various Concentration Camps a series of pharmacological experiments, working closely with his former employers. In these experiments he used Sulfonamide, a nitrous acid compound, Rutenol, and a combination formula containing an unknown substance labelled 'Secret Sign 3582' and prussic acid.

In 1947, he was indicted by an American Military Court, which established that in one of his experiments on 75 people who were treated with a new medication made available by Bayer, 40 died. Vetter was sentenced to death and he was executed on February 2, 1949.

VOLKENRATH, Elisabeth. Born on September 5, 1919, in Schönau. She served at Ravensbrück, Auschwitz-Birkenau and Bergen-Belsen Concentration Camps. She was tried by the British Army and found guilty of War Crimes and was executed on December 13, 1945.

VOSS, Peter, Born December 18, 1897, in Flensburg. He was in charge of the four crematoria in Birkenau. He was an *SS-Oberscharführer* in rank. He was replaced by Otto Moll, in May 1944, as the Camp command thought he was not ruthless enough to oversee the mass extermination of the Hungarian Jews. Filip Müller described Voss as in his mid-thirties, of medium height and stocky, with a small slightly hooked nose. He had a penchant for alcohol and valuables stolen from the victims murdered in the gas chambers. His fate is unknown.

WEBER, Dr. Bruno, Born on May 21, 1915, in Trier. He was the Director of the *SS* Hygiene Institute in Rajsko near Auschwitz. He also carried out numerous bacteriological and haematological research activities in Block 10. In January 1945, the Hygiene Institute was evacuated, to be rebuilt in Dachau Concentration Camp by Weber and his close colleague Dr. Hans Münch. Dr. Weber died on September 23, 1956.

WILKS, Martin, Born in 1916. He was chief accountant in the office of the *SS* garrison physician at Auschwitz Concentration Camp from October 1941, until the evacuation of the Camp in January 1945.

WIRTHS, Dr. Eduard, Born September 4, 1909, in Würzburg. He came from a Catholic family associated with Democratic Socialism and worked as a rural doctor after he completed his medical studies. In 1933, he joined the Nazi Party and the *SA*, and undertook official health-related assignments, as well as maintaining his practice. He became a member of the *Waffen-SS* in 1939, and served on the front-line in Norway and the Soviet Union.

Because of a heart ailment he was declared unfit for front-line service in April 1942, and was sent briefly to the Dachau and Neuengamme Concentration Camps, before being transferred to Auschwitz Concentration Camp in September 1942, where he performed the role of Garrison Doctor. All *SS* Camp Doctors were subordinate to him; he deployed them on the selection platform according to a hierarchical principle—he himself regularly participated in selections—so as to cultivate the discipline and self-image of his subordinates. Wirths himself was subordinate to Office D-III for Sanitation and Camp Hygiene in the *WVHA* in Berlin, which was directed after 1942, by the physician Enno Lolling. But he was also subordinate to the Commandant of Auschwitz, with whom he dealt with on a daily basis. It was Wirths who, within the camp hierarchy, insisted that an order from Berlin be followed that only doctors should carry out selections. Hence, Wirths had not only control over selections, he organized the system.

Wirths set in motion scientific experiments to be carried out in Auschwitz, aimed at the early detection of cervical cancer, but he never took part in these experiments, which frequently resulted in the death of the subjects. In 1945, Wirths was arrested by the British Army and he committed suicide in prison on September 20, 1945.

WÖNTZ, Rudolf Friedrich, Born on September 2, 1906, in Königsbach, Pforzheim district. By vocation he was a car mechanic and clerk. He joined the Nazi Party in 1932, and the *SS* in 1938. Wöntz served in Auschwitz Concentration Camp in Department IV—*Technische Abteilung* from March 1941 as an electrician, and later in the *Baubetriebdienststelle*.

ZOLLER, Viktor, Born on June 22, 1912, in Ravensburg, Bavaria. He was the son of a local tradesman, Josef Zoller. After completing his schooling he attended a college for three years where he obtained a degree in building and construction.

In June 1931, he began work as an apprentice with a master builder and trained to be a civil engineer. He spent just over a year in an architects office and attended a vocational school for two terms learning the masonry trade. On April 1, 1933, he was recruited into the *Reichsarbeitsdienst (RAD)*, where he was employed in the construction office until April 13, 1934.

During April 1933, he joined the Nazi Party and the *Allgemeine-SS*. From April 13, 1934, he was assigned to the 1st *Totenkopfstandarte* 'Oberbayern', and was attached to the Dachau Concentration Camp. On April 20, 1938, he was appointed a platoon commander and was promoted to the rank of *SS-Untersturmführer*. Zoller remained at Dachau until September 1, 1941, when he was posted to the Mauthausen Concentration Camp in Austria. He served there until May 1942, as commander of the *SS* Sentry units and later as camp adjutant.

On May 1, 1942, Viktor Zoller was transferred to the 3rd *SS* Panzer Grenadier Regiment *'Totenkopf.'* He saw active service on the Russian Front from May 11 until July 17, 1942, when he returned to the Regimental Headquarters as an adjutant.

On September 1, 1942, he was posted as a staff officer to an *SS* Motorcycle Replacement Battalion, while attached to the 3rd *SS* Panzer Division *'Totenkopf'* and he remained at this post for two months.

In November 1942, he was transferred from active service to serve in the *SS* Central Command Office in Vienna. He was then posted during the last days of October 1943, to the *SS-WVHA* Headquarters in Berlin. This was a short-lived appointment, because on November 2, 1943, Zoller was assigned to the Auschwitz Concentration Camp as an adjutant to Commandant Rudolf Höss, for a brief time. When Höss was replaced by Arthur Liebehenschel, on November 11, 1943, Zoller continued as adjutant.

With Liebehenschel falling into a depressed state, Zoller became a real figure of power within the camp, he was present at many executions at the 'Black Wall' in Block 11. On May 8, 1944, Liebehenschel was posted to the Lublin Concentration Camp and Rudolf Höss returned to oversee the mass extermination of the Hungarian Jews. Rudolf Höss had little time for an adjutant who thought he was the Commandant. So it came as no surprise that on May 25, 1944, Zoller was posted again to Mauthausen Concentration Camp. Zoller was transferred once more to work in the *SS-WVHA* Headquarters in Berlin, and he was there when the Second World War came to an end. Viktor Zoller was captured at the end of the War in Bavaria by American Forces and he was imprisoned at the Mindelheim internment camp. On December 23, 1945, he was charged with War Crimes committed whilst at Mauthausen Concentration Camp.

The trial took place at the former Dachau Concentration Camp and it commenced on March 7, 1946. He was found guilty of all charges on May 11, 1946, and he was sentenced to death on May 13, 1946. Viktor Zoller was executed in the courtyard of Landsberg-am-Lech Prison on May 28, 1947.

ZORN, Werner, Born on January 2, 1915, in Tetlow, near Berlin. He served in the *Stahlhelm* from March 1932, and joined the *Reichsheer* in October 1935, serving with the 25th Infantry Regiment, rising to the rank *of Leutnant der Reserve*. He was also at this time a member of the local *SA* unit and a leader with the Hitler Youth.

On December 1, 1938, he joined the *Allgemeine-SS* and was appointed platoon Commander of the 2nd *SS-Totenkopfstandarte* 'Brandenburg' based at Buchenwald Concentration Camp for nearly three years until September 15, 1941, when he was transferred to the *Waffen-SS*. He was assigned to the 3rd *SS* Infantry Regiment 'Totenkopf,' but he only spent two weeks in this command, before being posted to the Auschwitz Concentration Camp on October 1, 1941.

At Auschwitz, he was immediately put in command of the 2nd and 5th *SS* Sentry Companies. His task was to train these companies and restore discipline in its ranks. He was selected for this task, as he was an experienced and professional soldier.

On November 25, 1941, Zorn returned to the Front with the *SS* 3rd Infantry Regiment and saw active service on the northern sector of the Eastern Front. In August 1942, he was posted to the 2nd *SS* Panzer

Division '*Das Reich*,' and was appointed Company Commander with the 2nd Replacement Battalion '*Deutschland*.'

On November 12, 1942, Zorn was assigned to the SS Infantry School 'Doberitz' where he trained as a Battalion Commander. On December 16, 1942, he was posted to the 2nd SS Panzer Grenadier Reconnaissance Battalion, and took part in the heavy fighting in Kharkov and later on in Kursk in July 1943. In November 1943, his battalion suffered heavy casualties during the fighting at Kiev. He remained with this command unil February 1944, before it was moved to the Normandy area in France.

On February 8, 1944, Zorn was transferred to the 17th SS Panzer Division '*Goetz von Berlichtingen*' and was assigned to the post of Commander of the 3rd Battalion of the 37th SS Infantry Regiment.

In early November 1944, Zorn took part in the 'Battle of Metz' and he was reported missing in action, presumed dead. He was declared 'killed in action' on December 8, 1944.

Chapter XII
Transports to Auschwitz Remembrance, Survivors and Victims

In this chapter, a massive Roll of Remembrance for the Jewish people sent to Auschwitz, as included in my other books about the Aktion Reinhardt Camps would simply be too overwhelming. Over 1 million people lost their lives in Auschwitz-Birkenau, many of them of Jewish origin. So a more selective path has been chosen.

Records have been consulted to include, where possible, the details of transports to Auschwitz from various countries throughout Europe, and some brief biographies and accounts of the terrible journeys suffered by the Jews, which for most was a one way ride to oblivion. No one person is greater or lesser than another, simply everyone cannot be listed, so I apologize in advance if your story or one of your relatives is not included.

Deportations to Auschwitz Concentration Camp required the co-ordination of numerous German government ministries and state organizations including the Reich Main Security Office (*RSHA*), the Ministry of Transport, and the Foreign Office. The *RSHA* co-ordinated and directed the deportations; the Ministry of Transport organized train schedules; and the Foreign Office negotiated with the officials of the occupied countries regarding the handing over of their Jews. Adolf Eichmann's office was responsible for organizing the deportation trains for Jews, and Eichmann's railroad expert and liaison with the Ministry of Transport was Austrian Franz Nowak. Other members of Eichmann's office included Anton Brunner, Theodor Dannecker, Hans Günther, Rolf Günther, Otto Hunsche, Hermann Krumey, Dr. Heinz Röthke and Dieter Wisliceny. These 'engineers of human misery' will feature frequently in the following chapter:

Transports From The Altreich

Transports from the *Altreich* started in October 1939, with transports from Vienna to Nisko in Poland, as co-ordinated by Adolf Eichmann's office, and Vienna featured again from February 1941, until March 1941, with a number of transports to various Polish locations such as Kielce and Opatów.

During October 1941 and early November 1941, there were a spate of deportations of Jews from major cities to the *Litzmannstadt* Ghetto in Poland, such as Berlin, Frankfurt am Main, Cologne, Hamburg, Düsseldorf, Prague and Vienna.

Between November 1941 and February 1942, there were a host of deportations from major German cities such as Hamburg, Düsseldorf, Frankfurt am Main, Berlin, Bremen, Munich, Breslau, Nuremberg, Stuttgart, Cologne, Munster, Osnabruck, Hannover, Leipzig, Dresden, Dortmund and others to Minsk, Kovno, and Riga, where many were killed directly in shooting '*Aktions*' in specially prepared mass graves.

From March 17, 1942, a whole series of deportations took place from the *Altreich* to the so-called Transit Ghettos in the Lublin District, such as Izbica, Krasnystaw, Piaski, Rejowiec, Włodawa and Zamość, as well as the Warsaw Ghetto. These transports came from Koblenz, Mainz, Darmstadt, Gelsenkirchen, Berlin, Munich, Vienna, Breslau, Magdeburg, Düsseldorf, Würzburg, Stuttgart, Theresienstadt, and Frankfurt am Main. The deportees from Germany usually went to the Bełżec and Sobibor death camps, which were part of the mass murder program controlled by Odilo Globocnik, the *SS* and Police Leader for the Lublin District.

During June and July 1942, a large number of transports left the *Altreich* for the Theresienstadt Ghetto, which will be covered more significantly, further on in the book. During the months of May and June 1942, the first transports went directly to the Auschwitz Concentration Camp, from locations in Silesia such as Gleiwitz and Beuthen. These commenced on May 16, 1942:

Transports From the Altreich Direct to Auschwitz 1942–1944

Date	Deportation From	Number of Deportees	Arrival At Auschwitz
16 May 1942	Gleiwitz	54	
20 May 1942	Gleiwitz	167	20 May 1942
28 May 1942	Gleiwitz	145	28 May 1942
2 June 1942	Beuthen	133	2 June 1942
8 June 1942	Gleiwitz	33	8 June 1942
13 June 1942	Beuthen	134	13 June 1942
15 June 1942	Beuthen	147	15 June 1942
16 June 1942	Gleiwitz	3	16 June 1942
23 June 1942	Gleiwitz	116	23 June 1942
29 June 1942	Gleiwitz	57	29 June 1942
11 July 1942	Hamburg / Bielefeld / Berlin	697	
17 July 1942	Vienna	995	18 July 1942
29 November 1942	Berlin	998	
8 December 1942	Vienna	9	
9 December 1942	Berlin	994	10 December 1942
14 December 1942	Berlin	815	
12 January 1943	Berlin	1196	13 January 1943
29 January 1943	Berlin	1004	30 January 1943
3 February 1943	Berlin	952	4 February 1943
19 February 1943	Berlin	997	20 February 1943
26 February 1943	Berlin	1095	27 February 1943
27 February 1943	Halle	2	
1 March 1943	Berlin	1722	2 March 1943
1 March 1943	Stuttgart / Trier / Düsseldorf / Dortmund	1500	2 March 1943
2 March 1943	Berlin	1750	3 March 1943
2 March 1943	Paderborn / Hannover / Erfurt / Dresden	1500	3 March 1943

3 March 1943	Berlin	1726	4 March 1943
3 March 1943	Vienna	75	5 March 1943
4 March 1943	Berlin	1120	6 March 1943
4 March 1943	Breslau	1405	6 March 1943
6 March 1943	Berlin	721	7 March 1943
12 March 1943	Berlin	941	13 March 1943
13 March 1943	Munich	219	
31 March 1943	Vienna	85	
19 April 1943	Berlin / Potsdam	681	20 April 1943
19 April 1943	Frankfurt am Main	17	
17 May 1943	Berlin	406	19 May 1943
17 May 1943	Stuttgart	13	
17–18 June 1943	Nuremberg / Würzburg	73	
28 June 1943	Berlin	314	29 June 1943
4 August 1943	Berlin	100	5 August 1943
10 September 1943	Berlin	49	11 September 1943
14 September 1943	Stuttgart	2	
28 September 1943	Berlin	73	
7 October 1943	Vienna	21	
12 October 1943	Stuttgart	?	
14 October 1943	Berlin	78	
29 October 1943	Berlin	50	
8 November 1943	Berlin	50	
1 December 1943	Vienna	25	
7 December 1943	Berlin	54	
7 December 1943	Stuttgart	?	
20 January 1944	Berlin	48	
22 February 1944	Berlin	32	
24 February 1944	Vienna	41	
7 March 1944	Stuttgart	?	
9 March 1944	Berlin	32	11 March 1944
18 April 1944	Berlin	31	19 April 1944
26 April 1944	Vienna	19	

3 May 1944	Berlin	26	4 May 1944
19 May 1944	Berlin	24	
15 June 1944	Berlin	29	16 June 1944
27 June 1944	Vienna	22	28 June 1944
28 June 1944	Vienna	38	29 June 1944
12 July 1944	Berlin	31	13 July 1944
10 August 1944	Berlin	39	12 August 1944
21 August 1944	Vienna	2	
1 September 1944	Vienna	29	4 September 1944
6 September 1944	Berlin	39	7 September 1944
5 October 1944	Vienna	100	
12 October 1944	Berlin	31	
24 November 1944	Berlin	27	

Source: Das Bundesarchiv—Memorial Book Online Resource

Inge Deutschkron, who was born in Berlin and who lived in Berlin throughout the Second World War and went into hiding in February 1943, recalled in a conversation with Claude Lanzmann, for the film *Shoah*:

> I remember the day when they made Berlin *Judenrein*. The people hastened in the streets, no one wanted to be in the streets, you could see the streets were absolutely empty. They didn't want to look, you know. They hastened to buy what they had to buy—they had to buy something for the Sunday, you see. So they went shopping and hastened back into their houses.
> And I remember this day very vividly because we saw police cars rushing through the streets of Berlin taking people out of the houses. They had herded the Jews together, from factories, from houses, wherever they could find them and had put them into something that was called 'Klu.' Klu was a dance restaurant, a very big one. From there they were deported in various transports. They were going off not very far from here on one of the tracks at the Grünewald station, and this was the day when I suddenly felt so utterly alone, left alone, because now I knew we would be one of the very few people left, I didn't know how many more would be underground. This also was the day when I felt very guilty that I didn't go myself and I tried to escape fate that the others could not escape.

There was no more warmth around, no more soul akin to us, you understand. And we talked about this. What happened to Elsa? To Hans? And where is he and where is she? My God, what happened to the child? These were our thoughts on that horrible day. And this feeling of being terribly alone and terribly guilty that we did not go with them. Why did we try? What made us do this? To escape fate—that was really our destiny or the destiny of our people.[296]

Kitty Hart-Moxon was born Kitty Felix on December 1, 1926, in the Southern Polish town of Bielsko-Biała. On August 24, 1939, Kitty and her family moved to Lublin and tried to escape to Russia, but the attempt failed at Dorohusk. They returned to Lublin, and with the aid of false papers, Kitty and her mother Rosa, went to work at the I. G. Farben Company in Bitterfeld.

On March 13, 1943, they were betrayed to the *Gestapo*, and at a trial they were both sentenced to hard labor for life, for endangering the security of the Third Reich.... illegally entering Germany with false papers. Kitty and her mother were told by an official, *'Nur Morgen geht es nach Auschwitz.'* They were transferred from Leipzig to Dresden, where they and the rest of those arrested waited in a transit cell to take them to Auschwitz:

> In the morning all the occupants of Cell 13 were taken in small groups down a spiral staircase... bringing up the rear was a wardress who looked less of a bully than some of them. I risked asking her: 'This Auschwitz place, what's it really like?' 'It's not for you to ask questions.' We were loaded into another Black Maria, with all its windows blacked out. When we emerged we found ourselves in a railway siding, besides an enormously long train of smart newly painted passenger coaches.
> The windows of the coaches, like those of the prison van, had all been painted over and barred. The interior consisted of a narrow central corridor dividing rows of tiny locked cages. Each cell had been designed for two or four people, but six of us were pushed into one of them. Mother and I managed to stay together. After the cages were filled, the whole

---

[296] Claude Lanzmann, *Shoah*, Pantheon Books, New York 1985, pp. 50–51.

coach was shut. It was gloomy and depressing. Individual cells were unlit, and the only illumination came from a dim electric bulb in the corridor ceiling.[297]

The journey began:

> It was ages before the train began to move. With no change between darkness and daylight, nothing but that electric bulb feebly on all the time, we had little sense of time and no way of working out how far we travelled. I was drowsing, propped against the wire mesh, when the train slowed and finally clanked and grated to a halt. The familiar screaming and bellowing started up right away. 'Everybody Out, Off the train. Get a move on!' We scrambled down awkwardly in near-darkness. It was still night, but in the distance was a hint of dawn. There were hundreds of people stumbling about, trying to find their footing on the lumpy ground. We were dazed, unable to get our bearings. Guards moved in, screaming and shoving us into columns. We marched off along the railway line, tripping and lurching as we went. Mother and I stayed side by side.[298]

They had arrived at Auschwitz, Kitty Hart continued:

> We came to a gate with the motto above it in iron lettering, silhouetted against the sky: *ARBEIT MACHT FREI*—Work Brings Freedom. Men who must have been in a different part of the train were taken in through the gate, along with some of the women... the rest of us were formed into fives and went staggering on, picking our way with the help of the erratic glare from three layers of illuminated, electrified fencing. Above them stood a rank of high watchtowers.
> The railway line petered out. We kept going until we were halted at another gate and a guardhouse. This was in fact the entrance to Auschwitz II, or Birkenau, though at the time we knew nothing of the names or significance of any part of this bewildering place. A dank chill caught us. The whole area was shrouded in a clinging grey mist. But dawn was breaking.... A reddish glow through the mist was flickering in the weirdest way, and there was a sickly, fatty, cloying smell. Mother and I glanced at each other, baffled. Who could be roasting meat, great quantities of it, at this hour of the morning?[299]

---

[297] Kitty Hart, *Return to Auschwitz*, Granada Publishing, St. Albans 1983, pp. 76–77.
[298] Ibid., p. 78.
[299] Ibid., pp. 78–79.

The date was April 2, 1943, when Kitty and her mother Rosa entered Birkenau:

> We stumbled on our way and were driven into a long narrow building which we later heard referred to as the sauna. Women with short hair were pacing up and down, wearing striped jackets and trousers or baggy striped garments which could hardly be described as dresses. Each had a large green triangle on her left breast, identifying her as a German criminial prisoner. There was no uniformed German in sight.
> We were ordered to strip and our clothes were thrown into large vats for decontamination. We ourselves were left under a row of cold showers for some time and then dipped in a foul-smelling, bluish-green fluid. While we were still shivering and stinging from this, the *Fryzerki*, the hairdressers, got to work, 'Arms and legs out.' We had to stretch arms and legs wide while they shaved our heads, under our armpits, and between our legs. We looked ridiculous—but even more ridiculous when we were issued with new clothing..... I got a pair of khaki breeches several sizes too large for me, a blouse with odd sleeves, two old stockings and a pair of clogs. When I turned to look for my mother, I couldn't make her out at first and when we did recognize each other, we burst out laughing.... The uniforms, we discovered later, came from 20,000 Russian Prisoners of War, who had been massacred just before our arrival.
> We were bullied into a long line and shuffled towards desks where a number of girl clerks sat... they were methodically taking down particulars of all the newcomers. I was just behind my mother, and while my documentation was being completed another woman tattooed her forearm. Mothers number was 39933. I became 39934.[300]

Transports from Theresienstadt to Auschwitz

Theresienstadt, the German name for Terezin, was founded in the late 18th century when Emperor Josef II decided to build a fortress at the confluence of the Labe and Ohre Rivers, some 30 miles North West of Prague, in what is now called the Czech Republlic, but during the occupation this area was known as the Protectorate of Bohemia and Moravia.

---

[300] Ibid., pp. 80–81.

The fortress town was named after his mother—Maria Theresa, and the stronghold took ten years to build. It consisted of the Main and Small Fortress, alongside a fortified area. These fortifications used a number of elements, massive bastions, bulwarks and an extensive network of underground passage-ways.

After the German occupation in 1938, Terezin was renamed by the Germans as Theresienstadt and in March 1940, Dr. Walther Stahlecker , Commander of the Security Police and Security Service in Prague sought approval from Reinhard Heydrich in Berlin to establish a prison in the Small Fortress in Theresienstadt. In June 1940, the prison was established under the control of the *Gestapo* in Prague.

Reinhard Heydrich, when he became Deputy Protector of Bohemia and Moravia on October 10, 1941, summoned Adolf Eichmann from the Reich Main Security Office and Gerhard Mauer from *Amtsgruppe D* of the *WVHA* to meet him and Karl Hermann Frank in Prague. Heydrich informed those present that he had already selected Theresienstadt and other fortified sites to become a Ghetto. He used the terms *Sammellager* and *Zentralstelle* and on November 24, 1941, a Ghetto was indeed established in the town itself in former Austrian barracks.

On January 20, 1942, Heydrich announced at the Wannsee Conference in Berlin that Theresienstadt was under consideration to become a special Ghetto for Jews over 65 years of age and Jews with serious wounds or those who had been awarded with high decorations during the First World War. Thus Theresienstadt was seen as the Ghetto for privileged Jews, but it never lost sight of its original purpose, that is as a transit camp for Jews from the Old Reich and Jews from the Protectorate of Bohemia and Moravia.

With the departure of the original Czech residents in June 1942, the first of the 'privileged' Jews from the '*Altreich*' started to arrive in Theresienstadt. From June 2, 1942, a spate of transports departed from Berlin, Munich and Vienna. These were mainly Great War veterans and the elderly. Other categories included Jews married to Aryans, half Jews who belonged to the Jewish faith. What then followed was a flood of deportees who had simply brought their exemptions. For example during 1942, Theresienstadt received 32,988 Jews from the *'Altreich,'* 13,922 Jews from Austria and 54,827 from the Protectorate of Bohemia and Moravia. Some of these transports ended up in the *Aktion Reinhardt* death camps of Bełżec, Sobibór and Treblinka, whilst many found their way to Auschwitz.

Transports From Theresienstadt to Auschwitz 1942–1944

Date	Transport Designation	Number of Deportees
26 October 1942	By	1866
20 January 1943	Cq	2000
23 January 1943	Cr	2000
26 January 1943	Cs	1000
29 January 1943	Ct	1000
I February 1943	Cu	1001
6 September 1943	Dl	2479
6 September 1943	Dm	2528
5 October 1943	Dn*	1196
5 October 1943	Dn a	53
15 December 1943	Dr	2504
18 December 1943	Ds	2503
20 March 1944	Dx	45
15 May 1944	Dz	2503
16 May 1944	Ea	2500
18 May 1944	Eb	2500
1 July 1944	Eh	10
28 September 1944	Ek	2499
29 September 1944	El	1500
1 October 1944	Em	1500
4 October 1944	En	1500
6 October 1944	Eo	1550
9 October 1944	Ep	1600
12 October 1944	Eq	1500

16 October 1944	Er	1500
19 October 1944	Es	1500
23 October 1944	Et	1715
28 October 1944	Ev	2038

* Dn – *Kindertransport* – Childrens Transport
Source: Terezin Gedenkbuch

Included in Transport Ep on October 9, 1944, was Felice Rahel Schragenheim who was born on March 9, 1922, in Berlin. She was arrested on August 21 and deported from Berlin on September 5, 1944 to the Theresienstadt Ghetto, near Prague.

She was deported to Auschwitz Concentration Camp on October 9, 1944, and was deported to the Bergen Belsen Concentration Camp in Germany, where she died in March 1945, according to the *Bundesarchiv Gedenkbuch*, though other sources list her date of death as December 31, 1944.

Felice Schragenheim was a Jewess and a lesbian and she worked for a Nazi newspaper and lived and worked using the name Felice Schrader. Felice fell in love with Elisabeth 'Lilly' Wust, who was the wife of a German soldier, Gunther Wust, and the mother of four boys, who lived at *Friedrichshaller Straße 23*, in Berlin.

Felice was part of an underground network who worked to procure identification documents for Jews in hiding or those who wished to leave the Reich. Felice moved in with Lilly on May 2, 1943, and the next day Lilly requested a divorce from Gunther. Gunther Wust was killed in action and the two women raised the four children, until Felice was arrested on August 21, 1944.

Lilly visited Felice in Theresienstadt in a vain attempt to bring about her release, and Lilly was interrogated by the *Gestapo* following her visit to Theresienstadt, probably the only thing that saved her, was her status as a Nazi mother, who had been awarded the *Ehrenkreuz der Deutschen Mutter* for producing four Aryan sons. The two women wrote to one another constantly, before Felice's death. Some of the letters along with four of Lilly's personal journals have been donated to Yad Vashem.

In 1981, Lilly Wust was awarded the German Federal Cross for assisting Jews during the War and their love story like so many others would probably never have been told, if it were not for a book written about their lives called *'Aimee and Jaguar, A Love Story, Berlin 1943'*, by Erica Fischer. Aimee and Jaguar were their pet names for each other, and five years later in 1999, a film of the same name was released, based on the book directed by German Director, Max Farberböck. The film was a critical and commercial success, being nominated for a Golden Globe Award and was Germany's official submission for a Best Foreign Language Film Academy Award.

Lilly Wurst died on March 31, 2006, and was buried at Dorfkirche Giesendorf, Berlin, and on her gravestone, there is also written 'In Memoriam' to Felice Schragenheim.[301]

The next person we shall cover is Max Block, who was born on December 14, 1889, in Bochum, Germany. He was the fourth of Bendix and Therese Block's twelve children. Max moved to Berlin in 1917, where he worked as a banker. On March 31, 1930, he married Gertrud Hildegard Rosenthal.

They emigrated to Holland during February 1936, and they were registered at Beethovenstraat 64, and a year later they moved to Brahmsstraat 11, and then to Watteaustraat 21, on November 3, 1938. During November 1938, Max wrote a report about the treatment of his mother who was seventy-eight years old. Therese Block, during the program that became known as *'Kristallnacht,'* was awakened by the Nazis at 3 o'clock in the morning on November 12, 1938, and was told she had six hours to leave. She emigrated to Los Angeles, where two of her daughters lived. The report is housed in the Wiener Library in London.

In March 1939, Max moved back to Brahmsstraat 11, and on July 11, 1939, he was divorced from Gertrud, who remarried and settled in England in 1940. Max Block was deported from Westerbork to Theresienstadt on April 22, 1943, and he was further deported on

---

[301] www.Medium.com

Transport Eq on October 12, 1944, to Auschwitz Concentration Camp, where he was murdered on October 14, 1944.[302]

Transports From Belgium

Towards the end of July 1942, the *SS* established the Dossin *Kaserne* in Malines as a *Sammellager für Juden*—Collection Camp for Jews. The barracks were constructed in the 18th century and were located half-way between Brussels and Antwerp, the two cities where most of the Jews in Belgium were living. Furthermore, adjacent to the barracks was a railway line linking Brussels and Antwerp running via Louvain to Germany and beyond.

One account worthy of a mention was the event of April 19, 1943, when Belgian railway-workers contrived to leave some doors open when the cattle cars departed from the Dossin *Kaserne*. Other railway workers held up the train between Tirlemont and Vise, where the resistance group, the so-called '*Comité de defence des Juifs*' had organized an ambush. The gun-fire of the *SS* guards was returned, and 231 Jews were able to escape, though twenty were killed and more than a hundred were wounded.

Transports From Malines in Belgium to Auschwitz 1942–1944

Date	Number of Deportees	Arrival in Auschwitz
4 August 1942	998	5 August 1942
11 August 1942	999	13 August 1942
15 August 1942	1000	17 August 1942
18 August 1942	998	20 August 1942
25 August 1942	995	27 August 1942
29 August 1942	1000	31 August 1942
1 September 1942	1000	3 September 1942
8 September 1942	1000	10 September 1942

---

[302] Thomas Nowotny, *The Story of Max Block* www.Holocaustresearch-project.org, 2012.

12 September 1942	1000	14 September 1942
15 September 1942	1048	17 September 1942
26 September 1942	1742	28 September 1942
10 October 1942	1679	12 October 1942
24 October 1942	995	26 October 1942
31 October 1942	1937	3 November 1942
15 January 1943	1632	18 January 1943
19 April 1943	1631	22 April 1943
31 July 1943	1563	2 August 1943
20 September 1943	1433	22 September 1943
15 January 1944	657	17 January 1944
4 April 1944	625	7 April 1944
19 May 1944	507	21 May 1944
31 July 1944	563	2 August 1944

Source: Das Bundesarchiv—Memorial Book Online Resource

On the transport which left Malines on January 15, 1944, was the Polish-born Jew, Meir Tabakman and his wife Raizl. Tabakman had been deported some months earlier, but he had jumped off the train. Subsequently he had been re-captured and now branded as a *'Flitzer'* (one who had tried to flee), he was locked in a special goods wagon with other former escapees. His wife later recalled, 'not one of them entered the camp, all went straight to the gas chambers'.[303]

Transports From France

From August 1941, the Germans commenced using Drancy as a *Sammellager für Juden*—Collection Camp for Jews. The Camp was located in a public housing project built between the years 1932 to 1936, and the project was known as Cité de la Muette. Prior to the Second World War it was used as a public housing project, but was later used as a barracks for the French police and then a Transit Camp for the Jews of France.

---

[303] www.HolocaustresearchprojectS.org.

The Camp measured 200 by 400 meters with barbed wire fences and watchtowers at each corner; the Camp held some 4,500 people and was guarded initially by members of the French police, but they were replaced by members of the SS on July 2, 1943. The Commandant was Alois Brunner, one of Adolf Eichmann's top aides, and he was assisted by four other SS members who also served on Eichmann's staff. Two other members of Eichmann's staff deserve a special mention for the parts they played in the deportation and murder of the Jews of France, they were Theodor Dannecker and Heinz Röthke. Theodor Dannecker was moved from Paris to Bulgaria in order to mastermind the deportations in 1943, and in Italy during 1944. He committed suicide in a US prison camp in Bad Tölz on December 10, 1945. Dr. Heinz Röthke, who took Dannecker's place in Paris in July 1942, was never brought to trial.

Some 65,000 people passed through Drancy, being taken by bus to the nearby railway station of Le Bourget-Drancy to the death camps in Poland, mostly to Auschwitz. Deportations also took place from other transit camps such as Pithiviers, Beaune-la-Rolande, Compiègne, as well as Angers and Lyon. The first transport to Auschwitz from Drancy left on March 27, 1942, and these ran until July 1944. A couple of transports in August 1944 went from Lyon to Auschwitz and the last transport from France on August 15, 1944 went from Drancy to Buchenwald Concentration Camp in Germany.

One of the most tragic events regarding the Holocaust in France was the destruction of the children's home in Izieu on April 6, 1944 by a *Gestapo* detachment led by the notorious Klaus Barbie. The following day, on April 7, 1944, *Obersturmführer* Barbie of the Lyons *Gestapo* reported the dissolution of the Jewish *Colonie des Enfants* at Izieu-Ain. 'Captured—forty-one children, aged from three years to ten, and ten attendants. The transport will leave for Drancy tomorrow.'

Among the Jewish children deported from Izieu to Auschwitz via Lyons and Drancy was the eleven-year old Liliane Berenstein, who before leaving, wrote a letter to God, the letter read as follows:

> God? How good you are, how kind, and if one had to count the number of goodnnesses and kindnesses you have done us he would never finish.

God? It is you who command. It is you who are justice, it is you who reward the good and punish the evil. God? It is thanks to you that I had a beautiful life before, that I was spoiled, that I had lovely things that others do not have. God? After that, I ask you one thing only: MAKE MY PARENTS COME BACK, MY POOR PARENTS, PROTECT THEM (even more than you protect me) SO THAT I SEE THEM AGAIN AS SOON AS POSSIBLE. MAKE THEM COME BACK AGAIN. Ah! I could say that I had such a good mother and such a good father! I have such faith in you that I thank you in advance.[304]

None of the children survived, only one of the supervisors at the children's home survived Auschwitz and that was Lea Feldblum, who was twenty-seven years old.[305]

Transports From France to Auschwitz 1942–1944

Date	Deportation From	Number of Deportees	Arrival At Auschwitz
27 March 1942	Compiègne	1112	30 March 1942
5 June 1942	Compiègne	1000	7 June 1942
22 June 1942	Drancy	1000	24 June 1942
25 June 1942	Pithiviers	999	27 June 1942
28 June 1942	Beaune La Rolande	1038	30 June 1942
17 July 1942	Pithiviers	928	19 July 1942
19 July 1942	Drancy	1000	21 July 1942
20 July 1942	Angers	827	23 July 1942
22 July 1942	Drancy	1000	24 July 1942
24 July 1942	Drancy	1000	26 July 1942
27 July 1942	Drancy	1000	29 July 1942
29 July 1942	Drancy	1000	31 July 1942
31 July 1942	Pithiviers	1049	5 August 1942
3 August 1942	Pithiviers	1034	5 August 1942
5 August 1942	Beaune La Rolande	1014	7 August 1942
7 August 1942	Pithiviers	1069	9 August 1942
10 August 1942	Drancy	1006	12 August 1942
12 August 1942	Drancy	1007	14 August 1942

---

[304] M. Gilbert, *The Holocaust*, Collins, London 1985, pp. 666–667.
[305] www.Jewishvirtuallibrary.org

14 August 1942	Drancy	991	19 August 1942
17 August 1942	Drancy	997	19 August 1942
19 August 1942	Drancy	1000	21 August 1942
21 August 1942	Drancy	1000	23 August 1942
24 August 1942	Drancy	1057	26 August 1942
26 August 1942	Drancy	1000	28 August 1942
28 August 1942	Drancy	1000	31 August 1942
31 August 1942	Drancy	1000	2 September 1942
2 September 1942	Drancy	1000	4 September 1942
4 September 1942	Drancy	1000	6 September 1942
7 September 1942	Drancy	1000	9 September 1942
9 September 1942	Drancy	1000	11 September 1942
11 September 1942	Drancy	1035	13 September 1942
14 September 1942	Drancy	1000	16 September 1942
16 September 1942	Drancy	1003	18 September 1942
18 September 1942	Drancy	1000	20 September 1942
21 September 1942	Pithiviers	1015	23 September 1942
23 September 1942	Drancy	1006	25 September 1942
25 September 1942	Drancy	1028	27 September 1942
28 September 1942	Drancy	904	29 September 1942
30 September 1942	Drancy	211	2 October 1942
4 November 1942	Drancy	1010	6 November 1942
6 November 1942	Drancy	1000	8 November 1942

9 November 1942	Drancy	1000	11 November 1942
11 November 1942	Drancy	745	13 November 1942
9 February 1943	Drancy	1000	11 February 1943
11 February 1943	Drancy	998	13 February 1943
13 February 1943	Drancy	1000	15 February 1943
2 March 1943	Drancy	1000	4 March 1943
23 June 1943	Drancy	1018	25 June 1943
18 July 1943	Drancy	1000	20 July 1943
31 July 1943	Drancy	1000	2 August 1943
2 September 1943	Drancy	1000	4 September 1943
7 October 1943	Drancy	1000	9 October 1943
28 October 1943	Drancy	1000	30 October 1943
20 November 1943	Drancy	1200	23 November 1943
7 December 1943	Drancy	1000	10 December 1943
17 December 1943	Drancy	850	20 December 1943
20 January 1944	Drancy	1153	22 January 1944
3 February 1944	Drancy	1214	6 February 1944
10 February 1944	Drancy	1500	12 February 1944
7 March 1944	Drancy	1501	10 March 1944
27 March 1944	Drancy	1025	30 March 1944
13 April 1944	Drancy	1500	16 April 1944
29 April 1944	Drancy	1004	1 May 1944
20 May 1944	Drancy	1200	23 May 1944
30 May 1944	Drancy	1004	2 June 1944
30 June 1944	Drancy	1150	4 July 1944
31 July 1944	Drancy	1300	3 August 1944
11 August 1944	Lyon	430	

Source: Das Bundesarchiv—Memorial Book Online Resource

One of those transferred from France is David Olere who was born on January 19, 1902, in Warsaw. After completing his studies at the Academy of Fine Arts in Warsaw, at the age of 16, he moved to Danzig, today Gdańsk in Poland, and then to Berlin. In Berlin he exhibited woodcuts. He relocated to Paris in 1923, and he became involved in the motion picture industry, working as a designer of sets, costumes and posters.

On February 2, 1943, David Olere was arrested and incarcerated in the transit camp at Drancy. Exactly one month later on March 2, 1943, he was deported to Auschwitz Concentration Camp. On arrival he was selected to live and due to his excellent language skills he was used by the *SS*. The Germans also took advantage of his talents as an illustrator, writing letters to their family members which contained drawings.

He was tattooed with the prisoner number 106144, and was a member of the *Sonderkommando,* employed in the crematoriums.[306] On January 19, 1945, he was evacuated from the Camp on the forced marches, and he eventually found himself in Mauthausen Concentration Camp in Austria. He was moved to the sub-camp of Melk and on May 6, 1945, he was liberated by the American Forces. Upon his return to France, David Olere produced some fifty drawings documenting his experiences in Auschwitz and Mauthausen. He died on August 21, 1985, near Paris.[307]

Transports From Greece to Auschwitz 1943–1944

Drawing on various source materials, including train tickets printed in Greek and German which were found at the Oswiecim railway station after the War, Danuta Czech concluded that 48, 533 Jews arrived from Salonika during the period from March 20 to August 18, 1943.

---

[306] Shlomo Venezia, *Inside the Gas Chambers,* Polity Press, Cambridge 2009, p. 197.
[307] www.gfh.org.il

In 1944, another 6,000 Jews were transported from Athens and the islands of Corfu and Rhodes. When added together, these two figures give an approximate total of 55,000 Jews deported from Greece to Auschwitz.

The Germans began the destruction of the Jewish community in Salonika by destroying the vestiges of Jewish history. They destroyed the archives and the Jewish gravestones from the enormous Salonika cemetery on December 6, 1942, when *Sturmbannführer* Robert Wulff, one of Eichmann's representatives conducted a preliminary survey. Shortly afterwards, Adolf Eichmann and his deputy, Rolf Günther visited Salonika. The deportations were to be conducted by two more of his trusted associates: Dieter Wisliceny and Anton Brunner, who arrived from Vienna on February 6, 1943.

The Jews of Salonika were ordered to wear the Jewish Star of David and three Ghettos were created. One of them, the 'Baron Hirsch' quarter, which was enclosed, housed Jews from the Macedonian hinterland. The 'Baron Hirsch' quarter was a Camp with huts near the railway station, which was constructed in 1903, for Jewish refugees from the Mogilev and Kishinev pogroms, and was inhabited by 2,000 of the poorest Jewish inhabitants of Salonika. While the establishment of 'Baron Hirsch' was taking place, Wisliceny and his associates took up residence in two Jewish villas in the Hodos Velissariou.

On March 14, 1943, it was announced that the 2,800 Jews held in 'Baron Hirsch' were to be sent to Kraków. A train of forty boxcars departed on March 15, 1943, and it arrived five days later in Auschwitz, on March 20, 1943. Out of the total of 2,800 Jews deported, 2191 were gassed on arrival.[308]

Shlomo Venezia was born on December 29, 1923, in Salonika, Greece. There were five children in his family, his older brother Maurice, and his sisters Rachel, Marcia and Marta. His father, Isacco Venezia, died in 1934 or 1935, leaving his wife Doudon Angel to bring up five children as a widow. In July 1943, the family transferred to

---

[308] G. Reitlinger, *The Final Solution*, Sphere Books, London 1971, pp. 399–400.

Athens. It was from the Haidari Prison where the whole family was deported to Auschwitz on April 1, 1944. Also deported with him were his cousins Dario and Yakob Gabbai. Schlomo recalled the deportation in his memorable book, 'Inside the Gas Chambers,' published in Paris in 2007:

> It was cunning of the Germans to get us together in our families. When you're alone, the idea of escaping is more tempting. But how can you think of abandoning your parents or your children? And yet a few people managed to escape, almost by chance. On the path between the prison and the freight station the trucks carrying us followed along one after the other. A German guard was seated near the driver and kept an eye on the passengers in the truck ahead. One of these trucks broke down and so, of course, the one ahead of it didn't have anybody to keep an eye on the rear. Five or six young boys jumped off and escaped, but the Germans soon had everything under control again.
>
> We finally arrived on the platforms. There were cattle cars waiting for us. The Germans pushed us brutally into the wagons. Inside there was nothing, just planks on the floor, a big empty can in the middle, and a smaller one with water. In a corner, I saw three crates of raisins and carrots. The space was very limited, and as soon as everyone had climbed aboard, we saw that it would be impossible to stretch out, at best we would need to stay seated throughout the journey. I immediately sat in a corner near the window.[309]

Shlomo's account continued:

> Looking out of the window, I saw an *SS* officer starting to get angry with some people who seemed to be from the Red Cross. I thought they were there because they wanted to free us. But they simply wanted to hand out some food for our journey. I believe they knew what our final destination was, since they wouldn't have taken any trouble if it had been just a short trip, even in those conditions. Eventually they came to an agreement, and the *SS* officer allowed the Red Cross trucks to follow the train until it stopped outside the city. Through the window, I could see the trucks following us at a distance. The train stopped out in the open country, so that the Red Cross personnel could distribute parcels of food and blankets.....

---

[309] Shlomo Venezia, *Inside the Gas Chambers*, Polity Press, Cambridge 2009, pp. 26–27.

> The Red Cross people tried to give us as many as they could, and the important thing was to grab hold of them. I picked up the parcels and the blankets, and threw them back to my brother and cousin, who were making room in the carriage.... In fact I had picked up thirty-eight parcels and several blankets. In every parcel there were wheat wafers, powdered milk, chocolate, cigarettes, and other useful things to keep us going throughout the journey. Of course we shared with the other people in the carriage.[310]

En-route to Auschwitz, Shlomo received an ominous warning from someone he knew:

> From Athens the train was meant to go via Salonika, which was an important railway junction in the North. The train stopped near the station to replenish its coal and water. I went up to the skylight to see if there was anyone outside I might recognize. German soldiers were posted every ten yards along the train. As chance would have it, the railwayman who was checking the track was a young fellow I did know. His name was Gyorgos Kaloudis.... His father had also worked on the railways and was a known communist. The older man had been arrested by the Germans as soon as they entered Salonika. Gyorgos had replaced his father on the railways. His work consisted of ensuring that the brakes didn't block the wheels, and adjusting them with a long hammer.
>
> When he saw me, he appeared very surprised and slipped over, pretending to be working on my carriage. Without being noticed by the Germans, he said in Greek, 'What's going on? You here too? Try to get the hell out of here; where they're taking you, they just kill everybody!' He told me that we were going to Poland..... When the train began to move again, I immediately told my brother and my cousins what Gyorgos had just told me.

But Shlomo could not bring himself to leave his mother and sisters behind, so any escape attempts had to be abandoned. The nightmare journey continued, the convoy left Greece, travelled through Yugoslavia, then Austria and Slovakia. They stopped in Brno, in Slovakia, and Shlomo received another warning:

> In Brno, the train stopped again. I remember the place, as I'd found the name of the town distinctly odd. We were begging the Germans to let us have a little water. Instead of that, a drunkard stopped in front of my

---

[310] Ibid., pp. 27–28.

> carriage and motioned to us in a very explicit dumb show, telling us we were all going to be killed, hanged. He was completely drunk, but seeing him waving his hands around like that made me so angry that I spat in his face the minute he came to our carriage. Eventually a German soldier showed him away…. After Brno we took another two days to reach the *Judenrampe* in Auschwitz-Birkenau.[311]

Shlomo Venezia's transport was unloaded at the site of the *Judenrampe*, which was located 1 kilometer south east of the entrance of the camp at Birkenau. The date was April 11, 1944:

> The train hadn't blown its whistle when the transport had stopped en route. So when I heard that peculiar whistle and felt the train suddenly braking I immediately realized that the convoy had finally reached its destination. The doors opened onto the Judenrampe, just opposite the potato sheds….. as soon as the train stopped, the *SS* opened the doors of the carriage and started yelling '*Alle runter! Alle Runter!*' 'Everyone Out!' 'Everyone Out!'
> We saw men in uniform pointing their sub-machine guns, and Alsatians barking at us. Everyone was in a stupor, numb after the journey—and all of a sudden, fierce yells and a whole infernal din to throw us off our guard, and prevent us knowing what was going on. I happened to be near the door, so I was among the first to climb out. I wanted to stay near the door to help my mother get out. We had to jump for it, as the carriage was high and the terrain was sloping. My mother wasn't that old, but I knew the journey had worn her out and I wanted to help her. While I was waiting for her, a German came up behind and struck me two heavy blows on the back of my neck with his stick. He lashed out with such force, I thought he'd split my skull…. Seeing that he was going to start hitting me again, I ran off to join the others in the queue…. So that's what I did, and when I turned around to try and find my mother, she wasn't there anymore. I never saw her again. She wasn't there, and neither were my two little sisters, Marcia and Marta.[312]

The selection for those who were to die and those who were to live now took place:

---

[311] Shlomo Venezia, *Inside the Gas Chambers*, Polity Press, Cambridge 2009, p. 32.
[312] Ibid., pp. 34–35.

> As soon as we jumped out of the train, the Germans with their whips and blows, made us get into two queues, sending the women and children to one side and all the men without distinction, to the other. They beckoned us into place: '*Männer hier und Frauen hier!*' 'Men here and women here!' We stepped into place like robots, in response to their yells and orders.......
> They immediately made us all line up in front of a German officer. Another officer arrived shortly afterwards. I don't know if it was the famous Dr. Mengele; it may have been, but I'm not sure. The officer barely looked at us and made a gesture with his thumb indicating 'Links, rechts!' Left, right!' and depending on the direction he sent us, each of us had to go one way or the other.... I found myself on the side where there were fewer people. In the end there were just three hundred and twenty men left. All the others set off, without knowing it, for immediate death in the gas chambers at Birkenau. My brother and my cousins also ended up on the right side with me. Our group was sent on foot to Auschwitz I.[313]

The next chapter was about to begin for Schlomo, his brother and their cousins in Auschwitz Concentration Camp:

> We walked the distance just over a mile or so, from the *Judenrampe* to the Camp at Auschwitz I, while the others unsuspectingly headed off to the gas chambers at Birkenau. I remember that, before entering the Auschwitz I main gate, with the inscription '*Arbeit Macht Frei*'—'Work Makes Free,' I noticed a sign placed near the barbed wire fence. It read '*Vorsicht Hochspannung Lebensgefahr*,' meaning 'Beware, high tension, danger of death.'
> Once inside, immediately on the left was Block 24, we later discovered that it served as a brothel for the soldiers and a few privileged non-Jews. In the windows we could see pretty women laughing..... we saw in the distance, prisoners who tried to come across to us and find out where we were from and if by any chance we had any news of their families. All at once, I heard a voice calling, 'Schlomo!' 'Schlomo!' Looking towards the prisoners, I spotted the fiancé of my sister Rachel, Aaron Mano, who was trying to attract my attention. He wanted to know if Rachel had been arrested too. I told him that, unfortunately, she had

---

[313] Shlomo Venezia, *Inside the Gas Chambers*, Polity Press, Cambridge 2009, p. 35–37.

been deported with us, but I didn't know what had happened to her since.[314]

Then an unusual event took place:

> Finally, the Germans ordered us to line up in groups of five in a narrow space between two blocks, opposite the kitchens. Here there were two Germans waiting for us, with a movie camera. They told one of the prisoners who had been deported with us to go over so they could film him. I remember that man clearly, as he had the same family name as I, Venezia, Baruch Venezia, but he wasn't from my family. He was a very tall man, with the hooked nose and typical face of southern Jews.
> His features were tired and drawn after the journey. He hadn't shaved for several days; this and his defeated expression, made him look even more miserable. I heard one of the Germans telling the other to film him, as he had a 'perfect Jewish profile.'
> We had to wait for an officer to come and give us instructions. We stood there motionless for a long time. Before the officer arrived, a Greek interpreter whom I knew from Salonika came over to us and warned us that the German was going to ask us a few questions. He advised us to answer without thinking twice, and to say that we were in good health, without any lice, and ready to work. This man's name was Salvatore Cunio.
> Finally, when the officer arrived, night had already fallen. He asked us the anticipated questions; we answered in the way the interpreter had indicated. Then the officer gave the order: 'Alle nach Birkenau.' 'Everyone to Birkenau.' So we turned around and set off for Birkenau. It was dark and there was a thick fog; one could see just a few lights in the distance. It must have been ten o'clock by the time we arrived in Birkenau.
> We entered by the central tower, where the trains later started to come in. But, at the time of our arrival, the tracks leading right into the Camp, designed to cope with the massive deportation of Hungarian Jews, were still under construction.... Once I was in the Camp, I don't know if we continued straight on, passing in front of Crematorium II and III to come in from behind, or whether instead we passed down the *Lagerstraße*. Through the fog, all I could make out were the huts lit up by little lights on the right and left of the road. At the time, I didn't yet know who or what was in those buildings, so I didn't pay much attention.

---

[314] Ibid., pp. 37–38.

We eventually entered the *Zentralsauna*, a big brick structure used to disinfect people and clothes. The first thing we had to do was take off all our clothes... at the far end of the room we saw two doctors, SS officers in white coats. They watched us as we walked naked in front of them. Every now and then they would motion to one of us to stay on the side. In this way they put some fifteen to eighteen people 'on the side.' Among them was a cousin of my father's. He had always seemed fragile and unhealthy.

The reception process continued:

Those who hadn't been put aside continued on, and passed into the following room. In this room, 'hairdressers' were lined up to shave our heads and entire bodies. Since they didn't have adequate tools, or any shaving foam, they pulled our skin off until we bled. In the following room were the showers. This was a big room with pipes and shower heads above us. A rather young German controlled the taps of hot and cold water. To amuse himself at our expense, he quickly changed from scalding hot to freezing cold water. The minute the water became too hot, we moved away so as not to get burned, and then he started howling like an animal, beat us and forced us to get back under the scalding water.....

Schlomo explained how the prisoners received their numbers:

Still soaking wet and naked, I followed the queue until I reached the tattooing room. There was a long table at which several prisoners had been put to tattoo our identity numbers on our arms. They used a sort of ball-point pen with a sharp point that pierced one's skin and made the ink go in under the epidermis. They had to make these little penetrations until the number appeared on one's arm. It was extremely painful. When the man tattooing me finally dropped my arm, I immediately rubbed the front of my arm to lessen the pain.
When I looked to see what he'd done to me, I couldn't make anything out under the mixture of blood and ink. I was suddenly frightened that I might have wiped the number out. With a bit of spit, I wiped my arm clean and I saw the number that had been correctly injected: 182727, my identity.[315]

---

[315] Shlomo Venezia, *Inside the Gas Chambers*, Polity Press, Cambridge 2009, p. 38–41.

After that, we had to wait for the clothes that were to be handed out to us. For some time now, new prisoners had not been given striped uniforms. Instead we received disinfected clothes left by the prisoners who had arrived before us. They were handed out without anyone bothering to give us clothes that fit. We were given a jacket, a pair of trousers, underpants, shoes and socks. The clothes were often frayed and full of holes.

Several of the new arrivals couldn't get their trousers on, and others had been given trousers that were much too big. There was no way we could go and ask those who'd distributed the clothes for things of our own size. They might well have beaten us, even if they, too were prisoners. So we tried to sort it out among ourselves by swapping clothes. But you needed to be lucky, especially with the shoes—so many of them had holes in their soles. I managed to get reasonable clothes, even if everything was a bit too large for me.[316]

Transports From Hungary 1944

At the beginning of March 1944, according to Dieter Wisliceny—one of Adolf Eichmann's most trusted associates, almost all of the staff of Eichmann's Jewish Deportation Office assembled at Mauthausen Concentration Camp to plan the proposed implementation of the 'Final Solution' to the Jewish question in Hungary.

The German forces moved into Hungary on March 19, 1944, and Eichmann arrived at the end of March 1944, and set up his headquarters in the Hotel Majestic, in the charmingly named Rose Hill suburb of Budapest. On March 20, 1944, Hermann Krumey and Dieter Wisliceny visited the leaders of the Jewish community in their offices of the *kehillah* in Pest and issued an order that the notables should assemble there the next day. This was the same Hermann Krumey who had been Head of the Central Resettlement Office, *Umwandererzentralstelle (UWZ)* in Łódź. He had been responsible, along with Odilo Globocnik, for deporting Polish farmers and their families, from the Zamość Lands to Auschwitz, during 1942 and 1943.

---

[316] Ibid., p. 42.

The following day, Hermann Krumey and Dieter Wisliceny reappeared at the *kehillah* and informed the notables who had attended, that they must form a Jewish Council and that all matters relating to the Jews would be handled now by the Germans, dealing exclusively through the Jewish Council.

On March 31, 1944, Eichmann held the first meeting with the new Jewish Council in the Hotel Majestic, and he declared at the meeting; 'I am a bloodhound.' He also informed the members of the Jewish Council that 'they may sleep in their beds at night, he asked to see the Jewish museum and library, matters that had interested him since 1934.' Samuel Stern, who ran a successful Milk and Dairy product marketing company and a refrigeration business during the First World War was appointed the Head of the Jewish Council. He survived the Holocaust, but died in 1946.

A week before this meeting, Ernst Kaltenbrunner, Head of the Reich Main Security Office left Budapest on March 24, 1944, having secured three appointments to aid the Germans in their savage quest to achieve the 'Final Solution' in Hungary. The three men appointed were László Baky, László Endre and László Ferenczy. All three men were active in the Arrow Cross, the Hungarian National Socialist movement. Baky and Endre ran the Jewish Commissariat in the Ministry of the Interior. Whilst Major Ferenczy was to act as a go-between for the Hungarian Gendarmerie and the German Security Services.

According to the testimony of Dieter Wisliceny, László Ferenczy went to Eichmann's office as early as April 20, 1944, and he implored Eichmann to 'take the Jews off the hands of the Ministry of the Interior and Wisliceny confirmed that Eichmann had German Railway officials waiting in the next office and that Rolf Günther at once telegraphed *Gruppenführer* Glücks, the Inspector of Concentration Camps, to get ready at Auschwitz.

Between April 24 and April 28, 1944, Endre went with Eichmann and Wisliceny on an inspection tour at Kassa (Košice), Ungvár, Munkács, and Mamaros-Sziget, Holding Camps. At all of these places, between 15,000 to 25,000 Jews were huddled miserably in brickfields and Endre allowed himself to be convinced by Eichmann that these Jews should be deported from Hungary.[317]

Two transports from Hungary, the first sent from Budapest on April 29, 1944, arrived in Auschwitz on May 2, 1944. The second transport was sent from Topoly. After the selection 486 men and 616 women were admitted to the Camp, the remaining 2,698 men and women were murdered in the gas chambers.[318]

On May 15, 1944, the main deportations began, and at Auschwitz Concentration Camp a period of frenzied mass murder took place. Some 380,000 Jews were deported by June 30, 1944.

The deportation of the Hungarian Jews to Auschwitz resulted in one of the most bizarre episodes of the Second World War. On May 5, 1944, Eichmann sent for Joel Brand, a Jewish representative of the Joint Distribution Committee. Brand, along with Dr. Reszo Kastner met with Eichmann at the Hotel Majestic. Eichmann informed Brand and Kastner that he had a proposal to put to them, that had been approved by *Reichsführer-SS* Heinrich Himmler. The proposal was to exchange one million Jews for goods, such as 10,000 trucks, to be used on the Eastern Front. Joel Brand was allowed to leave Hungary and inform the Allies of this proposal.

Brand accompanied by Andor (Bandi) Grosz, arrived in Istanbul, Turkey on May 19, 1944, four days after the mass deportations of Hungarian Jews to Auschwitz had commenced, it was here that they met local representatives of the Joint Rescue Committee of the Jewish Agency. Grosz was arrested by the British forces on June 1, 1944, shortly after crossing the Syrian border.

Brand left for Palestine on June 5, 1944, but he too was arrested by the British at Aleppo on June 7, 1944. Three days later, on June 10, 1944, he was able to reveal the plight of the Hungarian Jews under the Nazis, and Eichmann's 'Jewish Lives for Goods' proposal, to Moshe Sharrett, Head of the Jewish Agency's Political Department.

---

[317] G. Reitlinger, *The Final Solution*, Sphere Books, London 1971, pp. 455–457.

[318] Danuta Czech, *Auschwitz Chronicle*, Henry Holt and Company, New York 1990, p. 618.

The day earlier, back in Budapest, Eichmann told Kastner, 'that if he did not receive an answer from Brand in three days, he would let the mills grind in Auschwitz.' In fact the mills were already grinding with deadly consequences.

Moshe Sharrett and Ira Hirschmann of the War Refugee Board informed the top Jewish leaders and also leading figures of the British and American governments of what Brand had told them. The British government decided against having any dealings with the *Gestapo* and they refused to let Brand return to Hungary. On July 19, 1944, the BBC made public the Nazi proposal and claimed 'this monstrous offer was a loathsome attempt to blackmail the Allies.'

Joel Brand thus realized that his mission to rescue some of his fellow countrymen and women was doomed. He testified at the trial of Adolf Eichmann in 1961, and he died three years later on July 13, 1964, in Tel Aviv, Israel.[319]

Transports From Hungary—Deportation Trains Passing Through Kassa in 1944

Date	Deported From	Number of Deportees
May 14 1944	Nyíregyháza	3200
May 14 1944	Munkács	3169
May 16 1944	Kassa	3055
May 16 1944	Beregszász	3818
May 16 1944	Máramarossziget	3007
May 16 1944	Munkács	3629
May 16 1944	Kassa	3629
May 17 1944	Kassa	3352
May 17 1944	Ungvár	3455
May 17 1944	Ökörmező	3052
May 17 1944	Munkács	3306
May 18 1944	Máramarossziget	3248
May 18 1944	Beregszász	3569
May 18 1944	Sátoraljaújhely	3439

[319] www.Holocaustresearchproject.org.

May 18 1944	Munkács	3025
May 19 1944	Felsővisó	3032
May 19 1944	Mátészalka	3299
May 19 1944	Szatmárnémeti	3006
May 19 1944	Munkács	3222
May 20 1944	Máramarossziget	3104
May 20 1944	Nagyszőllős	3458
May 20 1944	Munkács	3026
May 21 1944	Felsővisó	3013
May 21 1944	Sátoraljaújhely	3290
May 21 1944	Munkács	2861
May 22 1944	Máramarossziget	3490
May 22 1944	Ungvár	3335
May 22 1944	Szatmárnémeti	3330
May 22 1944	Mátészalka	3299
May 23 1944	Felsővisó	3023
May 23 1944	Nyíregyháza	3272
May 23 1944	Munkács	3269
May 23 1944	Nagyvárad	3110
May 24 1944	Beregszász	2602
May 24 1944	Kassa	3172
May 24 1944	Huszt	3328
May 24 1944	Munkács	3080
May 25 1944	Ungvár	3334
May 25 1944	Nagyvárad	3148
May 25 1944	Kolozsvár	3130
May 25 1944	Aknaszlatina	3317
May 25 1944	Felsővisó	3006
May 26 1944	Huszt	3249
May 26 1944	Szatmárnémeti	3336
May 27 1944	Sátoraljaújhely	3325
May 27 1944	Nagyszőllős	3415
May 27 1944	Nyíregyháza	2708

May 27 1944	Ungvár	2988
May 27 1944	Marosvásárhely	3183
May 28 1944	Tecso	2208
May 28 1944	Des	3150
May 28 1944	Nagyvárad	3227
May 29 1944	Beregszász	860
May 29 1944	Mátészalka	3299
May 29 1944	Kolozsvár	3417
May 29 1944	Szatmárnémeti	3306
May 29 1944	Nagyvárad	3166
May 30 1944	Kisvárda	3475
May 30 1944	Marosvásárhely	3203
May 30 1944	Nagyvárad	3187
May 30 1944	Szatmárnémeti	3300
May 31 1944	Ungvár	3056
May 31 1944	Kolozsvár	3270
May 31 1944	Nagybánya	3073
May 31 1944	Szilágysomlyó	3106
June 1 1944	Mátészalka	3299
June 1 1944	Kisvárda	3421
June 1 1944	Nagyvárad	3059
June 1 1944	Szatmárnémeti	2615
June 2 1944	Huszt	2396
June 2 1944	Beszterce	3106
June 2 1944	Kolozsvár	3100
June 3 1944	Nagyszőllős	2967
June 3 1944	Kassa	2499
June 3 1944	Nagyvárad	2972
June 3 1944	Szilágysomlyó	3161
June 4 1944	Szászrégen	3149
June 4 1944	Sátoraljaújhely	2567
June 5 1944	Nagyvárad	2527
June 5 1944	Mátészalka	3100

June 5 1944	Nyíregyháza	2253
June 5 1944	Nagybánya	2844
June 6 1944	Huszt	1852
June 6 1944	Des	3160
June 6 1944	Beszterce	2875
June 6 1944	Szilágysomlyó	1584
June 8 1944	Des	1364
June 8 1944	Kolozsvár	1784
June 8 1944	Marosvásárhely	1163
June 9 1944	Kolozsvár	1447
June 11 1944	Maklár	2794
June 12 1944	Diósgyőr	2675
June 12 1944	Balassagyarmat	2810
June 12 1944	Diósgyőr	2941
June 12 1944	Érsekújvár	2899
June 12 1944	Diósgyőr	3051
June 13 1944	Hatvan	2961
June 13 1944	Komárom	2790
June 13 1944	Salgótarján	2310
June 14 1944	Miskolc-Diósgyőr	3968
June 14 1944	Balassagyarmat	1867
June 15 1944	Leva	2678
June 15 1944	Miskolc	2829
June 15 1944	Érsekújvár	1980
June 16 1944	Győr	2985
June 16 1944	Komárom	2673
June 16 1944	Dunaszerdahely	2969
June 25 1944	Debrecen	2286
June 26 1944	Szeged	3199
June 27 1944	Debrecen	3842
June 27 1944	Kecskemét	2642
June 27 1944	Nagyvárad	2819
June 27 1944	Békéscsaba	3118

June 28 1944	Bácsalmás	2737
June 29 1944	Kecskemét	2790
June 29 1944	Szolnok	2038
June 29 1944	Debrecen	3026
July 5 1944	Sárvár	3105
July 5 1944	Szombathely	3103
July 6 1944	Kaposvár	3050
July 7 1944	Soprom	3077
July 7 1944	Papa	2793
July 7 1944	Paks	1072
July 7 1944	Monor	3549
July 7 1944	Óbuda	3151
July 7 1944	Sárvár	2204
July 8 1944	Pécs	2523
July 8 1944	Óbuda	2997
July 9 1944	Monor	3065
July 9 1944	Óbuda	3072
July 9 1944	Budakalász	3072
July 9 1944	Monor	3079
July 9 1944	Békásmegyer	1924
July 20 1944	Rákoscsaba	1230

The above data was collected by the Railway Command of Kassa—List made available by Miklós Gaskó.

Source: The Politics of Genocide – Volume 2

One family that was part of the above deportations was the Lok family from Sárvár, close to the Hungarian-Austrian border. On June 20, 1944, Teresz Lok, who was born in 1902, in Sárvár, was deported with her two daughters and two sons, and her grandfather. Her grandfather Adolf Schwarz, (who was born in Sárvár in 1872), along with the two girls, Edith (who was born on October 10, 1927, in Budapest), and Alice, (who was born on February 7, 1929, in Sárvár) and the two boys, Imre, (who was born in 1935) and Ocsi, (who was five years old), all marched to the railway station at Sárvár. Alice described the scene:

> When we saw the cattle trains I told my sister, it's a mistake, they have cattle trains here, they don't mean we should go in cattle trains, grandfather cannot sit on the floor in a cattle train. The railroad station was a wonderful memory always, because father had a business office in Budapest and he would go every week to his business office and we would always accompany him and always wait for him, Thursday night coming home. He would go on Monday and come back Thursday and he would always bring us something; and it was so wonderful to go to the railroad station expecting father to come. Then going there and seeing cattle trains. Cattle trains!
>
> 'They don't mean to put us in cattle trains,' I said to my sister Edith..... and so we found ourselves in the cattle train. They closed the door on us and they left a bucket for sanitary use, and a bucket for water. And I told Edith, 'I will never use the sanitary-use bucket in front of these people, no matter what happens to me.'
>
> I see grandfather on the floor, all our baggage sitting very uncomfortably and from time to time mother would want to give us something to eat and it was starting to be smelly and sweaty and hot in the June day. I didn't want to eat anything or drink anything. We were pushed into a corner, Edith and I, and we couldn't move, we couldn't go anywhere. And around four days later we arrived in Auschwitz. When we arrived I told Edith, 'Nothing can be so bad like this cattle train. I am sure they will want us to work, let's go and we will work.'[320]

The selection of the new arrivals was about to take place, Alice recalled what happened next:

> I went to that group with the children and I was very tall for my age and suddenly a German soldier he asked me, '*Haben sie Kinder?*'—Do you have children? And I said, 'No, I am just fifteen,' in German. And then he put me in to another group. And now I was very far away from Edith. I didn't see mother, I didn't see grandfather.

Alice Lok and her sister Edith were selected to live, but her grandfather, mother, and two younger brothers were all murdered in the gas chambers. Edith was separated from Alice, who was housed in

---

[320] www.WW2History.com

Block 12, Camp C, but by a miracle they were re-united, and were never again apart in Auschwitz.

Alice and Edith were evacuated to Guben Labor Camp and were then moved to Bergen-Belsen Concentration Camp. Edith passed away probably in a Red Cross hospital after the Camp was liberated by the British Forces in April 1945[321]. Alice never saw her again, and she emigrated to Israel where she married Rabbi Moshe Cahana. They eventually settled in the United States of America and raised three children.

Transports From Italy

The first mass transport from Italy left Rome on October 18, 1943, bound for Auschwitz. There is a slight discrepancy in the number of Jews deported. In the Auschwitz Chronicle the figure is 15 higher than the number quoted in the book by Lillianna Picciotto. The figures quoted in the Auschwitz Chronicle state that out of the number who arrived, 839 were taken to the gas chambers and murdered.

Transports From Italy To Auschwitz 1943–1944

Date	Deportation From	Number of Deportees
16 September 1943	Merano	35
18 October 1943	Rome	1020*
9 November 1943	Florence / Bologna	93
6 December 1943	Milan / Verona	249
30 January 1944	Verona	605
22 February 1944	Fossoli	510
5 April 1944	Fossoli / Mantova / Verona	609
16 May 1944	Fossoli	581
26 June 1944	Fossoli / Verona	523

---

[321] The Yad Vashem Central Database of Shoah Victims online resource incorrectly lists Edith's date of death as July 1944.

| 2 August 1944 | Verona | 246 |
| 24 October 1944 | Bolzano | 133 |

Source: IL Libro Della Memoria

One of the most famous of Holocaust survivors was Primo Levi. He was deported to Auschwitz on February 22, 1944, and what follows is a short biography of his life:

Primo Levi was born on July 31, 1919, in Turin, Italy. He was the eldest of two children, born to middle-class Italian-Jewish parents, whose ancestors had settled in Italy centuries earlier to escape the Spanish Inquisition.

In 1937, Primo Levi completed his primary schooling and entered the University of Turin. With the help of a sympathetic Professor, Dr. Nicola Dallaporto he was able to complete his studies and in 1941, he graduated with his honours degree in chemistry.

Using a false identity and forged papers, he found employment as a chemist with a mining company and then worked for a Swiss pharmaceutical company in Milan. He returned to Turin after his father died in 1942. A year later in 1943, Primo Levi and his mother and sister fled to the hills of Amay, and he joined an Italian resistance group. He was arrested by Fascist forces and he was incarcerated in the Camp at Fossoli di Capri, near Modena.

On February 22, 1944, he was deported by the Germans, who had taken control of the camp from the Italians. On arrival at Auschwitz, he was tattooed with the prisoner number 174517. Primo Levi managed to secure himself a position as an assistant in I. G. Farben's Buna-Werke laboratory, that researched the production of synthetic rubber.

Shortly before the Camp was liberated by the Red Army, Primo Levi became ill with scarlet fever and he was placed in the Camp's hospital. The illness spared Primo Levi from the forced 'death marches' and it was in the hospital that he was liberated by the Russian Army on January 27, 1945.

Primo Levi returned to Turin and he found work at the Duco paint factory which was part of the Du Pont company. There he started to write the first draft of his book, 'If This Is A Man,' which was published in Italy in October 1947.

He married Lucia Morpurgo and they had two children, Lisa and Renzo, and he left his job to concentrate on writing. In 1975, his book 'The Periodic Table' was published in Italy. This book was a collection of twenty-one autobiographical stories that each use a chemical element as its starting point. The accounts covered everything from Primo Levi's childhood, schooling, his stay in Auschwitz, and his life after being liberated from the camp. This book was critically acclaimed as his finest work. In 1986, he published his last work 'The Drowned and the Saved' again about his life and his experiences.

On April 11, 1987, the concierge in his apartment building, where Primo Levi had been born and lived for most of his life, found him dead at the bottom of the stairwell. The coroner ruled that his death was suicide. Some of those who knew Primo Levi well maintained his death was an accident, saying that he had suffered recently from dizzy spells.[322]

Transports From Trieste to Auschwitz

Trieste was a former Austrian city that was incorporated into the Reich on September 23, 1943. It was the capital of a new *Gau* (District) Trieste-Küstenland. Friedrich Rainer became the Gauleiter and his old friend from the Austrian Anschluss days, Odilo Globocnik, who had been dismissed as the Police Leader of Lublin, returned to the place of his birth as Higher *SS* and Police Leader for the Adriatic Coastal Region. Before the Second World War, there were more than 5,000 Jews living in Trieste, but less than half remained behind when the Germans took over. There was a round-up on October 9, 1943, and a second on January 19, 1944, when Dr. Morpurgo, the Secretary of the Community Council was taken, and the home for the elderly, the Pia Casa Gentilomo was liquidated.[323]

---

[322] www.biography.com.
[323] G. Reitlinger, *The Final Solution*, Sphere Books, London 1971, p. 383.

The seventy inmates were kept until the transport left for Auschwitz on January 28, 1944, in the rice warehouse in the San Sabba suburb. The rice warehouse in San Sabba—through Christian Wirth, the former Commandant of the Bełżec death camp in Poland, and the Inspector of the *SS Sonderkommando Aktion Reinhard*—into an interrogation and execution center, where not only Jews but also Italian and Yugoslavian partisans were tortured, beaten to death or simply shot. Their bodies were cremated in a specially installed furnace in the courtyard. The human ashes were dumped in the Adriatic Sea.[324]

Transports From Trieste to Auschwitz 1943-1944

Date	Transport Designation	Number of Deportees
7 December 1943	21	160
6 January 1944	22	27
28 January 1944	23	61
26 February 1944	24	4
29 March 1944	25	120
27 April 1944	26	36
1 June 1944	27	9
12 June 1944	28	37
21 June 1944	29	24
undated	30	2
11 July 1944	31	5
31 July 1944	33	71
11 August 1944	34	6
undated	35	5
undated	36	1
2 September 1944	37	48
3 October 1944	38	20
18 October 1944	39	6
1 November 1944	40	4

Source: IL Libro Della Memori

---

[324]   C.Webb, *The Bełżec Death Camp*, Ibidem, Stuttgart 2016, p. 8.

Transports From Luxemburg To Auschwitz

Date	Deportation From	Number of Deportees
12 July 1942	Luxemburg	24
17 June 1943	Luxemburg	11

The listing of the transport dated June 17, 1943, shows the destination as Theresienstadt / Auschwitz

Source: Das Bundesarchiv—Memorial Book Online Resource

Transports From the Netherlands

The Nazis established a transit Camp for the Jews of the Netherlands at Westerbork, which was located some 80 miles north of Amsterdam in the province of Drenthe. This Camp was originally a refugee camp built in 1939, to house the flood of refugees coming from Germany. At the end of 1941, the Germans decided that Westerbork would become a transit Camp for Jews, prior to being deported to the east. The Camp measured 500 by 500 meters, and was surrounded by a barbed-wire fence with seven watchtowers, guarding twenty-four large wooden barracks. The Camp was extended on a massive scale, eventually there were 107 such barracks each designed to hold 300 people. The costs of this massive undertaking were financed from the proceeds of confiscated Jewish property.

On July 1, 1942, the Camp came under the control of the *Befehlshaber der Sicherheitspolizei und des SD* and on July 14, 1942, the transfer of Jews from Amsterdam to Westerbork began and the first transport to Auschwitz commenced on July 15, 1942.

Albert Konrad Gemmeker took over as the Camp Commandant on October 12, 1942, but the timetable, the size of trains and eventual destination were determined by Adolf Eichmann's office—IV B4 in Berlin. The deportation trains to the east usually left Westerbork on a Tuesday. Philip Mechanicus, one of the inmates, wrote a description in his diary of a deportation on Tuesday June 1, 1943. This transport went to the Sobibór Death Camp in Poland, but is an important historic account, and the deportations to Auschwitz were no different:

Tuesday June 1. The transports are as loathsome as ever. The wagons used were originally intended for carrying horses. The deportees no longer lie on straw, but on the bare floor in the midst of their food supplies and small baggage, and this applies even to the invalids who only last week got a mattress. They are assembled at the hut exits at about seven o'clock by *OD* men, the Camp Security Police, and are taken to the train in lines of three, to the Boulevard des Misères in the middle of the Camp.

The train is like a long mangy snake, dividing the camp in two and made up of filthy old wagons. The Boulevard is a desolate spot, barred by *OD* men to keep away interested members of the public. The exiles have a bag of bread which is tied to their shoulders with a tape and dangles over their hips, and a rolled up blanket fastened to the other shoulder with string and hanging down their backs. Shabby emigrants who own nothing more than what they have on and what is hanging from them. Quiet men with tense faces and women bursting into frequent sobs. Elderly folk, hobbling along, stumbling over the poor road surface under their load and sometimes going through pools of muddy water. Invalids on stretchers carried by *OD* men.

On the platform the Commandant with his retinue, the 'Green Police,' Dr. Spanier, the Medical Superintendent, in a plain grey civilian suit, bareheaded and very dark, with his retinue, Kurt Schlesinger, the head of the Registration Department, in riding breeches and jackboots, a nasty face and straw-coloured hair with a flat cap on it. Alongside the train doctors, holding themselves in readiness in case the invalids need assistance.

The deportees approaching the train in batches are surrounded by *OD* men standing there in readiness to prevent any escapes. They are counted off a list brought from the hut and go straight into the train. Any who dawdle or hesitate are assisted. They are driven into the train, or pushed, or struck, or pummelled, or persuaded with a boot, and kicked on board, both by the 'Green Police' who are escorting the train and by *OD* men. Noise and nervous outbursts are not allowed, but they do occur. Short work is made of such behaviour—a few clips suffice. The OD men base their uncouth behaviour on that of their German colleagues, who are lavish in the use of their fists and inflict quick, hard punishment with their boots. The Jews in the Camp refer to them as the Jewish *SS*. They are hated like the plague and people would gladly flay many of them alive if they dared.

Men, women, old and young, sick and healthy, together with children and babies, are all packed together into the same wagon. Healthy men and women are put in amongst others who suffer from the complaints associated with old age and are in need of constant care, men and women who have lost control over certain primary physical functions, cripples, the old, the blind, folk with stomach disorders, imbeciles, lunatics. They all go on the bare floor, in amongst the baggage and on it, crammed tightly together. There is a barrel, just one barrel for all these people, in the corner of the wagon where they can relieve themselves publicly. One small barrel not large enough for so many people. With a bag of sand next to it, from which each person can pick up a handful to cover the excrement. In another corner there is a can of water with a tap for those who want to quench their thirst.

When the wagons are full and the prescribed quota of deportees has been delivered, they are closed up. The commandant gives the signal for departure—with a wave of his hand. The whistle shrills, usually at about eleven o'clock and the sound goes right through everyone in the Camp, to the very core of their being. So the mangy-looking snake crawls away with its full load. Schlesinger and his retinue jump up on the footboard and ride along for a little bit for the sake of convenience, otherwise they would have to walk back. That would wear out their soles. The commandant saunters contentedly away. Dr. Spanier, his hands behind his back and his head bent forward in worried concentration, walks back to his consulting room.[325]

Philip Mechanicus was born in Amsterdam on April 17, 1889. He travelled to the Dutch East Indies, where he worked as a reporter and a newspaper editor. On his return to Amsterdam, he wrote several books and edited the *Algemeen Handelsblad* and when the Germans banned Jews from working on newspapers, he stayed on and worked under a pseudonym.

When seen on a tram without wearing a Jewish Star, he was reported and arrested and imprisoned in *Amstelveensweg* and sent to Amersfoort Camp, where he was tortured and brutally beaten. He was injured so badly he spent nine months in hospital in Westerbork Camp from November 7, 1942.

---

[325] D. Slier and I.Shine, *Hidden Letters*, Star Bright Books, New York 2008, pp. 146–147.

He was deported from Westerbork to Bergen-Belsen Concentration Camp on March 8, 1944, but he was transferred to the Auschwitz Concentration Camp on October 9, 1944. He was shot and killed there three days later on October 12, 1944.[326]

Transports from the Netherlands to Auschwitz 1942–1944

Date	Deportation From	Number of Deportees	Arrival At Auschwitz
15 July 1942	Westerbork	1135	16/17 July 1942
16 July 1942	Westerbork	895	17 July 1942
21 July 1942	Westerbork	931	22 July 1942
24 July 1942	Westerbork	1000	25 July 1942
27 July 1942	Westerbork	1010	28 July 1942
31 July 1942	Westerbork	1007	1 August 1942
3 August 1942	Westerbork	1013	4 August 1942
7 August 1942	Westerbork	987	8 August 1942
10 August 1942	Westerbork	559	11 August 1942
14 August 1942	Westerbork	505	15 August 1942
17 August 1942	Westerbork	506	18 August 1942
21 August 1942	Westerbork	1008	22 August 1942
24 August 1942	Westerbork	519	25 August 1942
28 August 1942	Westerbork	608	30 August 1942
31 August 1942	Westerbork	560	1 September 1942
4 September 1942	Westerbork	714	5 September 1942
7 September 1942	Westerbork	930	8 September 1942
11 September 1942	Westerbork	874	12 September 1942
14 September 1942	Westerbork	902	16 September 1942
18 September 1942	Westerbork	1004	20 September 1942
21 September 1942	Westerbork	713	22 September 1942
25 September 1942	Westerbork	928	26 September 1942

---

[326] Ibid., p. 146.

28 September 1942	Westerbork	610	30 September 1942
2 October 1942	Westerbork	1014	3 October 1942
5 October 1942	Westerbork	2012	7 October 1942
9 October 1942	Westerbork	1703	11 October 1942
12 October 1942	Westerbork	1711	14 October 1942
16 October 1942	Westerbork	1710	18 October 1942
19 October 1942	Westerbork	1327	21 October 1942
23 October 1942	Westerbork	988	25 October 1942
26 October 1942	Westerbork	841	27 October 1942
30 October 1942	Westerbork	659	1 November 1942
2 November 1942	Westerbork	954	4 November 1942
6 November 1942	Westerbork	465	7 November 1942
10 November 1942	Westerbork	758	12 November 1942
16 November 1942	Westerbork	761	
20 November 1942	Westerbork	726	21 November 1942
24 November 1942	Westerbork	709	26 November 1942
30 November 1942	Westerbork	826	2 December 1942
4 December 1942	Westerbork	811	6 December 1942
8 December 1942	Westerbork	927	10 December 1942
12 December 1942	Westerbork	757	14 December 1942
11 January 1943	Westerbork	750	13 January 1943
18 January 1943	Westerbork	748	20 January 1943
22 January 1943	Apeldoorne	921	24 January 1943
23 January 1943	Westerbork	516	24 January 1943
2 February 1943	Westerbork	890	4 February 1943
9 February 1943	Westerbork	1184	11 February 1943
16 February 1943	Westerbork	1108	18 February 1943
23 February 1943	Westerbork	1101	25 February 1943
24 August 1943	Westerbork	1001	26 August 1943
31 August 1943	Westerbork	1004	2 September 1943
7 September 1943	Westerbork	987	9 September 1943
14 September 1943	Westerbork	1005	16 September 1943

21 September 1943	Westerbork	979	23 September 1943
19 October 1943	Westerbork	1007	21 October 1943
15 November 1943	Vught	1149	
16 November 1943	Westerbork	995	17 November 1943
25 January 1944	Westerbork	948	27 January 1944
8 February 1944	Westerbork	1015	10 February 1944
3 March 1944	Westerbork	732	5 March 1944
23 March 1944	Westerbork	599	25 March 1944
5 April 1944	Westerbork	240	7 April 1944
19 May 1944	Westerbork	453	21 May 1944
3 June 1944	Vught	496	
3 September 1944	Westerbork	1019	5 September 1944

Source: Das Bundesarchiv—Memorial Book Online Resource

On the very last transport from Westerbork on September 3, 1944, was the Frank family, who were to become known throughout the world because one young Jewish girl kept a diary whilst in hiding in Amsterdam. That young girl was Anne Frank. Below is the story of the Frank family:

Otto Frank was born on May 12, 1889, in Frankfurt am Main, Germany. He was born on Frankfurt's *Westend,* a well-to-do district. After attending high school he briefly studied art at the University of Heidelberg. He accepted a job offer in the United States of America, and worked between 1908 and 1909 at Macy's Department Store in New York. When his father died, Otto Frank returned to Germany and worked for a metal engineering company in Düsseldorf until 1914. During the First World War, Otto and his two brothers, Herbert and Robert served in the German Army, and Otto attained the rank of lieutenant. After the defeat of Germany he worked in his late father's bank. Whilst working at the bank he became acquainted with Edith Höllander, the daughter of a manufacturer, who was born on January 16, 1900, in Aachen. Otto and Edith married in 1925 and settled in Frankfurt. They had two daughters, Margot, born on February 16, 1926, and Anne, whose full name was Annelies Marie, who was born on June 12, 1929.

In 1933, after Hitler seized power and anti-Jewish measures took hold, Otto Frank left Germany for Holland, where he started a branch of the German Opekta firm in Amsterdam, and soon Edith, Margot and Anne joined him. The Frank family moved into a house on the Merwedeplein, in the southern part of the city. Anne and Margot attended the Montessori School which was nearby. This carefree life was interrupted by the Nazi invasion during May 1940.

During 1941, the Nazis increased the number of anti-Jewish measures and Otto Frank prepared to take his family into hiding with the help and co-operation of a number of his staff. Such individuals as Victor Kugler, (referred to under the name of Victor Kraler), Johannes Kleiman (Mr. Koophuis), Hermine Santruschitz (Miep Gies) and Elizabeth Voskuijl (Elli Vossen) made a hiding place for the Franks, which became known as the 'Secret Annex' and was located behind Otto Frank's company on 263 Prinsengrecht, in Amsterdam.[327]

The catalyst for the flight into hiding was that on July 5, 1942, Margot Frank received a notification to report for a 'work force project' and the following day on Monday July 6, 1942, the Frank family went into hiding. They were joined in the 'Secret Annex' one week later by the van Pels family. The van Pels family were also German Jews who had emigrated from Osnabrück, on June 26, 1937. The father Hermann was born on March 31, 1898, in Gehrde, Germany. His wife Auguste van Pels was born on September 29, 1900, in Buer, Germany. Their son Peter van Pels was born on November, 8, 1926, in Osnabrück. On November 16, 1942, Fritz Pfeffer joined the two families in hiding at the 'Secret Annex.' Fritz Pfeffer was born on April 30, 1889, in Giessen, Germany. He emigrated to Holland in December 1938. Fritz was Miep Gies' dentist and he knew the Frank family well.

In hiding, Anne kept a diary and her entry for December 24, 1943, is especially poignant:

---

[327] *Anne Frank In The World*, Anne Frank Stichting, 1985, pp. 10, 64 and 104.

Believe me, if you have been shut up for a year and a half, it can get too much for you some days. In spite of all justice and thankfulness, you can't crush your feelings. Cycling, dancing, whistling, looking out into the world, feeling young, to know that I'm free—that's what I long for; still I musn't show it, because I sometimes think if all eight of us began to pity ourselves, or went about with discontented faces, where would it lead us?[328]

On 4, August 1944, the *SD* conducted a raid on the Prinsengrecht offices. Dutch workers Johannes Kleiman, Miep Gies, and Victor Kugler identified the Dutch *SD*-detectives as Gezinus Gringhuis and Willem Grootendorst, who were both given life sentences after the War. The officer in charge of the raid was *SS-Oberstabsfeldwebel* Karl Joseph Silberbauer. The eight people in hiding and Victor Kugler and Johannes Kleiman were taken by truck to the *SD* prison on Euterpestraat.[329]

The arrested Jews were taken on August 8,1944, to the central train station in Amsterdam and transferred to Westerbork by passenger train. They were incarcerated in S Barrack Number 67 and awaited deportation to the east. On September 3, 1944, the inhabitants of the 'Secret Annex' were deported to Auschwitz. This in fact was the last transport from the Westerbork Transit Camp to Auschwitz. This transport arrived in the Auschwitz Concentration Camp on September 5, 1944. Out of the 1,019 Jews on the transport, 549 prisoners were murdered in the gas chambers.[330]

Hermann van Pels was the first of the eight to die. Hermann was selected to work in a *Kommando* that worked outside and a few weeks later he was murdered in the gas chambers, the precise date was unknown. Fritz Pfeffer was the next one of the group to pass

---

[328] Ibid., p. 109.
[329] *Anne Frank House, A Museum with a Story*, Anne Frank Stichting 2001, pp. 176–193.
[330] Danuta Czech, *Auschwitz Chronicle*, Henry Holt and Company, New York 1990, p. 702.

away. In October 1944, he was transferred to the Neuengamme Concentration Camp near Hamburg. He died in the Neuengamme sick-bay barrack on December 20, 1944.[331]

Edith Frank and her two daughters Margot and Anne were selected for work, but the two girls were transferred to Bergen-Belsen Concentration Camp probably on October 28, 1944. Edith remained in Birkenau. At the end of November 1944, Edith was sent to the sick-bay barrack where she died on January 6, 1945. Margot Frank died from typhus in Bergen-Belsen some time during March 1945. A few days after her sister Margot died, Anne Frank also died from typhus in Bergen-Belsen.[332]

Auguste van Pels was selected for work in Auschwitz, but she was transferred on November 26, 1944, to Bergen-Belsen, where she met up with Margot and Anne. It was Auguste who arranged for Anne's long-time friend Hannah Goslar, who was incarcerated in the *Sternlager* in the Camp, to meet up through the barbed wire. On February 6, 1945, Auguste was sent to the Raghuhn Labor Camp, a sub-Camp of Buchenwald Concentration Camp. Auguste died enroute or just having arrived at Theresienstadt some time either in April or May 1945.[333]

Peter van Pels was selected to live on the ramp in Birkenau and worked in the postal department, which was much more favourable than an outdoors working group. Because of his job, he was able to share food with other prisoners, including Otto Frank. He was transferred to the Mauthausen Concentration Camp and he arrived there on January 25, 1945. He died there on the day the Camp was liberated on May 5, 1945.[334]

Otto Frank was the only one of the group of eight that sought refuge in the 'Secret Annex' to survive Auschwitz and the other Camps. He worked in an outside *Kommando*, until he became sick

---

[331] *Anne Frank House, A Museum with a Story*, Anne Frank Stichting 2001, pp. 198–200.
[332] *Anne Frank House, A Museum with a Story*, Anne Frank Stichting 2001, pp. 204 and 206.
[333] Ibid., pp. 207 and 210.
[334] Ibid., p. 212.

and was sent to the Camp hospital. Peter van Pels visited Otto daily and cared for him, until he was evacuated from the Camp. Otto was still in the Camp hospital when the Soviet Army liberated the Camp on January 27, 1945. Otto finally was able to return to Holland by June 1945.[335]

Upon his return to Amsterdam, Otto Frank eventually discovered in July 1945, that Anne and Margot had died in the Camps and shortly after this, Miep Gies gave him Anne's diary, and other papers that she had rescued from the Annex on the day the families were arrested. She handed the diary and notebooks with the words, 'Here is your daughter Anne's legacy to you.' Anne had been given the diary as a present by her parents in June 1942.

Friends of Otto Frank persuaded him to publish Anne's diary and the book was published on June 25, 1947, under the title '*Het Achterhuis*' – The Annex, with a print run of 1,500 copies. The book was well received in the Netherlands and in December 1947, a second edition was published.

To date, more than fifty different editions have been published and more than 18 million copies have been sold. In 1953, Otto Frank married Elfriede Markovits, also a survivor of Auschwitz. They settled in Basel, in Switzerland. Otto Frank died from lung cancer on August 19, 1980 in Basel. The house where Anne and the others lived in hiding is now a museum, managed by the Anne Frank Foundation, which was founded in 1957.[336]

Transports From Poland to Auschwitz

At the Adolf Eichmann Trial in Jerusalem, at Session 99, which took place on July 17, 1961, Eichmann testified in some detail who was responsible for the deportations within the *Generalgouvernment,* the German name for the parts of Poland that had not been incorporated into the Reich. To clarify this point for the readers this is what he stated:

---

[335] Ibid., p. 214.
[336] *Anne Frank In The World*, Anne Frank Stichting 1985, p. 134.

In the matters of resettlement within the *Generalgouvernement*, because Himmler had given special orders to the Senior SS and Police Leader, to whom the SS and Police leaders were subordinate. But in other matters—say involving border security, sabotage and other matters of importance to the Reich—Müller could doubtless issue orders to the *Generalgouvernment*. But not in the matters of resettlement. In that area the Senior SS and Police Leader had overall responsibility.[337]

Transports of Jews To Auschwitz From Poland within Pre-War Borders

Date of Arrival	Originated From	Number of Deportees
May 5 1942	Dąbrowa	630
May 12 1942	Sosnowice	1500
May 1942	Zawiercie	2000
May 1942	Będzin	2000
June 17 1842	Sosnowiec	1000
June 20 1942	Sosnowiec	2000
June 1942	Bielsko-Biała	5000
June 1942	Olkusz	3000
June 1942	Krzepice	1000
June 1942	Chrzanów	4000
August 1–3 1942	Będzin	5000
August 15 1942	Sosnowiec	2000
August 16 1942	Sosnowiec	2000
August 17 1942	Sosnowiec	2000
August 18 1942	Sosnowiec	2000
November 7 1942	Ciechanów	2000
November 8 1942	Ciechanów	1000
November 8 1942	Białystok	1000
November 9 1942	Białystok	1000
November 14 1942	Ciechanów	2500
November 14 1942	Białystok	1500
November 18 1942	Grodno	1000
November 19 1942	Ciechanów	1500

---

[337] www.Nizkor.org.online–resource.

November 22 1942	Ciechanów	1500
November 25 1942	Grodno	2000
November 28 1942	Ciechanów	1000
November 30 1942	Ciechanów	1000
November 1942	Grodno	1000
December 2 1942	Grodno	1000
December 3 1942	Płońsk	1000
December 6 1942	Mława	2500
December 8 1942	Grodno	1000
December 10 1942	Małkinia	2500
December 12 1942	Małkinia	2000
December 14 1942	Nowy Dwór	2000
December 17 1942	Płońsk	2000
January 7 1943	Augustów	2000
January 13 1943	Zambrów	2000
January 14 1943	Łomża	4000
January 15 1943	Zambrów	2000
January 16 1943	Zambrów	2000
January 16 1943	Łomża	2000
January 17 1943	Łomża	2000
January 18 1943	Zambrów	2000
January 19 1943	Kraków	400
January 20 1943	Grodno	2000
January 21 1943	Grodno	2000
January 22 1943	Grodno	3650
January 23 1943	Grodno	2000
January 24 1943	Grodno	2000
January 26 1943	Sokółka Jasionówka	2300
January 28 1943	Wolkowysk	2000
January 30 1943	Wołkowysk Prużany	2612
January 31 1943	Orańczyce	2450
January 31 1943	Prużany	2834
February 2 1943	Prużany	1265
February 5 1943	Zamość	417
February 6 1943	Białystok	2000
February 7 1943	Białystok	2000

February 8 1943	Białystok	2000
February 18 1943	Chrzanów	1000
March 13 1943	Kraków	2000
March 16 1943	Kraków	1000
March 31 1943	Sieradz	1000
March 31 1943	Ostrowiec	3000
March 31 1943	Sosnowiec	1000
June 6 1943	Kraj Warty	1000
June 20 1943	Sosnowiec	45
June 24 1943	Sosnowiec	1600
June 25 1943	Częstochowa	1000
June 25 1943	Będzin	2500
August 1 1943	Będzin	2000
August 1 1943	Będzin	2000
August 1 1943	Będzin	4000
August 1 1943	Sosnowiec	4000
August 2 1943	Będzin	2000
August 3 1943	Sosnowiec	3000
August 3 1943	Sosnowiec	3000
August 3 1943	Sosnowiec	3000
August 5 1943	Sosnowiec	3000
August 5 1943	Sosnowiec	1000
August 6 1943	Sosnowiec	3000
August 10 1943	Sosnowiec	3000
August 12 1943	Sosnowiec	1000
August 21 1943	Pomorze	500
August 23 1943	Koło	2000
August 26 1943	Zawiercie	1500
August 27 1943	Zawiercie	1500
August 27 1943	Wolsztyn	1026
August 28 1943	Kostrzyn	800
August 29 1943	Rawicz	2000
August 29 1943	Koluszki	1600
August 31 1943	Bochnia	3000
September 2 1943	Tarnów	5000
September 2 1943	Przemyśl	3500

September 2 1943	Bochnia	3000
September 19 1943	Dąbrowa	1300
October 15 1943	Poznań	38
October 18 1943	Zawiercie	1000
October 28 1943	Pabianice	348
November 2 1943	Szopienice	1870
November 3 1943	Szopienice	1203
November 5 1943	Szebnie	4237
November 12 1943	Śląsk	191
November 1943	Rzeszów	1000
December 17 1943	Będzin	800
January 13 1944	Będzin / Sosnowiec	2000
February 7 1944	Sosnowiec	40
February 26 1944	Sosnowiec	64
March 4 1944	Sosnowiec	27
March 9 1944	Bielsko	7
March 14 1944	Sosnowiec	39
March 16 1944	Bielsko	6
March 28 1944	Borysław	600
April 9–16 1944	Górny Śląsk	295
April 22 1944	Sosnowiec	21
April 23 1944	Śląsk	248
May 16 1944	Sosnowiec	17
May 29 1944	Sosnowiec	10
June 22 1944	Borysław	700
June 29 1944	Sosnowiec	61
July 12 1944	Sosnowiec	23
July 18 1944	Sosnowiec	47
July 19 1944	Sosnowiec	317
July 23 1944	Sosnowiec	12
July 27 1944	Pustków	1700
July 30 1944	Radom	1707
July 30 1944	Radom	5
July 31 1944	Tarnów	3000
July 31 1944	Pionki	3000
August 1 1944	Kielce	94

August 2 1944	Kielce	547
August 3 1944	Ostrowiec	307
August 4 1944	Ostrowiec	1443
August 6 1944	Galicja	2
August 8 1944	Pustków	137
August 8 1944	Radom	2
August 15 1944	Łódź	244
August 15 1944	Galicja	7
August 16 1944	Łódź	400
August 16 1944	Galicja	35
August 16 1944	Łódź	270
August 18 1944	Radom	510
August 21 1944	Łódź	131
August 22 1944	Łódź	66
August 24 1944	Łódź	222
August 30 1944	Łódź	75
September 2 1944	Łódź	393
September 2 1944	Łódź	500
September 18 1944	Łódź	2500
August–September 1944	Łódź	55,000–65,000

Source: Franciszek Piper, *How Many Perished, Jews, Poles, Gypsies*, Yad Vashem Studies Vol XXI, Jerusalem 1991.

One man who was deported from Grodno to Auschwitz on January 21, 1943, was Dr. Jacob Gordon of Vilna. At Auschwitz he was tattooed with the prisoner number 92627, and he described his expulsion from Grodno and his journey to the Camp:

> The liquidation of the Ghetto in Grodno began on January 19, 1943,[338] and lasted five days. On the morning of the twenty-first, German police came into my room and drove my family and me out into the street. A large group of Jews was already collected there. Many dead men, women and children were lying in the street. They had been shot by the Germans. We were taken into a big synagogue building, where several thousand people were already assembled.

---

[338] Incorrectly stated as June 19, 1943. See above entries for Grodno.

After a short time we were taken out again, put in rows of five and driven under a strong guard to the Lososna station, where a train consisting of about thirty-five goods trucks waited for us. We were packed 120 of us into a truck; we were so crowded together that most of us had to stand. We found a few loaves of bread and some sausage in our truck, half-a-kilo of bread and 25 grammes of sausage per person, but there was no water, and we suffered agony from thirst. The German guards shot at the peasants when they wanted to give us water or snow.

On the night of January 22, we arrived at Oświęcim. The train stopped just outside Brzezinka. We were turned out of the trucks with loud shouts of 'Raus! Los! Schneller! and we were hastened by blows. We had to leave behind all our belongings that we had brought with us. All the new arrivals were then filed up and divided into four groups. Group one, young healthy men for work in the Camp: Group two, young girls from sixteen to twenty, for work in the women's Camp: Group three, men either too old or too young: Group four, old women or women with children.

Our transport consisted of 3,650 people; 265 were put into Group one, 80 into Group two, and the rest over 3,000 in number, were loaded into motor lorries and driven straight off, as we afterwards learned, to the crematorium, where they were gassed or burned. Among them were my wife, my son, my father, and my mother. My brother and I were sent to the Camp.[339]

Transports From Slovakia to Auschwitz

The transports of Jews from Slovakia to Auschwitz in March 1942, were in fact the first transport of Jews to arrive in Auschwitz from outside of Poland. Back in the autumn of 1941, the Nazis had asked the Slovak government to provide forced laborers to work in the Reich. In February 1942, the Slovaks offered them whole families, some 20,000 Jews in total.

The president of Slovakia, Josef Tiso, a Catholic priest and leader of the Slovak People's Party of Hlinka had no desire to retain the women and children after their breadwinners had departed for the

---

[339] Dr. Filip Friedman, *This Was Oświęcim*, The United Jewish Relief Appeal, London 1946, pp. 21 and 23.

Reich. It was more beneficial for them, if all of the Jews were deported, but the Germans only wanted those who could work.

To resolve this matter, a meeting was held during February 1942, in Bratislava, the capital of Slovakia, between the Prime Minister of Slovakia, Vojtech Tuka, the chief of his office Dr. Izidor Koso, and Adolf Eichmann's representative in Slovakia *Hauptsturmführer* Dieter Wisliceny.

Wisliceny and Tuka on trial after the War and Tuka under oath testified that the Slovakians put forward the view that to separate the breadwinner from the rest of the family was un-Christian, since after the resettling of the Jewish workers in the Reich, the families would have 'no one to look after them.'

Wisliceny on the other hand testified that the Slovaks were primarily worried about the 'financial considerations' that would result from the Nazis receiving the workforce, while the families were left behind with no means of support. To break the impasse, the Slovaks suggested they might compensate the Germans for the 'expenses' incurred if the families went along with the breadwinners. The matter was resolved in Berlin. The Slovak government agreed to pay the Germans 500 *Reichsmarks* for every Jew deported, on condition that they never came back to Slovakia and that no claim was made by the Germans on the property or other assets they had left behind.[340]

There took place in Bratislava on March 23, 1942, a big round-up of Jews conducted by the police and the nationalist militia the Hlinka Guard. The Jews were taken to a labor camp at Sered', and two days later the first train left for Auschwitz, which was only 130 miles away.[341]

Otto Pressburger, who was on one of the early transports from Slovakia recalled his arrival:

> From the station we had to run to Auschwitz I in groups of five. They (the SS) shouted *'Schnell laufen! Laufen, laufen, laufen!'* And we ran. They killed on the spot those who could not run. We felt we were less

---

[340] Laurence Rees, *Auschwitz—The Nazis and the Final Solution* – BBC Books London 2005, pp. 107–108.
[341] G. Reitlinger, *The Final Solution*, Sphere Books, London 1971, p. 418.

than dogs. We had been told that we were going to work, not that we were going to a Concentration Camp.[342]

The next morning, after a night with no food or drink, Otto Pressburger, his father and the rest of the Slovak transport of around 1,000 men were made to run from the main Camp up to the building site that was Birkenau. Otto estimated that around 70–80 people were killed on the way and that Birkenau, deep in mud and other filth, was an appalling place.[343]

---

[342] Laurence Rees, *Auschwitz—The Nazis and the Final Solution*, BBC Books London 2005, pp. 111.
[343] Ibid., p.111.

Chapter XIII
War Time Reports About Auschwitz-Birkenau

The Polish underground movement fed reports about Auschwitz and the Nazi persecution of the Jews and Poles, to the Allies throughout the occupation. The Polish Ministry of Information in London, published a regular fortnightly publication called 'Polish Fortnightly Review.'

What follows are a number of these articles, as they appeared in print. The articles have been faithfully re-produced, as they appeared to the British public. The first two reports about the Camp seem to cover the same ground, to some extent, but nevertheless give the reader a detailed look at day to day life and death in Auschwitz, and are of important historical value.

Polish Fortnightly Review—June 1 1941
The Concentration Camp At Oświęcim

Telegrams arriving from the Camp in Oświęcim, reporting the deaths of those imprisoned there, first focussed the attention of all Poland on this place of torture at the end of last year. The death rate among the Poles interned there rose to some 20 or 25 per cent; so high a death rate is due in part to the mass executions carried out for disobedience or with the object of terrorising the prisoners, but mainly because of the gaoler's treatment of the inmates and the exceptionally abominable conditions in which the prisoners have to live.

This Camp was opened only last summer. It is composed of several blocks, each for 400 persons. Among those interned there are Germans, Czechs and Poles. Every national group is numbered separately. The number of Poles interned there exceeds 6,500.

When the prisoners reach the Camp, their own clothes, including underwear and footwear, are taken away and Camp shoes, shirts and prison suits made of striped alpaca bearing the Camp number and the letter P are given to them. The prisoners did not receive shoes until September 19, 1940. Before that date they had to go barefoot. Headgear and overcoats were distributed only after November 1st. Before that, the prisoners had to work bareheaded and clothed only in their thin alpaca suits.

Living conditions are appalling. 100 men are herded into a room that should accommodate only 50. It is forbidden to sleep in day clothes; these, though often wet have to serve as pillows. In the morning prisoners put them on again, still wet. There is one rug for every two prisoners. The prisoners have to get up at 4.30 a.m. and, whatever the weather, wash in the open, naked to the waist, and without soap. There is one towel for 20 people. After washing comes the roll-call, at which all must be present. Then at 6 o'clock, after a breakfast consisting only of *ersatz* (substitute) coffee, the prisoners go to work.

The work varies: it may be extracting sand or gravel from the River Soła, or loading and unloading trucks, or again it may be quite useless work such as carrying poles from one spot to another. At 11 o'clock the prisoners return to the Camp for what is called dinner. Actually this consists of a half-hour's break, during which no food is provided except a litre of soup. The food is quite insufficient for men engaged in hard physical work.

Those who have a temperature of above 39 degrees C are sent to the Camp hospital. Those who ask to see the prison surgeon with a lower temperature are regarded as saboteurs and are beaten. Beatings are administered on all possible occasions. Prisoners are beaten with clubs on their faces and all over their bodies. Slackness in carrying out orders is regarded as sabotage. Furthermore, the 'Sachsenhausen gymnastic' is applied. This consists in jumping with bent knees for 20 minutes or longer. Those who faint are pushed aside. As punishment the so-called pole is applied, a method of torture known in the Austrian army before the War of 1914–18: the delinquent is hung by the armpits over a pole, so that the tips of his feet touch the earth, but give him no support. Another punishment is to subject prisoners to a stream of water from a hose. This may kill a weak person in a few minutes. For instance, Dr. Aleksander Rajchman, a Fellow of the University of Warsaw, was killed in this way, in ten minutes. There are also roll-calls in the courtyards, sometimes lasting several hours. For even small delinquencies, prisoners are transferred to the penal section, which is completely separated from the rest of the Camp. There the most ingenious tortures are applied: prisoners are frequently awakened at night for instance, on the pretext of inspections, or of ascertaining whether the clothes are in their proper place, and so on.

Night inspections take place in all barracks. As in Mauthausen, criminal prisoners from Germany play the parts of gaolers; the more inhumanly they behave towards the Polish and other prisoners, the more are their own sentences reduced. In such conditions it is hardly surprising that the death rate is very high. Prisoners die from illnesses contracted through the cold, and even more often from heart failure resulting from overwork and nervous strain.

The post brought to Warsaw large numbers of letters informing the next-of-kin of the deaths of their relatives in the Camp at Oświęcim. Families are entitled to receive urns containing the ashes of the deceased. A case is recorded in which a family was informed of the death of a relative and received his ashes twice. In another case the family received two urns from two different places. In yet another case analysis of the ashes proved that the urn contained merely dust and rubbish.

So far, only about 200 prisoners have returned to Warsaw from the Camp in Oświęcim. Generally only those are released from Oświęcim, who are sufficiently broken. Before releasing a prisoner, the *Gestapo* ascertains whether he or she is known to belong to a political party; if so, he cannot hope to be released. Before his release, a prisoner has to sign a promise: (1) that he will not tell anyone about the conditions prevailing in the Camp; (2) that he will be loyal to the Germans and that he will not take part in any action directed against Germany; (3) that he will report to the German police all anti-German activities which may come to his knowledge. The prisoner is given his own clothes. After his return home, he must register with the *Gestapo*. A released prisoner is as a rule a sick man, tuberculosis and with a weak heart, and in a state of nervous collapse.[344]

Polish Fortnightly Review—November 15 1941
Oświęcim Concentration Camp

The Concentration Camp at Oświęcim, which is the largest in Poland, merits a detailed description. The journeys to this Camp may take from three to five days, according to distance and travelling conditions. During the journey rations consisting of bread and noodles, which in wintertime were frozen together in a solid mass, were put through the ventilation window. Sometimes as many as ten bodies are removed from the trucks, which have been held in sidings for some days, while in the winter some forty percent of the other prisoners had frostbitten hands and feet. It was common for those still alive to remove the clothes from the dead to wear for the sake of warmth.

At Oświęcim railway station the trucks are shunted on to a siding with a platform specially built for the purpose. One end slopes sharply downwards, and in wintertime it was very slippery, covered with ice and frozen snow. The trucks are kept sealed until nightfall, when the doors are opened and dazzling arc lights are switched on. Blinded, numbed with cold, hungry, and dizzy with the sudden fresh air, they are unable to step out immediately, and the police help them out with rifle butts and kicks. The older men fall and slide down the ramp. Prisoners unable to get up from the floor of the truck are dragged out by their feet or hands and flung down the ramp. The corpses are left in the truck, and are afterwards burnt in the crematorium. The prisoners are then packed into lorries, being beaten incessantly the while.

On arrival at the Camp they are ordered to fall in line, in order of size. Those who cannot stand are laid out on the ground. After the list has been checked, which usually takes a couple of hours or more,

---

[344] *Polish Fortnightly Review*, June 1, 1941, Polish Ministry of Information.

they are allotted to the various barracks. The barracks are unheated, and there are innumerable chinks in the walls. At one time a man was hanged over the door of one of the barracks, and his body was left hanging for some time. He was one of a group who planned to organize a hunger strike to protest against prisoners being driven out to work dressed only in wet overalls during frosts.

There is so little room for sleeping that if any prisoner turns over he disturbs his neighbours. There is only one palliasse for every three prisoners. All towels have to be kept in a single heap, so that no prisoner has his own towel and the danger of infectious diseases is greatly increased. Many persons suffering from venereal diseases are deliberately sent to the Camp. Rising time is about 5 a.m. and three minutes are allowed for washing under a cold shower, cleaning clothes and dressing.

Sick prisoners must work as though they were quite well. No one may report sick unless he has a temperature of over 100.4 Fahrenheit. If anyone reports sick with a lower temperature he is sent to the punishment squad. The prisoners live in dread of illness, as there is no proper medical care for them.

The jailers in charge of the barracks are chiefly criminals who have been given life sentences, but among them are a couple of German Communists. The jailers are degenerates, and have absolute sway over the lives of the prisoners in their charge. The prisoners are forced to do exhausting labor, frequently entirely useless. On one occasion a group of five men, including two priests, was ordered to do stonebreaking. One of them tried to warm his hands by clapping them against his body, and the guard sentenced him to stand with his hands above his head for half an hour. While performing their task they were not allowed to kneel or squat down. When one of the priests, an old man, knelt down to pick up the hammer-head, which had come off the handle, the guard ran up and kicked the priest so hard that blood came.

One group of prisoners was given heavy blocks of wood, with which they had to smooth the surface of stone blocks, which were to be used for sculpture. A medallion with a stamp of the Blessed Virgin slipped out of the open neck of one man's shirt, and a *Gestapo* man at once ran up, kicked him in the face, tore the medallion away and ordered him to eat it.

Another group was ordered to construct a pond. As the prisoners may not ruin their boots and socks, they were ordered to work barefoot in the snow and on the frozen mud. All the prisoners of this group were from the intellectual class. One day they were unable to stand any more, and attacked their two guards, trampling them in the mud. The next day a large number of prisoners were taken out to the open field and ordered to run. The guards opened fire from machine-guns. Those who were killed were at once cremated.

In the centre of the Camp is a square used as a place for punishment exercises. In the middle of the square is a post. One day some fifteen men had to perform special gymnastics consisting of squatting and rising at the order of a *Gestapo* man behind them. The prisoners held one another's hands, so that the stronger could help the weaker. This kind of exercise is continued for hours at a time. The *Gestapo* men in charge are changed, but the prisoners have to go on. Frequently prisoners can be seen pushing wheelbarrows loaded with stones around the square at the double. Behind them a guard rides on a cycle, using a whip on those who do not keep running. Prisoners frequently die on this exercise, as no one yet succeeded in running around the circle more than 25 times.

Sometimes the prisoners are ordered to set out stones in a pattern, and then collect them again; often they have to carry piles of stones from one spot to another, and then shift them back the next day. They also have to build their own walls, level the ground, and so on.

The prisoners are fed very badly. Three times a day they are given 20 grammes of bread (less than an ounce), at noon they get soup and in the evening a brown fluid called coffee. The food has to be consumed in a very short, fixed period, and when instead of soup they are given potatoes in their jackets, they have to eat the skins as well, as they have no time to peel them. Large numbers suffer from digestive troubles, and they suffer all the more because they are allowed to use the toilet only three times a day.

It happened one day that a prisoner ate two portions of dinner. When it was discovered he was led out before the entrance gate, near the crematorium. By the gate two rows of guards with knouts were lined up. One of them told the prisoner that as he had shown so much ingenuity and cleverness in eating an additional portion, he was to be released. The gate was open and he could run out to freedom. But as stealing was a punishable offence, he must first run the gauntlet of the two rows of guards. He started to run between the line, being beaten mercilessly on the head and legs with the knouts. Near the end of the line he began to stagger, but he summoned up all his strength and ran out through the gate. Then a machine-gun opened fire, and he was wounded in the belly.

The guards called to a man with a wheelbarrow working close by, threw the wounded man on the barrow and ordered him to be taken to the crematorium. The prisoner was sufficiently conscious to see where he was being taken, and in a frenzy of despair tried to say something to the crowd of guards watching the sight. But they only laughed and made their way to the crematorium. There he was thrown into the furnace, where there were already two half-burnt bodies. The sight of his struggles aroused only jeers and laughter among the onlookers. The two guards in charge of the crematorium were ordered to divide the ashes into three, as the last victim had moved and so had disturbed the ashes of the other bodies.

The least misdemeanour is punished by public whipping and the principle of collective responsibility is imposed. If any one is missing at the roll-call, the entire group is kept standing for hours in the frost. One day, when one prisoner was missing, a large group of men was stopped after their work and kept standing in their wet clothes from 12 to 6 p.m. of the following day. Any one who moved was at once beaten. During this period 86 men died under the torture. In order to lengthen the period of torture, when any prisoner swooned he was carried under a pump, and brought around by having water pumped over him, and then he was returned to the line to be beaten.

Until the middle of September, all prisoners had to go barefoot, though the paths were made up of sharp stones. Every prisoner had his own clothing, which consisted of striped cotton overalls, like pyjamas. They were not allowed to wear any head covering. All heads were clean shaven.

At the end of November 1940, there were some 8,000 Poles in the Oświęcim Camp. Theoretically, they are divided into three groups: political prisoners, criminals and priests and Jews. This last group is the one worst treated, and no member of this group leaves the Camp alive. Every month the Warsaw postal authorities send out several hundred notices of death of people in Oświęcim.

During last winter the mortality in the Camp was terribly high, an average of 70 to 80 persons dying every day. On one day 156 people died. Even the Germans were forced to arrange for the inspection of the Camp by a sanitary commission, after which the mortality fell somewhat, and during the spring and summer was some 30 daily. During the winter months, three crematorium furnaces were insufficient to cope with the bodies to be cremated.

The Oświęcim Camp is built to hold 40,000 persons. All around the Camp is a great strip of 'neutral' area, beyond which is a triple wall. Before the wall, posts are set up at every fifty yards bearing the inscription: 'Neutral zone. Anyone crossing this line will be fired on without warning.'[345]

Polish Fortnightly Review—May 1 1945
An Eye-Witness Account of the Women's Camp
At Oświęcim-Brzezinka
Autumn 1943 to Spring 1944

At the outset, I want to say that the details given below are strictly true and authentic. They are not dictated by any desire for propaganda, by hatred, or love of exaggeration. On the contrary, instead of making the picture more glaring, I shall try to tone it down, to make it more credible. For the reality I have to write about is so horrible that it is difficult to expect that anyone who hasn't seen it

---

[345] *Polish Fortnightly Review*, November 15, 1941, Polish Ministry of Information.

should believe it. Yet it is the reality. Please believe this short account of that reality, and believe my words as you would believe someone returned from the dead.

The women's Concentration Camp at Oświęcim has officially no connection with the men's Camp. They are two separate worlds. The data concerning either of them does not apply to the other. Founded a year or more after the men's Camp had been started, the women's Camp is at present passing through that same process of successive horrors which the men's Camp had already experienced. The results are still more terrible, for women have less powers of resistance and are more helpless than men.

Some Figures

The serial number of the women at present in the Camp runs into the eighty thousands. Of this number, 65,000 women of various nationalities have died during the past two years. The majority of the deaths have been Jewesses, but several other nations have contributed large quotas. The total number of Polish women who have passed through the Camp is estimated at fifteen to sixteen thousand. Of these, 5,500 are still alive. The others are dead. The number of released women are insignificant and do not amount to one percent of the total.

The women's Camp is an abyss of misery, a horrible slaughter house for thousands upon thousands of women. Their ages range from ten to seventy. The crimes for which they are incarcerated are equally varied: In addition to serious political cases, and women soldiers captured with arms in hand, there is a Poznań woman who refused to sell her favourite cat to a German woman. Her hard bed is shared by a twelve-year-old girl who, while collecting her father's geese, happened unknowingly to cross the frontier, so-called, near Częstochowa. She has been here for two years as a serious political criminal. The nationalities are just as varied: Polish, Russian, Ukrainian, Yugoslavian, German, French and Jewish. The Jewesses are the most numerous and most unfortunate of all.

At first the conditions at Brzezinka were so horrible that very few of those who came to the Camp in the early days are still alive. A great transport of a thousand women, brought from the Fordon prison two years ago, is recalled by only four women still alive. There are very few low serial numbers left in Brzezinka, and they are very rare. When one listens to the stories of those still left one is seized with indescribable horror. Although there has been a great improvement in conditions since then, the mortality continues to be enormous. For instance, out of a number of prisoners transferred from the Pawiak prison in Warsaw on October 5, two-thirds have died. In the winter the women are decimated by typhus. In the summer by malaria. All through the year bad hygienic conditions, starvation and a horrible, ruthless, humiliating regime prevail.

Conditions of Work

Seven hundred Polish women work in the Camp itself, in the kitchen, the laundry, the tailoring department, the packing department, the clothing warehouse, the office and so on. They are all privileged individuals, for they work with a roof over their head and in a moderate temperature. All the others, with the exception of five hundred at present 'parked' in hospital, go to work out of doors. This work is compulsory, winter and summer. Frost, rain, snow, heat, nothing holds up the march of the columns for work in the fields. Only when there is dense mist are they kept in the barracks, for fear they should escape. This is the only rest they have, as Sunday is not observed.

The work assigned to the women is very hard. In the winter the rivers Vistula and Soła were cleaned up, and the women digging out the channels stood up to their knees in water all day. Another group carried stones and paving for roads. Heavy artillery wagons, no longer in service since the army was motorized, and so transferred by the Wehrmacht to the Camps, were hauled along by the women. The work lasts twelve hours each day. It should not be forgotten that the workers are inadequately clothed, have no outdoor clothes, and go winter and summer in the same clothing which they wear in the barracks, and are undernourished into the bargain.

The food at Brzezinka is terrible: a quarter kilogramme of bread each day, five dekagrammes of margarine or sausage, a decotion of leaves and herbs morning and evening (unsweetened), soup made of turnips in the afternoon. Never of anything else but turnips, and prepared in a specially repulsive fashion. It is really horrible, and after it the soup given in other prisons seems tasty. It has no fat or any other positive elements, and is completely valueless. Such food is not sufficient for a day's work. And so it is only the food parcels which keep the women alive, and only ten per cent of them receive parcels.

Distinguishing Marks

On arrival at the Camp every woman is at once tattooed with her number on the left forearm. The shaving of the head, which was compulsory until recently, has been stopped. Then all her clothes are taken and all articles in exchange for the striped Camp uniform. The number is repeated on the clothes, striped with the addition of a triangle and a letter indicating the woman's nationality. A red triangle indicated political 'criminals,' a green one thieves, and a black one anti-social behaviour, i.e. sabotage and prostitution. The Jewesses are given stars. They do not wear the striped garment, but ragged civilian clothing, with a great red cross painted with oil paint between the shoulders. They are not entitled to receive parcels or write letters. It is worth mentioning here that the Jewesses who are given numbers amount to some ten per cent of the total number of Jewish women brought to Brzezinska. Of the transports of Jews that arrive every day from all over Europe, ten per cent of each group who go to the Camp are given numbers and live out their lives in a barrack, to perish successively in the monthly 'selections.' The other ninety percent go straight from the railway to the gas chamber and the crematorium. They suffer a more ephemeral torment. How many there have been of these condemned it is impossible to calculate. The ten per cent mentioned above numbered a total of almost forty thousand.

The Camp Authorities

Birkenau is divided into Camp A and Camp B. The Camp Commandant is the notorious murderer and executioner Adolf Taube. That name must not be forgotten. He has on his conscience the lives of many thousand women. Just as notorious are the *Ober*, Dreschel and her assistant Hasse. These are the lowest dregs. Under them are two 'Camp Seniors' (*Lagerälteste*). In Camp A she is 'Bubi' the former President of a Lesbian club in Berlin. In Camp B she is 'Stenia,' a very cruel woman with sadistic instincts.

The immediate authority over the prisoners is the 'block.' She may be a German, a Polish woman, a Czech, a Yugoslavian. In general they are bad types, though among them are some outstanding women. It depends on them whether the life of a prisoner is tolerable or not, for they can even make for a certain alleviation of the prisoner's lot. The other categories of officials, the *Kapo*, work supervisors, are the same as in the men's Camp.

The Camp

The Camp covers an enormous area. It is adjacent to the Gypsy Concentration Camp, in which there are swarms of gypsies, who like the Jews, have been brought here from all parts of Europe. At the moment they are not being slaughtered, but the mortality among them is very high. They have no rights and they are not allowed to go to the hospital.

Within the bounds of Brzezinka there are six 'chimneys' or crematoria, which are always in use, and belch smoke all day, and flame all night. The living barracks or 'blocks' are of two kinds. The old ones are of brick and the new ones of wood. It is warmer in the brick barracks in the winter time, but instead of beds they have the notorious bunks, which hold up to eight persons. In these suffocating lairs sometimes twelve to fourteen women have to lie. In the summer-time that is an indescribable torture. The wooden barracks are better, for instead of the bunks they have three-tiered beds, but on the other hand it is as cold inside these barracks as outside. The sanitary arrangements are a nightmare of Camp life. A permanent defect of the Camp is the repeated and chronic shortage of water. There have been times when the prisoners could not wash themselves for weeks, or even months.

The Camp is surrounded by a trench and by wire, which is said to be charged with a high tension current. Said to be, because in fact the current is rarely switched on, owing to the necessity for economy. So that this fact may not come to light, the guards in the guardhouses are ordered to shoot anyone who goes anywhere near the wire. They may not allow a suicide to approach the barrier. Only recently the guard had a day off as reward for killing a prisoner.

The ground at Brzezinka is marshy and full of clay. The Women's Camp covers an area of well over a thousand acres, is built on a swamp, or saturated clay leas. The Camp had previously been the scene of the terrible death of several tens of thousands of Soviet prisoners of War, who were killed by starvation. These unhappy wretches chewed the grass and had to resort to cannibalism. Their bodies were sucked down into the swamp, and they had no other form of burial. Then the marshy soil, which constituted one enormous grave, was covered over with rubble and the barracks built on it. Streets were marked out and Brzezinka came into being.

In addition to the normal malaria which had been chronic in the district for many years, innumerable infections caused by the decay of human bodies buried only just under the surface spread in the area. And as there is no other water in Brzezinka except that lying above the subsoil, one can imagine the sanitary conditions which prevail. All over the Camp not a blade of green is to be seen. Nothing ever grows on the clay earth, which is trampled over by thousands of feet. There are too many tears and so much blood in this soil for it to produce anything.

Only lice and rats multiply on it. The lice became a plague of the Camp, for there was no way of escaping them. They were everywhere. After the last typhus epidemic, which carried off Germans too, energetic steps were taken to delouse the Camp and there was a decided reduction in the number of lice. There remained the other plague of rats. They were innumerable and loathsome, they gnaw at the corpses waiting to be taken to the crematorium, they attack the sick and deprive the healthy of all possibility of sleep.

The railway station of Oświęcim lies just over a mile from Brzezinka. A sideline has recently been built over which the trains loaded with prisoners run right into the Camp through the wire.

The Hospital

A large part of the Camp is occupied by the 'park' as the hospital is called. It consists of over a dozen barracks. This hospital, unique in its kind, calls for extensive description separately. It is distinguished by its primitive and anti-hygienic conditions and the complete absence of medicaments.

There are doctors, the majority of them Polish women, who work with incredible devotion and self-sacrifice, but their labor and goodwill are not of much benefit, for they have not even the simplest and most essential of medical supplies. Last winter, during a terrible typhus—there is a typhus epidemic every year—the 'park' became a scene of moving tragedy. The sick were crowded in it so much that the feverish half-delirious women lay four to each narrow bed. About 300 women died every day—some 9,000 monthly. The bodies were dragged out of the block and flung in a heap, like piles of wood. A heap of these emaciated, distorted bodies with wide open eyes and mouths lay in front of every hospital building.

Before the lorries arrived each evening to remove this daily contribution and take it to the crematorium the bodies were gnawed by the rats, of which there are numberless multitudes in the Camp, and pecked by the rooks. At this period, when the head doctor, a German came to inspect the blocks, he paid not the least attention to the piles of bodies or to the doctor's requests for medicines, but closely examined the walls to see if there was any dust or spider's webs anywhere. And if he noticed anything of this kind he talked threateningly about the necessity to observe hygienic conditions. But why raise the question of medical supplies for that matter, when there was even a lack of water in the hospital and the sick died of thirst?

In the February the typhus epidemic died away by itself, having carried off over twenty thousand victims. The mortality in the Camp has dropped for the time being, but an outbreak of ordinary summer malaria is expected soon, and that will continue until September. The only preventative against malaria is quinine, but there is none whatever in the Camp.

The Prisoners Powers of Endurance

Oświęcim takes its greatest toll of life among the youngest of its inmates. Proportionally girls up to the age of twenty have the greatest mortality rate—and there is a huge number of such girls in the Camp, together with women over fifty. The middle ages best survive the long starvation and hard labor. Members of the intellectual classes die more rapidly than those of the working class.

Among the nationalities of which so many are represented at Brzezinka, the French women proved to have the lowest powers of resistance—there are only 26 of them alive in the Camp and at one time they numbered several hundred, while the Russians and the Yugoslavians are the strongest and have the greatest powers of endurance.

Among the more outstanding women who died in the Camp last winter was the wife of General Dragoljub Mihailović, the Commander-in-chief in Yugoslavia, and among the Polish women were Maria Sadowska (Stronska), Natalia Hiszpanska, Zofia Kraczkiewicz, Lucia Charewiczowa (Docent of Lwow University), and the painter Jewniewiczowa. Deaths last year included Emilia Grocholska, the well-known publicist, Zarzycka, the writer, and the grey-haired poetess Savitri (Anna Zaborska), who was left to die outside a block, after being beaten up with sticks.

Escapes

Many minds are occupied with the thoughts of possible escape. There are frequent escapes from the men's Camp, and eighty percent of them are successful. Up to a hundred escape each month and last January, when mists were especially common, some 160 prisoners got away. Almost every day while a roll-call is being held, the sirens begin to wail to announce that someone's escape has been discovered. At the sound, patrols composed of *Kapo's*, guards and others go off to seek the prisoners. They do not appear to be very fervent in their searches.

On the other hand, escapes from the Women's Camps are very rare, and only a few cases have known to have occurred.

Degradation

Are the starvation and everyday torments of life as we have described it the worst side of a stay in Brzezinka? Does the horror of the Camp system depend on them?

No. There are still worse things. The horror derives from the complete denial and destruction of humanity. Once a prisoner has arrived at the Camp she ceases to be a human being, she is only a number, an animal, and less than an animal. Everything will rather be forgiven her than any display of human dignity, of shame, of noble indignation. The Germans carry through their programme of dehumanisation, of humiliation and subjection with incomparable consequentiality and with the systematic order peculiar to that nation.

Despite their stupidity, the Germans have realized that the nature of women determines the nature of the nation. To destroy the woman is to destroy the morrow of their hated neighbours. So the few who do not die must go back home mutilated. Feminine modesty is a powerful moral factor, it is equivalent to the conception of feminine virtue. So let modesty and honour perish. This is the purpose of the mass compulsion on the prisoners to strip themselves bare and to march naked past Germans.

And so a line of beautiful naked girls, naked pregnant mothers, naked old and exhausted women walks along. They are scarlet with shame. An *SS* man calls out jeeringly: 'Forwards the political ladies! Forwards!" (*Loss die politsche Damen!*). The tears pour down the faces of some of the girls and fall on their bare breasts. A gang of men from the Men's Camp is working mending the road along which the procession marches. Their naked wives, sisters, mothers pass them by only a few paces away. And something fine and moving happens: without a word of command all the men turn and stand with their backs to the road. Not one of them moves, or turns his head until the women have passed.

Like the old story of Lady Godiva. The procession reaches the bath, called 'Sanna' and the water of the showers washes away the tears. A group of *SS* men come up and watch the bathing women, looking for volunteers for 'Puf,' the brothel. At present women can apply voluntarily. But if there were no volunteers, the *SS* men would select their victims.

A crowd of naked girls from Lowicz district huddles in terror in one corner like an anxious, frightened herd. But a German woman, a former cabaret singer, breaks away from the larger crowd, and proudly displays her still not entirely ravaged body, while she sings pornographic German songs. Encouraged by her example another, a withered gypsy, starts out and begins to dance a fiery Cossack dance. She is lissom, her bare thighs swing round, she drops to a squatting position to kick out her legs, the two dry pieces of skin, which were once breasts smack together. The *SS* men laugh aloud in their amusement and lash at the dancer with their whips when she halts breathless. The Lowicz girls weep loud.

Part of the system of dehumanizing the prisoners consists in compelling them to perform even the most intimate physiological necessities in public. There is no chance of isolation in the Camp, and a moment of solitude is an empty dream. The woman slave is always one of an animal herd, always surrounded by a crowd, incessantly hunted, cuffed, heaped with the most horrible expressions. This slave, a living number, does not possess a change of underlinen, cannot call the least thing her own, and has an unchallenged right to only one thing: to death. And the inhabitants of the Camp avail themselves abundantly of that right.

Like Slaves in Ancient Egypt

Rain falls very often in Oświęcim, the district has the heaviest rainfall in all of Poland. Through the slanting streams of cold autumn rain one sees a long row of great, heavy ex-artillery wagons loaded with rubble or rubbish moving along a '*Lagerstraße*' (Camp street). These wagons are drawn by undernourished, emaciated women in striped overalls. Twenty pull at the shafts and traces, sixteen—eight on each side—turn the spokes of the wheels with the movement known to the world from the slaves depicted on Egyptian bas-reliefs.

They work like that all day, wet through. Their miserable clothing, made of wood-pulp, is soaked through in an instant. On the other hand it takes long to dry out. When after the roll-call the laborers return to their barracks they are glad to throw off their wet rags, and to wrap themselves in dry blankets. But the clothing does not get dry during the night, and when they have to get up at daybreak the next morning, they draw on a wet overall, put on soaking wet boots. They will shiver with the cold until the kindly sun has pity on them, warming and drying them. But suppose the downpour lasts several days!

When the gleam of the sunset shines on the accursed high-tension wires surrounding the Camp, when the evening roll-call brings all the inhabitants of the Camp without exception together, the mortally weary columns of women workers move up from all directions. Some of them are carrying burdens on stretchers. Others haven't stretchers, so they drag their burdens along the ground.... What are those burdens? The dead bodies of their comrades who have died at work that day. Sometimes one or two, sometimes more. The stretchers are short. The legs and arms hang stiffly, helplessly. A band playing a lively march comes out to meet them, involuntarily the slaves' weary legs fall into step. The rhythm is communicated to the dead, and the hanging hands, the helpless feet begin to keep time.

Death in Oświęcim

In November last year the annual typhus epidemic broke out in Brzezinka. It was especially violent in its course. In November, December and January the deaths amounted to nine thousand per month. Three hundred women every day. The hospital blocks were overcrowded. Four sick women lay on each narrow pallet. Try to imagine the picture of four women in a high fever, pressed close together, unable to stir, with bodies covered all over with the itch and ulcers, eaten alive with lice and fleas. There could be no thought of fighting the epidemic, for there were no medical supplies. They did not exist at all, not even the simplest and most primitive. Nothing.

And of what avail was the devotion and goodwill of the doctors, most of them Polish women, when all they could do was to certify the disease and had nothing with which to treat it. And so the sick died, died without religious consolation, without a friendly word of farewell.

Young girls died for whom mothers were waiting yearningly at home, mothers died for whom little children were waiting for them at home. Some departed with resignation, others clung desperately for life: "I can't die, I promised mother I'd come back for certain," one dying girl complained. The block personnel carried out the bodies and flung them down in the yard outside the doors. By evening, a large pile of bodies was gathered, lying in the mud or snow, naked, yellow and blue, fearfully emaciated, arms flung out, flung down carelessly, legs straddled, with staring eyes. For death in Oświęcim, the death which is the comrade of every prisoner, is entirely lacking in piety, beauty and respect. It is as ugly as if Satan himself, the Lord of the Camp, were playing with humanity and its after-death hopes.

The bodies lay in the yard all day, for the lorry carrying them to the crematorium came only in the evening. All this time the rats rummaged among them. But once it happened that the rats gnawed at the forearm of a dead woman and destroyed the number there tattooed, the only proof of her identity, and owing to the bureaucratic complications this caused, the Camp authorities ordered that the lorry was to come twice a day, so as not to leave so much time for the rats.

The epidemic was at its height at Christmas time. A huge fir tree hung about with electric lamps shining brilliantly stood in the *'Lagerstraße.'* The light picked out the pile of dead bodies, but the merry sound of music came from the *'Sauna.'* The local band was giving a concert. The death-wires rang with the frost. As though that sound had a suggestive power, more than one desperate woman made her way towards it that night. The guards in various parts of the Camp opened fire again and again. The 'posts' sitting in their towers were firing, for they were not allowed to let a suicide get near the wire. They had to shoot her first. A year ago a 'post' got a week's leave for shooting a prisoner. They were lucky. Every time they wanted to visit their girls, they watched for a woman prisoner getting too close to the wire, and their leave was assured.

The Jews

Health and strength, honour and life—it is not sufficient to deprive the prisoners of these in order to consummate the work of dehumanizing them: the prisoners must be robbed of their heart. Perhaps the greatest torment of a stay in the Camp was the sight of the terrible tragedy of the Jews, which was open for all of the Camp to see.

In Brzezinka there were six 'chimneys,' or crematoria. They were never idle. Not an evening passes without the prisoners seeing the flames leaping out of the broad chimneys, sometimes to a height of thirty feet. Not a day passes without heavy billows of smoke pouring from them. The cremating of the bodies of those who die in the Camp is only a small part of the crematoria's functions. They are intended for the living rather than the dead. And every day trains draw into the Camp along the sideline bringing Jews from Bulgaria, Greece, Rumania, Hungary, Italy, Germany, Holland, Belgium, France, Poland, and until recently, from Russia.

The trains bring men, women and children, and old people. Ten percent of the women in each train are sent to the Camp, are given a number tattooed on them, a star on their clothing, and the numbers of the Camp are thus increased. The others are sent straight to the gas chambers. The scenes which take place there defy all powers of description. But as ten percent of the transports brought to the Camp amount to over thirty thousand Jewish women, what is the total figure of the victims whom the crematoria have consumed?

It is terrible to think, terrible to watch when lorries pass through the *Lagerstraße,* carrying four thousand children under ten years of age—children from the Ghetto in Terezin in Bohemia—to their death. Some of them were weeping calling 'mummy,' others were laughing at the passers by and waving their hands. Fifteen minutes later not one of them was left alive and the gas-stupefied little bodies were burning in the horrible furnaces. But who will believe that this is true? Yet I swear that it was so, calling on the living and the dead as my witnesses.

'Stupefied by gas...' Yes, for gas was dear, and the 'special command'—*Sonderkommando* servicing the death chamber, used it very economically. The amount of gas used kills the weaker organisms, but only sends the stronger organisms to sleep for a little while. The latter revive on the crematoria lorries and are flung alive into the roaring fires.

The fact that they are transferred to the Camp and given a number does not save the ten percent of Jewish women from death: it only postpones death. Every month a 'sorting' or selection goes on in the Camp. Irrespective of the weather and the time of year all the Jewish women have to report naked at the roll-call. The Camp authorities examine them and assign a certain proportion to the 'chimneys.' Who can say what governs the decision as to the choice? They select not only old sick women, but young girls with healthy, handsome bodies. As the selection takes some days, those condemned do not go straight to the 'chimneys,' but remain for the time being locked up in the notorious 'Block No. 25.' There they await their fate, naked and despairing.

They get nothing more to eat or drink. And so through the grated window comes a terrible howl of despair, an imploring wail: 'Water, water for God's sake water! If you believe in Christ give us water!'

But anyone who gives them water, or even approaches a window, is in danger of death herself. Even so, there were Polish women who did not hesitate to give the condemned water or snow at night. This heroism was rather of service in demonstrating to themselves that they were still human, for what did even a few buckets of water mean to the thousand condemned? The despairing wail, the wail of dying animals, did not cease for several days and nights in the summer. It rent the heart. Until at last silence fell. Lorries drove up and executioners went in to the death block. They seized each woman in turn by the arms and legs, swung the bodies and flung them on to the lorry. The head crashed hollowly against the floor or side. When full, the lorry set off to take its terrible load to the chamber.

I am writing the truth, the very truth that I have seen all this time with my own eyes and even that is a small part of what I have seen. I pass over in silence a number of no less horrible facts: the misery of the mothers, the 'regulation' killing of newly-born babies, the sombre 'Block 10' in which women are subjected to horrible and murderous experiments as though they were rabbits, the weekly selection of Aryan women in the hospital, compulsory until recently.

If I wanted to tell everything, I should never finish.[346]

Whilst reports by the Polish Home Army about Auschwitz are numerous, reports by members of the *SS* are less so. One such report that has survived, is the detailed report by *SS-Sturmbannführer* Albert Franke Gricksch, who accompanied his superior *SS-Gruppenführer* Maximillian von Herff on a journey through Poland. Maximilian von Herff was the head of the *SS*-Personnel Main Office, and had previously served in the *Deutschen Afrika Korps*. The journey travelled through places such as Kraków, Lvow, Lublin and Warsaw. The journey visited a number of labor Camps and Concentration Camps, such as Lublin and Poniatowa. The first place visited was Auschwitz Concentration Camp:

---

[346] *Polish Fortnightly Review, May 1, 1945*, Polish Ministry of Information.

Report on the Duty Journey through Poland from the 4th to 16th May 1943 by *SS*-Sturmbannführer Albert Franke Gricksch.

The Journey

On Tuesday 4th May 1943, at 9.15am, the plane left the Tempelhof Aerodrome. We landed at the aerodrome at Kraków at 11.40am after having a pleasant trip from Kottbus and Breslau. The Commandant of the Aerodrome reported to *SS-Gruppenführer* Herff.[347] *SS-Obersturmbannführer* Höss,[348] Commandant of the Concentration Camp at Auschwitz, reported immediately after.

Auschwitz

We carried on immediately and went to Auschwitz Camp. At 13.00 hrs. we arrived at Auschwitz, the leaders of the Camp were assembled and introduced to the *Gruppenführer*. Amongst those were *SS-Oberführer* Caesar, who is in charge of all agricultural dimensions as *Stbf*. After the *Gruppenführer* had addressed the leaders and informed them of the purpose of his visit, he joined them at dinner.

In order to get a clear picture of the Camp, its structure and purpose, SS-*Obersturmbannführer* Höss drove us around the whole Camp area. The Camp itself was an old Austrian hutted Camp which had been extended to a small town by the work of *SS-Obersturmbannführer* Höss. Auschwitz is the biggest Concentration Camp in Germany. It covers about 18,000 morgens and has at the moment 54,000 inmates. Out of these 18,000 morgens, 8,000 are arable, 1,000 are fishbreeding and 3,000 are used for market gardening and greenhouses. They are breeding their own horses and keep their own poultry farms.

---

[347] In the report HERSS is stated but it seems more logical that this is his superior Maximillian von Herff.

[348] In the report HERSS is stated, but this should be Rudolf Höss, The Commandant of Auschwitz.

In 1932 (should probably read 1942) the breeding measures have produced 32,000 chicks. Besides, the Camp has its own kennels with 500 picked animals specially trained to guard prisoners. The Camp is to be gradually extended to hold 200,000 prisoners. It has got its own leather tannery, a factory for brushes, a butchers shop, bakery, cobblers shop, blacksmiths, a place for breeding pheasants, their own research institute (a research for diseases of plants), nurseries, plants of rubber, testing fields for different kinds of corn, suitable for Eastern purposes. The best methods to get the most out of the soil are tried out in the Camp in order to gain experience for the settlement. Special cold resisting fruit trees are being planted, and corn usually used in the *Kauhasus* is being developed for the East.

The actual Concentration Camp is sub-divided into blocks for 10,000 each, and the *Ustbf.* Is to be in charge of each block. The inmates are Jews, Gypsies, Poles and Women. The Camp has its own orchestra, which is conducted by the former Warsaw Radio Orchestra conductor. The whole Polish Intelligentsia remain in this Camp for life, and will be employed in laboratories and science research institutes, according to their knowledge. The Jewish women who work in the chemical laboratories are students from the Sorbonne University.

Because of the Krupp-works in Essen having been practically destroyed, the transfer of these to Poland and the Auschwitz district has taken place. Three new factory sheds have been created in a comparatively short time in the Camp, which will after a month, take over two-thirds of the Krupp production of matches and will be run entirely by prisoner labor. The sheds are constructed in accordance with modern principles and give a clean and friendly impression.

In the agricultural sphere, they have succeeded in producing nice large fields by creating a large network of draining systems. This does not only enable them to work these fields very extensively but also to work it on a profitable basis. The small Polish farms and villages have been expropriated and the Polish farmers settled in different areas. Near the completely neglected fishponds, dykes are being built by women, and in that way thousands of morgens of swampy meadow have been drained and the foundations for a new fishbreeding ground have been laid.

The guarding of the prisoners is done by a '*Wachkommando*' consisting of 13 companies each having 200 men. Each company has got a leader—an officer and the 13 companies form a so-called *Lagersturmbann*, which is commanded by a *Stbf* and one assistant.

The personnel reports of the Camp Commandant are very interesting. It is a very difficult task to cope with the individual groups of prisoners. The Gypsies have to be treated differently from the Poles, and the Poles differently from the Ukrainians. The hygienic question is a very heavy responsibility for the Administration; nearly all the inmates, especially the Jews from the East and South East have to be trained in this respect, for they show a particular fear of keeping themselves clean. In parts there have to be very strict measures in order to train the prisoners out of superstition. When having a shower bath they wrap up their lice in a piece of paper and hide it in their mouth in order to have them in their new clothes, as they are of the opinion that whoever has lice will not become ill.

After the inspection of the Camp we drove through Auschwitz. It is a completely neglected small town which had at one time 11,000, of which 8,000 were Jews who have left now. The town has changed completely under German leadership. It is typical of Polish mismanagement, the sanitary conditions at Auschwitz. An Artillery Regiment was stationed there for six years. There was neither light nor water laid on, but only open wells which are dug near the latrines. These latrines were closed up when they were full and new ones opened a few yards further on, so a rather interesting circulation, sewer, drinkwater, sewers, was a consequence. Neither the Polish Military authorities nor the medical officers have ever drawn the attention to the danger for the health of the troops.

Not far from Auschwitz we saw a wonderful sign of the German strength in the 4th year. The *HG* built in a very short time, industrial works which extended over 12 kms square. These works were run mainly on foreign labor with the aid of prisoners. This establishment is one of the largest chemical works in Germany and will commence production within a few months. They produce Buna (artificial rubber) petrol and a considerable amount of gases.

After a short talk with the Camp Commandant in his flat, we left Auschwitz and arrived in Kraków after a two hours trip.[349]

---

[349] National Archives Kew, WO 309/374.

Chapter XIV
Post War Testimonies

This chapter will include post War testimony from the highest ranking SS officer to ordinary prisoners who survived incarceration in one of the most deadly places ever created by man. We start with the testimony of Camp Commandant Rudolf Höss, awaiting trial in Poland. Some of what he states has already been covered in this book, but it has to be reproduced in full, to give the complete picture. Rudolf Höss recalled his life and role in one of the greatest crimes ever committed:

Translation of the Deposition of Rudolf Franz Ferdinand Höss—alias Franz Lang

I, Rudolf Franz Ferdinand Höss, alias Franz Lang, hereby declare, after having been warned accordingly, that the following statement is true:

I was born on the 25th November 1900. I am the son of the merchant Franz Xaver Höss in Baden-Baden. I have two married sisters, who are living at present in Mannheim and Ludwigshafen.

Addresses
Buehler, Maria Ludwigshafen-Oggersheim on the Rhine, 31 Bruckenweg
Grete Mannheim-Feudenheim, 16, Feldstraße

After I finished the preparatory school, I visited the humanistic '*Gymnasium*' at Mannheim until I reached the '*Untersecunda.*' On the 1 August 1916, I volunteered for the '*Badische* Dragon Regiment 21' and joined the replacement squadron in Bruchsal, Baden. After a short training I was sent to the Asia Corps in Turkey. I remained there until the end of 1917, in Mesopotamia, and was then, until the armistice, on the Palestine Front. I was twice wounded, suffered from malaria and I was repeatedly decorated.

After my return to Germany in January 1919, I volunteered for the *Ostpreussische Freiwilligenkorps*, was sent to the *Freikorps* Rossbach, and participated in the battles in the Balticum, Ruhrgebiet and Oberschlesian. Afterwards I learned agriculture in Silesia, and Schleswig-Holstein (Hornsdorf bei Schlammersdorf, *Kreis* Segeberg-Farmer Boeckmann 1922). I was a member of the *Arbeitsgemeinschaft* Rossbach, in this capacity I later had an *Arbeitsgruppe* in Mecklenburg.

In June 1923, I was arrested for taking part in a murder and I was sentenced in 1924 to ten years imprisonment. The man in question was Walther Kadow, Occupation: Schoolteacher, who betrayed Schlageter to the French. The murder was committed during the end of May in a wood near Parchim. Myself and three others took part in the murder. After five years imprisonment I got an amnesty.

I joined the *Bund der Artamanen* and was, during the years 1929 to 1934, in charge of different *Landienstgruppen* in Brandenburg and Pommern. Himmler, Heinrich, was a member of the *Bund der Artamanen (Gauführer Bayern)*. In 1929, I got married in Heuhasen, near Löwenburg, on the Nordbahn. My wife's name is Hedwig Hensel from Neukirch, Oberlausits. The names of my wife's four brothers are: Fritz Hensel, at present in Flensburg, Helmut Hensel, at present in Botzen, Gerhard Hensel near Königsbruck in Sachsen, Rüdolf Hensel in a Prisoner of War Camp in Bayern (*SS-Oberscharführer*).

In 1922, I joined the *NSDAP* in Munich. I have not got the golden Party badge, neither have I been awarded the Blood Order, for having been imprisoned.

In 1933 I formed a squadron of horses on the *SS* farm Sallentin in Pommern. I was detailed by the Party and by landowners to do this, as I have been in the cavalry. My Party number is 3240. Himmler noticed me during an inspection of the *SS* in Stettin—we knew each other from the *Bund der Artamanen*—and he arranged that the administration of a Concentration Camp was given to me. I came to Dachau in November 1934 where, after additional military training, I was employed as a a *Blockführer* in the *Schutzhaftlager*. Later on I did the job of a *Rapportführer* and *Gefangeneneigentumsverwalter*.

When I came to Dachau I held the rank of *SS-Scharführer* and was promoted in 1935, to *SS-Untersturmführer*. In 1938, I was sent, as Adjutant to the Camp Commandant of Sachsenhausen, *Oberführer* Baranowski. In November 1938, I was made *Schutzhaftlagerführer* holding the rank of a *SS-Hauptsturmführer* until my transfer to Auschwitz on the 1st May 1940.

I was given the order, by an higher authority, to transform the former Polish Artillery Barracks near Auschwitz into a quarantine Camp for prisoners coming from Poland. After Himmler inspected the Camp in 1941, I received the order to enlarge the Camp and to employ the prisoners in the to be developed agricultural district and to drain the swamps and inundation area on the Weichsel. Furthermore he ordered to put 8–10,000 prisoners at the disposal of the building of the new Buna Works of the I. G. Farben. At the same time he ordered the erection of a POW Camp, for 100,000 Russian prisoners, near Birkenau.

The number of prisoners grew daily in spite of my repeated interventions that billets were not sufficient, and further intakes were sent to me. Epidemic diseases were unavoidable because medical provisions were inadequate. The death rate rose accordingly. As prisoners were not buried, crematoriums had to be installed.

In 1941, the first intake of Jews came from Slovakia and Upper Silesia. People unfit to work were gassed in a room of the crematorium in accordance with an order which Himmler gave me personally.

I was ordered to see Himmler in Berlin in June 1941 and he told me, approximately, the following: The *Führer* ordered the solution of the Jewish question in Europe. A few so-called *Vernichtungslager* are existing in the *Generalgouvernement*—Bełżec near Rawa Ruska, Ost Polen, Treblinka near Malkinia on the River Bug, and Wolzek near Lublin.[350]

---

[350] Bełżec, Treblinka and Sobibór were three death Camps built as part of *Aktion Reinhardt*, the mass murder program of Polish Jewry, named in honor of Reinhard Heydrich, under the control of Odilo Globocnik, the SS and Police Leader for the Lublin District. Höss in

These Camps come under the *Einsatzkommando* of the *Sicherheitspolizei* under the leadership of high *SIPO* officers and guard companies. These Camps were not very efficient and could not be enlarged. I visited the Camp Treblinka in Spring 1942³⁵¹to inform myself about the conditions. The following method was used in the process of extermination: Small chambers were used equipped with pipes to induce the exhaust gas from car engines. This method was unreliable as the engines, coming from old captured transport vehicles and tanks, very often failed to work. Because of that the intakes could not be dealt with according to the plan, which meant to clear the Warsaw Ghetto.

According to the Camp Commandant of Treblinka, 80,000 people have been gassed in the course of half a year.³⁵² For the above mentioned reasons, Himmler declared the only possibility to extend this Camp, in accordance with the plan, was Auschwitz, as it was a railway junction of four lines and, not being thickly populated, the Camp area could be cut off completely. This is the reason why he decided to do the mass exterminations in Auschwitz, and I had to make the preparations at once. He wanted the exact plan in accordance with this instruction in four weeks.

---

	his statement gives the wrong date, the Camps were not constructed until much later. Bełżec was constructed from November 1941, and became operational in March 1942. Sobibór, incorrectly named as Wolzek, and Treblinka were not constructed until the spring of 1942. So Himmler could not have stated this in June 1941, and it is more probable that Höss met Himmler in the summer of 1942.
351	Treblinka was not operational until July 23, 1942, Höss visited Treblinka in September 1942, as part of his fact finding tours of Chełmno, to learn about improved methods of corpse disposal, which were later introduced in Auschwitz-Birkenau, with immediate effect.
352	At the time of Höss's visit to Treblinka, it had been operational for less than 3 months. But between July and September some 250,000 Jews had been deported from the Warsaw Ghetto alone. There were also mass transports from Częstochowa, Siedlce, Radom and Kielce, so it would appear that Höss is deliberately understating the murderous efficiency of Treblinka.

Furthermore he said this task is so difficult and important that he cannot order just anybody to do it and he had the intention to give this task to another high ranking *SS* officer, but he did not consider it advisable to have two officers giving orders whilst on a construction job. I was then given the definitive order to carry out the destruction of the intakes sent from *RSHA*. I had to get in touch with *SS-Obersturmbannführer* Eichmann of *Amt 4* (*Dienststelle* commanded by *SS-Gruppenführer* Müller) concerning the sequence of incoming transports.

At the same time transports of Russian POW's arrived from the area of the *Gestapo Leitstelle* Breslau, Troppau and Kattowitz, who, by Himmler's written order to the local *Gestapo* leaders, had to be exterminated. As the new crematoriums were only to be finished in 1942, the prisoners had to be gassed in provisionally erected gas-chambers and then had to be burned in pits.[353] I am now going to explain the method of gassing.

Two old farm buildings, which were situated rather out of the way near Birkenau, were made airtight and provided with strong wooden doors. The transports were unloaded on a siding in Birkenau. Prisoners fit to work were picked out and brought to the Camps. The luggage was left and was later on taken to the store. The others, who were meant to be gassed, were marched to the one km. distant plant. The sick and people unfit to walk were taken there in lorries. In front of the farmhouses everybody had to undress behind walls made from branches. On the door was a notice saying '*Desinfectionsraum*' (Disinfection Chamber). The *Unterführer* on duty had to tell the prisoners to watch their kit in order to find it again after having been deloused. This prevented disturbances.

When they were undressed, they went into the room according to size, 200–300 at a time. The doors were locked and one or two tins of *Zyklon B* were thrown into the room through holes in the wall. It consisted of a rough substance of Prussic acid. It took, according to the weather 3–10 minutes. After half an hour the doors

---

[353] The four purpose built crematoria were not fully operational until June 1943.

were opened and the bodies were taken out by the *Kommando* of prisoners, who were permanently employed there, and burned in pits. Before being cremated, gold teeth and rings were removed. Firewood was stacked between the bodies and when approximately 100 bodies were in a pit, the wood was lighted with rags soaked in paraffin. When the fire had started properly more bodies were thrown on to it. The fat which collected in the bottom of the pit was put into the fire with buckets to hasten the process of burning when it was raining. The burning took 6–7 hours. The smell of the burned bodies was noticed in the Camp even if the wind was blowing from the west.

After the pits had been cleaned the remaining ashes were broken up. This was done on a cement plater where prisoners pulverized the remaining bones with wooden hammers. The remains were loaded on lorries and taken to an out of the way place on the Weichsel and thrown into the river.

After the erection of the new big crematorium the following method was used:

After the first two big crematoriums were finished in 1942 (the other two were finished half a year later) mass transports from Belgium, France, Holland and Greece started. The following method was used. The transport trains ran alongside an especially built ramp with three lines, which was situated between the crematorium, store and camp Birkenau. The sorting out of the prisoners and the disposing of the luggage was done on the ramp. Prisoners fit to work were taken to one of the various Camps, prisoners to be exterminated were taken to one of the new crematoriums.

There the first went to one of the big underground rooms to undress. This room was equipped with benches and contraptions to hang up clothing, and the prisoners were told by interpreters that they were brought here to have a bath and be deloused and to remember where they put their clothing. Then they went on to the next room which was equipped with water pipes and showers to give the impression of a bath. Two *Unterführers* remained in the room until the last moment to prevent unrest.

Sometimes it happened that the prisoners knew what was going to be done. Especially the transports from Belsen knew that they were most likely taken to the place of extermination. When transports from Belsen arrived, safety measures were strengthened and the transport was split up into smaller groups which was sent to different crematoriums to prevent riots. SS men formed a strong cordon and forced resisting prisoners into the gas chambers. That happened very rarely as prisoners were set at ease by the measures we undertook.

I remember one incident especially well. One transport from Belsen arrived, approximately two-thirds, mostly men, were in the gas chamber, the remaining third was in the dressing room. When three or four armed *SS Unterführers* entered the dressing room to hasten the undressing, mutiny broke out. The light cables were torn down, the SS men were overpowered, one of them stabbed and all of them were robbed of their weapons. As the room was in complete darkness wild shooting started between the guard near the exit door and the prisoners inside.

When I arrived I ordered the doors to be shut and I had the process of gassing the first party and then went into the room together with the guard carrying small searchlights pushing the prisoners into one corner from where they were taken out singly into another room of the crematorium and shot, by my order, with small calibre weapons. It happened repeatedly that women hid their children underneath their clothing and did not take them into the gas chamber. The clothing was searched by the permanent *Kommando* of prisoners under the supervison of the SS and children who were found were sent into the gas chamber. After half an hour the electric air conditioner was started up and the bodies were taken up to the cremating stove by lift. The cremation of approximately 2,000 prisoners in five cremating stoves took approximately 12 hours. In Auschwitz there were two plants, each of them had five double stoves. Furthermore there were another two plants, each having four bigger stoves and provisional plants as described above.

The second provisional plant had been destroyed. All clothing and property of prisoners was sorted out in the store by a *Kommando* of prisoners which was permanently employed there and was also billeted there. Valuables were sent monthly to the *Reichsbank* in Berlin. Clothing was sent to armament firms, after having been cleaned, for the use of forced labor and displaced persons. Gold from teeth was molten down and sent monthly to the medical department of the *Waffen-SS*. The man in charge was *Sanitätsfeldzeugmeister SS-Gruppenführer* Carl Blumenreuter.

I personally never shot anybody or beat anybody. Owing to the mass intakes, the number of prisoners fit to work grew immensely. My protests to the *RSHA* to slow down the transports, which means to send fewer transports, was rejected everytime. The reason given was the *Reichsführer-SS* had given an order to speed up extermination and every *SS Führer* hampering some will be called to account. Owing to the immense over-populating of existing barracks and owing to the inadequate hygienic installations, epidemic diseases like spotted fever, typhus, scarlet fever and diphtheria, broke out from time to time, especially in the Camp Birkenau.

Doctors came under the Camp Commandant from a military point of view. As far as the medical decisions went they had their own routine and came under the *Chef des Sanitätswesens des WVHA SS-Standartenführer* Dr. Lolling, who again came under *Reichsarzt SS-Obergruppenführer* Dr. Grawitz. In one respect the above mentioned rule has been broken. Local *Gestapo* leaders were given orders by the *RSHA* to get in touch with me. Prisoners who were kept in Concentration Camps for the *Gestapo* and who have not been sentenced out of political reasons, were allowed to be removed by any other means. I received the names of the persons, personally, from the leader of the *Gestapo* and I passed them on again to the respective doctor for finishing off. This, usually, was an injection of petrol. The doctor had orders to write an ordinary death certificate. Regarding the reason of the deaths, he could put any illness.

During the time as Commandant we made the following experiments:

Professor Clauberg, chief of the Womens Hospital, Königshutte, in Upper Silesia, made sterilization experiments. This was done as follows. He got in contact with the doctor of the Womens Camp to find him suitable persons. They were put in a special ward of the hospital. Under a special x-ray screen he gave them a syringe with a special liquid which went through the womb into the ovary. This liquid, as he said, definitely blocked the ovary and caused an inflammation. After a few weeks he gave them another injection which could tell him that the ovary was definitely blocked. These experiments were made by order of the *Reichsführer SS*.

Similar sterilization experiments on women were made by Doctor Schumann, a doctor of the *Reichskanzlei*[354] but his experiments were not successful.

Against spotted fever they had certain methods of lice. They took healthy but lousy persons which were wrapped in with certain stuff, one called *Lausetto*, which was made from horse dung. The results of it were recorded afterwards.

Doctor Wirths, *Sturmbannführer* and Camp Doctor, looked for women with cancer in the beginning stages and operated on them. He worked on experiments of his brother who worked in a hospital in Hamburg. He also put persons to death with prussic acid injections. Those people have been condemned to death by the *Gestapo*. I also know during my work in *Amstgruppe D* of activities of Professor Doctor Schilling from Munich and Doctor Rascher[355] *Stabsarzt der Luftwaffe*. Prisoners condemned to death were put under air pressure experiments to see how the human organs react. The same doctors also put people in cold water to see how long they can exist.[356]

354	Incorrectly stated as Dr. Schumacher. See the Biography of Dr. Horst Schumann.
355	Incorrectly stated as Dr Rasche. This was Dr Sigmund Rascher, who was executed on Himmler's orders in Reichenau Camp in February 1945.
356	National Archives Kew, WO 374/62109.

A number of survivors provided statements to the British Forces who liberated Bergen-Belsen Concentration Camp, which was located near the city of Celle, Lower Saxony in Northern Germany, on April 15, 1945. A number of those liberated had been sent to Bergen-Belsen when Auschwitz was evacuated, and they provided statements about their incarceration in Auschwitz, and about some of the *SS* who guarded them and ill-treated them:

In the Matter of War Crimes and Atrocities At Auschwitz and Other Camps

Deposition of Henry Florczyk, late of Marzalkowska, 69, Warsaw, Poland, sworn before me, Major Geoffrey Smallwood, Major-Legal Staff, an Officer of the Staff of the Judge Advocate General to the Forces.

I am 41 years of age and was arrested on 24th June 1940, because I was a professor of mathematics and had written a number of books. I was taken to prison in Warsaw and transferred to Auschwitz on 15th August 1940. On 12th March 1943, I was transferred to Buchenwald and on 8th September 1943, to Dora Camp, Nordhausen. On 9th April 1945, I came to Belsen.

While I was at Auschwitz I knew an *SS* Officer, *Lagerführer* Mayer, whose description is as follows: Height about 6ft, round face, and well built. He would call the sick on *Appell* every evening and would ask them if they were ill. When they replied yes, he would have them beaten with a stick until they fell down. On one occasion a Pole who was sick with dysentery came late to an *Appell* and Mayer ordered him to be given 25 strokes on the back. He died a few days later.

At Auschwitz, *Lagerführer SS Obersturmführer* later *Hauptsturmführer* Fritzsch was directly responsible for many people being beaten especially Jews and Priests from the *Strafkompanie*. At *Appell* the dead would be brought on parade by his orders and would be laid on the ground in front of those still standing. Sometimes people received a card ordering them to report to his office and when they were reported they were shot.

Between 8th October 1941, and November 1941, about 10,000 Russians entered the Camp as Prisoners of War. They were ill-treated and only given clothes for use at *Appell* whilst they were working. Many died from typhus and many were given injections of phenol, so that they died within a few minutes. By March 1942, only 500 of them were left. I know this is true since I was then the Secretary of the Russian Hospital. Those who died from injections I was ordered to put down as having died from T.B. or one of 10–20 illnesses excluding typhus. Fritzsch was the Commandant until February 1942. His description is: Age about 50, height 5ft 7ins, very thin face and grey hair.

I name the following *SS* men working with Fritzsch:

SS-Hauptscharführer	Palitzsch	Height 6ft, light hair, round face, pale complexion
SS-Scharführer	Hössler	Photo 9–1
SS Officer	Schwarz	Height 6ft, fat round face
SS Officer	Seidler	Height 6ft, well built
SS Officer	Grabner	Height 6ft, slim, elegant appearance, thin faced

In February 1942, Fritzsch was superseded by *SS-Hauptsturmführer* Aumeier of Flossenburg Camp and the same conditions continued including injections of Phenol and subsequent deaths which I was told to attribute to other causes. Aumeier's hospital chief was *SS-Unterscharführer* Klehr, whose description is: age about 55, height about 6ft, round faced. Aumeier's description is: Height 5ft 4 ins, thin face, long nose.

Another Doctor responsible for the selection of those to be injected was *SS*-Doctor Entress whose description is: Height 6ft, slim build, straight nose, long face. I think he was one of those with the medical goods factory at Leverkusen near Cologne, called Bayer.

In the summer of 1942, there was a bad typhus epidemic and many who suffered from it were sent to the gas chambers. Many also were sent who had minor disabilities such as swollen feet and these sometimes would be chosen by *Arbeitsdienstführer* Vlies[357] whose description is: Height about 6ft 3 ins, ugly long face, big nose and well built.

At the end of October 1942, as a reprisal for alleged atrocities by Polish partisans at Lublin I personally saw *SS-Hauptscharführer* Palitzsch shoot 280 prisoners.

Sworn by Henry Florczyk this 18th day of May 1945 at Belsen Camp

Before Me Major Geoffrey Smallwood.[358]

In The Matter of War Crimes And The Gas Chamber At Auschwitz

Deposition of Regina Plucer (Female) late of 4, Lagowinska, Łódź, Poland, sworn before Captain Alfred James Fox, General List, D.A.P.M. 86 Special Investigation Section, Corps of Military Police.

I am 32 years of age and was arrested in 1941 at Gostynin near Łódź because I was a Jewess. I was taken to Bruchfelde Labor Camp where I remained until August 1943, when I was transferred to Auschwitz. I came to Belsen in January 1945.

In October 1944, I was employed at Auschwitz with a party detailed to dismantle the No.1 gas chamber and crematorium. The dismantling was apparently ordered because of the nearness of the advancing Russian Army. The work was done very carefully, various stones had to be stacked separately, and doors, window frames, fittings and so on were given numbers so that I gathered that the building was to be re-assembled elsewhere. During these operations I had access to all the departments of the building and I am able to describe the interior in a general way. The actual method of operat-

---

[357] This is probably Arbeitsdienstführer Fries as included on the list of Auschwitz personnel – National Archives Kew, WO 208/4296.
[358] National Archives Kew, WO 311/1326/1.

ing the gas chamber and the crematorium was told to me by members of the *Sonderkommando*—special party employed in the building when it was in use.

The building was surrounded by a wire fence over which blankets were draped apparently to screen the events which took place therein from outside view. A garden also surrounded it which was of considerable depth and again assisted in the screening process. The building itself consisted of a basement, ground floor and attic. In the basement was the undressing room, access to which from the outside was gained either by a flight of steps or a chute. The chute was used for sick and weak people but often when lorry-loads of victims came, they were tipped directly from the lorry down the chute. The capacity of the undressing room was such that I estimate it would hold about three thousand persons. The second room in the basement was the gas chamber itself holding about one thousand persons.

The ground floor was divided into two compartments. The first was the doctors' experimenting and vivisection room. In this room I saw a large glass container filled with some liquid in which were apparently human organs, I took these to be brains and spleens.

Th second compartment which was immediately above the undressing room, contained 15 separate ovens which were in line. They were about six feet long, six feet high and three feet wide. The corpses were conveyed from the gas chamber by means of an elevator to this room, where they were loaded into trolleys which ran on rails parallel with the ovens. The trolleys would then be unloaded and the bodies placed in the various ovens. The fuel used in the ovens was wood.

Immediately above the gas chamber was part of the garden and from here ten small chimneys led down into the gas chambers. Each one showed above the earth about a foot and was about a foot square. Each was fitted with a lid. Into these chimneys were put green coloured powders and some chemical action would take place and the gas developed would descend into the gas chamber.

The attic was used as living quarters by members of the *Sonderkommando*. Up to the time that the building was dismantled *Obersturmführer* Moll was in charge.

Sworn by the said Deponet Regina Plucer at Belsen this 30th day of May 1945 before me A.J. Fox, Captain.[359]

In the Matter of War Crimes and Atrocities At Drancy Prison, Paris and Auschwitz.

Deposition of Renee Erman (Female) late of 80 Rue des Menilmonatre, Paris, sworn before Captain Alfred James Fox, General List, D.A.P.M. 86 Special Investigation Section, Corps of Military Police.

I am 31 years of age and was arrested in Paris in April 1943 by the Germans because I was a Jewess. I was then taken to Drancy Prison in Paris and on 20th April 1943 I went to Auschwitz. I was transferred to Belsen on 25th January 1945.

Whilst at Drancy Prison there was an *SS* man named Brenner in charge. This man was responsible for many deaths. In my presence I have seen him beat, kick and throw stones at prisoners for no apparent reason apart from the fact that they were Jews. I know that two prisoners at whom this man threw stones died as a result of the injuries they received. I called at the Hospital on one occasion to see some friends and I was told by them that prisoners admitted the day before, suffering from head wounds inflicted by this man, were dead. I cannot state whether they were men or women who had died. It was not an unusual occurrence to see persons severely wounded by this man's brutality.

On arriving at Auschwitz I worked as a nurse in the experimental laboratory in Block 10. I was present on many occasions when *SS* doctor Weber experimented by taking blood from women for soldiers at the front. This process was often repeated until the person became very weak. He also took blood from a woman of one blood group which he injected into a woman of a different blood group.

---

[359] National Archives Kew, WO 311/1326/1.

This often caused very serious illness. In one case a woman died in the laboratory due to this operation.

This Doctor also carried out experiments in rheumatism and I know that one woman had 45 injections by the Doctor measuring the change of her heart. This made her very ill. Persons coming into Block 10 were always the fittest and sometimes up to 300 were in this block. They were kept whilst a course of experiments was carried out and then sent away. I should state that, the Camp in which this experimental block was situated was a Men's Camp and women were only brought there for experimental purposes. When they left this block they were sent to Birkenau where a selection was made to find those fit for work. Most of the people who left this experimental block were not in a fit condition for work. I have been told by friends that these sick people were always sent to Block 25 which meant that they subsequently went to the gas chamber.

I also knew a Doctor Schumann who experimented on young Greek girls (virgins) for sterilization. These girls were taken to another block where they were subjected to very strong X-rays which resulted in their sexual organs being dried up. These operations did in fact sterilize these girls and many of the weaker ones died as a result of them. Those that survived were brought back in batches of 10 or 12 for inspections. They were again operated on and the female sex organs removed which resulted in their deaths in 4 or 5 days. I did not myself see the actual operations performed but I did see the results as it was my duty to dress the wounds of the women. The girls who had these operations carried out on them came to Block 10 after the operation, the operations having been carried out in a different block. I saw 4 Greek girls die as a result of operations by this Doctor.

There was also an SS doctor Wirths.[360] He used to experiment on women between the ages of 40 and 50 who were having their menopause, apparently looking for a kind of Cancer. He used to take part of the womb out for examination under the microscope. The women

---

[360] Incorrectly stated as Wirtz in the report.

became very ill as a result of this. I did not see any of these operations carried out but heard of them from patients who had been experimented on and nurses who were present at the operations. These operations were carried out in Block 10, but not in my part of the Block. Similar operations were carried out by Doctor Samuel, a prisoner.

There was another SS doctor by the name of Professor Clauberg who carried out experiments.[361] This was a famous Doctor from Berlin. I have been present during his experiments and have seen him inject something into the womb of women and then place an electric plate on their stomachs. The current was then turned on. This was done while the patients were still conscious and no anaesthetic was used. This experiment did not take long, but must have caused a great deal of pain to the person experimented on, because I have heard them shout and cry with pain. Many found it impossible to walk afterwards and had to go to bed. None of these people died in hospital as a result of these experiments but as I have said before it is certain that they went to Birkenau; they went to the gas chamber as I am sure they could not work.

Many of the prisoners who were in this block were very sick but tried hard not to show it as they knew that they would be sent immediately to Birkenau and then to the gas chamber. Those that remained in the Block had this experiment made on them two or three times. Four or five injections were also given to the prisoners by this Doctor. The object, according to Professor Clauberg was to sterilize but I cannot say whether it did in fact result in sterilization. Most of this Doctor's experiments were carried out on the younger and more beautiful women so that when photographs were taken, the best results were obtained. The photographs were of the lower part of the trunk and it is natural that from an experimental point of view they would be better on the young than on the old. These photographs were taken 24 hours after the experiment. Professor Clauberg was assisted by an SS doctor Goebel in these experiments. Goebel was also responsible for carrying out similar operations.

---

[361]   Incorrectly stated as Globerg in the report.

In the summer of 1944, I witnessed the public hanging of 4 women under the supervision of *SS* man Hössler, whom I identify as No 1 on photo 9. At this time Block 10 had been moved from the Men's Camp to the Women's Camp nearby and renamed Block 1 Women's Camp. Hössler was in charge of this Camp. The persons hung were accused of assisting other persons to destroy the crematorium. Some explosives had been stolen from a store outside the Camp and the four girls were the persons in charge of this store. They were therefore held responsible for the loss and were hung.[362]

In prison Block 11 at Auschwitz were kept political prisoners including women and children. I myself have seen on many occasions batches of about 100 taken out naked and put against the wall and shot. The shooting was done by *SS* guards on the orders of Commandant Schwarz.

I recognise *SS* doctor Klein in photo 9 No.5. In my presence at Auschwitz he selected victims for the gas chamber.

Sworn by the said Deponet Renee Erman at Belsen Camp this 26th day of May 1945, before me Captain A.J. Fox. General List.[363]

Summary of Examination of Amalie Wernecke of Germany, duly sworn statement

I am 33 years of age of German nationality born at Berlin-Weissensee. My permanent address is *Bahnhofstraße 88, München*, Germany. I am now living at Block RB 1, Room 8, Hohne (Belsen) Camp, Germany.

I was arrested by the Nazis at my home on 7th March 1943, because I was a Gypsy, and was sent to Auschwitz-Birkenau. In August 1944, I was transferred to the Isolation Camp (Quarantine) Auschwitz, where I remained until October 1944, when I was sent to the Ravensbrück Concentration Camp. On 28th March 1945, I was taken

---

[362] This hanging was probably the hanging carried out not in the summer of 1944, but on January 6, 1945.
[363] National Archives Kew, WO 309/ 739.

to the Belsen Concentration Camp where I was liberated on 15th April 1945.

I have today been shown a number of photographs and from these I have picked No.1 on Photograph FC/4 as being a man I know by the name of Schwarzhuber. He was Deputy Camp Commandant of the Auschwitz-Birkenau Camp and I also saw him later at Ravensbrück.

At Auschwitz-Birkenau I was employed as a nurse at the Revier. I was frequently on night duty and nearly every night between midnight and 2 o'clock in the morning Schwarzhuber came to the Revier, carrying a pistol in one hand and a heavy walking stick in the other. He went in the room where the nurses slept and there he raped whoever pleased him.

He was nearly always drunk when he came in and usually he stayed for one or two hours. During one of his nightly visits in May 1943, he came up to me, gave me a cigarette and told me that he would send a sentry to take me to his quarters as he wanted to sleep with me. When the sentry came for me about half an hour later, I refused to go. The following night Schwarzhuber came up to me and asked me why I had not come. I told him that I was married and that my husband was at Auschwitz. He then shouted 'You are a prisoner and as such have no rights but must do what I say,' and beat me severely with his heavy stick. My back bled a lot and I collapsed. Schwarzhuber then told me to get up, but I was unable to do so. He then kicked me with his heavy boots all over my body. I was confined to bed for six weeks after the beating.

When I was not on night duty I slept with my husband in Block 4. Schwarzhuber would often come into our Block at night and make the married women get up from the beds they shared with their husbands. They then had to strip completely and in full view of their husbands were made to dance before Schwarzhuber. He would then pick out the one who was best looking and take her into the room of the Block-Leader for immoral purposes.

One night in early May 1943, Schwarzhuber came into the Revier around about 1 o'clock. I was on duty at the children's ward. The children were very restless and some cried. Two little boys of about

4 were sitting on a chamber relieving themselves and they started to cry too as Schwarzhuber came in. I saw him go up to them shouting 'You ... brats, you should not be alive,' and he hit them savagely with his heavy walking stick over the head. Their heads split wide open and they both died instantaneously. Schwarzhuber then ordered me to pick up the dead bodies and carry them to the death hall at the Revier, which I did so. He also told me that I must not mention the fact that he had killed the children to anyone.

Signed: With a X
Undated

In the Matter of War Crimes and An SS Man Named Schreier

Deposition of Sophie Seyfarth commonly known as Sasha (Female) late of 47 Werderstraße, Bremen, sworn before Captain Alexander Mackinlay Forbes Royal Artillery, Legal Staff, No. I War Crimes Investigation Team.

I am of German nationality and my age is 25. I was arrested at Bremen on 5th August 1941, by the *Gestapo*. I was put in a cell in the local police prison at Bremen, where I remained for about a month. The reason for my arrest was that I had refused to work at the Focke Wolf factory. I was then transferred to Ravensbrück, where I remained until 26th March 1942. From there I was taken to Auschwitz and I remained in Auschwitz until January 1945 when I was transferred to Ravensbrück for a short time and was finally brought to Belsen in March 1945. On 17th June 1945, I was arrested by the British and confined in the local prison.

In the year 1943, I was employed as a *Kapo* at Auschwitz and I recognise No.1 on Photograph Q/4/1 as an *SS-Oberscharführer* whom I knew as Spezi. I have now been told that he is known as Heinrich Schreier, but I do not think that is his real name.[364]

When I first met Schreier he was in charge of the arrest block and on one occasion in or about the end of March 1942, Schreier was

---

[364] The name on the report was Henrich, it should be Heinrich.

present when a group of men were lined up for selection. I saw the men selected taken upstairs into a certain room where it was well known that shootings took place. On this occasion I saw that when Schreier and the other *SS* men returned from the room one of them was still wearing a glove which was covered in blood. I was told by another *Kapo*, whose name is Jakob, that the men selected by Schreier and other *SS* men were taken up and shot. I did not see any of the selected men again.

In the first week of February 1943, I was questioned by an *SS* man named Hoyer about an escape I had made from Auschwitz in October 1942. I was recaptured in December 1942. Hoyer attempted to find out who had sheltered me during that period and I refused to tell him. I was bent over a table and given a large number of strokes across my back with a heavy wooden club. Schreier and some other *SS* men carried out the beating. I was then placed in the bunker and remained there until the end of March 1943. I was very ill and I still have scars on my back. It was necessary for me to have an operation in June 1943, as a big wound on my back had not healed properly. Schreier was generally very bad to the internees and I have often seen him give frequent beatings.

Hoyer was an *SS-Unterscharführer* at Auschwitz and I would describe him as age about 30, height 5ft 7 inches, weight 130 lbs approximately, hair dark brown, thick, face oval shaped, complexion brown, brown eyes, straight pointed nose, high pitched voice, and good teeth.

Jakob was a *Kapo* at Auschwitz. I would describe him as aged about 35, height 5 ft 11 inches, weight 200 lbs approximately, dark hair, round face, brown complexion, dark blue eyes, flat nose, small ears with slight cauliflower, deep voice, good physique. He stated that he was a professional boxer.

Sworn by the said Deponet Sophie Seyfarth at Belsen this 30th day of June 1945 before me A.M. Forbes, Captain. RA.[365]

---

[365] National Archives Kew, WO 309/ 739.

In the Matter Of War Crimes and in the Matter of Brutality At Auschwitz Camp By SS Woman

Deposition of Klara Lebowitz of Certis Czechoslovakia, sworn before me Major P. Ingress Bell, D.A.A.G. Legal Staff, an Officer of the Staff of the Judge Advocate General to the Forces.

I am 31 years of age and a Jewess of Czechoslovakian nationality. I was sent to Auschwitz in April 1944 and transferred to Belsen on 4th January 1945.

I worked in the kitchen and though I was dismissed from *Appells* after a few minutes in order that I might go to work, whilst working in the kitchen I could see what happened at the *Appells*.

SS woman Grese was in charge of the *Appells* which took place twice a day, these lasted at least two hours and more often three or four hours. If a mistake was made in counting the internees, they were made to stand until the missing one was found and this often meant all day. No time was allowed for food and people used to fall unconscious as a result of this.

When the woman Grese attended these *Appells* she often made the internees go on their knees for hours on end or hold stones in their hands, high above their heads. If an internee did not stand upright because she was weak or for any other reason, she would beat her with a rubber truncheon, sometimes until she was unconscious. She would kick persons lying on the ground and many people were taken to hospital as a result of her treatment. The internees were not allowed to carry anything in their pockets and this woman Grese would often stop and search internees whom she would beat unmercifully, if she found anything on them, even a handkerchief.

I have often seen the woman Grese with Dr. Mengele selecting people for the gas chamber and for forced work in Germany. If the woman Grese saw a mother and daughter or sisters trying to get together in selections for forced work in Germany, she would beat them until they were unconscious and leave them lying on the ground.

Sworn by the above Klara Lebowitz this 12th day of May 1945 at Belsen, before me the said Major P. Ingress Bell.[366]

In The Matter of War Crimes and In The Matter Of The Extermination of Greek Jews

Deposition of Allegre Kalderon of Andigonidon 11, Salonika, sworn before me Major P. Ingress Bell, DAAG, Legal Staff, an Officer of the Staff of the Judge Advocate General to the Forces.

I am 20 and a Jewess of Greek nationality. I was arrested about three years ago and taken to Auschwitz. I know of my own knowledge that in four months, 45,000 Greek Jews were taken to Auschwitz. Thousands of us were exterminated by the gas chamber and otherwise on arrival. 16,000 women remained and selections were made from time to time until only about 150 survived. Ultimately about 60 of us were transferred about 7 months ago to Belsen Camp and out of the original 45,000, there are only some 60 women survivors.

I survived principally because I was employed as a dress-maker and I escaped a great deal of ill-treatment owing to my occupation.

A number of Germans took part in the selection of victims for the gas chamber, but I did not know their names. I can recollect, however, the names of Taube, Klein, Mengele. I also name as persons whom I have personally seen committing brutal and savage assaults on internees. *SS* woman Juana Bormann, whom I identify as No.3 on Photo 19. I also name Franz Hössler and Theodore Hueschkel whom I identify as 1 and 2 respectively on Photo 9. I have seen these men repeatedly administer savage and brutal treatment to half-starved internees.

I am the Block Leader at present of No. 4 block S.T. and I am well acquainted with the surviving internees. I have been asked to select three reliable witnesses who are able to name the persons responsible for the atrocities at Auschwitz and bring them to make statements. This I will endeavour to do.

---

[366] National Archives Kew, WO 311/ 1326/1.

Sworn By The Above Named Allegre Kalderon this 15th day of May 1945 At Belsen Camp, Before Me the said Major P. Ingress Bell.[367]

The next series of statements cover the forced evacuation of Poles from the Zamość Lands, which is part of the Lublin district in Southeastern Poland. These forced evacuations were part of the German racial policy of evicting Polish farmers, thus freeing up these areas for settlers from the Reich. Many of the farmers and their families were deported to Auschwitz Concentration Camp, under the program that was co-ordinated by the Central Resettlement Office, *Umwandererzentralstelle (UWZ)* headed by Hermann Krumey in Łódź, in co-operation with Odilo Globocnik, the *SS* and Police Leader for the Lublin District, who was also responsible for this ethnic cleansing in the Lublin district.

The total number of Polish inhabitants evicted from the Zamość region between November 1941, and August 1943, amounted to circa 110,000 people from 297 villages, which equated to 31% of the number of Poles earmarked for resettlement. Included in this number were 30,000 children, of which 4,500 were sent to Germany to be Germanized.[368]

Testimony of Anna Hanas, former female prisoner of *KL* Auschwitz on her eviction from the village of Mokre, her internment in the Zamość Camp and then in Auschwitz *KL*, on November 22, 1967, in Zamość.

During the occupation of 1939–1945, I lived in the village of Mokre in the Zamość powiat. The day before December 9, 1942, we heard news that people had been evicted from the surrounding villages. We assumed that our village could be evicted too, and so prepared ourselves for it.

---

[367] National Archives Kew, WO 311/ 1326/1.
[368] Helena Kubica, *The Extermination at KL Auschwitz of Poles Evicted from the Zamość Region in the Years 1942–1943*, Auschwitz-Birkenau State Museum 2006, p. 24.

In the early morning of December 9, 1942, the Germans surrounded our village. Next, they entered each house and told everyone to leave within 15 minutes, to take food and head for the village administration building. My parents, my younger 14-year old brother and I took some food and went to the village centre. There we joined some 300 other people who had been rounded up like us. The Germans were brutal. I saw one of the soldiers beat Stefania Brochner with a rubber truncheon for trying to defend her father.

At around 9.00am, the Germans started loading people onto wagons and whilst doing this they shoved and beat the people regardless of whether they were children or women. The whole transport was bound for Zamość, for Okrzeja Street, where there was a Camp for evictees. The evictions were concluded with the help of *SS* units. I don't know who commanded this particular unit. At around 11.00am, we found ourselves in the said Camp.

We were immediately put before a commission that held office in a barrack. It comprised of *SS* men. Their procedure was as follows: they examined the people standing in front of them; they ordered the people to move their heads and paid special attention to their facial features, their eyes and also their height, then one member of the family was handed a card with a block number. I wanted to add that the commission examined whole families together. There were cases of children being separated from parents. I saw them take three children away from Mr. and Mrs. Szabtowski; there were many more cases like that.

After selection I went to a block—a barrack where we remained until morning, sleeping on bare bunks. The barrack was unheated. We received nothing to eat. The following day we were hustled out into the square. The names of some 1,500 people were read out and thus a group was formed to be sent to Auschwitz. Whilst in the Zamość Camp I witnessed cases of Camp staff persecuting those evicted. There was an incident just after our arrival where a woman called Cebula holding a small child in her arms was beaten and together with her child pushed off the wagon into the mud. This happened to her because she was getting off the wagon too slowly. I also saw children who had been separated from their parents try to return to them and the staff use rubber truncheons to chase them away.

The journey to Auschwitz lasted two days. We travelled in freight cars, 70–80 of us crammed into each one. They gave us no food for the journey and we were forbidden to beg. Throughout the journey we were kept locked up inside the cars, unable to get out or receive anything from the outside. For those two days on that train we had nothing to eat or drink. I arrived at Auschwitz on December 12 and remained there until January 18, 1945. My family, who were taken with me to Auschwitz, perished there; my mother and brother died of exhaustion, and my father was gassed.[369]

Testimony of Stanislaw Glowa given before Regional Judge Jan Sehn on September 30, 1946, in Kraków.

I was a prisoner of the Auschwitz Concentration Camp from August 18, 1941, to August 30, 1944, when I was put into a penal transport and sent to the Concentration Camp in Sachsenhausen, where I remained until May 3, 1945.

At Auschwitz I, my number was No. 20017. Initially I worked as a mower. In October 1941, I came down with Concentration Camp diarrhoea and was put in Block 20, which then served as a hospital for infectious diseases. After my recovery I remained at the block as a gofer in the *Durchfall* (diarrhoea) suffers' ward. For several weeks I was the night watchman there.

Most of those killed with injections were Jews. Nonetheless, Aryans of all nationalities were also murdered in this way. In the winter of 1942/43 *Rapportführer* Palitzsch brought two boys from the Zamość transport over from Birkenau. Initially he put them in Block 11, and then the following day he took them to Block 20, where Panszczyk 'pricked' both of them. The boys' names were Mieczyslaw

---

[369] Helena Kubica, *The Extermination at KL Auschwitz of Poles Evicted from the Zamość Region in the Years 1942–1943*, Auschwitz-Birkenau State Museum 2006, p. 242.

Rycaj and Tadeusz Rycyk. The parents and the young siblings of both of these boys were gassed.

Only some 90 boys aged 8–14 were selected from that entire transport. Rycyk and Rycaj were from that very group. The rest of these 90 or so boys were later brought over to Block 20 and there they were killed with injections that NCO nurse Scherpe administered. That was because Panszczyk broke down after killing Rycyk and Rycaj, stopped administering injections and was put in a transport to Neuengamme.[370]

Recollections of Waclawa Kedzierska, known in the Camp as Kropornicka, a 14-year old girl evicted with her family from Skierbieszów.

A sharp whistle broke the night silence. The Auschwitz-Birkenau Camp prisoners were abruptly reawakened of course, those who were still alive. The block and the room overseer began to shout at and beat prisoners, and throw them off the bunks. That day we did not even receive our lukewarm herbal tea. We were the only ones driven out to the roll call.

So these human shadows, skeletons in Concentration Camp language called 'Muselmen', were pushed out of the blocks and, swaying on their feet, made to stand in ranks five deep. Grandmothers stood alongside mothers and daughters; here age, education and social status were insignificant. They were just numbers; these were striped uniforms, not people. This was the memorable day February 6, 1943.[371] That day there was a general roll call in both Auschwitz and Birkenau.

We were driven out of the blocks at five in the morning, it was dark, and so we had to wait until it got light. There was a bitter frost and we were dressed just in our Camp issued underwear and striped uniforms. We wore clogs, the type without soles, and very thin scarves on our shaven heads. Those who lacked the strength to go

---

[370] Ibid., pp. 244–245.
[371] In the statement listed as February 7, 1943.

remained in the Camp along with the corpses. Hungry and cold, we stood in the meadow until 3 in the afternoon; some of the prisoners collapsed and lay in the snow. It was impossible to help them because we ourselves were so weak and cold that we could barely stand on our own feet.

I remember the hunger hurt the guts and the cold so penetrating that even the heart shivered. Whilst we stood there, every so often *SS* women or *SS* men would come and beat us with sticks. In the Camp they loaded both the corpses and the living from the Death Block and the camp hospital onto trucks and drove them to the crematorium.

Once the Camp was empty, *SS* men positioned themselves in a row in front of the gate and let us back in, in single file, each block separately. We were jostled and beaten. Anyone who no longer had the strength or whose mere look they did not like was pulled away from the rest and left at the gate. Their fate was sealed; they were all to go to Block 25, to the Death Block. There, either hunger or cold would finish them off or alternatively they would be taken to the crematorium alive.

At the time I was 14. I had arrived with my parents in a transport from the Zamość region. It was a terrible experience; I feared what might happen to me, but was even more fearful for my parents. So as not to be blue from the cold and somehow still look strong and healthy, I tried to redden my face by rubbing it with my uniform, but as it was frostbitten, this action caused wounds to appear. Shaking from the cold and from fear, I passed through the entrance on stiff legs, receiving only a couple of blows to the head with a stick.

Mother was behind me and I was very scared; in front of me, a friend and another friend's mother had been selected. I feared that they would also take my mother and was determined to then go with her. But fate had decided otherwise, we both passed this selection successfully to continue to suffer from the hunger, cold, humiliation and work that many would not survive. Various diseases, dirt, lice, fleas, and other inhuman conditions were the things we were destined to endure.³⁷²

Testimony of former prisoner Janina Wojcik on her eviction from the village of Labunki, her deportation to *KL* Auschwitz and the birth of her child in the Camp.

On December 28, 1942, I, together with my husband and two children aged 4, and 2, was evicted from the village of Labunki. At the Camp in Zamość, the Germans took my children away from me and my husband and they were put in Barrack 9.

Five weeks later, we were transported to Auschwitz and there I was separated from my husband. In Auschwitz in April 1943, I gave birth to my third child. The Germans provided no help to either me or my child and I gave birth whilst suffering from typhus.

A Polish woman washed my child and then let it lie beside me. Four days later my child died. My two older children died in the Zamość Camp. More than once in Auschwitz I saw the Germans receive transports of adults and children, i.e. parents and their children, who were then all marched off to the gas chamber and killed.

During roll calls in Auschwitz there was a German we used to call Taube³⁷³, who would select people to go to the gas chamber. I do not know what his real name was or where he came from. He could have been around the age of 35, tall, who wore a *Gestapo* type of uniform.³⁷⁴

---

³⁷² Helena Kubica, *The Extermination at KL Auschwitz of Poles Evicted from the Zamość Region in the Years 1942–1943*, Auschwitz-Birkenau State Museum 2006, pp. 245–246.
³⁷³ This was Adolf Taube. See the Perpetrators Biographies.
³⁷⁴ Helena Kubica, *The Extermination at KL Auschwitz of Poles Evicted from the Zamość Region in the Years 1942–1943*, Auschwitz-Birkenau State Museum 2006, p. 243.

Chapter XV
Post War Trials

Nuremburg 1945/1946—IMT

The International Military Tribunal was held in the German city of Nuremburg, during 1945 and 1946. Here, some of the leading figures of Nazism stood trial, before the victorious Allied nations. Those who stood in the dock were Hermann Göring, Rudolf Höss, Hans Frank, Ernst Kaltenbrunner and Julius Streicher, along with other members of the defeated regime.

Rudolf Höss, the Commandant of Auschwitz took the stand on April 15, 1946, in defence of Ernst Kaltenbrunner, who had succeeded Reinhard Heydrich as head of the Reich Main Security Office. Rudolf Höss spoke in a completely apathetic voice, with the utmost frankness at the genocide perpetrated under Himmler's orders at Auschwitz. In spite of Kaltenbrunner claiming that his personal intervention with Himmler during October 1944 had ceased the gassings, and his denials against all of the charges against him, Kaltenbrunner was found guilty of War Crimes and was hanged on October 16, 1946 in Nuremburg prison.

Although Auschwitz figured heavily in the trial itself, Hans Frank, the Governor-General of Poland denied ever having visited the Camp. He had tried to do so, but his car was diverted from the Camp, as there was supposed to be an epidemic. Hans Frank even complained to Adolf Hitler about being denied access, who then suggested that Hans Frank take the matter up with Heinrich Himmler.

One of the eyewitnesses who gave testimony at Nuremburg was Marie Claude Vaillant-Couturier, who stood in the dock on January 28, 1946:

> **Marie Claude Vaillant-Couturier:** We saw the unsealing of the cars and the soldiers letting men, women and children out of them. We then witnessed heart-rending scenes; old couples forced to part from each

other, mothers made to abandon their young daughters, since the latter were sent to the Camp, whereas mothers and children were sent to the gas chambers. All these people were unaware of the fate awaiting them. They were merely upset at being separated, but they did not know that they were going to their death. To render their welcome more pleasant at this time—June to July 1944, an orchestra composed of internees, all young and pretty girls dressed in little white blouses and navy blue skirts, played during the selection, at the arrival of the trains, gay tunes such as 'The Merry Widow,' the 'Barcarolle' form 'The Tales of Hoffmann,' and so forth. They were then informed that this was a Labor Camp and since they were not brought into the Camp they saw only the small platform surrounded by flowering plants. Naturally, they could not realize what was in store for them. Those selected for the gas chamber, that is the old people, mothers and children, were escorted to the red-brick building.

M. Dubost: These were not given an identification number?
Marie Claude Vaillant-Couturier: No.
M. Dubost: They were not tattooed?
Marie Claude Vaillant-Couturier: No. They were not even counted.
M. Dubost: You were tattooed?
Marie Claude Vaillant-Couturier: Yes, look—the witness showed her arm. They were taken to a red-brick building, which bore the letters *'Baden,'* that is to say 'Baths.' There, to begin with they were made to undress and given a towel before they went into the so-called shower room. Later on, at the time of the large convoys from Hungary, they had no more time left to play-act or to pretend; they were brutally undressed, and I know these details as I knew a little Jewess from France who lived with her family at the 'Republic' district.
M. Dubost: In Paris?
Marie Claude Vaillant-Couturier: In Paris. She was called 'Little Marie' and she was the only one, the sole survivor of a family of nine. Her mother and her seven brothers had been gassed on arrival. When I met her she was employed to undress the babies before they were taken into the gas chamber. Once the people were undressed they took them into a room, which was somewhat like a shower room, and gas capsules were thrown through an opening in the ceiling. An *SS* man would watch the effect produced through a porthole. At the end of 5 or 7 minutes, when the gas had completed its work, he gave the signal to open the doors; and men with gas-masks—they too were internees—went into the room and removed the corpses. They told us that the internees must have

suffered before dying, because they were closely clinging to one another and it was very difficult to separate them.

After that a special squad would come to pull out gold teeth and dentures; and again, when the bodies had been reduced to ashes, they would sift them in an attempt to recover the gold. At Auschwitz there were eight crematoria but, as from 1944, these proved insufficient. The SS had large pits dug by the internees, where they put branches sprinkled with gasoline, which they set on fire. Then they threw the corpses into the pits. From our block we could see after about three-quarters of an hour or an hour after the arrival of a convoy, large flames coming from the crematorium, and the sky was lighted up by the burning pits. One night we were awakened by terrifying cries. And we discovered, on the following day, from the men working in the *Sonderkommando*—the 'Gas Kommando'—that on the preceeding day, the gas supply having run out, they had thrown the children into the furnaces alive.

M. Dubost: Can you tell us about the selections that were made at the beginning of winter?

Marie Claude Vaillant-Couturier: During Christmas 1944—no, 1943, Christmas 1943—when we were in quarantine, we saw, since we lived opposite Block 25, women brought to Block 25 stripped naked. Uncovered trucks were then driven up and on them the naked women were piled, as many as the trucks could hold. Each time a truck started, the infamous Hössler[375] ran after the truck and with his bludgeon repeatedly struck the naked women going to their death. They knew they were going to the gas chamber and tried to escape. They were massacred. They attempted to jump from the truck and we, from our own block, watched the trucks pass by and heard the grievous wailing of all those women who knew they were going to be gassed. Many of them could very well have lived on, since they were suffering only from scabies and were, perhaps, a little too undernourished.

Since the Jewesses were sent to Auschwitz with their entire families and since they had been told that this was a sort of ghetto and were advised to bring all their goods and chattels along, they consequently brought considerable riches with them. As for the Jewesses from Salonika, I remember that on their arrival they were given picture postcards bearing the post office address of '*Waldsee*,' a place which did not exist, and a printed text to be sent to their families, stating, 'We are doing very well here; we have work and we are well treated. We await your arrival.' I myself saw the cards in question, and the *Schreiberinnen*, that is, the

---

[375] Incorrectly stated in the testimony as Hessler.

secretaries of the block, were instructed to distribute them among the internees in order to post them to their families. I know that whole families arrived as a result of these postcards.[376]

Warsaw—The Trial of Rudolf Höss

During the years 1946–48 seven trials were held before the Supreme National Tribunal in Poland, two of which dealt with the Concentration Camp at Auschwitz. The first of these, lasting from March 11, 1947, to March 29, 1947, saw the first Commandant of Auschwitz, Rudolf Höss stand trial in Warsaw.

In his prison cell during the period before the trial, Rudolf Höss wrote his memoirs, fully aware that the weight of evidence against him was enormous. He explained the extermination process in great detail.

The proceedings were simultaneously translated into English, Russian, French and German. The trial was attended by many observers from different countries and journalists. The eight-man American delegation included the assistants of General Telford Taylor, Chief Prosecutor of the US Military Tribunal in Nuremburg.

Investigations were conducted on behalf of the Polish authorities by the Kraków Regional Commission for the Investigation of Nazi Crimes presided over by Judge Jan Sehn, who was a member of the Main Commission for the Investigation of Nazi Crimes in Poland. Some 21 volumes of material were gathered, which included the depositions of witnesses, the statements of the accused Rudolf Höss, the testimony of experts and the most important documents of the Camp's history that had survived.

The Supreme National Tribunal sentenced Rudolf Höss to death by hanging on April 2, 1947. The sentence was carried out on April 16, 1947, at the former Concentration Camp in Oświęcim, adjacent to the former Commandant's office.[377]

---

[376] Michael Marus, *The Nuremburg War Crimes Trial 1945–46*, Bedford Books, Boston, New York 1997, pp. 155–158.
[377] Kazimierz Smolen, *Auschwitz*, Interpress, Warsaw 1985, pp. 184–188.

Kraków—The Trial of the SS Garrison: Liebehenschel, Grabner and Others

The second trial held before the Supreme National Tribunal was held from November 25, 1947, until December 16, 1947, in Kraków. There were 40 members of the former SS garrison put on trial. These included: Arthur Liebehenschel, who succeeded Rudolf Höss as Commandant; Maximillian Grabner, former Head of the Political Department; Hans Aumeier, former *Lagerführer*; Karl Ernst Möckel, Head of the supply department; Marie Mandel, formerly in charge of the Women's Camp in Birkenau; Franz Xaver Kraus, Assistant to the *Lagerführer*; Dr. Johann Paul Kremer, Camp Doctor; Heinrich Josten, Deputy *Lagerführer*; Dr. Hans Münch, of the SS Hygiene Institute at Auschwitz; Erich Mühsfeldt, Head of the crematorium; Hermann Kirschner, overseer; Karl Seufert, overseer; Hans Koch, overseer, Wilhelm Gerhard Gehring, overseer; Ludwig Plagge, *Rapportführer*; Otto Latsch, *Rapportführer*; Fritz Wilhelm Buntrock, *Rapportführer*; August Reimond Bogusch, *Blockführer*; Kurt Hugo Müller, *Blockführer*; Paul Goetze, *Blockführer*; Paul Szczurek, *Blockführer*; Richard Albert Schröder, *Blockführer*; Herbert Paul Ludwig, *Blockführer*; Eduard Lorenz, *Blockführer*; Therese Brandl, Wardress in the Women's Camp; Alice Orlowski, Wardress in the Women's Camp; Luise Danz, Wardress in the Women's Camp; Hildegard Marthe Luise Lachert, Wardress in the Women's Camp; Hans Hoffmann, member of the Political Department; Arthur Johann Breitweiser, member of the works department; Hans Schumacher, member of the works department; Adolf Medefind, member of the works department; Franz Romeikat, member of the works department; Anton Lechner, overseer; Josef Kollmer, overseer; Detlef Nebbe, overseer; Alexander Bülow, overseer; Erich Dinges, Driver; Johannes Weber, overseer; and Karl Jeschke, overseer.

The trial in Kraków was held from November 25, 1947, until December 16, 1947, and the trial proceedings were based on the same material used in the case against Rudolf Höss, supplemented by additional depositions of witnesses. Those on trial here did not however, like Höss, assume full responsibility for their crimes, they attempted to pass responsibility onto those who were not on trial, or onto Rudolf Höss, stating that they were only following orders from a superior. They frequently gave false testimony, for example the infamous Maximillian Grabner, the former Head of the Political Department—the Camp *Gestapo* assured the court that 'they had no power in the Camp!'[378]

The sentences were announced on December 22, 1947. Twenty-three of the accused were sentenced to death, six to life imprisonment, seven to fifteen years imprisonment each and two to ten and a half years, one to three years and one of the accused, Hans Münch was acquitted. Those sentenced to death were Liebehenschel, Aumeier, Grabner, Möckel, Mandel, Kraus, Plagge, Buntrock, Gehring, Latsch, Josten, Kollmer, Mühsfeldt, Kirschner, Schumacher, Bogusch, Brandl, Szczurek, Goetze, Ludwig, Müller, Kremer and Breitweiser. The sentences of Johann Kremer and Arthur Johann Breitweiser were later reduced to life imprisonment.

Other War Crimes Trials of Concentration Camp Personnel Involving Former Auschwitz Personnel

When the Allied Forces liberated the many Concentration Camps in the Reich, they brought to trial a number of *SS* men, who had previously served in Auschwitz Concentration Camp and had been transferred to other Camps.

Bergen-Belsen Concentration Camp Trial

The trial of Bergen Belsen Concentration Camp personnel included some senior *SS* members of the Auschwitz Garrison, such as Josef Kramer, Dr. Fritz Klein, Franz Hössler, Irma Grese, Peter Weingärtner, Elizabeth Volkenrath, Juana Bormann, Heinrich Schreler.

The trial began on November 17, 1945 and lasted for 54 days. On November 17, 1945, the court sentenced 11 of the defendants to death

---

[378] Ibid., pp. 188–189.

by hanging. All the above were sentenced to death, with the exception of Heinrich Schreier, who was sentenced to serve 15-years in prison.

Dachau Concentration Camp Trial

The trial of Dachau Concentration Camp personnel took place during 1945, and out of the 40 men accused, 36 were sentenced to death on December 13, 1945. Among those charged were former members of the SS Garrison at Auschwitz, such as major figures: Hans Aumeier, Otto Moll. Hans Aumeier was in fact extradited to Poland and he faced War Crimes charges at the Supreme National Tribunal in Kraków during November 1947. The most notorious figure Otto Moll was found guilty of War Crimes and was sentenced to death on December 13, 1945. He was executed at Landsberg on May 28, 1946. Another member of the SS Garrison, Vinzenz Schoettl, who served in Auschwitz from 1944 to 1945, was also tried and found guilty of War Crimes. He was also executed on May 28, 1946.

Ravensbrück Concentration Camp Trial

The first trial of Ravensbrück Concentration Camp personnel took place from December 5, 1946, until February 3, 1947, with 16 members of the SS Garrison at the Curiohaus Court in the Rotherbaum district of Hamburg. Of the 16 defendants tried, these included Johann Schwarzhuber. He was found guilty and executed on May 3, 1947.

Frankfurt am Main—Robert Mulka and Others

One of the most significant trials of SS personnel who had served at Auschwitz Concentration Camp was held in West Germany between December 20, 1963, and August 20, 1965, in Frankfurt am Main. The preliminary investigation took several years and originally included 24 suspects. This included Richard Baer, the last Commandant of

Auschwitz, but he died before the trial began, and Hans Nierzwicki who did not take the stand due to illness.

The 22 who appeared in the dock were Robert Mulka, Karl Höcker, Wilhelm Boger, Hans Stark, Klaus Dylewski, Pery Broad, Johann Schoberth, Bruno Schlage, Franz Hoffmann, Oswald Kaduk, Stefan Baretzki, Heinrich Bischoff, Arthur Breitweiser, Dr. Franz Lucas, Dr. Willi Frank, Dr. Willi Schatz, Dr. Viktor Capesius, Josef Klehr, Herbert Scherpe, Emil Hantl, Gerhard Neubert, and *Kapo* Emil Bednarek.

As the trial proceedings dragged on for months, two of the accused were judged unfit to continue, and on March 13, 1964, Bischoff was excluded from the trial and on July 13, 1964, the same fate befell Neubert.

Dr. Hans Laternser, the German Lawyer who headed up the Defence Counsel and was vastly experienced in representing former *SS* personnel in War Crimes Trials, was often abusive to the former Camp inmates who gave testimony. His often arrogant remarks frequently dismayed the President of the court Dr. Hans Hofmeyer and the members of the Prosecution team. Equally, this behaviour was repeated by the former *SS* men standing trial. They often accused the witnesses of lying, or simply said "That is not true."

On June 8, 1964, the civil prosecutor Dr. Henry Ormond proposed a visit to the former Concentration Camp. He justified the trip by saying "that even the most precise depositions by witnesses, sketches and photographs were no substitute for seeing with one's own eyes." The visit took place on December 14, 1964, where twenty-three persons comprising of Walter Hotz from the panel of judges, all the prosecutors, eight members of the defence counsel and one of the accused Dr. Franz Lucas.

In the administrative building of the State Museum at the former Camp at Oświęcim, a room was made available where sessions were held. Present at the sessions were Professor Jan Sehn, plenipotentiary of the Minister of Justice, the Director of the Museum, former prisoner Kazimierz Smolen, the co-plaintive Miecyslaw Kieta and his counsel Henry Ormond.

The aim of the visit was to find answers to 32 questions raised from the depositions of both individual witnesses and the accused. The visit concluded on December 16, 1964, with the signing of a protocol, which was read out during the trial itself in Frankfurt.[379]

Some of the accused, namely Josef Klehr and Emil Bednarek and the Counsel for the Defence stated reservations about certain aspects of evidence put forward by ex-prisoner and now the Oświęcim Director of the museum, Kazimierz Smolen.

Dr. Hermann Stolting, an expert for the Defence Counsel, thus requested that another visit should be made to Auschwitz, which was supported by other members of the Defence Counsel, Benno Erhard, and Hans Laternser. In view of these reservations, Kazimierz Smolen was summoned once again to the Court House, in Frankfurt am Main.

During the course of his cross-examination, however, it became clear that all of the explanations put forward by Kazimierz Smolen were correct. Thus the motion for a second visit was rejected. It was noted by the President of the Court, Dr. Hans Hofmeyer, that neither Laternser or Stolting attended the proceedings, and that should be emphasized in the records.

Clearly the Defence Counsel were simply playing for time. On August 19, 1965, the sentences were finally passed:

Defendant	Sentence Passed
Robert Mulka	14 Years at Hard Labor
Karl Hocker	7 Years at Hard Labor
Wilhelm Boger	Life and an additional 5 Years at Hard Labor
Hans Stark	10 Years
Karl Dylewski	5 Years at Hard Labor
Pery Broad	4 Years at Hard Labor
Bruno Schlage	6 Years at Hard Labor
Franz Hoffmann	Life at Hard Labor

---

[379] Kazimierz Smolen, *Auschwitz*, Interpress, Warsaw 1985, pp. 184–88.

Oswald Kaduk	Life at Hard Labor
Stefan Baretzki	Life and an additional 8 Years at Hard Labor
Dr Franz Lucas	3 Years and 3 Months at Hard Labor
Dr. Willi Frank	7 Years at Hard Labor
Dr. Victor Capesius	9 Years at Hard Labor
Josef Klehr	Life and an additional 15 Years at Hard Labor
Herbert Scherpe	4 Years and 6 Months at Hard Labor
Emil Hantl	3 Years and 6 Months at Hard Labor
Johann Schöberth	Acquitted
Arthur Breitweiser	Acquitted
Dr. Willi Schatz	Acquitted
Emil Bednarek—*Kapo*	Life at Hard Labor

Source: Auschwitz by Bernd Naumann

Frankfurt am Main—Gerhard Neubert and Others

A second trial was also held in Frankfurt am Main, the so-called Trial II, before the *Schwurgericht* and this lasted from December 14, 1965 until September 16, 1966. The three former *SS* men accused were Gerhard Neubert, Wilhelm Burger and Josef Erber, who was also known as Josef Hustek. All three men were found guilty of War Crimes. Erber was sentenced to life imprisonment; Burger was sentenced to eight years in prison; Neubert was sentenced to three-and-a-half years imprisonment.

Berlin—Dr. Horst Fischer

During March 10, 1966 and March 25, 1966, Dr. Horst Fischer, one of the Auschwitz Camp medical Doctor's was tried by the Supreme

Court of the German Democratic Republic in Berlin. A welter of documents were supplied by the Polish Authorities and depositions were made by dozens of witnesses from a number of countries.

Dr. Fischer admitted that he had taken part in selections for the gas chambers and executions by phenol injections. The Court sentenced him to death for his participation in the deaths of 80,000 people. He was executed by guillotine on July 8, 1966, in Leipzig.

Frankfurt am Main—Bernhard Bonitz and Josef Windeck

Two former *Kapo's* Bernhard Bonitz and Josef Windeck from Auschwitz were finally brought to trial in Frankfurt am Main, in the so-called Trial III. This took place between August 30, 1967, and June 14, 1968. The two men were both sentenced to life imprisonment.

Frankfurt am Main—Alois Frey and Willi Sawatzki

Two former members of the *SS*-Garrison at Auschwitz, Alois Frey and Willi Sawatzki were brought to stand trial, in the so-called Trial IV. This took place between December 18, 1973, and February 3, 1976. Both men were accused of participating in the liquidation of the Gypsy Camp and the murder of prisoners during the evacuation of the Camp during January 1945.

On November 25, 1974, Alois Frey was released for lack of evidence, and on February 3, 1976, the Prosecutor dropped the charges against Sawatzki. Thus the trial collapsed and both men were not tried.

Chapter XVI
Epilogue

My Visits to Auschwitz by Chris Webb

In July 2004, I made my first trip to Auschwitz-Birkenau as part of the ARC website group. We left the Hotel Demel, at Glowackiego Street 22, in the district of Bronowice. We, that is Paul Denton, Artur Hojan, Carmelo Lisciotto and I suffered a rather long delay in a Kraków bank trying to cash some Travellers Cheques. Nowadays thankfully, these have been relegated to just a distant memory, and we finally made our way back to the hotel, and boarded the minibus on our way to Auschwitz.

At Przegorzały village we passed the hilltop residence of Otto Wachter, the Governor of Kraków, this impressive building was later on requisitioned by Hans Frank, and became a hospital for the *SS*.

After a brief stop in the town of Auschwitz, our minibus made its way to the memorial for the Camp at Monowitz, and the houses built by the Germans for the workers there. Then we visited the modern train station in Oświęcim, and stopped for a coffee in the the *Skorpion* restaurant that had been built on the site of the former *Deutsches Haus*, opposite the station. During the War, *SS* officers stayed in the *Deutsches Haus* before reporting for duty at the Camp, and Himmler visited there for dinner on the evening of July 17, 1942, after his inspection tour.

We then drove in the minibus to the former Auschwitz Main Camp, and walked under the sign at the main gate, '*Arbeit Macht Frei*.' As you walked through the gate, the red-brick buildings looked impressive and robust, a site that was built to last, the former Camp streets were swarming with visitors, most were silent, the mood was sombre.

Our guide, who was one of our tour members was Borje Hallstrom, and he showed us the kitchen and open air water storage tank. Then we made our way to Blocks 10 and 11. There was a feeling of dread on entering Block 11, where the hundreds of black and white portraits of prisoners stared into the corridor. This was an oppressive building, the cells, the room where the Special Court sat, the dreadful standing cells, which left a grim impression.

We then left Block 11 by the side entrance and stood in the courtyard between Blocks 10 and 11 with the windows boarded up. At the end of the courtyard was the 'Black Wall' where *Rapportführer* Gerhard Palitzsch carried out thousands of executions. We walked through the Camp and made our way to Block 28, where members of our group Lukasz Biedka and Melvyn Conroy and myself saw the Jewish Exhibition, which was extremely moving.

Our small group then made its way to the former crematorium and gas chamber next to the gallows where Rudolf Höss was executed on April 16, 1947. The crematorium in the main Camp stopped burning corpses in July 1943, when the four large Crematoriums in Birkenau were all fully operational. At first the building was used for storage and then designated as an air-raid shelter. The furnaces, chimney and some of the walls had been demolished, and the openings in the roof where the *SS* poured in the *Zyklon B* crystals were plastered over. After the Second World War had ended the Auschwitz-Birkenau State Museum carried out a partial re-construction. The chimney and the two ovens were re-built using original components.

We left the Camp and re-assembled in the car park, where we boarded the mini-bus and our driver Joe took us back to the modern railway station, to take some photographs, before making our way to the old Jewish ramp near Birkenau. The site is very neglected as are the nearby storage buildings where potatoes were stored. There appears to be just one railway line now, with rusted signals. It is hard to think that at this site during the years 1942 and 1943, many thousands of Jewish deportees arrived, to be selected either to work or to be gassed immediately.

Some of our group decide to walk to the Birkenau Camp, whilst others prefer to travel in the mini-bus, and we park in the car park, right by the infamous substantial main gate entrance. Some of us decide to climb the tower which gives a panoramic view of the whole

Camp, with the brick barracks to the left, the railway tracks and ramp—which was operational for the arrival of the Jews from Hungary in May 1944, and to the right the vast area with the wooden barracks, though many have disappeared completely.

After some photographs are taken on the ramp, we proceed to the brick blocks in the former Women's Sector BIa, where we see the infamous 'Block of Death' which was located in Block 25. This is a truly depressing block, earthern floor, cramped wooden bunks, with a private room for the Block Leader. This is where the women waited for days, without food, water or heating, naked. They were in the ante-chamber of death, just waiting for the lorries to take them to the gas chamber.

Borje leads Cameron Munro, Artur Hojan and myself next to the Penal Colony barracks where on the wall there is a wonderful wartime painting showing the Penal Company *Kommando* digging the *Königsgraben*—the "Kings Ditch", complete with excavator, small-gauge railway train and guards. We also visit a block with toilets and a washroom, now empty and silent, we walk through the barracks struggling to take it all in.

We walk through Birkenau and arrive at the ruins of Crematorium II, looking at the remains of the red brick structure it really hits home, that this huge factory of death was the industrialized efficient killing machine of the Third Reich. We go through the entrance gate of Crematorium III, which is a mirror of Crematorium II.

After some photographs are taken we head towards the Sauna, which was built in late 1943, where new arrivals were given showers, tattooed with their own prisoner number and given Camp clothes. We pass by the disinfection chambers and the shower room and enter a room where hundreds of photographs are on display. They show Jewish individuals, and family groups, couples. Some of the people are shown wearing the 'Yellow Star,' this is a truly moving and tragic exhibition of people, who lost their lives due to the Holocaust.

We leave the Sauna building and make for Crematoriums IV and V, which were smaller than Crematoriums II and III, and nearby we see the pond where the ashes of the victims murdered in the gas chambers were dumped, in order to erase all traces of the mass murder committed here among the birch trees.

The last sites we see are the ruins of the 'White House', or Bunker II, as it was known during its operation. This was the second gas chamber bunker, converted from a Polish farmhouse, which was put into operation in June 1942, and where Heinrich Himmler witnessed the gassing of a transport of Jews from the Netherlands. Nearby are the foundations of the two barracks, where Jews undressed before entering the 'Little White House,' and the area where the bodies were first buried, then cremated by the *Sonderkommando*.

We walk on and the last thing we see is the site of Bunker I, the so-called 'Red House,' which was demolished probably in March 1943. Apart from a well, there is nothing to see here, no foundations, just an empty field.

We walk along the Camp road, heading towards the impressive looking *Kommandantur,* with a cross, as the building had been used as a convent. We turn right and walk back through the former Camp area, looking at the vast, now empty space that used to be known as '*Kanada*,' where the clothes and possessions of the Jews who arrived at the Camp, were sorted and stored.

We reach the ramp, and walk up to the main gate, pausing one last time to take in the final view of the most infamous killing fields known to man. Once seen—never forgotten.

Twelve years later on Tuesday 8, March 2016, half of the student group, and staff from Teesside University plus myself board the bus outside the Hotel Wyspianski, in Westerplatte 15, in the city of Kraków. Today we are going to visit the Auschwitz Concentration Camp. We cross the Vistula and the imposing Wawel Castle, and leave the city. At Przegorzały village, on the right we pass the house of Otto Wachter, that I remembered from 2004, high on the hill—it still looks impressive.

We arrive at the car park and eventually gain access through what was the Reception block, where headphones are collected and our female guide leads the group through the main gate, with the '*Arbeit Macht Frei*' sign above us. The group excursion leads us through a tour of pre-selected blocks, and Professor Matthew Feldman, who has been on the guide a number of times suggest we visit the Slovak-Jewish Exhibition, in one of the blocks. The exhibition is a fine one, with numerous photographs and documents detailing the Holocaust in Slovakia, and the transports to Auschwitz, for the Slovak Jews. We rejoin the group in one of the blocks and continue on with the rest of the tour of the Main Camp.

This time, I am able to see Rudolf Höss' former house, which is just outside the Camp, before we are taken to see the re-constructed Crematorium and the gas chamber opposite the former *SS* sick bay. This building is visited at lightning pace and we are soon led out of the Camp, and back on the bus, ready to start the second part of the tour, which is to visit Birkenau.

Rather than provide the reader with a re-run of what I saw in 2004, I will just cover what I hadn't seen before. Half-way down the ramp, was a symbolic single cattle car, opposite the *SS Blockführerstube (SS* Administration Building). We then followed our guide to the so-called 'Children's Block' in Sector BIa. This barrack is numbered 16a and has two drawings, showing a boy going to a school building and children walking, drawn by a fellow Camp inmate, just to make the barrack a little more pleasant for the children. This housed the Polish children deported from Zamość, which was covered in some detail in the book.

After visting the four major crematorium sites, the Sauna looked closed, so we did not go in and so Professor Feldman led the group to the site of Bunker 2 and then to a small site that has a memorial to the Russian Prisoners of War murdered at Auschwitz, and then onto Bunker 1, which is just an empty field, with houses in the near distance. We leave the Camp through the Main Gate entrance and board the bus, to pay a visit to the *Alte Juden Rampe*, which is nearby.

This has changed considerably, the area has been tidied up, there is a single wooden cattle car on the track, with an explanation sign, which was new to me. The potato storage sheds look even more dilapidated than in 2004, they are slowly crumbling away and it cannot be long before they are reclaimed by nature.

On Wednesday 9 March, 2016, with lecturer Lucy Jolly in charge, we take the second half of the forty-strong group to Auschwitz. Today we have a male guide, and it is interesting to compare the different styles. One was keen to focus on the human stories, another one less so, I leave it up to the reader to guess who adopted which approach.

Before we entered the Camp, I wanted to see the original railroad siding and ramp where the prisoners were unloaded, before going into the Auschwitz Main Camp. A small group of intrepid explorers agreed to go with me. We left the large park and crossed the main road and headed for an industrial area. We found the railway line, and headed north and saw the ramp to the left of a large white building, which was formerly part of the Polish Tobacco Monopoly. I recognized the ramp and building from photographs I had already seen. Just enough time to take a couple of photographs, before he have to head back to the Reception building, for our timed-tour.

This tour of both Auschwitz and Birkenau were identical, and we bade farewell to our official guide after seeing the 'Children's Block' in Sector BIa, in Birkenau. The students were very moved by this block. I then led the group back into the Camp and went to see all the major sites. This time by chance as we neared the Sauna building, a member of the Camps ground-staff walked by, and I asked him if the Sauna was open? He nodded and we went in, unlike the previous day. This was more or less the same as in 2004, although there was a small metal cart on rails that I could not recall from my earlier visit. Everyone was moved by the photographic display, which I had first seen in 2004. It is still powerful and moving.

We have time today to visit one of the wooden barracks, the huge barrack built for horses, to the right of the main entrance, in Sector BIIa, the men's quarantine Camp. We visit the Latrines and one of the wooden barracks. We pay a visit to the *Alte Juden Rampe*, nearby and make our way back to Kraków and our hotel. The bus is very quiet, everyone is lost in their thoughts of what they have seen today.

On Thursday January 19, 2017, once again I was kindly invited by Teesside University to accompany the students and staff on a trip to

Kraków and Auschwitz. What was very different this time was the weather. Kraków had enjoyed temperatures of minus twenty five the week before, now it was minus nine, and the landscape was white and it was snowy and picturesque.

As this was my third visit in two years, the guided tour followed a well-worn path, though this year I did ask him to show us the swimming pool by Block 6, which he kindly took us to. It is one thing reading about Auschwitz and the inhuman conditions the inmates experienced. But to see the mounds of shaving brushes, the suitcases with names and addresses, the mounds of shoes and human hair, really brings home to you, what this place stood for. I asked our guide if he could take us to the Jewish Block, to see the exhibition there, but he said we sadly did not have enough time. We spend until lunch time at Auschwitz Main Camp.

We meet up with the guide in Birkenau, for the shorter tour of the major Auschwitz Camp complexes. We spend quite a lot of time by the substantial memorial at the end of the ramp, after visting the wooden cattle car situated on there, where photographs were taken. It is bitterly cold, there is a large Jewish group walking down the ramp, and we are dressed in coats, jumpers and thermals, it makes you appreciate how poorly the prisoners were clothed, in these freezing temperatures, this is something you have to experience for yourself, you will never get that from just reading about it.

After visiting Crematorium II, our guide takes us to the 'Block of Death' in Block 25, which in fact is the official end of the tour. I ask him if he will kindly take us to the 'Children's Block,' which he does. I ask him, why the block is not lit, and he replied that it is deliberately kept the way it was. After that he leads us out of the Camp, and bids us farewell. It is very cold indeed and a lot of the students return to the coach.

A proposal is discussed between Lucy, one of the students Sue, and myself, with one proposal being that the group return to Kraków if they want to, and some of us will stay and new transport will be arranged. Sue is disappointed that we have seen so little of Birkenau with the official guide, though suggests that rather than complicate the travel arrangements, the students can either return to the Camp, sit on the bus, or go to the Museum café. I will act as the guide, which I am very happy to do.

I spoke to the students about the proposal, and about half of the group decide, despite the cold, that they want to see more of Birkenau, and so we set off through the main entrance and walk down the ramp, heading for Crematorium III. We have about an hour, and after Crematorium III, we skirt the modern memorial, past the sewage treatment plants and head for the Sauna. Unfortunately, due to the forthcoming Holocaust Memorial Commemorations, the Sauna is closed.

We proceed at pace to Crematoriums IV and V, and see the outline in the snow of the ponds where the ashes of those murdered in the gas chambers were dumped. Sue was particularly keen to see the ponds, but due to the snow, we can only see the outline. I tell her, to visit again in the summer, but the snow does give the place an eerie, atmospheric feel, which is an experience in itself.

We abandon plans to find Bunker I, and as we walk through the Camp, a number of wild deer are spotted. We reach the ramp and as the sun starts to fade, I take some photographs of the watchtowers, fences and barracks. One of these pictures has been used as the cover of this book.

Sadly we do not have time to visit the wooden barracks in Sector BIIa, which was another thing Sue and the others wanted to see, we have been beaten by the clock, and make our way back to the bus.

Our memorable trip to the greatest cemetery without a grave is over.

Back in the UK, I invited the students of Teesside University to give me their thoughts and observations about our trips to Auschwitz-Birkenau, and these seem a fitting way to close this book, as to what Auschwitz means 77 years after it was established.

Here are those thoughts and observations, and I want to thank Professor Matthew Feldman, and all the students who kindly provided this material, I am extremely grateful:

Ryan Dixon

My main impression of Auschwitz-Birkenau was that I did not know how to feel. I found it very difficult, despite years of study, to comprehend and rationalize the Camp. Walking around both Camp systems with people taking photographs, listening to tour guides and visitors talking amongst themselves, it felt too surreal to imagine that over 70 years ago, human beings were either exterminated or worked to death here. This feeling was quickly overtaken by sadness and the fear that one human component could do this to another individual kind in order to create their vision of a utopia.

The visit has actually motivated me more and inspired me to do more and understand the Holocaust as a wider subject. The visit also helped put things into perspective as it is easy to see the Holocaust as a numerical data base, whereas this visit really drove home that human beings were actually involved.

The most memorable thing about Auschwitz-Birkenau for me was that the 'Final Solution' was ultimately *not* the final solution. Hearing about the differing manner of exterminations and the various ways they attempted to get rid of the bodies (for example: mass graves, open-air fires and so on) was the most memorable, because there is a lasting image of a systematic, perfected machine, whereas in reality, it was almost a series of trial and error, to find the most efficient solution.

I would like to implore anyone, that if they get the opportunity to visit Auschwitz-Birkenau or any other Nazi Concentration Camp, to do so. Although it is not the happiest memories to take away from a trip, it is a truly remarkable journey back in time and one which needs to be understood and needs to act as a warning to future generations.

Although the memory of Nazi genocide will never diminish, visiting the 'headquarters' of this atrocity really drives home a poignant point. My lasting feeling of this trip is that visiting Auschwitz-Birkenau perversely gave me hope, hope in that the lessons we can learn from the Nazi death Camps, means that we can never let this happen again.[380]

James Urwin

The first impression I had, was the enormity of the Camp at Birkenau, I thought it would have been more concentrated. It also came across as something I would not have looked twice at. If I drove past the buildings in the UK, I would not look twice if I did not know how infamous the buildings were.

The visit has helped me understand the gravity of mass genocide. I cannot think of many other places where people were so brutally treated and murdered in such a high volume in a singular location. Often after reading a book that explains the severity of War, you easily forget about it—ultimately it is words on paper—you know what happened thanks to the books, but not necessarily 'understand' what has happened. Visiting a place like Auschwitz can really hit one hard and give you a much bigger taste of how real the genocide was.

The most memorable thing I saw was the gas chambers and walking through a building that, step by step, explained how the victims were led to their inevitable murder. An image showing the burning of the dead bodies in the open stuck in my mind too.

I would advise people to go to these places, because it gives a perspective that nothing else can. No matter how much I read, visiting Auschwitz-Birkenau helped me realize, not just the Holocaust, but what humans are really capable of, even if they have created a seemingly civilized society

---

[380] Tania Muhlberger's pointed out that this was said by my father, Professor Detlef Muhlberger, so many times—as he spent his lifetime in studies and lecturing to illustrate the Nazis as a warning from history, and that we must definitely NEVER allow this barbarity to occur ever again

Josh Axe

The first impression I got of Auschwitz-Birkenau was the sheer size of the Camp. Birkenau was huge, and even empty, one could imagine the horrors there, with the help of photographs alongside the buildings and ruins, and with the exhibits. I had seen photographs of the site previously, but visiting it in person really nails down the scale of which people were persecuted by the Nazis.

Another was seeing the shock of the items stored at the Auschwitz Main Camp. The huge amounts of hair, personal belongings, and jewellery that the Nazis took from their victims, put into perspective the amount of people that had passed through there and suffered. Whether they went on to other Camps such as Anne and Margot Frank going to Belsen, or dying at Auschwitz, it showed the suffering that these people must have gone through.

Thirdly an impression I got was the state of which people had to survive. We visited in the winter, all wrapped up in huge coats and thermals and still people were shaking from the cold. Those who were interned there had to survive the weather whilst working on minimal food and in little to no clothing. I could not even imagine the scale of what these people suffered in these conditions.

The visit has aided my studies as I am using Auschwitz as an example in my dissertation which is about the memory of the Holocaust and mainly focuses on Bergen-Belsen. The most memorable thing I saw during the visit to the Main Auschwitz Camp was the standing cells, which left a deep impression. The cells that barely looked big enough for one person, having three plus people standing in them for days at a time with no food or water, must have been horrific. It made me realize that those interned did suffer even more horribly than I first thought, as these cells were not something I was aware of before the visit.

I would like to add that the most memorable part of my visit to Birkenau, was the time after the official tour ended, Chris took a group of us back into the Camp to look around some sites that we had missed, including where the 'White House' was, as well as the

Ash Pond. Visiting these places, that we would have not seen otherwise, was very informative, and one of the more thought provoking parts of the whole site. This was by far the most interesting part of the trip as Chris gave us information that would otherwise not have been available, and the interest and dedication to the subject was apparent, which made listening to the information given all the more intriguing.

Adam Brunskill

Auschwitz-Birkenau was an extremely chilling place, the idea that the construction was not even finished was shocking. The sheer scale of Auschwitz-Birkenau was overwhelming in a sense.

The visit definitely helped put more perspective on what actually happened at Auschwitz-Birkenau and helped me with my studies. Visiting the Camp gave me an insight into what it was like and what happened there from physical examples.

Hannah Smith

My main impression of Auschwitz-Birkenau was a vast area surrounded by coldness. The way in which there was no wildlife and an eerie silence that was there created a strong impression which made it feel like the wildlife knew something horrendous had happened there.

I feel I never understood the true scale of Auschwitz-Birkenau until visiting the site, as it is much larger than I thought. This shook me, as at the moment of visiting the Camps, it made me realize just how large this dreadful crime was.

The visit has helped me significantly with my studies as it has allowed me to widen my knowledge of the Holocaust. It has also encouraged my studies into Jewish culture and their lifestyle before the War. I want to research more elements of the genocide and the life in the ghettos, due to visiting the Jewish Galicia Museum in Kraków.

The visit has also changed my outlook on life, as it has made me realize how much we must fight to stop prejudice around the world, beginning with even the smallest acts of discrimination, in order to prevent anything like the Holocaust happening again. By fighting even the smallest elements of hostility and xenophobia can be a way to move towards more equality. The visit also made me want to protect different cultures because by having these variable cultures within the world, they provide us with much more vitality and vibrancy to life.

The most memorable thing that I saw in Auschwitz was the mural that had been painted on the wall of the children's barrack in Birkenau, by another prisoner. I found it an amazing thing to see, as it showed how adults wanted to do anything to protect the children who were having to live in the horrors of the Camp everyday. It tried to demonstrate to the children some sort of colour and normality, even in such a horrendous place

Mike Jukes

I visited Auschwitz-Birkenau in March 2016, as part of a study trip with Teesside University. I did not know what to expect or how I would feel when we got there. We were told that some of us would be physically emotional and others would be reflective and quiet— it turned out, for me personally, it would be both. This would be my first visit to Auschwitz-Birkenau, but it will not be my last.

The first section of our tour took place in Auschwitz I, which I found unusually busy, very much like a tourist site rather than a Memorial. As we walked around the grounds with our headsets on listening to our guide, I found myself drifting from our group and wanted my experience of Auschwitz to reflect how lucky I am in my own life. My wife and I had very recently welcomed our son into the world—our second child.

When our group arrived in the room in Auschwitz which contained the belongings of the children of the Holocaust, my heart sank. Shoes, teddy bears, cardigans were visible, surviving this terrible period of history, whilst the owners, innocent children, were brutally taken and killed. I pictured my own children in those shoes and I broke down. I had to take a moment outside and compose myself. Many emotions ran through me on this visit—anger, sorrow, and an overwhelming feeling of 'why did this happen?' At this moment I knew I had made the right decision to come on this trip. I wanted to be there to pay my respects and to understand the terrible atrocities that had occurred.

The second part of our tour took us to Birkenau. This site was calm, peaceful and eerily quiet. The views I was seeing, were the final views of so many innocent people, and again I reflected on my own life and how lucky I am.

During our time in Auschwitz-Birkenau I connected and bonded with many of the university group—people who I had not spoken to before—became my friends and still are. We shared emotional moments that can only be explained by sharing a visit to this precious and sacred site in history.

The visit to Auschwitz has not only changed my vision on my studies, for example, looking at how people have denied the Holocaust is beyond ridiculous, but it has also changed my outlook on life. I do not take my life for granted and I cherish every day I have to spend with my family.

Jess Oman

Auschwitz-Birkenau provides a unique insight into one of the darkest periods in history. During a recent trip to the Camp I found that there were two features of the memorial site that startled me the most. The railway, which has become an iconic symbol of the Holocaust, was particularly harrowing, as I felt that the remnants of a system which was used to transport millions of men, women, and children to their deaths, represents the National Socialists disregard for human life. I struggled to comprehend how humanity could construct such a villainous and unethical system that was dedicated to the extermination of one group of people.

I also found that the size of the Camp was especially nauseating, as the magnitude of space committed to the genocide of the Jews and also the free area that was intended to encompass an extension, is incomprehensible. As I walked the distance of the Camp, I felt emotionally drained and a deep sense of sadness that will continue to haunt my memory and my research.

The trip to the Camp has deeply impacted on my studies, as I feel a wholehearted sense of sorrow and compassion for the victims and their families. I was inspired by a surviving drawing of children inside one of the barracks in Birkenau, to research medical experiments on children in the Camp, for my undergraduate dissertation.

As part of this research I also travelled to Kraków to interview Lidia Maksymowicz, who was a 'test' subject for Dr. Josef Mengele, at the age of three-years old. It was an honour to interview Lidia as she provided me with a detailed insight into her history as well as that of the Camp.

Auschwitz-Birkenau has undoubtably made me feel like I have an obligation to ensure people remember the atrocities that were committed there and the millions of victims who never had the chance to leave the Camp.

For me the most memorable aspect of the Camp was the defiant attitude of the victim's families who had returned to the gravesite of their loved ones. The Camp is filled with candles and flags from all over the world, left by people who are determined to preserve the memory of their friends and relatives. I believe this is a key feature of the Camp, as although the eradication of the Jews and other 'undesirable' victims was the core element of Nazi policies, even in death, their victims fight on in the form of the love of those who mourn them.

It is crucial that life in Auschwitz-Birkenau is remembered to prevent a re-occurrence of the atrocities committed by the National Socialists, and to ensure that the victims of their crimes are remembered.

Illustrations

Fig. 1. Auschwitz Town Main Street 1941 (Chris Webb Private Archive)

Fig. 2. Auschwitz Town Main Street July 1941 (Chris Webb Private Archive)

Fig. 3.   Oświęcim Railway Station 1905 (Chris Webb Private Archive)

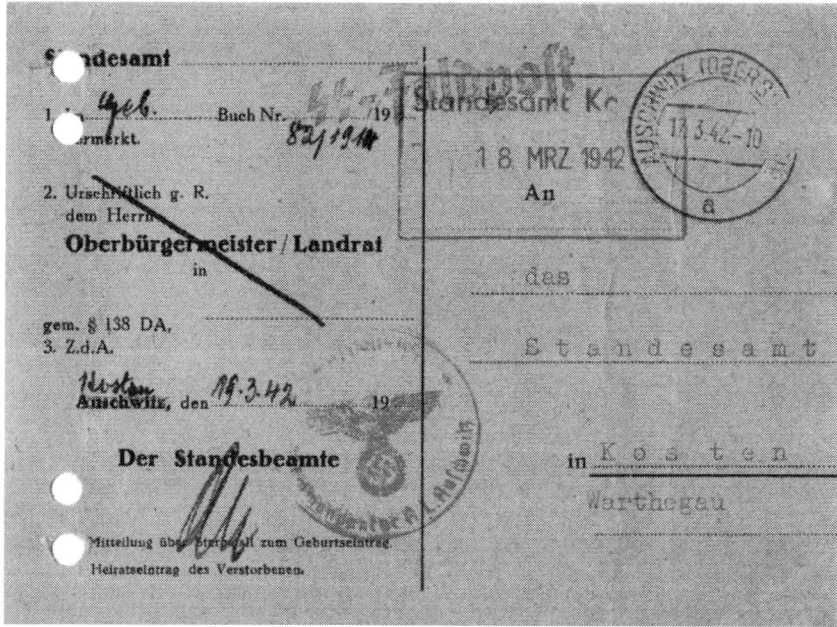

Fig. 4.   Death Notice To Standesamt Kosten (Chris Webb Private Archive)

Standesamt Auschwitz Auschwitz, den 22. November 194..

Mitteilung gem. § 292, DA.

zum Geburtseintrag Nr. 82/1914 zum Heiratseintrag Nr. ?

Vorname und Familienname des Verstorbenen: Wlodzimierz Idzinski

röm.kath. - ledig

geb. am 25.2.1914 in Kosten

(Standesamt .... Nr. ....

verstorben am 17.11.1941 in Auschwitz O/S

(Standesamt Auschwitz O/S Nr. 4405/19..)

Der Standesbeamte

In Vertretung

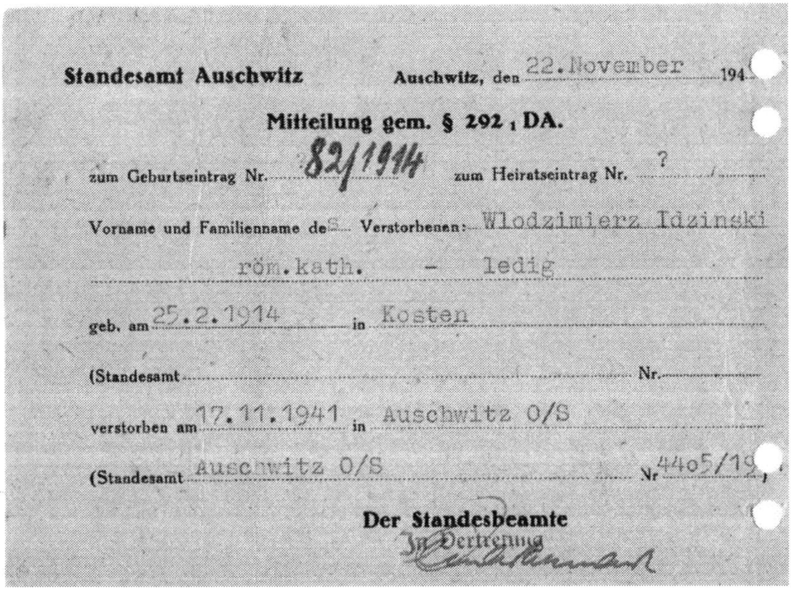

Fig. 5. Death Notice For Wlodzimierz Idzinski—Kosten (Chris Webb Private Archive)

Konzentrationslager Auschwitz

Folgende Anordnungen sind beim Schriftverkehr mit Gefangenen zu beachten:

1.) Jeder Schutzhaftgefangene darf im Monat zweimal von seinen Angehörigen Post empfangen und an sie absenden. Die Briefe an die Gefangenen müssen gut lesbar mit Tinte geschrieben sein und dürfen nur zwei Seiten je 15 Zeilen enthalten. Briefumschläge müssen ungefüttert sein. In einem Brief dürfen nur Briefmarken von 12 Pfg. beigelegt werden. Alles Andere ist verboten. Postkarten haben 10 Zeilen. Lichtbilder dürfen als Post nicht verwendet werden.

2.) Geldsendungen sind gestattet.

3.) Es ist darauf zu achten, dass bei Geld- oder Postsendungen die genaue Adresse, bestehend aus: Name, Geburtsdatum, und Gefangenen-Nummer, auf die Sendungen zu schreiben ist. Wenn die Adresse fehlerhaft ist, geht die Post an den Absender zurück oder wird vernichtet.

4.) Zeitungen sind gestattet, dürfen aber nur durch die Poststelle des K.L. Auschwitz bestellt werden.

5.) Pakete dürfen nicht geschickt werden, da die Gefangenen im Lager alles kaufen können.

6.) Entlassungsgesuche aus der Schutzhaft an die Lagerleitung sind zwecklos.

7.) Sprecherlaubnis und Besuche von Gefangenen im Konzentrationslager sind grundsätzlich nicht gestattet.

Der Lagerkommandant.

Absender:

Meine Anschrift:

Name:

geboren am:

Gef.-Nr.:

Postkarte

An Frau

Borodajko Wanda

Sandomierz

Opatowska 5

Generalgouvernement

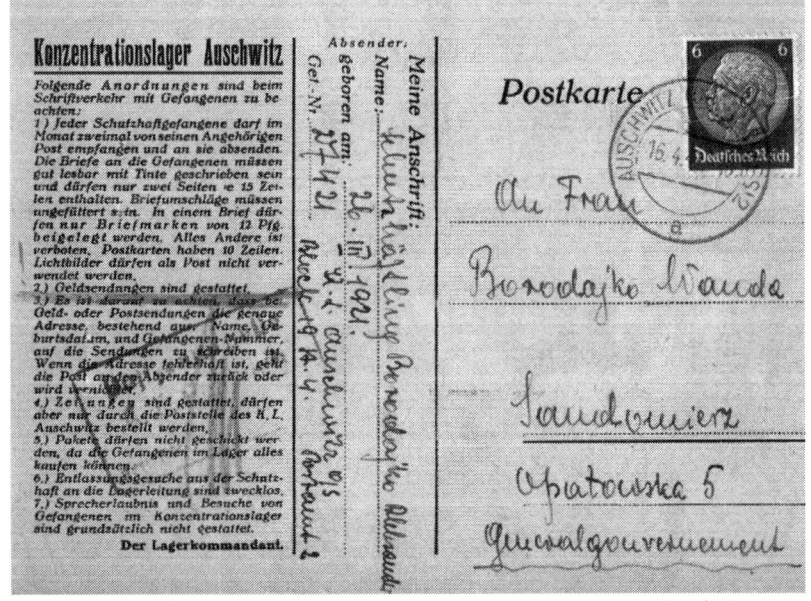

Fig. 6. Postcard From An Auschwitz Prisoner: A. Borodayko (Chris Webb Private Archive)

Fig. 7. Military Concert In Auschwitz Town (Chris Webb Private Archive)

Fig. 8. Unidentified SS-Man—Auschwitz (Chris Webb Private Archive)

Fig. 9.   Auschwitz—KZ Gate 2004 (Chris Webb Private Archive)

Fig. 10.   Auschwitz—Swimming Pool 2004 (Chris Webb Private Archive)

Fig. 11.   Auschwitz Kitchens 2004 (Chris Webb Private Archive)

Fig. 12.   Birkenau Alte Juden Rampe 2004 (Chris Webb Private Archive)

Fig. 13. Birkenau—The Author 2004 (Chris Webb Private Archive)

Fig 14. Birkenau—The Ramp 2004 (From The Main Gate Tower) (Chris Webb Private Archive)

Fig. 15. Birkenau—General View 2004 (ditto) (Chris Webb Private Archive)

Fig. 16. Birkenau—General View Right 2004 (ditto) (Chris Webb Private Archive)

Fig. 17. Birkenau—Artur Hojan Lost In Thought 2004 (Chris Webb Private Archive)

Fig. 18. Birkenau—Drawing Of The Königs Graben In The Penal Company 2004 (Chris Webb Private Archive)

Fig. 19. Auschwitz—Main Reception 2016 (Chris Webb Private Archive)

Fig. 20.   Professor Matthew Feldman And Guide 2016 (Chris Webb Private Archive)

Fig. 21.   Auschwitz—Block 24 2016 (Chris Webb Private Archive)

Fig. 22.   Auschwitz—Block 10 2016 (Chris Webb Private Archive)

Fig. 23.   Auschwitz—Block 11 Courtyard 2016 (Chris Webb Private Archive)

Fig. 24.   Auschwitz—The Black Wall In Block 11 Courtyard 2016 (Chris Webb Private Archive)

Fig. 25.   Auschwitz—Fences 2016 (Chris Webb Private Archive)

Fig. 26.   Auschwitz—Barracks 2016 (Chris Webb Private Archive)

Fig. 27.   Auschwitz—Crematorium 2016 (Chris Webb Private Archive)

Fig. 28. Auschwitz—The Villa Of Commandant Rudolf Höss 2016 (Chris Webb Private Archive)

Fig. 29. Birkenau—Cattle Car On The Ramp 2016 (Chris Webb Private Webb)

Fig. 30. Birkenau—Ruins Of The Little White House Gas Chamber 2016 (Chris Webb Private Archive)

Fig. 31. Birkenau—Ruins Of The Little Red House Gas Chamber 2016 (Chris Webb Private Archive)

Fig. 32. Birkenau—The Ponds Where The Ashes Were Dumped 2016 (Chris Webb Private Archive)

Fig. 33. Birkenau—Kommandantur 2016 (Chris Webb Private Archive)

Fig. 34. Birkenau—The Interior Of One Of The Brick Barracks 2016 (Chris Webb Private Archive)

Fig. 35. Birkenau—A General View 2016 (Chris Webb Private Archive)

Fig. 36. Auschwitz—The Main Gate 2016 (Chris Webb Private Archive)

Fig. 37. Birkenau—The Main Entrance 2016 (Chris Webb Private Archive)

Fig. 38.   Birkenau—Crematorium II Ruins 2016 (Chris Webb Private Archive)

Fig. 39.   Birkenau—Sauna 2016 (Chris Webb Private Archive)

Fig. 40.   Birkenau—Crematorium Ruins 2016 (Chris Webb Private Archive)

Fig. 41.   Birkenau—The Interior Of A Wooden Barracks 2016 (Chris Webb Private Archive)

Fig. 42. Auschwitz—The Main Gate 2017 (Chris Webb Private Archive)

Fig. 43. Auschwitz—Entrance From Inside The Camp 2017 (Chris Webb Private Archive)

Fig. 44.   Auschwitz—Block 24—The Camp Brothel 2017 (Chris Webb Private Archive)

Fig. 45.   Auschwitz—Block 20—The Camp Hospital 2017 (Chris Webb Private Archive)

Fig. 46. Auschwitz—The Entrance To Block 11 2017 (Chris Webb Private Archive)

Fig. 47. Auschwitz—Barracks 2017 (Chris Webb Private Archive)

Fig. 48.   Auschwitz—Barracks In The Snow 2017 (Chris Webb Private Archive)

Fig. 49.   Auschwitz—Auschwitz Fences 2017 (Chris Webb Private Archive)

Fig. 50. Birkenau—Blockführerstube On The Ramp 2017 (Chris Webb Private Archive)

Fig. 51. Birkenau—Ramp In The Snow 2017 (Chris Webb Private Archive)

Fig. 52. Birkenau—Tracks By The Ramp 2017 (Chris Webb Private Archive)

Fig. 53. Birkenau—Painting In The Children's Barrack 2017 (Chris Webb Private Archive)

Fig. 54. Birkenau—Watchtower 2017 (Chris Webb Private Archive)

Fig. 55. Birkenau—The Gate To The Crematorium 2017 (Chris Webb Private Archive)

Fig. 56. Birkenau—Chris Webb, Lucy Jolly, Mark Handscomb 2017 (Chris Webb Private Archive)

Documents, Drawings, Maps and Sources

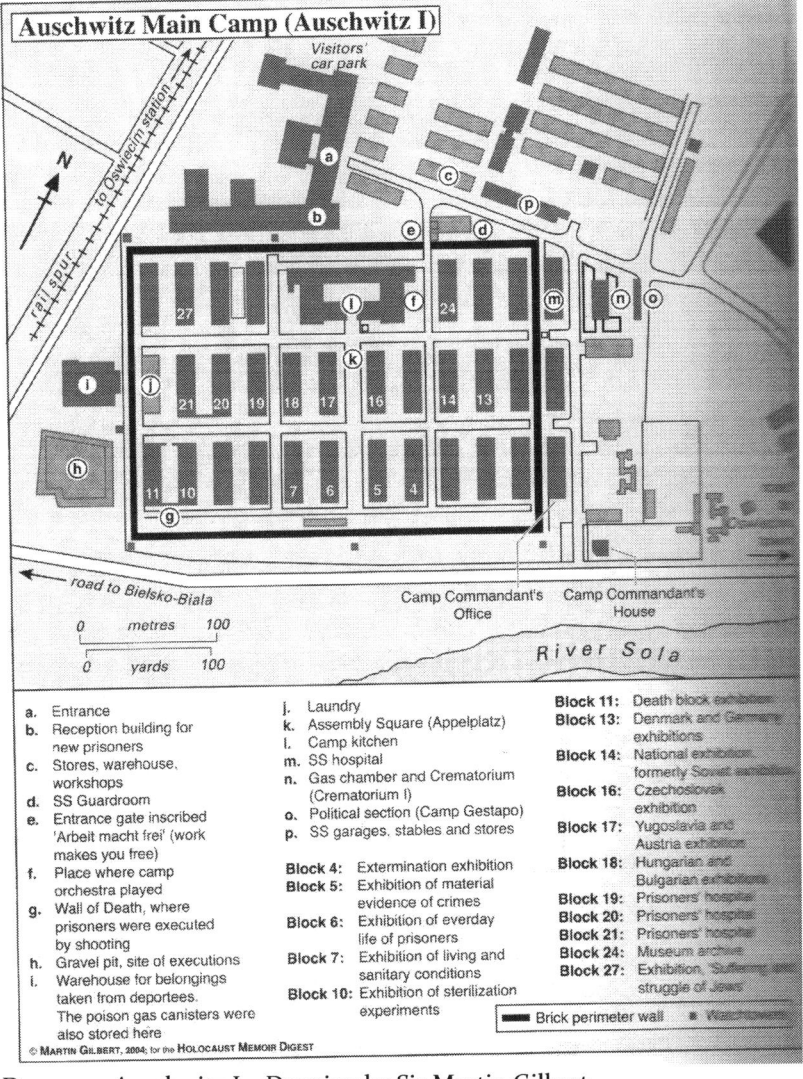

Doc. 1.   Auschwitz I—Drawing by Sir Martin Gilbert

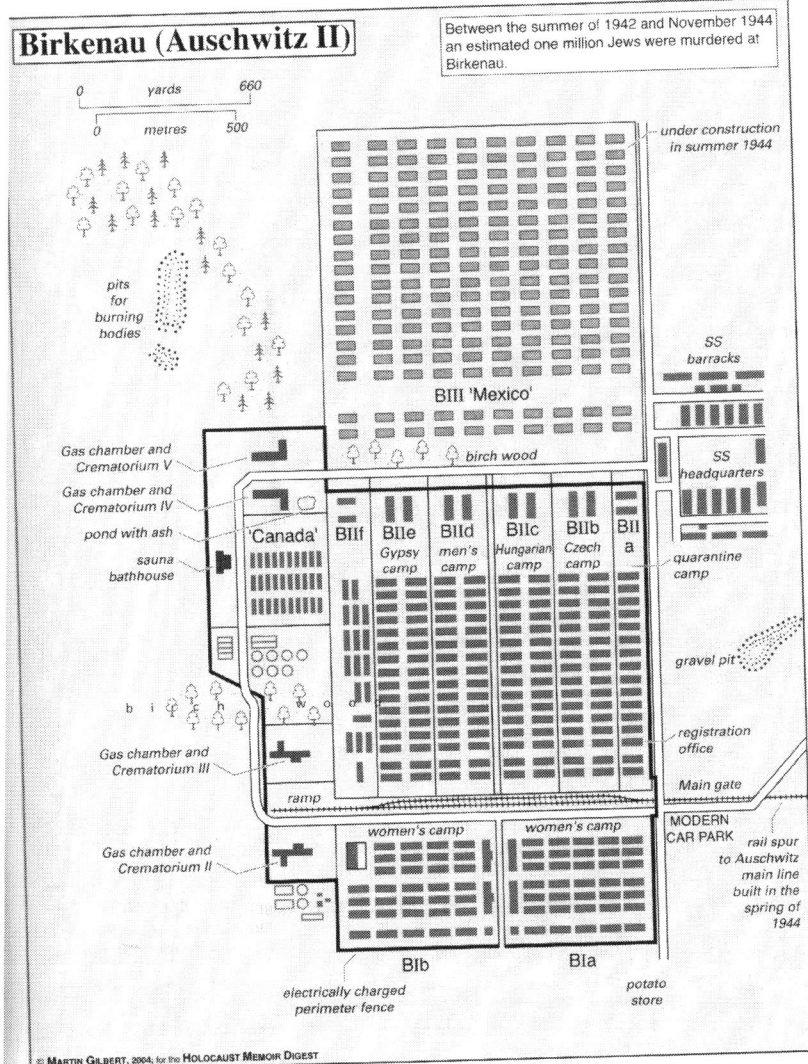

Doc. 2. Auschwitz II—Drawing by Sir Martin Gilbert

- 6 -

1	2	3	4	5	6	7
122	Psn 21 C	6/7.2.	Pj 109	Bialystok 9.00	Auschwitz 12.10	2000
		8/9.2.	Lp 110	Auschwitz	Bialystok	
		10.2.	Pj 129	Bialystok 9.00	Treblinka 12.10	2000
		10.2.	Lp 130	Treblinka 21.18	Bialystok 1.30	
		12.2.	Pj 133	Bialystok 9.00	Treblinka 12.10	2000
		12.2.	Lp 134	Treblinka 21.18	Grodno	
		14.2.	Pj 163	Grodno 5.40	Treblinka 12.10	2000
		14.2.	Lp 164	Treblinka	Scharfenwiese	
123	Psn 21 C	7/8.2.	Pj 111	Bialystok	Auschwitz	
		8.2.	Lp 112	Auschwitz	Myslowitz	
126	Gedob 1 BC 16 C	25/26.1.	Po 61	Zamocz 8.20	Berlin Whgen 17.30	1000
		29/30.1.	Da 13	Berlin Mob 17.20	Auschwitz 10.48	1000
		31.1/1.2.	Lp 14	Auschwitz	Zamocz	
		3/4.2.	Po 65	Zamocz	Auschwitz	1000
		4.2.	Lp 66	Auschwitz	Myslowitz	
127	Gedob 1 BC 16 C	29/30.1.	Po 63	Zamocz 8.20	Berlin Whgen 17.30	1000
		2/3.2.	Da 15	Berlin Mob 17.20	Auschwitz 10.48	1000
		4/5.2.	Lp 16	Auschwitz	Litzmannstadt	
125	Dre 21 C 1 G	20/21.1.	Da 101	Theresienst.	Auschwitz	2000
		21/22.1.	Lp 102	Auschwitz	Theresienstadt	
		23/24.1.	Da 103	Th	Au	2000
		24/25.1.	Lp 104	Au	Th	
		26/27.1.	Da 105	Th	Au	2000
		27/28.1.	Lp 106	Au	Th	
		29/30.1.	Da 107	Th	Au	2000
		30/31.1.	Lp 108	Au	Th	
		1/2.2.	Da 109	Th	Au	2000
		2.2.	Lp 110	Auschwitz	Myslowitz	

Doc. 3. Railway Circulation Plan January–February 1943 (Wiener Library)

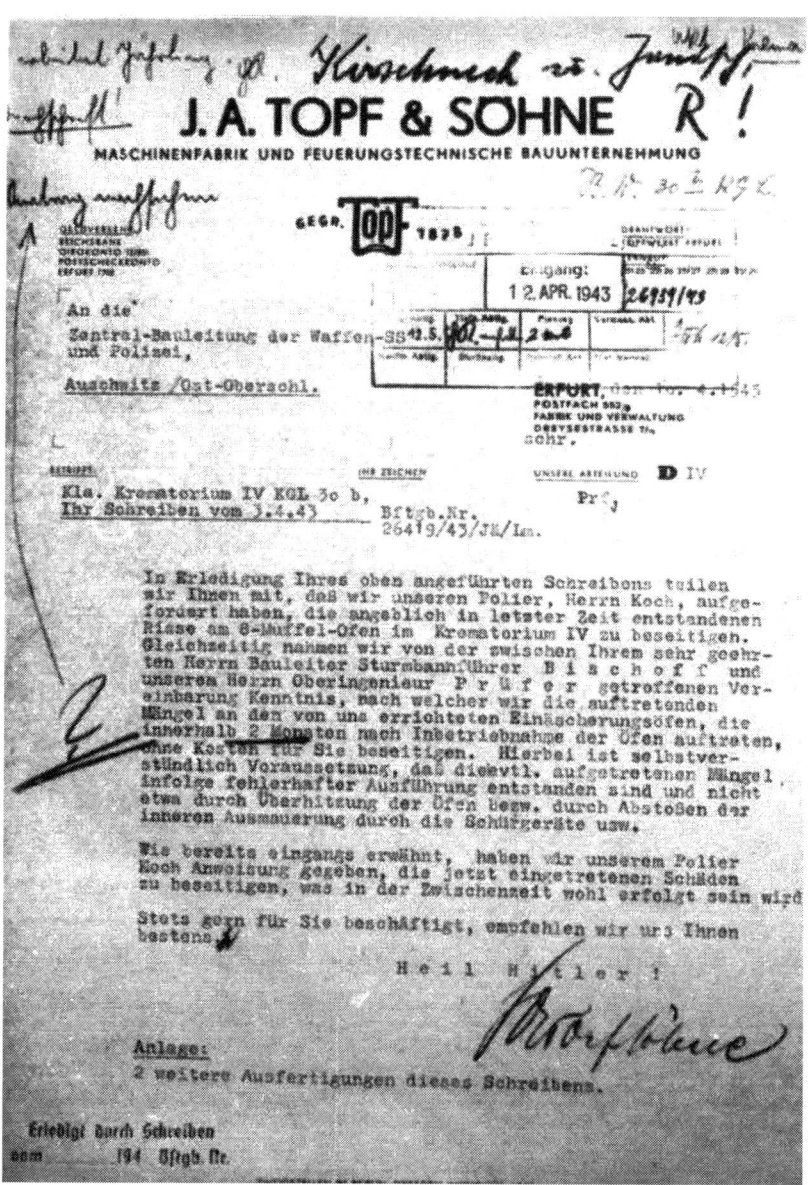

Doc. 4.   J. A. Topf Letter – Crematorium IV (Wiener Library)

B.13.

    Meine Mutter, eine Dame von beinahe 80 Jahren, war bis zu den Pogromen in Deutschland im Altersheim in A. untergebracht. Das Heim war eine jüdische Privatstiftung. Es waren etwa 40 bis 50 Herren und Damen untergebracht. Das Alter der Insassen dürfte etwa zwischen 70 und 85 Jahren liegen.

    In der Nacht vom 11. zum 12. November wurden sämtliche Insassen um 3 Uhr nachts geweckt mit der Anweisung, ihre Sachen zu packen, um bis 9 Uhr morgens das Haus zu verlassen. Sofern sie in dem Orte, in dem wenig Juden wohnen, Angehörige hatten, wurden sie dort untergebracht oder in der näheren Umgebung. Man muss allerdings berücksichtigen, dass infolge der Pogrome die Unterbringung sehr beschränkt war. Wo die Greise und Greisinnen untergebracht sind, die keine Angehörigen in der Nähe hatten, entzieht sich meiner Kenntnis.

Max Block
Amsterdam,
Waterau - Straat

Doc. 5.   Report by Max Block about the treatment of his mother on Reichskristallnacht (Wiener Library London)

Doc. 6.   Registration Card at Theresienstadt for Felice Schragenheim (ITS Archives Bad Arolsen. Courtesy of Robert Parzer)

FEDERACE ŽIDOVSKÝCH OBCÍ V ČESKÉ REPUBLICE

Maiselova 18
P.O.B. 297
110 01 Praha 1

V Praze dne 30.5.97

ÚSTŘEDNÍ KARTOTÉKA — TRANSPORTY

R. č. 4373

Brichta Heřman

Rodné datum: 6.5. 1897

Adresa před deportací: PRAHA XI, Na Kopečku 1915

1. transport TEREZÍN
dne: 13 VII 1943
Di č. 554

2. transport
dne: 29.9.1944
číslo: El-270
do: Osvětím

FEDERACE ŽIDOVSKÝCH OBCÍ
V ČESKÉ REPUBLICE
110 01 Praha 1, Maiselova 18

Doc. 7. Transport Record of Hermann Brichta from Theresienstadt to Auschwitz

FEDERACE ŽIDOVSKÝCH OBCÍ V ČESKÉ REPUBLICE

Maiselova 18
P.O.B. 297
110 01 Praha 1

V Praze dne 20.5.97.

ÚSTŘEDNÍ KARTOTÉKA — TRANSPORTY

R č. *379*

Brichtaová Tonča

Rodná dne: 22.6.1892

Adresa před deportací: PRAHA XI, Na Kopečku 1915

1. transport - TEREZÍN	2. transport
dne: 13 VII 1943	dne: 12.10.1944
Di č. 555	číslo: Eq - 823
	do: Osvětim

FEDERACE ŽIDOVSKÝCH OBCÍ
V ČESKÉ REPUBLICE
110 01 Praha 1, Maiselova 18

Doc. 8. Transport Record of Toni Brichta from Theresienstadt to Auschwitz

FEDERACE ŽIDOVSKÝCH OBCÍ V ČESKÉ REPUBLICE

Maiselova 18
P.O.B. 297
110 01 Praha 1

V Praze dne 30. 5. 97

ÚSTŘEDNÍ KARTOTÉKA — TRANSPORTY

R. č. V. 370

Brichta František

Rodná data: 7. 10. 1923

Adresa před deportací: PRAHA XI, Na Kopečku 1915

HLÁŠEN OPĚT DO EVIDENCE

1. transport - TEREZÍN
dne: 13. VII 1943
Di č. 556

2. transport
dne: 12. 10. 1944
číslo: Eg - 824
do: Osvětim

FEDERACE ŽIDOVSKÝCH OBCÍ
V ČESKÉ REPUBLICE
110 01 Praha 1, Maiselova 18

Tel 00422/24 81 10 90
/24 81 01 30
Fax 00422/24 81 09 12

Bankovní spojení:
Česká spořitelna
Pařížská 9, Praha 1
č. účtu 6060553 - 018/0800

Devizové konto:
Živnostenská banka
Praha 1, Na příkopě 20
No - 3483 - 6044

IČO:
00 438 341

Doc. 9. Transport Record of Franciszek Brichta from Theresienstadt to Auschwitz (Kindly Supplied by Frank Bright to the Author)

R. u. S.-Fragebogen
(Von Frauen sinngemäß auszufüllen!)

Richard Baer

Dienstgrad: ⚡-Ostuf.   ⚡-M44

Sip. Nr. **302172**

Einschreiben!

Name (leserlich schreiben): B a e r , Richard

in ⚡ seit 7.7.32   Dienstgrad: ⚡-Obersturmführer   ⚡-Einheit: 9.⚡-T.J.B.

in SA von — bis —, in HJ von — bis —

Mitglieds-Nummer in Partei: 454 991   ⚡-Nr.: 44 225

geb. am 9. Sept.1911 in F l o s s ?? Kreis: Oberpfalz

Land: Bayern   jetzt Alter: 29 1/2   Glaubensbekenntnis: gttgl.

Jetziger Wohnsitz: im Felde   Wohnung:

Beruf und Berufsstellung:

Wird öffentliche Unterstützung in Anspruch genommen?

Liegt Berufswechsel vor?

Außerberufliche Fertigkeiten und Berechtigungsscheine (z. B. Führerschein, Sportabzeichen, Sportauszeichnung):

Führerschein 1 u. 3   SA = u. Reichssportabz. br.

Staatsangehörigkeit: Dtsch.

Ehrenamtliche Tätigkeit:

Dienst im alten Heer: Truppe ... von ... bis

   Freikorps .... von
   Reichswehr .... von
   Schutzpolizei ..... von
   Neue Wehrmacht ... von

Letzter Dienstgrad:

Frontkämpfer: ... bis ... verwundet:

Orden und Ehrenabzeichen, einschl. Rettungsmedaille:

Personenstand (ledig, verwitwet, geschieden — seit wann):

Welcher Konfession ist der Antragsteller? ggl.   die zukünftige Braut (E
(Als Konfession wird auch außer dem herkömmlichen jedes andere gottgläubige Bekenntnis angesehen.)

Ist neben der standesamtlichen Trauung eine kirchliche Trauung vorgesehen? Ja — nein.
Hat neben der standesamtlichen Trauung eine kirchliche Trauung stattgefunden? Ja — nein.
Gegebenenfalls nach welcher konfessionellen Form?
Ist Ehestands-Darlehen beantragt worden? Ja — nein
Bei welcher Behörde (genaue Anschrift)?

Wann wurde der Antrag gestellt?
Wurde das Ehestands-Darlehen bewilligt? Ja — nein.
Soll das Ehestands-Darlehen beantragt werden? Ja — nein
Bei welcher Behörde (genaue Anschrift)? Finanzamt Hamburg-Bergedorf

Doc. 10.   Baer Fragebogen (Yad Vashem)

Doc. 11. Liebehenschel Fragebogen (Yad Vashem)

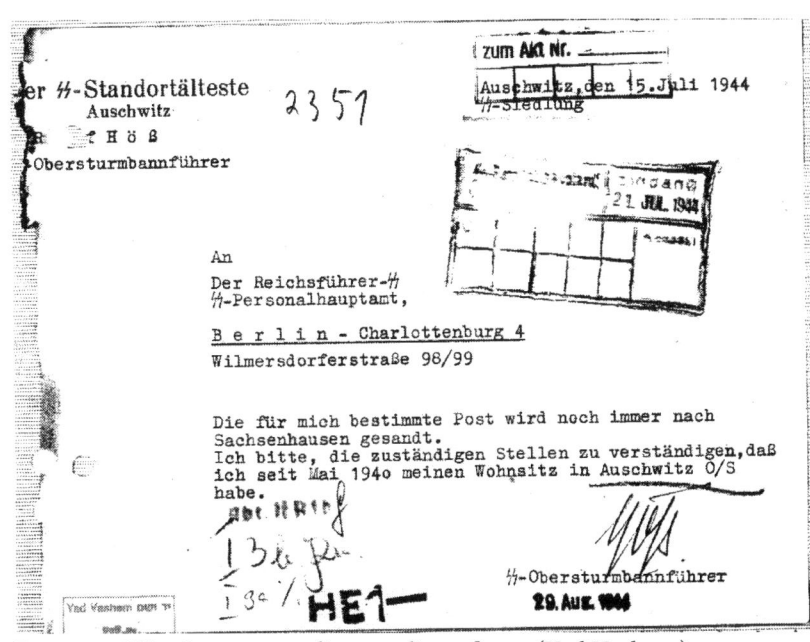

Doc. 12.   Höss Letter regarding sending of post (Yad Vashem)

Fragebogen

(Anlage zum Antrag auf Aufnahme in die Nationalsozialistische Deutsche Arbeiterpartei)

A

Vor- und Zuname (bei Frauen auch Mädchenname): Karl, Ludwig, Robert Mulka
Beruf oder Art der Tätigkeit '): Export- Handelsvertreter.
Wohnort '): Hamburg 13. Wohnung: Ise Straße Nr. 127 hpt.
Geburtsort: Hamburg Geburtsdatum (Tag, Monat, Jahr): 12.April 1895.
Staatsangehörigkeit: D.R. Wenn staatenlos, frühere Staatsangehörigkeit: entfällt.
Sind Sie erbgesund? Ja.
Vor- und Zuname des Vaters: Matthes Mulka
Geburtsort des Vaters: Kolkwitz b/Cottbus Geburtsdatum des Vaters (Tag, Monat, Jahr): 30.Jan.1857
Volkszugehörigkeit des Vaters: Deutschblütig.
Vor- und Zuname der Mutter (Mädchenname!): Marie, geb. Bock.
Geburtsort der Mutter: Beeskow. Geburtsdatum der Mutter (Tag, Monat, Jahr): 31.März 1867.
Volkszugehörigkeit der Mutter: Deutschblütig.

B

Familienstand (ledig, verheiratet, verwitwet, geschieden): Verheiratet.
Vor- und Zuname des Ehegatten (bei Frauen Mädchenname!): Erna, geb.Beckenbach.
Geburtsort des Ehegatten: Altona/E. Geburtsdat. d. Ehegatten (Tag, Monat, Jahr):26.Mai 1895.
Ist der Ehegatte frei von jüdischem oder farbigem Rasseeinschlag? Ja.
Waren Sie früher mit einem nichtarischen Ehegatten verheiratet? Nein.
Wodurch ist diese Ehe beendet worden? (Tod oder Scheidung) entfällt.
Wann? entfällt. Bei Scheidung, durch welches Gericht? entfällt.
Sind Kinder aus dieser Ehe vorhanden? entfällt. Wieviele? entfällt.

C

Haben Sie früher einer Freimaurerloge angehört? Nein. Welcher? entfällt.
Tag des Eintritts? entfällt. Tag des Austritts? entfällt.
Welches Amt und welchen Grad haben Sie in der Loge bekleidet? entfällt.
Haben Sie früher einer logenähnlichen Vereinigung (Odd Fellows und Druiden-Orden) oder einem Geheimbund angehört? Nein. Welcher oder welchem? entfällt.

Doc. 13.   Robert Mulka Fragebogen (NARA)

MOST SECRET.

ZIP/GPDD 259b/25-10-42

KEPT UNDER LOCK AND KEY: NEVER TO BE REMOVED FROM THE OFFICE.

This document is to receive CX/MSS Security Treatment

GERMAN POLICE DECODES Nr.3 TRAFFIC : 7.10.42

I B TRAFFIC

1/4. OMA de OMF   0700   239 249 250 46
RSHA IV B 4 BERLIN, zu Händen SS Obersturmbannführer EICHMANN, nachrichtlich an die Amtsgruppe D, ORANIENBURG, zu Händen SS Obersturmbannführer LIEBEHENSCHEL.
Betr: Abbeförderung von Juden aus den poln-czech-niederländischen Gebieten nach AUSCHWITZ. Bezug: dort. Fs. vom 5.10.42, Nr. 181212, 1755 Uhr ... Geheim. Bezüglich der aufgegebenen Judentransporte aus HOLLAND wird noch am Abgabe der Zugnummern und der voraussichtlichen Ankunftszeiten durch Funk gebeten, um auf Grund dieser Unterlagen bei der Reichsbahndirektion OPPELN veranlassen zu können, dass diese Transporte in KOSEL nicht anhalten, sondern nach AUSCHWITZ durchfahren, um Sie, wie vereinbart, von dem Zugriffe der Beauftragten der Schmeldtaktion zu bewahren.
Gez. HOESS, SS Obersturmbannführer.

5/6. ? de ?   0740   239 21 7
Chef Amt D III.
Es wird gemeldet, dass SS Obersturmführer ENTRESS am 6.10.42 Nachmittag auf dem Motorrad einen Unfall erlitten hat, mit Platzwunden ...... Schürfwunden am Hinterkopf und starker Prellung des linken Ellenbogen. .... Seine ..corrupt groups... nachweisbar. Es ist mit einigen Tagen Dienstunfähigkeit und weiterhin mit beschränkter Dienstfähigkeit zu rechnen.
Gez. I.V. ENTRESS, SS Obersturmführer.

Doc. 14.   Höss—Adolf Eichmann Decode (National Archives Kew)

7/8. OMA de OMF 0830 ? 180
Betr: Beförderungen. Bezug: dort. Funk vom 7.11.42. Die
Kdtr. KL. AU. bittet um Mitteilung durch Fs., ob die
Beförderung der SS Untersturmführer Arie MOEHLMANN zum SS
Obersturmführer, SS Hauptscharführer Gerhard PALITZSCH zum
SS Untersturmführer, SS Hauptscharführer Konrad WIEGAND zum
SS Untersturmführer, SS Oberscharführer Georg GRUENBERG
zum SS Untersturmführer abgelehnt wurde, oder ob noch mit
einer Beförderung zu rechnen ist.
Gez. HOESZ.

9. OMI de OMU 0835 220
Betr: Überstellung von Häftlingen nach KOELN. Bezug: dort.
Funk vom 6.11.42. Der Transport mit 185 Häftlingen geht heute,
den 9.11.42 in WEIMAR ab, wie bereits fernmündlich dem
Amtsgruppenchef gemeldet.
Gez. PISTER.

10/11. OMA de OMF 0900 250 120
Betr: Besichtigung des Haarverwertungsbetriebes, Firma
HELD in FRIEDLAND, Bezirk BRESLAU. Bezug: dort.
Funk vom 30.9.42. Die Kdtr. KL. AU. erbittet neuerlich
Fahrgenehmigung für SS Untersturmführer HOESSLER und SS
Untersturmführer SELL mit Pkw. oder Bahn nach FRIEDLAND zur
Besichtigung des Haarverwertungsbetriebes HELD in FRIEDLAND,
Bez. BRESLAU.
Gez. HOESZ.

12. OMF de OMA 1030 85
Funkstellenleiter.
Zur Beförderung ..corrupt groups...
DISTRIBUTION LIST:
1. M.I.14
2. Col. Hatton Hall.
3. Capt. Babbage
4. Wing Commander Jones
5. I.S.
6. B.M.
7. File.
8. File.

Capt. Jackson

Doc. 15. Palitzsch and Hössler Decode (National Archives Kew)

Der Chef der Sicherheitspolizei und des SD

IV B 4 a   3233/44g(1015)

Berlin SW 11, den 11. März 1942.
Prinz-Albrecht-Straße 8
Fernsprecher: 12 00 40

Schnellbrief

Geheim

Auswärtiges Amt
D III 257.9
Eing. 12. MRZ 1942

An das

Auswärtige Amt,
z.Hdn. von Herrn Legationsrat R a d e m a c h e r ,

Berlin W 35,

Rauchstrasse 11.

<u>Betrifft</u>: Evakuierung von Juden aus Frankreich.
<u>Bezug</u>: Hies.Schnellbrief vom 9.3.42
— IV B 4 a - 3233/41g (1550) —

     Im Nachgang zum hiesigen Schnellbrief vom 9.3.1942 wird mitgeteilt, daß außer der am 23.3.1942 vorgesehenen Evakuierung von 1.000 Juden aus Compiègne in Zeitkürze weitere 5.000 staatspolizeilich in Erscheinung getretene Juden aus Frankreich in das Konzentrationslager Auschwitz (Oberschlesien) abgeschoben werden sollen.

     Ich darf bitten, auch hierzu die dortige Zustimmung auszusprechen.

Im Auftrage:

Eichmann

261430

Doc. 16.   Adolf Eichmann Letter regarding the French Jews (National Archives Kew)

lfd. Nr.	Selbstverpfleger über 10 Jahren männlich	geboren	weiblich	geboren	Kinder von 3-10 Jahren Namen	geboren
1	Barth Josef	17.5.17	Barth Anna	22.6.20	---	
2	Bernstein Hans	23.10.15	Bernstein Margot	25.10.20	---	
3	Bott Hans	14.8.13	Bott Emma	21.12.19	---	
4	Brülls Fritz	27.2.07	Brülls Resi	2.3.15	Brülls Günter	26.1c
5	Busch Hubert	2.7.14	Busch Käte	30.4.16	---	
6	Florstedt Hermann	18.2.95	Florstedt Charl.	25.4.95	---	
7	Fräschholz Fritz	5.10.11	Frischholz Maria	10.9.10	Frischholz Inge " Fritz " Roland	5.2 23.5 23.10
8	Gerstenmeier Wilh.	17.1.08	Gerstenmeier Math.	8.12.17	Gerstenmeier Helga " Elke	2.8 2.8
9	Hanson Herbert	17.3.13	Hanson Luzie	6.12.18	---	
10	Hering Max	27.8.10	Hering Herta	23.5.15	---	
11	Jaitner Edmund	12.8.13	Jaitner Elisabeth	11.7.22	---	
12	Kaps Josef	17.11.14	Kaps Hilde	7.11.20	---	
13	Kasprusch Edmund	27.10.07	---		---	
14	Komarek Paul	11.4.94	---		---	
15	Laurich Emil	21.5.21	Laurich Lilly	3.5.17	---	
16	Lendzian Emil	7.3.02	---		---	
17	Lübbe Mathias	23.4.13	Lübbe Lieselotte	21.2.16	---	
18	Mattausch Franz	30.12.99	---		---	
19	Merkel Walter	15.3.14	Merkel Erna	22.7.14	---	
20	Möckel Herbert	4.12.14	Möckel Gertrud	9.3.08	---	
21	Mußfeld Erich	18.2.13	Mußfeld Herta	24.7.13	Mußfeld Rolf	15.4
22	Petrick Heinz	22.1.13	Petrick Ingeborg	15.1.21	---	
23	Ruppert Wilhelm	2.2.05	Ruppert Rosa	18.8.08	Ruppert Dieta	21.8.
24	Seufert Karl	1.11.13	Seufert Zenta	13.6.14	---	
25	Schütz Karl	11.3.06	Schütz Elfriede	15.9.12	---	
26	Schütze Helmut	21.11.13	Schütze Ruth	1.5.20	---	
27	Schwägler Eugen	16.3.09	Schwägler Antonie	31.5.08	Schwägler Ingeborg	16.9.
28	Sigl Leo	22.2.09	Sigl Anna	8.4.07	---	
29	Spitz Alois	6.12.11	Spitz Maria	22.3.19	---	
30	Strippel Arnold	2.6.11	Strippel Maria		---	
31	Weber Arnold	19.1.97	Weber Johanna Nagel Elfriede geb.Weber Weber Edith Weber Inge	2.4.98 28.9.20 21.10.27 7.5.30	---	
32	Worster Heinrich	2?.11.09	---		---	
33	Jannsen Iwer	8.3.20	Jannsen Gertrud	19.6.21		

Doc. 17. Mühsfeldt—Lublin KZ (Yad Vashem)

SS - Scharführer
Otto M o l l, Kommandanturstab
des Konz. Lagers Sachsenhausen.   Oranienburg, den 26. 9. 1939
SS - Nr. 277670.

Betrifft: Heiratsgenhmigung.
Bezug   : - ohne -
Anlagen : - keine -

An den
Reichsführer - SS, Rasse-und Siedlungshauptamt
<u>B e r l i n</u> SW 68,
Hedemannstraße 23/24.

Der SS - Scharführer Otto M o l l, geb. am 4. 3. 1915
zu Hohen-schönberg, Angehöriger des Kommandanturstabes
des Konz. Lagers Sachsenhausen, bittet um die Heiratsgenehmi-
gung mit Fräulein Elli U n r u h, geb. am 18. 10. 1915 zu Klein-
Ziethen, Angehörige des Kommandanturstabes des Frauenkonzen-
trationslagers Ravenbrück.

Da meine zukünftige Ehefrau sich in Schwangerschaft befindet,
möchte ich in absehbarer Zeit heiraten.
Es ist mir jedoch nicht möglich, bis zum 30. des Monats
die erforderlichen Unterlagen herbeizuschaffen.
Ich verpflichte mich, die Papiere in absehbarer Zeit
nachzureichen.

[signature]
SS - Scharführer.

Doc. 18.   Otto Moll (NARA)

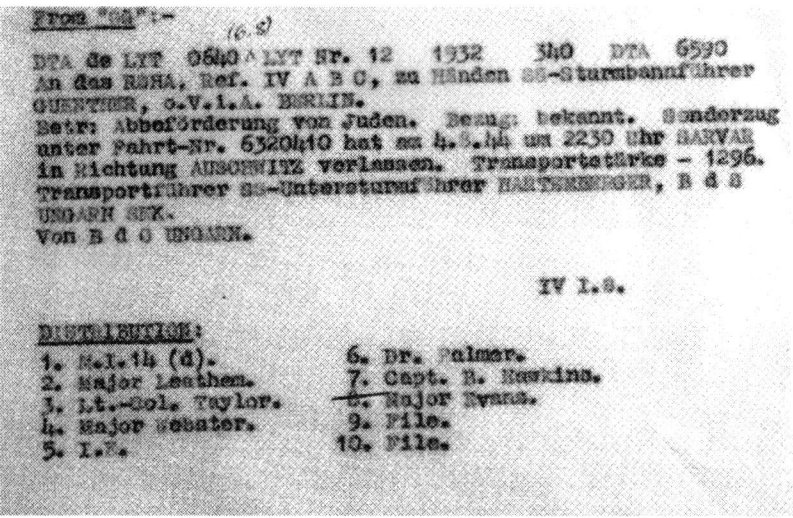

Doc. 19. Mittermeier SS Record (NARA)

Doc. 20. Sárvár—Auschwitz Decode (National Archives Kew)

Appendix I
Equivalent Ranks

SS-Reichsführer	Reichs Leader
SS-Oberstgruppenführer	General
SS-Obergruppenführer	Lieutenant General
SS-Gruppenführer	Major General
SS-Brigadeführer	Brigadier General
SS-Oberführer	Senior Colonel
SS-Standartenführer	Colonel
SS-Obersturmbannführer	Lieutenant Colonel
SS-Sturmbannführer	Major
SS-Hauptsturmführer	Captain
SS-Obersturmführer	First Lieutenant
SS-Untersturmführer	Second Lieutenant
SS-Sturmscharführer	Sergeant Major
SS-Hauptscharführer	Master-Sergeant
SS-Oberscharführer	Sergeant First Class
SS-Scharführer	Staff Sergeant
SS-Unterscharführer	Sergeant
SS-Rottenführer	Corporal
SS-Sturmmann	Acting Corporal
SS-Oberschütze	Private First Class
SS-Schütze	Private

Appendix II
Glossary of Nazi Terms

Abteilung: A branch, section or sub-section of a main department or office (*Hauptamt, Amtsgruppe* or *Amt,* q.v.) Also a military or paramilitary unit of up to battalion strength, i.e. approximately 700 men.

Aktion Reinhardt: The code name used in honor of Reinhard Heydrich for the mass murder of Polish Jewry.

Allgemeine-SS: General body of the SS consisting of full-time, part-time, and inactive or honorary members, as distinct from the *Waffen-SS* (see entry for *Waffen-SS*).

Amt: A directorate, or an office of a ministry.

Amtsgruppe: A branch of a *Hauptamt*.

Anschluß: Annexation of Austria to the German Reich in March 1938.

Arbeitslager: Labor/Work Camp.

Außenstelle/Außendienststelle: Out-station of an office, agency or ministry.

Befehlshaber der Sicherheitspolizei und des SD: Commander in Chief of the *SIPO* and *SD*.

Deutsches Ausrüstungswerk (DAW): German Armaments Factories.

Gau: One of 42 main territorial divisions of the Nazi Party.

Gauleiter: The highest ranking party official in a *Gau,* responsible for all of the political and economic activity, mobilization of labor, and civil defence.

Geheime Staatspolizei (Gestapo): Secret State Police which became *Amt IV* of the *RSHA* in September 1939. Headed by *SS-Obergruppenführer* Heinrich Müller.

Generalgouvernement: German-occupied Poland administered by Hans Frank from his headquarters in Kraków.

Hauptamt: A main or central office.

Höhere SS- und Polizeiführer: Higher *SS* and Police Leader. Himmler's personal representative in each military region. Also established in the occupied territories. Nominally the Commander of all *SS* and police units in his area, as well as acting liaison officer with the military and senior regional authorities.

Judenrat: Jewish Councils established by the Nazis for Jewish self-administraton, in all its various facets: food, housing, labor allocation, welfare, police, economic, and social, and so on.

Kapo: A prisoner-functionary in the Nazi Camps who was assigned by the *SS* Camp staff to supervise labor brigades, maintain discipline, or fulfil administrative tasks.

Kanzlei des Führers der NSDAP: Hitler's Chancellery.

Kommando: A brigade, squad, or detail.

Kommissariat: A Regional HQ of the police; also a political administration in the occupied eastern territories (for example: *Reichskommissariat Ukraine*).

Konzentrationslager: Concentration Camp.

Kreishauptmann: The principal district official in the *Generalgouvernement* and occupied territories.

Kriminalpolizei (Kripo): Criminal Police, the plain-clothed detective squads which together with the *Gestapo* formed the *Sicherheitspolizei*. In 1939 the *Kripo* became *Amt V* of the *Reichssicherheitshauptamt (RSHA)*. Headed by *Reichskriminaldirektor* Arthur Nebe.

Lagerälteste: Camp elder, a senior prisoner in a Nazi Camp.

Leitstelle: A Regional HQ of the *Gestapo* or *Kripo* established at the HQ of a Military District or capital of a county.

Oberkapo: Senior *Kapo* in a Nazi Camp.

Oberzugführer: Senior platoon leader; in charge of the platoon leaders.

Ordnungspolizei (Orpo): Order Police. The regular uniformed police, comprising the *Schutzpolizei (Schupo)*, *Gendarmerie* (rural constabulary), and *Feuerschutzpolizei* (fire-fighting police), together with certain technical and auxiliary services.

Organisation Todt: A paramilitary government organization used mainly for the construction of strategic highways and military installations.

Reichsgau: One of the eleven regions formed from territories annexed by the Reich.

Reichskanzlei: Chancellery of the Reich directed by Hans Lammers.

Referat: A sub-section within a *Gruppe*.

Referent: The official in charge of a *Referat*.

Reichsführer-SS: Reich Leader of the *SS*. Heinrich Himmler had this *SS* title from June 1936.

Reichskriminalpolizeiamt (RKPA): Berlin HQ of the *Kriminalpolizei (Kripo)* which in September 1939 became *Amt V* of the *Reichssicherheitshauptamt (RSHA)*.

Reichssicherheitshauptamt (RSHA): Reich Security Main Office, formed in September 1939 and combined the *Sicherheitspolizei* and the *Sicherheitsdienst (SD)*. It was both an *SS-Hauptamt* and a branch of the Reich Ministry of the Interior.

Schutzpolizei (Schupo): Protection Police. The regular uniformed municipal constabulary forming the bulk of the *Ordnungspolizei*.

Sicherheitsdienst (SD): Security Service. The intelligence branch of the *SS* headed by Reinhard Heydrich.

Sicherheitspolizei (Sipo): Security Police, comprising the *Kripo* and the *Gestapo*, headed by Reinhard Heydrich.

Sonderkommando: A special unit of the *SS* employed for police and political tasks in occupied territories. Also used to denote the special brigades of prisoners in Auschwitz who dealt with the corpses.

SS-Leibstandarte "Adolf Hitler": Hitler's bodyguard regiment. The oldest of the *SS* militarized formations, established in 1933. Commanded by Joseph "Sepp" Dietrich.

SS- und Polizeiführer: *SS* and Police Leader. In command of a district in the eastern occupied territories, subordinate to a *Höhere SS- und Polizeiführer*.

Standarte: *SS* or *SA* formation equivalent to a regiment, i.e. approximately 3,000 men.

Sturmabteilung (SA): Storm Detachment, also called the "Brown Shirts" after the colour of their uniform. The original Nazi paramilitary organization founded in 1921.

Sturmbann: An *SA* or *SS* unit, equivalent to a battalion, i.e. 750–1,000 men.

SS-Totenkopfverbände: *SS* Death's Head units that guarded the Concentration Camps. In 1939 they formed the nucleus of the *SS-Totenkopf* division, one of the first field formations of the *Waffen-SS*.

SS-Verfügungstruppen: The pre-war militarized formations of the *SS*, renamed the *Waffen-SS* in 1939.

Volksdeutsche: Ethnic Germans.

Volksliste: Ethnic German Resister.

Vorarbeiter: Foreman of a team of workers.

Waffen-SS: Fully militarized *SS* formations. Initially composed of the *SS-Verfügungstruppen* and the *SS-Totenkopf* units. During the Second World War it comprised of 40 divisions, both German and non-German units.

Wehrkreis: Military region, usually indicated on maps by a Roman numeral.

Wehrmacht: The German Armed Forces, i.e. the army, air force, and navy.

Wirtschafts und Verwaltungshauptamt (WVHA): Administration and Economic Main Office of the *SS*, formed from the *SS-Hauptamt Haushalt und Bauten* in 1940. Headed by Oswald Pohl, the *WVHA* supervised the *SS* economic enterprises and administered the Concentration Camps.

Zugführer: Military term for a platoon leader.

Selected Bibliography

Anne Frank In The World, Anne Frank Stichting, Amsterdam 1985.

Anne Frank House A Museum with a Story, Anne Frank Stichting, Amsterdam 2001.

ARAD, Yitzhak, *Bełżec, Sobibór, Treblinka*, Indianna University Press, Bloomington and Indianapolis 1987.

BAEDEKERS, *Das Generalgouvernement*, Leipzig 1943.

BRAHAM, Randolp L, *The Politics of Genocide—Volume 2—The Holocaust in Hungary*, Columbia University Press, New York 1994.

BROWN, Daniel Patrick, *The Camp Women*, Schiffer Military History, Atglen PA 2002.

CZECH, Danuta, *Auschwitz Chronicle*, Henry Holt and Company, New York 1989.

Der Dienstkalender Heinrich Himmler, Christians, Hamburg 1999.

DIXON, Jeremy, *Commanders of Auschwitz*, Schiffer Military History, Atglen PA 2005.

FRIEDMAN, Filip, *This Was Oświęcim*, United Jewish Relief Appeal, London 1946.

GARLINSKI, Jozef, *Fighting Auschwitz,* Fontana Collins 1975.

GILBERT, Martin, Final Journey, George Allen and Unwin Ltd. London 1979.

GILBERT, Martin, *The Holocaust,* Collins, London 1985.

HART, Kitty, *Return to Auschwitz*, Granada Publishing Ltd, St. Albans 1983.

HILBERG, Raul, *The Destruction of the European Jews*, Holmes and Meier, New York 1985.

HOLMES, Richard, *The World At War,* Ebury Press 2007.

HÖSS, Rudolf, *Commandant of Auschwitz,* Pan Books, London 1980.

JAROSZ, Barbara, *Auschwitz,* Interpress, Warsaw 1985.

KIELAR, Wiesław, *Anus Mundi,* Penguin Books, Harmondsworth 1980.

KLEE, Ernst *Das Kulturlexikon zum Dritten Reich,* Fischer S. Verlag GmbH 2007.

KLEE, Ernst, *Was sie Taten – Was sie Wurden,* Fischer Taschenbuch Verlag, 1986.

KLEE, Ernst, DRESSEN, Willi, RIESS, Volker, *The Good Old Days.* Hamish Hamilton, London 1991.

KUBICA, Helena, *The Extermination at KL Auschwitz of Poles Evicted from the Zamość Region in the Years 1942–1943,* Auschwitz-Birkenau State Museum 2006.

LANZMANN, Claude, *Shoah,* Pantheon Books, New York 1985.

MACLEAN, French L, *The Camp Men,* Schiffer Military History, Atglen PA 1999.

MARRUS, Michael R, *The Nuremberg War Crimes Trial 1945–1946,* Bedford Books, Boston and New York 1997.

MARSZALEK, Josef, *Majdanek,* Interpres, Warsaw 1986.

MÜLLER, Filip, *Eyewitness Auschwitz,* Ivan R. Dee, Chicago 1979.

NAUMANN, Bernd, *Auschwitz,* Pall Mall Press, London 1966.

NYISZLI, Dr. Miklós, *Auschwitz,* Granada Publishing, St. Albans 1973.

O'NEIL, Dr Robin, *Oskar Schindler—Stepping Stone To Life,* susaneking.com Texas 2010.

PELT, Robert van, and DWORK, Deborah, *Auschwitz 1270 To The Present,* Yale University Press, New Haven and London 1996.

PICCIOTTO, Liliana, *IL Libro Della Memoria,* Mursia, Milano 1991.

PIPER, Franciszek, *How Many Perished Jews, Poles, Gypsies*, Yad Vashem Studies Vol XXI, Jerusalem 1991.

REES, Laurence, *The Nazis and The Final Solution*, BBC Books, London 2005.

REITLINGER, Gerald, *The Final Solution*, Vallentine, Mitchell, London 1953.

SETKIEWICZ, Piotr, *The Private Lives of the Auschwitz SS*, Auschwitz Birkenau State Museum 1990.

SLIER, Deborah and SHINE, Ian, *Hidden Letters*, Star Bright Books, New York 2008.

SUHL, Yuri, *They Fought Back*, Schocken Books, New York 1975.

The Auschwitz Album, Yad Vashem / Auschwitz Birkenau State Museum 2002.

VENEZIA, Shlomo, *Inside the Gas Chambers*, Polity Press 2009.

WIERNICKI, John, *War in the Shadow of Auschwitz*, Syracruse University Press 2001.

WISTRICH, Robert, *Who's Who in Nazi Germany*, Routledge, New York 1995.

WEBB, Chris, *The Bełżec Death Camp*, ibidem-Verlag, Stuttgart 2016.

YEGER, Mark C, *Allgemeine-SS*, Schiffer Military History, Atglen PA 1997.

Sources and Acknowledgements

Websites

www.Bundesarchiv.de/gedenkbuch

www.holocaust.cz

www.deathcamps.org

www.holocausthistoricalsociety.org.uk

www.Holocaustresearchproject.org

www.Jewishvirtuallibrary.org

www.Joodsmonument.nl

www.nizkor

www.Yad Vashem Central Database of Shoah Victims

Archives

Auschwitz-Birkenau State Museum, Poland

Berlin Document Centre, Germany

Bundesarchiv, Berlin, Germany

Ghetto Fighters House, Israel

Holocaust Historical Society, UK

NARA Washington DC, USA

National Archives – Kew, UK

NIOD Amsterdam, Holland

Polish Library Hammersmith, London, UK

Tall Trees Archive, UK

Tiergarten 4 Association, Berlin, Germany

Wiener Library London, UK

Yad Vashem – Jerusalem, Israel

Private Correspondence

Frank Bright with the author

Acknowledgements

BRIGHT, Frank

GILBERT, Sir Martin, London, UK

HAARDT, Miriam – Wiener Library, London

HALLSTRÖM, Börje, Sweden

Hans from Alfstedt, Germany

HOJAN, Artur, Poland – Tiergarten 4 Association, Berlin, Germany

JOSAFAT, Samuel – Thessaloniki Jewish Community

KATZ, Lilli – Mai

KUBISZTAL, Pawel, Poland

LIEMPT, Martin van, Holland

LISCIOTTO, Carmelo – H.E.A.R.T.

MOSCOVITZ, Emmanuelle – Yad Vashem, Israel

MÜHLBERGER, Professor Detlef Willi

MÜHLBERGER, Tania Helene

MUNRO, Cameron – Tiergarten 4 Association, Berlin, Germany

NOWOTNY, Dr. Thomas

O'NEIL, Dr. Robin

PARZER, Robert – Tiergarten 4 Association, Berlin, Germany

SETKIEWICZ, Piotr – Auschwitz State Museum, Poland

SILBERKLANG, Dr. David – Yad Vashem, Israel

SPYRAKIS, Heather

SPYRAKIS, Mark

TURNQUIST, Tim

WEBB, Shirley

WONTOR-CICHY, Teresa – Auschwitz State Museum, Poland

Teesside University

AXE, Josh

BRUNSKILL, Adam

DIXON, Ryan

FELDMAN, Professor Matthew

HANDSCOMB, Mark

JOLLY, Lucy

JUKES, Mike

NIXON, Tom

OMAN, Jess

RICHARDSON, Sean

SMITH, Hannah

URWIN, James

Index of Names

A

Ackermann, Chaim 38, 219
Agrestowski, Jan 88, 201
Alinka, (A Girl in Auschwitz Christian Name is Unknown) 106
Ambros, Otto 29
Andreyev, (Christian Name is Unknown) 216, 217
Aumeier, Hans 40, 66, 67, 84, 85, 96, 227, 369, 391, 392, 393

B

Baer, Richard (Also Known as Karl Neumann) 39, 171, 202, 227, 243, 393, 451
Baky, László 303
Balut, Tadeusz 217
Barabasch, Alfred 217
Baranowski, Hermann 361
Baras, Jan 82
Barbie, Klaus 290
Baretzki, Stefan 109, 148, 394, 396
Barry, Charles 115
Bartosiewicz, Henryk 27
Bartoszewski, Wladyslaw 32
Baszrov, Gilmudin 221
Batko, Marian 33
Baworowski, Władysław 24
Bechert, Rudi 129
Beck, August 21
Bednarek, Emil 394, 395, 396

Beker, Djunio 22
Bell, P Ingress 379, 380, 381
Bendera, Eugeniusz (Also Known as Gienek) 45, 67
Berenstein, Liliane 290
Biedenkopf, Wilhelm 29
Bielski, Jerzy 26, 35
Bies, Albert 34
Bischoff, Heinrich 228, 394
Bischoff, Karl , 55, 69, 86, 91, 229, 235, 237, 246
Biskup, Wladyslaw 88, 201
Blau, Bela 126
Blobel, Paul 72, 73, 244
Block, Max 11, 287, 288, 447
Block, Therese 287
Blum, Leon 125
Blumenreuter, Carl 366
Bobla, Franciszek 33
Bock, Hans 24, 30, 36, 62
Bodmann, Franz 42
Boger, Friedrich Wilhelm 40, 109, 159, 229, 230, 231, 394, 395
Bogusch, August Reimond 391, 392
Bohm, Arno 130
Bölter, Florian 12
Bonigut, Paul 144
Bonitz, Bernhard 397
Borczyk, Boleslaw 86
Bordzic, Jerzy 213
Borenstein, Bar 81
Borenstein, Nojech 81
Bormann, Juana 211, 380, 392
Bormann, Martin 224

Borski, Stanislaw 38
Bracht, Fritz 32, 68, 69
Brack, Viktor 44, 69, 265
Brand, Joel, 304, 305
Brandl, Therese 391, 392
Brasse, Wilhelm 25
Braun, Ladislav 122
Braunschweig, Pierre 90
Breitweiser, Arthur Johann 231, 391, 392, 394, 396
Brenner, Karl Heinrich 372
Brichta, Frantisek (Also Known as Frank Bright) 1, 11, 186, 187, 190, 192, 193, 194, 195, 450, 474
Brichta, Hermann 448
Brichta, Toni 449
Broad, Pery 20, 48, 49, 55, 58, 74, 96, 232, 394, 395
Broch, Karl 184
Brochner, Stefania 382
Brodniewitsch, Bruno 21
Broszio, Karl 208
Brück, August 88, 92
Brunner, Alois 290
Brunner, Anton 276, 295
Budrowski, Alfons 213
Buki, Meilech (Also Known as Milton) 80
Bülow, Alexander 391
Buntrock, Fritz Wilhelm 109, 391, 392
Burger, Avri 126
Burger, Ernst 195, 199
Burger, Willi (Wilhelm) 255
Burski, Tadeusz 30
Busch, Hubert 138, 179, 180, 181

C

Caesar, Joachim 69, 232, 233, 355

Cahana, Moshe 311
Capesius, Victor 233, 234, 394, 396
Cebula, (A Girl in Auschwitz Surname is Unknown) 382
Charewiczowa, Lucia 347
Chruscicki, Captain (Christian Name is Unknown) 64
Chruscicki, Tadeusz 64
Ciesielski, Edward 27
Clauberg, Carl 42, 82, 201, 234, 235, 367, 374
Cohen, Leon 135, 141
Cunio, Salvatore 300
Cyrankiewicz, Jozef 71
Czuchajowski, Boleslaw 35

D

Dabrowski, (Christian Name is Unknown) 211
Dachdecker, Karl 65
Dacko, Ryszard 106
Dallaporto, Nicola 312
Danisch, Franz 134
Dannecker, Theodor 276, 290
Danz, Luise 391
Debski, Stanislaw 26
Dejaco, Walter 72, 235, 238, 244
Deresinski, Jozef 183
Dering, Wladyslaw 30, 31
Deutschkron, Inge 280
Diem, Rudolf 71
Dienstbach, Oskar 268
Dietrich, Marlene 197
Dinges, Erich 391
Dirlewanger, Oskar 197, 251
Domino, Marcin 34
Dorebus, Josef 183
Dragon, Avraham 136
Dragon, Szlama 60, 80

Draser, Hans 184
Dreschel, Margot Elisabeth 344
Dubois, Stanislaw 26
Dubost, M. 388, 389
Dusik, Franciszek 196
Dusik, Julian 196
Dylewski, Klaus (Also Known as Peter Schmidt) 235, 236, 394, 395

E

Eckardt, Josef 137
Edelstein, Jakob 107
Edelstein, Miriam 107
Eichenstein, Moses 38
Eichmann, Otto Adolf 48, 57, 58, 82, 99, 107, 144, 276, 277, 284, 290, 295, 302, 303, 304, 305, 315, 324, 331, 363, 455, 457
Eidenmüller, Horst 137
Eisenschmidt, Eliezer 96
Eisenstädter, Ludwig 133
Eisfeld, Walter 19
Emmerich, Wilhelm 79, 99, 100
Emperor Josef II 283
Endre, László 303
Engel, Miklos 125
Entress, Friedrich 30, 45, 369
Erber, Josef 396
Erler, Rudolf 184
Erman, Renee 372, 375
Ertl, Fritz Karl 237, 238

F

Farberböck, Max 287
Fediuszko, Wasyl 34
Feldblum, Lea 291
Ferenczy, László 303

Ferrer Ray, Margarita 114
Fischer, Erica 287
Fischer, Horst 396
Fischer, Otto 194
Florczyk, Henry 368, 370
Fogel, (A Slovakian Girl Christian Name is Unknown) 85
Forbes, Alexander Mackinlay 377, 378
Forschner, Otto 227
Fox, Alfred James 370, 372, 375
Frank, Annelies Marie 176, 320, 321, 322, 323, 324, 469
Frank, Edith 323
Frank, Hans 387, 398, 464
Frank, Karl Hermann 284
Frank, Margot 321, 323, 408
Frank, Otto 176, 320, 321, 323, 324
Frank, Willi 195, 238, 394, 396
Freese, Willi 184
Freimel, Rudolf 114, 195, 199
Frey, Alois 397
Fries, Jakob 370
Fritzsch, Karl 33, 35, 39, 40, 45
Furst, Rozsi 131

G

Gabbai, Yakob 296
Gajowniczek, Franciszek 35
Galinski, Edwards (Edek) 23, 157, 160
Galoch, Jan 196
Garbarz, Moshe Maurice 59
Garbowiecki, Mieczyslaw 86
Garlinski, Jozef 30, 31, 64, 66, 67, 71, 91, 103, 114, 116, 157, 176, 183, 196, 199, 224
Gartner, Ella 184, 185

Gaskó, Miklós 309
Gawel, Jozef 87
Gehring, Wilhelm Gerhard 391, 392
Gelermann, Aleksander 212
Gemmeker, Albert Konrad 315
Gerson, Kurt (Also Known as Kurt Gerron) 38, 197
Giermakowski, Adam 33
Glaue, Bernard 37
Globocnik, Odilo 81, 226, 277, 302, 313, 361, 381
Glogowski, Leon 31
Glowa, Stanislaw 383
Glücks, Richard 18, 19, 32, 71, 303
Goebbels, Josef 256
Goebel, Johannes 374
Goetze, Paul 391, 392
Gordon, Jacob 329
Gorges, Johannes 109, 111, 138, 179, 180, 181, 205
Göring, Hermann 29, 387
Gork, Kasimir 134
Goslar, Hannah 323
Goszkowski, Franciszek 96
Grabner, Maximillian 40, 49, 50, 74, 75, 84, 85, 96, 101, 102, 239, 267, 369, 391, 392
Gradowski, Zalman 183
Grawitz, Ernst Robert 366
Grell, Hermann 207
Gricksch, Albert Franke 354, 355
Gringhuis, Gezinus 322
Grocholska, Emilia 347
Groening, Oskar 240
Grootendorst, Willem 322
Gross, Emanuel 122
Gross, Wladyslaw 28
Grosz, Andor (Also Known As Bandi) 304

Grothmann, Werner 68
Grzesiak, Antoni 34
Grzybowska, Janina 214
Guarien, Paul 90
Günther, Gustav 211
Günther, Hans 276
Günther, Rolf 276, 295, 303
Guttman, Herbert 38
Gutwein, Juda 38

H

Habal, Erwin 215
Haemmerle, Albert 129
Halbreich, Eugenia 207
Halm, Hans 19
Halon, Edward 202
Hanas, Anna 381
Handelsman, Jankiel 184
Hantl, Emil 241, 394, 396
Harat, Andrezj 83
Harff, (Christian Name is Unknown) 219
Hart Moxon Kitty (Kitty Felix) 281, 282, 283, 469
Hartjenstein, Friedrich (Fritz) 39, 101, 136, 267
Hasse, Elisabeth 344
Hejduk, Roman 34
Henlein, Konrad 247
Hensel, Fritz 360
Hensel, Gerhard 360
Hensel, Hedwig 225, 360
Hensel, Helmut 360
Hensel, Rüdolf 360
Herff, Maximillian von 354, 355
Heydrich, Reinhard 29, 284, 361, 387, 463, 465, 466
Himmler, Heinrich 19, 27, 29, 31, 32, 55, 56, 57, 67, 68, 69, 72, 82,

96, 102, 146, 176, 197, 198, 225, 226, 227, 233, 234, 304, 325, 360, 361, 362, 363, 367, 387, 398, 401, 464, 465, 469
Hirsch, Friedrich (Fredy) 107, 111, 130, 295
Hirschmann, Ira 305
Hitler, Adolf 44, 66, 96, 191, 229, 232, 247, 250, 263, 274, 321, 387, 464, 466
Hlinka, Andrej 116, 330, 331
Höcker, Georg 242, 243, 251, 394
Höcker, Karl 242, 243, 251, 394
Hodys, Eleanore 100
Hoffmann, Ernst 101, 145, 388, 391, 394, 395
Hofmann, Franz Johann 40, 244, 245
Hofmeyer, Hans 394, 395
Hojan, Artur 1, 11, 398, 400, 422
Holblinger, Karl 62
Holik, (Christian Name is Unknown) 71
Holländer 137
Holz (Christian Name is Unknown) 125
Höss, Franz Xaver 359
Höss, Rudolf Franz Ferdinand (Code Name Franz Lang) 2, 19, 20, 27, 28, 31, 32, 33, 34, 37, 39, 41, 45, 47, 55, 56, 57, 58, 63, 68, 69, 72, 73, 77, 100, 101, 115, 136, 137, 171, 176, 224, 225, 226, 229, 235, 250, 252, 256, 274, 355, 359, 387, 390, 391, 399, 402, 428
Hössler, Franz 41, 45, 49, 50, 66, 72, 73, 80, 101, 185, 244, 245, 369, 375, 380, 389, 392, 456

Hotz, Walter 394
Hoyer, Wilhelm 378
Hunsche, Otto 276
Hustek, Josef (Also Known as Josef Erber) 109, 179, 396

I

Ilczuk, Jozef 201

J

Jacob, Lili 145, 146, 147
Jagiello, Konstanty (Also Known as Kostek) 26, 196
Jakubski, Antoni 31
Janisch, Josef 71, 248
Janowitz, Leo 107
Januszewski, Mieczyslaw 82
Jasiowka, Wladyslaw 201
Jaster, Stanislaw 67
Jaworski, Czeslaw 208
Jedlinski, Antoni 33
Jeschke, Karl 391
Jewniewiczowa, Wanda 347
Jossel, (Christian Name is Unknown) 127
Josten, Heinrich 245, 391, 392
Jothann, Werner 246
Jozek, (Surname is Unknown) 157
Jurek, (Surname is Unknown) 158, 159
Juszczyk, Franciszek 34

K

Kacperski, Lieutenant 27
Kadow, Walther 224, 360
Kaduk, Oswald 90, 247, 394, 396
Kahan, Adolf 124

481

Kahan, Esther 124
Kalderon, Allegre 380, 381
Kalniak, Ajzyk 183
Kaloudis, Gyorgos 297
Kaltenbrunner, Ernst 225, 303, 387
Kaminski, Jakob 94
Kaminski, Wladyslawa 213
Kammler, Hans 68, 69, 86, 229
Kammler, Heinz 91
Karcz, Jan 86
Karotynski, Karol 86
Karwat, Karol 35
Kastner, Reszo 304
Kastner, Rudolf 116
Katerzinski, Mieczislaw 129
Katz, Chaim 125, 133
Katz, Ludwig 126
Kauz, (Christian Name is Unknown) 96, 97
Kaytoch, Johanna 83
Kedzierska, Waclawa (Also Known as Kropornicka) 384
Kell 137
Kersten, Felix 68
Kielar, Wiesław 21, 22, 23, 24, 45, 47, 157, 158, 159, 160
Kiermaier, Josef 68
Kieszkowski, Waclaw 36
Kieta, Miecyslaw 394
Kirschneck, Hans 247, 248
Kirschner, Herbert 90, 391, 392
Kisniewicz, Stefan 36
Klarsfeld, Serge 147
Klehr, Josef 43, 77, 90, 236, 249, 369, 394, 395, 396
Kleiman, Johannes (Also Known as Mr Koophius) 321, 322
Klein, Alfred 129
Klein, Fritz 200, 392

Klemann, Hermann Christoph 209
Klipp, Kurt 214
Klodinski, Stanislaw 202
Klys, Helena 80
Knopp, Ladislaus 81
Kobylka, Stanislaw 201
Kocek, Stanislaw 36
Koch, (Christian Name is Unknown A Mechanic at Auschwitz) 71
Koch, Hans 391
Kohler, Robert 237
Kolbe, Maksymilian Rajmund 33, 35
Kolinski, Wiktor 86
Kolinski, Wlodzimierz 86
Kollmer, Josef 391, 392
Koso, Izidor 331
Koszewski, Marian 1
Kosztowny, Witold 31
Kozlecki, Henryk 36
Kozlowski, Wojeciech 217
Kraczkiewicz, Zofia 347
Krall, Jozef 82
Kramer, Josef 39, 136, 172, 250, 392
Krankemann, Ernst 26, 44
Kratzer, Theodor 250, 251
Kraus, Franz Xaver 213, 219, 391, 392
Kremer, Johann Paul 42, 77, 251, 270, 391, 392
Kreuzmann, Paul 67
Krolik, Feliks 34
Krumey, Hermann 81, 276, 302, 303, 381
Kuczbara, Boleslaw 82
Kugler, Victor (Also Known as Victor Kraler) 321, 322
Kukielka, Leon 78

482

Kulka, Erich 147
Kumuniecki, Karol 84, 86
Kurcweig, Herz 102
Kuroczkin, Pawel 221
Kurschuss, Albert 109, 111, 138, 205
Kurylowicz, Adam 71
Küsel, Otto 82, 98, 106
Kustra, Tadeusz 33

L

Lachert, Hildegard Marthe Luise 391
Lachmann, Gerhard 84, 90
Lachowicz, Henryk 64, 66
Lachowicz, Wlodzimierz 31
Lange, Herbert 72
Langefeld, Johanna 41, 69
Langfus, Lajb 183
Lanzmann, Claude 280, 281
Lasocka, Teresa 202
Laternser, Hans 394, 395
Latsch, Otto 211, 391, 392
Laufer, Meiloch 124
Lebowitz, Klara 379, 380
Lechner, Anton 391
Lejbisz, (Christian Names are Unknown) 212
Lempart, Jozef 67
Levi, Primo 2, 312, 313
Lewenthal, Salmen 81, 104, 105
Liebehenschel, Arthur 39, 101, 102, 136, 225, 226, 267, 274, 391, 392, 452
Lipka, Waclaw 201
Lok, Alice 310
Lok, Teresz 309
Lolling, Enno 258, 272, 366
Loposki, Witales 34
Lorenz, Eduard 391

Lubusch, Edward 157, 159
Lucas, Franz 252, 253, 394, 396
Luczak, Jozef 201
Ludwig, Herbert Paul 391

M

Maciag, Wladyslaw 36
Maier, Franz Xaver 39
Makalinski, Wlodzimierz 27
Maksymowicz, Lidia 412
Mandel, Marie 41, 391
Mandel, Zoltan 125
Mano, Aaron 299
Maringe, Stanislaw 64
Marketsch, Engelbert 206
Markiewicz, Stanislaw 34
Markovits, Elfriede 324
Markowiecka, Anna 209
Matjasinski, Kazimierz 201
Mauer, Gerhard 284
Mayer, Theodor Konrad 368
McCloy, John 116
McIntyre, Ian 115
Mechanicus, Philip 315, 317
Medefind, Adolf 391
Mengele, Carl 253
Mengele, Josef 42, 91, 167, 171, 174, 203, 257, 258, 412
Meyer, Max 39
Mieczyslaw, Francuz 82, 86, 88, 89, 201, 212, 217, 383
Mihailović, Dragoljub 347
Mikusz, Jozef 176
Mildner, Rudolf 96, 97, 98
Minkos, Herbert 40
Mira (Surname is Unknown) A Yugoslavian Girl 199

Miszutko, (Christian Name is Unknown A Slovakian Prisoner) 174
Möckel, Karl Ernst 255, 391, 392
Moll, Otto 41, 60, 61, 64, 65, 137, 138, 139, 169, 170, 172, 173, 176, 178, 255, 256, 271, 372, 393, 459
Morawa, Mieczyslaw (Also Known as Mietek) 88, 89, 93
Mordowicz, Czesław 144
Morgen, Georg Konrad 100, 102, 239, 267, 281
Morlawa, Mieczyslaw 201
Morpurgo, Lucia 313
Mühsfeldt, Erich 137, 162, 169, 173, 200, 259, 391, 392, 458
Mulka, Robert 256, 257, 393, 394, 395, 454
Müller, Andreas 133
Müller, Heinrich 72, 464
Müller, Kurt Hugo 391

N

Naumann, Bernd 21, 101, 224, 396
Nebbe, Detlef 391
Neubert, Gerhard 394, 396
Neuman, Julius 126
Neumann, Alexander 129
Neumann, Jozef 133
Nierzwicki, Hans 394
Nocko, Jozef 33
Nowak, Franz 276
Nyiszli, Miklós 152, 154, 155, 156, 161, 162, 163, 166

O

Obojski, Eugeniusz 45, 78, 86
Olere, David 294, 445

Opasiak, Stanislaw 33
Opel, Rubin 38, 96
Opilka, Jerzy 96
Oppel, Isaak 38
Oppenheimer, Alfred 214, 215
Orlowski, Alice 391
Ormond, Henry 394
Orzel, Roman 34
Osteringer, Rudi 129
Otulak, Stefan 33

P

Paczynski, Josef 54
Pajaczkowski, Henryk 65
Pajor, Jan 34
Palitzsch, Luise 80
Panszczyk, ??? 383, 384
Panusz, Lajb 183
Paszkowski, Aleksander 34
Perschel, Richard 158, 213
Pfeffer, Fritz 321, 322
Piasecki, Abraham 208
Piaty, Piotr 199
Piechowski, Kazimierz 67
Pinski, Boleslaw 33
Pizlo, Stefan 31
Plagge, Ludwig 391, 392
Pliszko, Lemke (Also Known as Chaim) 183
Plotnicka, Helena 90
Plucer, Regina 370, 372
Pohl, Oswald 225, 226, 467
Popiersch, Max 30, 42
Porazinski, Jerzy 64
Pressburger, Otto 73, 331, 332
Prozorowski, Piotr 34
Prüfer, Kurt 70, 86, 237
Ptasinski, Kazimierz 196
Puchala, Reinhold 177

Purke, Jozef 184

R

Rachberger, Stephan 95
Rackers, Bernhard 208
Radwanski, Tadeusz 86
Rahm, Karl 197
Rainer, Friedrich 313
Rainicke, Karl 95
Rajchman, Aleksander 335
Rajewski, Lucjan 178
Rascher, Sigmund 367
Rausen, Anschel 38
Raynoch, Zbigniew 195, 196
Reichmann, Walter 124
Reinicke, Otto 40
Reischenbeck, Wilhelm 210
Reiser, Arnost 190, 195
Rejowski, Wincenty 33
Ribbentrop, Joachim von 156
Rieck, Willi 40
Ring, Gerson 38
Robota, Roza 184, 185
Rodowicz, Wladyslaw 213
Roller, Franciszek 36
Romeikat, Franz 391
Rosenberg, Walter (Also Known as Rudolf Vrba) 84, 115, 116, 144
Rosenfeld, (Christian Name is Unknown) 211
Rosenthal, Gertrud Hildegard 287
Rosenwasser, Josef 126
Rosin, Arnost 144
Roth, Johann 195, 196, 199
Röthke, Heinz 276, 290
Rozanski, Zenon 64, 65
Rubin, Olmer 38
Rumkowski, Mordechai Chaim 175

Ruszczynski, Zbigniew 86
Rybinski, Franciszek 96
Rycaj, Mioeczyslaw 384
Rycyk, Tadeusz 384

S

Sadowska, Maria (Also Known as Stronska) 347
Safin, Regina 184, 185
Samuel, Maximilian 81, 303, 374, 474
Santruschitz, Hermine (Also Known as Miep Gies) 321, 322, 324
Sapheia, Adam 28
Sawatzki, Willi 397
Schatz, Willi 260, 394, 396
Scheffler, Jan 33
Schenk, A Director (Christian Name is Unknown) 208
Scherpe, Herbert 90, 261, 384, 394, 396
Schilling, Klaus Karl 367
Schillinger, Josef 79, 99, 100
Schindler, Oskar 216, 217, 470
Schlachter, August 47
Schlage, Bruno 262, 394, 395
Schlageter, Albert Leo 224, 360
Schlesinger, Kurt 316, 317
Schmauser, Ernst 32, 68, 69, 213
Schmidetzki, Walter 263
Schmidt, Elfriede 77
Schmidt, Max 212
Schmidt, Rudolf 28
Schöberth, Johann 263, 396
Schoettl, Vinzenz 393
Schönborn, (Christian Name is Unknown) 217

Schragenheim, Felice Rahel (Also Known as Felice Schrader) 286, 287, 447
Schreier, Heinrich 377, 378, 392, 393
Schröder, Richard Albert 391
Schulte, Wilhelm 264
Schumacher, Hans 367, 391, 392
Schumann, Horst 42, 44, 45, 79, 201, 265, 266, 367, 373
Schurz, Hans 40, 102, 266, 267
Schwarz, Adolf 309
Schwarz, Heinrich 39, 40, 101, 212
Schwarzhuber, Johann 41, 101, 109, 111, 112, 132, 134, 172, 376, 393
Schwela, Siegfried 42, 268
Sehn, Jan 383, 390, 394
Seidl, Siegfried 99
Seidler, Fritz 369
Seitz, Robert 138
Sentkeller, Doctor (Christian Name is Unknown) 155
Serafinski, Tomasz (Also Known as Witold Pilecki) 26, 27, 30, 64, 176
Seufert, Karl 391
Seyfarth, Sophie 377, 378
Sharrett, Moshe 304, 305
Siegruth, Johann 44
Silberbauer, Karl Joseph 322
Skierniewski, Jan 36
Slezak, Stanislaw 201
Smallwood, Geoffrey 368, 370
Smolen, Helena 178
Smolen, Kazimierz 36, 177, 213, 390, 394, 395
Sobanski, Tomasz 196
Sollmann, Ludwig 133
Sonneschein, Viliam 124
Spanier 316, 317

Speer, Albert 211
Spira, Richard 38, 129
Spitzer, Walther 133
Stahlecker, Walther 284
Stahler, Alois 129
Stark, Hans 40, 51, 52, 53, 268, 269, 394, 395
Stawiska, Cyla 170
Steinberg, Karl Fritz 109, 137
Steiner, Mikulas 126
Stenkin, Pavel 37
Stern, Samuel 303
Stirer, Henryk 86
Stolting, Hermann 395
Streicher, Julius 387
Stromberger, Maria 199
Strychowski, Jan 201
Studencki, Marian 86
Suliga, Antoni 33
Suligorski, Henryk 86
Superson, Kazimierz 86
Swierczyna, Bernard 195, 199
Szczepanek, Wojciech 34
Szczerbowski, Kazimierz 31
Szczurek, Paul 391, 392
Szpak, Natalia 199
Szwed, Tadek 22
Szymanski, Tadeusz 178

T

Tabakman, Meir 289
Taube, Adolf 161, 344, 380, 386
Tauber, Arnost 208
Tauber, Henryk 86, 88
Taylor, Telford 390
Teofil 45
The Harmata Family 60
The Wichaj Family 60

Thermann, Wilhelm Emil Edmund Freiherr von 31
Theuer, Adolf 50
Thilo, Heinz, 148
Tiso, Josef 330
Tods, Adam 201
Todt, Fritz 211
Tolinski, Marian 31
Tomczak, Jozef 36
Tomiczek, Wladyslaw 88
Trebaczowski, Jan 178
Trojanowski, Romek 22, 23
Tuka, Vojtech 331
Tyn, (Christian Name is Unknown) 129

U

Uhlenbrock, Kurt 42, 270
Ungier, Stanislaw 34

V

Vaillant Couturier, Marie Claude 387, 388, 389
Veesenmayer, Edmund 156, 166
Venezia, Baruch 300
Venezia, Isacco 295
Vesely, Ludwig 196, 199
Vetter, Helmuth 271
Vogel, Heinrich 27, 31
Volkenrath, Elisabeth 41, 392
Voskuijl, Elizabeth (Also Known as Elli Vossen) 321
Voss, Peter 100, 109, 111, 271
Votavova, Eva 63

W

Wachter, Otto 398, 401
Wajsblum, Ester 184, 185
Walter, Bernhard 145
Warszawski, Jozef 183
Wasowicz, Tadeusz 178
Weber, Johannes 391
Weil, Josef 215
Weingärtner, Peter 392
Weiss, Martin 226
Weiss, Naftali Zvi 146
Wernecke, Amalie 375
Wertheimer, Misi 126
Wetzler, Alfred 84, 115, 116, 144
Wiebeck, Gerhard 100
Wiejowski, Tadeusz 23, 24, 25
Wiernicki, Janusz (John) 148, 152
Wietschorek, Leo 24
Wigand, Arpad 18
Windeck, Josef Joachim (Also Known as Jupp) 160, 397
Wingoczewski, David 25
Winklemann, Otto 166
Wirth, Christian 314
Wirths, Eduard 42, 257, 272, 367, 373
Wisliceny, Dieter 276, 295, 302, 303, 331
Witamborski, Zdislaw 36
Wladyslaw, Glab 28, 30, 31, 32, 34, 36, 88, 201, 213
Wlodzimierz, Krat 27, 31, 34, 86, 415
Wojcik, Janina 386
Wolf, Joachim 176, 377
Wolff, Karl Friedrich Otto 31
Wolken, Otto 218, 221
Wöntz, Rudolf Friedrich 273
Wosnitza, Georg 74, 75
Wrobel, (Christian Name is Unknown A Polish Jew) 184, 185

Wroblewski, Zdzislaw 82
Wulff, Robert 295
Wust, Gunther 286
Wüst, Walther 68
Wysocki, Stanislaw 34

Y

Yana, A Girl in Auschwitz 114

Z

Zaborska, Anna (Also Known as Savitri) 347
Zakrzewski, Jan 95
Zaleski, Stanislaw 217
Zalesny, Heliodor 86
Zarzycka, Maria 347
Zasadzki, Stanislaw 213
Zawadzki, Mieczyslaw 217
Zelmanovic, Jozef 124
Zelmanovic, Max 147
Zimetbaum, Mala , 157, 160
Zimmer, Alexander 129
Zoller, Josef 273
Zoller, Viktor 101, 273, 274
Zolotov, (A Russian Prisoner in Auschwitz) 30
Zorn, Werner 275

ibidem.eu